THE OCCASIONAL
Margareader™
Food for thought, served Buffett style

*For the old gang at that little t-shirt shop
out there at the end of Margaret Street*

THE OCCASIONAL
Margareader™

Food for thought, served Buffett style

compiled & edited by
Donald W. Davidson

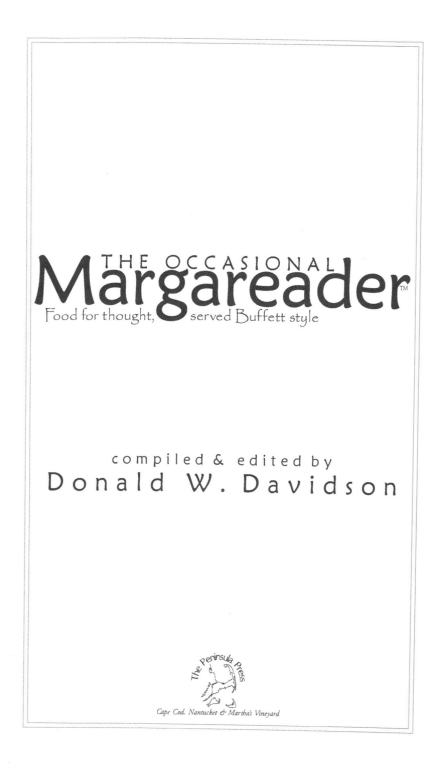

The Peninsula Press

Cape Cod, Nantucket & Martha's Vineyard

THE OCCASIONAL MARGAREADER:
Food for thought, served Buffett style

published by
The Peninsula Press · Cape Cod 02670 USA

Additional copies of this book may be ordered directly at
WWW.MARGAREADER.COM

Library of Congress Catalog Card Number: 10-80875
Davidson, Donald W., ed.
The Occasional Margareader: Food for thought, served Buffett style
The Peninsula Press, ©2010.
ISBN: 978-1-883684-99-0

First Edition published September, 2010
Manufactured in the United States of America

CONTENTS

TABLE OF CONTENTS

FOREWORD

THESE TWO ARE THE PAGES that most readers usually flip past on their way to the good stuff by the writers they know . . . or else by those writers whom they've heard of and think they should know. So, "hello there" and "thanks" for reading this far.

If you're at this line, though, then maybe you'll want to tag along a little further. There's nothing here of importance, but you might find something of interest. In a way, this book's like that old box of stuff that's been kicking around the family's attic for as long as anyone can remember, and these words you're reading right now are like something that someone scribbled on the outside. If nothing else, this scrawl has caught your attention.

Every now and then, somebody's moved that box, but no one's ever thrown it out, let alone even taken a peek inside. If anyone's bothered to open that box, this is the kind of stuff that someone might see: Little oval portraits of unknown ancestors, a dried flower, a packet of letters (each still in its original envelope) wrapped with a piece of violet ribbon, a souvenir plate brought back by some long-forgotten relative, a yellowed newspaper article mended on both sides with yellowed cellophane tape, a golf ball, a bottle cap, an old coin or two, and a well-worn wallet with nothing whatsoever within it. In short, the box contains things that mean little or nothing to anybody; or else, they mean the entire world to the one who's stored them there. If we took the time, we could start trying to make a little sense of it all.

Now, much like opening up that old cardboard box, opening up *The Occasional Margareader* is just another way of opening up Jimmy Buffett's trusty old mind. For years, I'd been making mental notes for myself about the literary references in his works. A remittance man here. An aviator there. And quite often a dreamer who refused to grow up. This process was nothing formal: no cards, no notebook, not even a marked-up album liner. Instead, in my mind's own attic there evolved a box full of literary allusions, all gathering dust until the proverbial right time. If ever that moment were to arrive, they'd all be read again, reflected upon, then arranged in some way that tried to make a little more sense of them all.

Apparently, that time now is here, and this volume contains a good number of those things that filled up that box in my mind. Of course, they first found their way inside there because Jimmy's spent decades cleaning out his own mind and putting this stuff into his stories and his songs. So, this book has become yet another storage box of sorts: "a collective memory" for stuff which our brains no longer have the space to contain. And, which we could never, ever bear to throw away.

Let me be clear that this "collective memory" concept about books is not anything that I thought up on my own. It's been under my memory's eaves since I first came across the notion in something by one Jimmy's favorites, John D. MacDonald. Between the writing of his last Travis McGee novel and his own unexpected passing, MacDonald had composed an essay entitled "Reading for Survival," which he described as an "affirmation of the ability of reading to empower and change lives." (Now those words certainly did not begin anywhere in *my* pencil box.)

"Reading for Survival" is a fascinating discussion between McGee and his best friend, Dr. Meyer. Through the course of a dozen or so pages, the two go back and forth over that "collective memory" thing before Meyer finally comes up with a line from Mark Twain: "The man who does not read good books has no advantage over the man who cannot read them." Ta-*daaaa!*

So, if you find yourself now looking for a reason to dig deeper inside this little box of a book, or you're just searching for some excuse to cast within a curious glance, then follow that sentiment passed along to us by the late John D. MacD. Just keep in mind that you don't need to read every page of this book, and you don't need to read them in the order that I've imposed. In fact, you don't even need to read them at all. Nonetheless, remember those few words from Mark Twain that you read on the second of these two pages. Maybe you should write them down and place them into a memory box of your own.

As for me, "thanks" for having read both pages, but it's time for you to move along now. There's nothing more to see here.

dwd
West Dennis, Cape Cod
18 August 10

JOSEPH CAMPBELL

OF ALL THE BOOKS that Jimmy's ever owned or read, there are very few that might merit the special place right alongside this one either on Jimmy's shelf, or in his heart.

"One of life's great pleasures is exchanging good books with close friends," Jimmy says, and this last work of Joseph Campbell's many volumes was a spontaneous gift from Ed Bradley back in 1988.

Jimmy had just returned from a concert tour of Australia, and he had brought home with him *The Songlines* by Bruce Chatwin, as well as Ainslie Roberts' *Echoes of the Dreamtime*. The oversized book was the most recent of the artist's "dreamtime" works that illustrated the Aboriginal myths, and Jimmy gave it to his longtime friend.

"Ed promptly took me to a bookstore in Aspen where he bought me a copy of *The Power of Myth* as a birthday present," recalls Jimmy. "I read the book, digesting it slowly like a crème brûlée, and made my New Year's resolution to start my own book." The immediate results of Jimmy's reading Campbell was not only *Tales from Margaritaville*, but also *Off to See the Lizard*.

To this day, Jimmy's affinity for Campbell's work continues to surface time and time again. "Joseph Campbell said that a good myth is like an old car that was built to last," Jimmy wrote when he revisited his songs for *Meet Me in Margaritaville*. "It just needs a good coat of paint every couple of years."

And not long after Jimmy had followed all those bubbles up from the *Lady of the Waters* to the surface of Nantucket's Madaket Harbor back in 1994, he returned home later that same August day to Long Island, where he found some comfort in watching – of all things – a few taped episodes of Campbell's PBS series with Bill Moyers called *The Power of Myth*. "Campbell," Jimmy explains, "looks at life and death as a timeless myth in which we all must find the role that suits us." Joseph Campbell himself had spent a great many years in search of that role, and his early life sort of parallels Jimmy's own upbringing.

Born in upstate New York in the early part of the twentieth century, the young Joe Campbell was raised in a strict Roman Catholic household; however, in his adolescence he was never exposed to anything like those Gulf Coastal pirate myths. Instead, he developed an intense interest in his own region's Native American culture and its related mythos. While he immersed himself in that kind of personal study, Joseph Campbell also excelled in his formal education and was, more or less, on a track to become an educator of one kind or another. By the time he was twenty-five, however, the Great Depression was at hand, and the idea of becoming a teacher was giving him what he called "the creeps."

"A lifetime to be spent trying to kid myself and my pupils into believing that the thing that we are looking for is in books!" he wrote in his journal. "I don't know where it is – but I feel just now pretty sure that it isn't in books," he said. "Where is it? And what is it, after all?"

His passion led him deeper into the myths that were to be found in cultures throughout civilization. After nearly two decades pursuing such ideas on his own, Campbell at last was able to develop his own idea of something he called the "monomyth." So, in *The Hero with a Thousand Faces*, he explained how the heroes of myths really served to represent some universal truths about each person's understanding of himself and of his role in society, as well as of just how those two faces of each person relate to one other. As heavy as all that might sound, it is with that sort of thinking that Jimmy has found himself growing as a husband, as a father, and as a teller of stories and tales.

Because *The Power of Myth* in book form is a basically a transcript of those conversations between Campbell and Moyers that served as the basis of the PBS program, it's just plain impossible to pluck out any one passage as a key to the role that myths play in civilizations around the world. After all, any transcript always reads more like a rough draft of something rather than like a polished volume of prose. Still, this brief selection does help to reveal a little further insight into the sorts of things that Jimmy's read regarding the powers of myths in general, along with the importance of relationships in particular.

Simply put, *The Power of Myth* is not just about how myths work; it's about why myths become necessary whenever you're trying to make some sense of it all.

Additional suggested works by Joseph Campbell:

— *The Hero with a Thousand Faces* (1949)

— *The Masks of God, Vol. 1: Primitive Mythology* (1959)

— *The Masks of God, Vol. 2: Oriental Mythology* (1962)

— *The Masks of God, Vol. 3: Occidental Mythology* (1962)

— *The Masks of God, Vol. 4: Creative Mythology* (1968)

— *Myths to Live By* (1972)

— *The Hero's Journey: Joseph Campbell on His Life and Work* (1990)

MYTH AND THE MODERN WORLD

a selection from
The Power of Myth/Chapter I

MOYERS: I CAME TO UNDERSTAND from reading your books – *The Masks of God* or *The Hero with a Thousand Faces*, for example – that what human beings have in common is revealed in myths. Myths are stories of our search through the ages for truth, for meaning, for significance. We all need to tell our story and to understand our story. We all need to understand death and to cope with death, and we all need help in our passages from birth to life and then to death. We need for life to signify, to touch the eternal, to understand the mysterious, to find out who we are.

CAMPBELL: People say that what we're all seeking is a meaning for life. I don't think that's what we're really seeking. I think that what we're seeking is an experience of being alive, so that our life experiences on the purely physical plane will have resonances within our own innermost being and reality, so that we actually feel the rapture of being alive. That's what it's all finally about, and that's what these clues help us to find within ourselves.

MOYERS: Myths are clues?

CAMPBELL: Myths are clues to the spiritual potentialities of the human life.

MOYERS: What we're capable of knowing and experiencing within?

CAMPBELL: Yes.

MOYERS: You changed the definition of a myth from the search for meaning to the experience of meaning.

CAMPBELL: Experience of life. The mind has to do with meaning. What's the meaning of a flower? There's a Zen story about a sermon of the Bud-

14

dha in which he simply lifted a flower. There was only one man who gave him a sign with his eyes that he understood what was said. Now, the Buddha himself is called "the one thus come." There's no meaning. What's the meaning of the universe? What's the meaning of a flea? It's just there. That's it. And your own meaning is that you're there. We're so engaged in doing things to achieve purposes of outer value that we forget that the inner value, the rapture that is associated with being alive, is what it's all about.

MOYERS: How do you get that experience?

CAMPBELL: Read myths. They teach you that you can turn inward, and you begin to get the message of the symbols. Read other people's myths, not those of your own religion, because you tend to interpret your own religion in terms of facts – but if you read the other ones, you begin to get the message. Myth helps you to put your mind in touch with this experience of being alive. It tells you what the experience is. Marriage, for example. What is marriage? The myth tells you what it is. It's the reunion of the separated duad. Originally you were one. You are now two in the world, but the recognition of the spiritual identity is what marriage is. It's different from a love affair. It has nothing to do with that. It's another mythological plane of experience. When people get married because they think it's a long-time love affair, they'll be divorced very soon, because all love affairs end in disappointment. But marriage is recognition of a spiritual identity. If we live a proper life, if our minds are on the right qualities in regarding the person of the opposite sex, we will find our proper male or female counterpart. But if we are distracted by certain sensuous interests, we'll marry the wrong person. By marrying the right person, we reconstruct the image of the incarnate God, and that's what marriage is.

MOYERS: The right person? How does one choose the right person?

CAMPBELL : Your heart tells you. It ought to.

MOYERS: Your inner being.

CAMPBELL: That's the mystery.

MOYERS: You recognize your other self

CAMPBELL: Well, I don't know, but there's a flash that comes, and something in you knows that this is the one.

PLENARY COUNCIL OF BALTIMORE

BEFORE YOU CRINGE at the mere thought of reading a little bit of doctrine from the Roman Catholic Church, maybe you should consider the opening eight words of Jimmy's life "(In Four Hundred Words or Less)," as he presents it. "I broke out of the grip of Catholicism . . . ," is how that begins, and it pretty much prepares the altar for this little morsel of food for thought.

Now, regardless of whether or not you think that religion's in the hands of some crazy-ass people, there can be no denying that every little altar boy has been told to read (perhaps memorize) *The Baltimore Catechism*. And the chances are pretty damn good that young Jimmy Buffett was among that little band of angels with dirty faces.

The Baltimore part of this catechism stems from the fact that it was proposed by the First Plenary Council in 1852. The United States at that time was still relatively compact and heavily populated along the eastern seaboard, so the Roman Catholics fell under the auspices of the Archbishop of Baltimore. The Plenary Council was simply a gathering of all the bishops in that one diocese. Among the earliest ambitions of the council was the creation of a small volume of Catholic doctrine that could be used for instructing and raising young Roman Catholics in North America. Otherwise, they would have to continue relying upon a translation of the *Small Catechism* written by Italy's Robert Bellarmine in the middle of the sixteenth century. But this American catechism did not happen.

A similar ambition was decreed by the Second Plenary Council in 1866, and that result was no different.

Not until the Third Plenary Council had convened in 1884 was any catechism for the New World ever produced, and that same one would remain in use among Catholics in the United State throughout the better part of the 1960s.

More likely than not, Jimmy had been instructed first to read and study the questions and answers in *The Baltimore Catechism* No. 1; then later, those in No. 2. The first of these books was a simplified version for the youngest Catholics, and the second was the main edition for young students. *The Baltimore Catechism* No. 3 was for older students, and an expanded version for the teachers of the catechism classes was No. 4.

Before we go any further, though, you might find it a bit interesting to remember that Jimmy's very first solo single from his *Down to Earth* LP was a somewhat biting little lyric called "The Christian?" which includes that question mark in its title. Having begun his solo career on that note, Jimmy never really passed up any chance to slip in some sort of religious references for quite a while thereafter. "The Missionary." "God's Own Drunk." Sister Mary Mojo. Mardi Gras. Mortal Sin. Carnival. Saints and Guardian Angels. When you add all those sorts of things to the eight little words at the outset of Jimmy's 400-word autobiography, you might see how glancing at *The Baltimore Catechism* just might lend you a little more insight into Bubba's own particular point of view.

Over the next few pages, you'll be introduced to the basics of sin (in all of its inescapable forms), the importance of confession and of absolution, as well as the mystery of the Holy Ghost. From the very outset, you might even be convinced that it's *all* your own damn fault, especially after you've read the prayer known as "Confiteor," the title of which is Latin for "I confess." That one begins: "I have sinned exceedingly . . . through my fault, through my fault, through my most grievous fault." Or, as they say in Latin, "Mea culpa, mea culpa, mea maxima culpa."

Ouch! Isn't there someone else they could blame?

THE BALTIMORE CATECHISM NO. 2

a selection from
Prayers / The Confiteor

I CONFESS TO ALMIGHTY GOD, to blessed Mary, ever Virgin, to blessed Michael the Archangel, to blessed John the Baptist, to the holy Apostles Peter and Paul, and to all the Saints, that I have sinned exceedingly in thought, word and deed, through my fault, through my fault, through my most grievous fault. Therefore, I beseech blessed Mary, ever Virgin, blessed Michael the Archangel, blessed John the Baptist, the holy Apostles Peter and Paul, and all the Saints, to pray to the Lord our God for me.

May the Almighty God have mercy on me, and forgive me my sins, and bring me to everlasting life. Amen.

May the Almighty and merciful Lord grant me pardon, absolution, and remission of all my sins. Amen.

a selection from
Lesson 6 / On Sin and Its Kinds

Q. HOW IS SIN DIVIDED?
A. Sin is divided into the sin we inherit called original sin, and the sin we commit ourselves, called actual sin. Actual sin is sub-divided into greater sins, called mortal, and lesser sins, called venial.

Q. In how many ways may actual sin be committed?
A. Actual sin may be committed in two ways: namely, by wilfully doing things forbidden, or by wilfully neglecting things commanded.

Q. What is our sin called when we neglect things commanded?
A. When we neglect things commanded our sin is called a sin of omission. Such sins as wilfully neglecting to hear Mass on Sundays, or neglecting to go to Confession at least once a year, are sins of omission.

Q. Is original sin the only kind of sin?

A. Original sin is not the only kind of sin; there is another kind of sin, which we commit ourselves, called actual sin.

Q. What is actual sin?

A. Actual sin is any wilful thought, word, deed, or omission contrary to the law of God.

Q. How many kinds of actual sin are there?

A. There are two kinds of actual sin — mortal and venial.

Q. What is mortal sin?

A. Mortal sin is a grievous offense against the law of God.

Q. Why is this sin called mortal?

A. This sin is called mortal because it deprives us of spiritual life, which is sanctifying grace, and brings everlasting death and damnation on the soul.

Q. How many things are necessary to make a sin mortal?

A. To make a sin mortal, three things are necessary: a grievous matter, sufficient reflection, and full consent of the will.

Q. What do we mean by "grievous matter" with regard to sin?

A. By "grievous matter" with regard to sin we mean that the thought, word or deed by which mortal sin is committed must be either very bad in itself or severely prohibited, and therefore sufficient to make a mortal sin if we deliberately yield to it.

Q. What does "sufficient reflection and full consent of the will" mean?

A. "Sufficient reflection" means that we must know the thought, word or deed to be sinful at the time we are guilty of it; and "full consent of the will" means that we must fully and wilfully yield to it.

Q. What are sins committed without reflection or consent called?

A. Sins committed without reflection or consent are called material sins; that is, they would be formal or real sins if we knew their sinfulness at the time we committed them. Thus to eat flesh meat on a day of abstinence without knowing it to be a day of abstinence or without thinking of the prohibition, would be a material sin.

Q. Do past material sins become real sins as soon as we discover their sinfulness?

A. Past material sins do not become real sins as soon as we discover their sinfulness, unless we repeat them with full knowledge and consent.

Q. How can we know what sins are considered mortal?

A. We can know what sins are considered mortal from Holy Scripture; from the teaching of the Church, and from the writings of the Fathers and Doctors of the Church.

Q. What is venial sin?

A. Venial sin is a slight offense against the law of God in matters of less importance, or in matters of great importance it is an offense committed without sufficient reflection or full consent of the will.

Q. Can we always distinguish venial from mortal sin?

A. We cannot always distinguish venial from mortal sin, and in such cases we must leave the decision to our confessor.

Q. Can slight offenses ever become mortal sins?

A. Slight offenses can become mortal sins if we commit them through defiant contempt for God or His law; and also when they are followed by very evil consequences, which we foresee in committing them.

Q. Which are the effects of venial sin?

A. The effects of venial sin are the lessening of the love of God in our heart, the making us less worthy of His help, and the weakening of the power to resist mortal sin.

Q. Which are the chief sources of sin?

A. The chief sources of sin are seven: Pride, Covetousness, Lust, Anger, Gluttony, Envy, and Sloth, and they are called capital sins.

Q. What is pride?

A. Pride is an excessive love of our own ability; so that we would rather sinfully disobey than humble ourselves.

Q. What effect has pride on our souls?

A. Pride begets in our souls sinful ambition, vainglory, presumption and hypocrisy.

Q. What is covetousness?

A. Covetousness is an excessive desire for worldly things.

Q. What effect has covetousness on our souls?

A. Covetousness begets in our souls unkindness, dishonesty, deceit and want of charity.

Q. What is lust?

A. Lust is an excessive desire for the sinful pleasures forbidden by the Sixth Commandment.

Q. What effect has lust on our souls?

A. Lust begets in our souls a distaste for holy things, a perverted conscience, a hatred for God, and it very frequently leads to a complete loss of faith.

Q. What is anger?

A. Anger is an excessive emotion of the mind excited against any person or thing, or it is an excessive desire for revenge.

Q. What effect has anger on our soul?

A. Anger begets in our souls impatience, hatred, irreverence, and too often the habit of cursing.

Q. What is gluttony?

A. Gluttony is an excessive desire for food or drink.

Q. What kind of a sin is drunkenness?

A. Drunkenness is a sin of gluttony by which a person deprives himself of the use of his reason by the excessive taking of intoxicating drink.

Q. Is drunkenness always a mortal sin?

A. Deliberate drunkenness is always a mortal sin if the person be completely deprived of the use of reason by it, but drunkenness that is not intended or desired may be excused from mortal sin.

Q. What are the chief effects of habitual drunkenness?

A. Habitual drunkenness injures the body, weakens the mind, leads its victim into many vices and exposes him to the danger of dying in a state of mortal sin.

Q. What three sins seem to cause most evil in the world?

A. Drunkenness, dishonesty and impurity seem to cause most evil in the world, and they are therefore to be carefully avoided at all times.

Q. What is envy?

A. Envy is a feeling of sorrow at another's good fortune and joy at the evil which befalls him; as if we ourselves were injured by the good and benefited by the evil that comes to him.

Q. What effect has envy on the soul?

A. Envy begets in the soul a want of charity for our neighbor and produces a spirit of detraction, back-biting and slander.

Q. What is sloth?

A. Sloth is a laziness of the mind and body, through which we neglect our duties on account of the labor they require.

Q. What effect has sloth upon the soul?

A. Sloth begets in the soul a spirit of indifference in our spiritual duties and a disgust for prayer.

Q. Why are the seven sources of sin called capital sins?

A. The seven sources of sin are called capital sins because they rule over our other sins and are the causes of them.

Q. What do we mean by our predominant sin or ruling passion?

A. By our predominant sin, or ruling passion, we mean the sin into which we fall most frequently and which we find it hardest to resist.

Q. How can we best overcome our sins?

A. We can best overcome our sins by guarding against our predominant or ruling sin.

Q. Should we give up trying to be good when we seem not to succeed in overcoming our faults?

A. We should not give up trying to be good when we seem not to succeed in overcoming our faults, because our efforts to be good will keep us from becoming worse than we are.

Q. What virtues are opposed to the seven capital sins?

A. Humility is opposed to pride; generosity to covetousness; chastity to lust; meekness to anger; temperance to gluttony; brotherly love to envy, and diligence to sloth.

&

ROBERT LOUIS STEVENSON

from
"A Baker's Dozen (Minus One)"
A Pirate Looks at Fifty
1998

THERE'S NO BETTER place to begin appreciating Jimmy's personal tastes in reading than with this classic tale which created the myth underlying practically everything that we've come to believe about pirates.

Listed as one of his favorite baker's dozen (minus one) of books, *Treasure Island* was the first hardcover volume that Jimmy ever owned. More importantly, it was a gift that his grandfather had brought back to him from a sailing voyage to Argentina.

On many occasions, Jimmy has claimed that it's this classic tale by Robert Louis Stevenson that first planted those seeds of adventure which grew eventually into his own nomadic and gypsy sort of life.

Jimmy has also said that when he captained *Euphoria* on a passage through the British Virgin Islands, he took his sailing companions on a side trip to Beef Island, just east of Tortola, and proclaimed, "We're sailing to Treasure Island!" To a great many historians, Beef Island is said to have been the inspiration and setting of this classic tale of adventure.

As for Robert Louis Stevenson himself, the world at large owes him a debt of gratitude for having the imagination to create those very notions we now hold about pirates sailing black schooners through tropical islands, moving in the company of one-legged sailors with parrots perched upon their shoulders, and daring to bury their treasures anywhere ashore, let alone on some deserted island. Indeed, it is Stevenson who gave us each one of those pieces of the pirate myth, as well as the very notion that a buried treasure might be marked with an X upon some map. Whether or not Stevenson's inspiration might have been Beef Island, the truth still remains that it was his own creativity that has given us that very term "treasure island."

The son of a son of a lighthouse engineer, Stevenson often expressed some guilt for having more or less abandoned his family's long and respected maritime lineage which seemed to encircle the globe from the ragged coastline of Scotland to the farthest reaches of the British Empire. Though he did attempt to study engineering at the University of Edinburgh, his endeavors simply were not successful. And so, he turned to travel and to writing. Still, it remains Stevenson's knowledge of the sea, of sailing, and of island life that provides the rich background for the adventure of young Jim Hawkins.

The idea of the island itself had begun as a map that he'd created for his stepson, Samuel Lloyd Osborne. Stevenson not only illustrated the piece quite intricately, but also embellished it further with bedtime tales that he'd make up about each aspect of this imaginary island. Then, after telling the youngster such a story, Stevenson would write down each one on paper as best as he could remember. In time, this colletion of tales would become Stevenson's first successful literary work: *Treasure Island*.

And though Robert Louis Stevenson will also be remembered for a handful of his other works, such as *Kidnapped*, *A Child's Garden of Verses*, and *The Strange Case of Dr. Jekyll and Mr. Hyde*, one of his most-quoted works is his personal favorite of all the verses he ever wrote. "Requiem" – which is Latin for "rest" or "peace" – is the poem that includes the verse he placed in his will for the headstone overlooking his own particular harbor within the island coastline of Samoa.

> Under the wide and starry sky,
> Dig the grave and let me lie.
> Glad did I live and gladly die,
> And I laid me down with a will.

ROBERT LOUIS STEVENSON

This be the verse you grave for me:
Here he lies where he longed to be;
Home is the sailor, home from sea,
And the hunter home from the hill.

Down through the years, Stevenson's works have inspired not only Jimmy, but also quite a few other writers, including J.M. Barrie and Ernest Hemingway. For the time being, though, here's the first part of the story that established the mythos of the pirates and that set Jimmy on the course that his heart still steers.

Additional suggested works by Robert Louis Stevenson:

— *A Child's Garden of Verses* (1885)

— *Kidnapped* (1886)

— *The Strange Case of Dr. Jekyl & Mr. Hyde* (1886)

— *South Sea Tales* (1893)

— *The Amateur Emigrant* (1896)

Treasure Island
Part Two/The Sea-cook
Chapter VII
I Go to Bristol

IT WAS LONGER than the squire imagined ere we were ready for the sea, and none of our first plans – not even Dr. Livesey's, of keeping me beside him – could be carried out as we intended. The doctor had to go to London for a physician to take charge of his practice; the squire was hard at work at Bristol; and I lived on at the hall under the charge of old Redruth, the gamekeeper, almost a prisoner, but full of sea-dreams and the most charming anticipations of strange islands and adventures. I brooded by the hour together over the map, all the details of which I well remembered. Sitting by the fire in the housekeeper's room, I approached that island in my fancy from every possible direction; I explored every acre of its surface; I climbed a thousand times to that tall hill they call the Spy-glass, and from the top enjoyed the most wonderful and changing prospects. Sometimes the isle was thick with savages, with whom we fought, sometimes full of dangerous animals that hunted us, but in all my fancies nothing occurred to me so strange and tragic as our actual adventures.

So the weeks passed on, till one fine day there came a letter addressed to Dr. Livesey, with this addition, "To be opened, in the case of his absence, by Tom Redruth or young Hawkins." Obeying this order, we found, or rather I found – for the gamekeeper was a poor hand at reading anything but print – the following important news:

Old Anchor Inn, Bristol, March 1, 17—

Dear Livesey – As I do not know whether you are at the hall or still in London, I send this in double to both places.

The ship is bought and fitted. She lies at anchor, ready

for sea. You never imagined a sweeter schooner – a child might sail her – two hundred tons; name, *Hispaniola*.

I got her through my old friend, Blandly, who has proved himself throughout the most surprising trump. The admirable fellow literally slaved in my interest, and so, I may say, did everyone in Bristol, as soon as they got wind of the port we sailed for – treasure, I mean.

"Redruth," said I, interrupting the letter, "Dr. Livesey will not like that. The squire has been talking, after all."

"Well, who's a better right?" growled the gamekeeper. "A pretty rum go if squire ain't to talk for Dr. Livesey, I should think."

At that I gave up all attempts at commentary and read straight on:

Blandly himself found the *Hispaniola*, and by the most admirable management got her for the merest trifle. There is a class of men in Bristol monstrously prejudiced against Blandly. They go the length of declaring that this honest creature would do anything for money, that the *Hispaniola* belonged to him, and that he sold it to me absurdly high – the most transparent calumnies. None of them dare, however, to deny the merits of the ship.

So far there was not a hitch. The work people, to be sure – riggers and whatnot – were most annoyingly slow; but time cured that. It was the crew that troubled me.

I wished a round score of men – in case of natives, buccaneers, or the odious French – and I had the worry of the deuce itself to find so much as half a dozen, till the most remarkable stroke of fortune brought me the very man that I required.

I was standing on the dock, when, by the merest accident, I fell in talk with him. I found he was an old sailor, kept a public-house, knew all the seafaring men in Bristol, had lost his health ashore, and wanted a good berth as cook to get to sea again. He had hobbled down there that morning, he said, to get a smell of the salt.

I was monstrously touched – so would you have been – and, out of pure pity, I engaged him on the spot to be ship's cook. Long John Silver, he is called, and has lost a leg; but that I regarded as a recommendation, since he lost it in his country's service, under the immortal Hawke. He has no pension, Livesey. Imagine the abominable age we live in!

Well, sir, I thought I had only found a cook, but it was a crew I had discovered. Between Silver and myself we got together in a few days a company of the toughest old salts imaginable – not pretty to look at, but fellows, by their faces, of the most indomitable spirit. I declare we could fight a frigate.

Long John even got rid of two out of the six or seven I had already engaged. He showed me in a moment that they were just the sort of fresh-water swabs we had to fear in an adventure of importance.

I am in the most magnificent health and spirits, eating like a bull, sleeping like a tree, yet I shall not enjoy a moment till I hear my old tarpaulins tramping round the capstan. Seaward, ho! Hang the treasure! It's the glory of the sea that has turned my head. So now, Livesey, come post; do not lose an hour, if you respect me.

Let young Hawkins go at once to see his mother, with Redruth for a guard; and then both come full speed to Bristol.

John Trelawney

Postscript – I did not tell you that Blandly, who, by the way, is to send a consort after us if we don't turn up by the end of August, had found an admirable fellow for sailing master – a stiff man, which I regret, but in all other respects a treasure. Long John Silver unearthed a very competent man for a mate, a man named Arrow. I have a boatswain who pipes, Livesey; so things shall go man-o'-war fashion on board the good ship *Hispaniola*.

I forgot to tell you that Silver is a man of substance; I know of my own knowledge that he has a banker's account, which has never been overdrawn. He leaves his wife to manage the inn; and as she is a woman of colour, a pair of old bachelors like you and I may be excused for guessing that it is the wife, quite as much as the health, that sends him back to roving.

J. T.

P.P.S. – Hawkins may stay one night with his mother.

J. T.

You can fancy the excitement into which that letter put me. I was half beside myself with glee; and if ever I despised a man, it was old Tom Redruth, who could do nothing but grumble and lament. Any of the under-gamekeepers would gladly have changed places with him; but such was not the squire's pleasure, and the squire's pleasure was like law. Nobody but old Redruth would have dared so much as even to grumble.

The next morning he and I set out on foot for the Admiral Benbow, and there I found my mother in good health and spirits. The captain, who had so long been a cause of so much discomfort, was gone where the wicked cease from troubling. The squire had had everything repaired, and the public rooms and the sign repainted, and had added some furniture – above all a beautiful armchair for mother in the bar. He had found her an apprentice also so that she should not want help while I was gone.

It was on seeing that boy that I understood, for the first time, my situation. I had thought up to that moment of the adventures before me, not at all of the home that I was leaving; and now, at sight of this clumsy stranger, who was to stay here in my place beside my mother, I had my first attack of tears. I am afraid I led that boy a dog's life, for as he was new to the work, I had a hundred opportunities of setting him right and putting him down, and I was not slow to profit by them.

The night passed, and the next day, after dinner, Redruth and I were afoot again and on the road. I said good-bye to Mother and the cove where I had lived since I was born, and the dear old Admiral Benbow – since he was repainted, no longer quite so dear. One of my last thoughts was of the captain, who had so often strode along the beach with his cocked hat, his sabre-cut cheek, and his old brass telescope. Next moment we had turned the corner and my home was out of sight.

The mail picked us up about dusk at the Royal George on the heath. I was wedged in between Redruth and a stout old gentleman, and in spite of the swift motion and the cold night air, I must have dozed a great deal from the very first, and then slept like a log through stage after stage, for when I was awakened at last it was by a punch in the ribs, and I opened my eyes to find that we were standing still before a large building in a city street and that the day had already broken a long time.

"Where are we?" I asked.

"Bristol," said Tom. "Get down."

Mr. Trelawney had taken up his residence at an inn far down the docks to superintend the work upon the schooner. Thither we had now to walk, and our way, to my great delight, lay along the quays and beside the great multitude of ships of all sizes and rigs and nations. In one, sailors were singing at their work, in another there were men aloft, high over my head, hanging to threads that seemed no thicker than a spider's. Though I had lived by the shore all my life, I seemed never to have been near the sea till then. The smell of tar and salt was something new. I saw the most wonderful figureheads, that had all been far over the ocean. I saw many old sailors, with rings in their ears, and whiskers curled in ringlets, and tarry pigtails, and a swaggering, clumsy sea-walk; and if I had seen as many kings I could not have been more delighted.

And I was going to sea myself, to sea in a schooner, with a piping boatswain and pig-tailed singing seamen, to sea, bound for an unknown island, and to seek for buried treasure!

While I was still in this delightful dream, we came suddenly in front of a large inn and met Squire Trelawney, all dressed out like a sea-officer, in stout blue cloth, coming out of the door with a smile on his face and a capital imitation of a sailor's walk.

"Here you are," he cried, "and the doctor came last night from London. Bravo! The ship's company complete!"

"Oh, sir," cried I, "when do we sail?"

"Sail!" says he. "We sail tomorrow!"

Chapter VIII
AT THE SIGN OF THE SPY-GLASS

WHEN I HAD DONE BREAKFASTING the squire gave me a note addressed to John Silver, at the sign of the Spy-glass, and told me I should easily find the place by following the line of the docks and keeping a bright lookout for a little tavern with a large brass telescope for a sign. I set off, overjoyed at this opportunity to see some more of the ships and seamen, and picked my way among a great crowd of people and carts and bales, for the dock was now at its busiest, until I found the tavern in question.

It was a bright enough little place of entertainment. The sign was newly painted; the windows had neat red curtains; the floor was cleanly sanded. There was a street on each side and an open door on both, which made the large, low room pretty clear to see in, in spite of tobacco smoke.

The customers were mostly seafaring men, and they talked so loudly that I hung at the door, almost afraid to enter.

As I was waiting, a man came out of a side room, and at a glance I was sure he must be Long John. His left leg was cut off close by the hip, and under the left shoulder he carried a crutch, which he managed with wonderful dexterity, hopping about upon it like a bird. He was very tall and strong, with a face as big as a ham – plain and pale, but intelligent and smiling. Indeed, he seemed in the most cheerful spirits, whistling as he moved about among the tables, with a merry word or a slap on the shoulder for the more favoured of his guests.

Now, to tell you the truth, from the very first mention of Long John in Squire Trelawney's letter I had taken a fear in my mind that he might prove to be the very one-legged sailor whom I had watched for so long at the old Benbow. But one look at the man before me was enough. I had seen the captain, and Black Dog, and the blind man, Pew, and I thought I knew what a buccaneer was like – a very different creature, according to me, from this clean and pleasant-tempered landlord.

I plucked up courage at once, crossed the threshold, and walked right up to the man, propped on his crutch, talking to a customer.

"Mr. Silver, sir?" I asked, holding out the note.

"Yes, my lad," said he; "such is my name, to be sure. And who may you be?" And then as he saw the squire's letter, he seemed to me to give something almost like a start.

"Oh!" said he, quite loud, and offering his hand. "I see. You are our new cabin-boy; pleased I am to see you."

And he took my hand in his large firm grasp.

Just then one of the customers at the far side rose suddenly and made for the door. It was close by him, and he was out in the street in a moment. But his hurry had attracted my notice, and I recognized him at glance. It was the tallow-faced man, wanting two fingers, who had come first to the Admiral Benbow.

"Oh," I cried, "stop him! It's Black Dog!"

"I don't care two coppers who he is," cried Silver. "But he hasn't paid his score. Harry, run and catch him."

One of the others nearest the door leaped up and started in pursuit.

"If he were Admiral Hawke he shall pay his score," cried Silver; relinquishing my hand, "Who did you say he was?" he asked. "Black what?"

"Dog, sir," said I. "Has Mr. Trelawney not told you of the buccaneers? He was one of them."

"So?" cried Silver. "In my house! Ben, run and help Harry. One of those swabs, was he? Was you drinking with him, Morgan? Step up here."

The man whom he called Morgan – an old, grey-haired, mahogany-faced sailor – came forward pretty sheepishly, rolling his quid.

"Now, Morgan," said Long John very sternly, "you never clapped your eyes on that Black – Black Dog before, did you, now?"

"Not I, sir," said Morgan with a salute.

"You didn't know his name, did you?"

"No, sir."

"By the powers, Tom Morgan, it's as good for you!" exclaimed the landlord. "If you had been mixed up with the like of that, you would never have put another foot in my house, you may lay to that. And what was he saying to you?"

"I don't rightly know, sir," answered Morgan.

"Do you call that a head on your shoulders, or a blessed dead-eye?" cried Long John. "Don't rightly know, don't you! Perhaps you don't happen to rightly know who you was speaking to, perhaps? Come, now, what was he jawing – v'yages, cap'ns, ships? Pipe up! What was it?"

"We was a-talkin' of keel-hauling," answered Morgan.

"Keel-hauling, was you? And a mighty suitable thing, too, and you may lay to that. Get back to your place for a lubber, Tom."

And then, as Morgan rolled back to his seat, Silver added to me in a confidential whisper that was very flattering, as I thought, "He's quite an honest man, Tom Morgan, on'y stupid. And now," he ran on again, aloud, "let's see – Black Dog? No, I don't know the name, not I. Yet I kind of think I've – yes, I've seen the swab. He used to come here with a blind beggar, he used."

"That he did, you may be sure," said I. "I knew that blind man too. His name was Pew."

"It was!" cried Silver, now quite excited. "Pew! That were his name for certain. Ah, he looked a shark, he did! If we run down this Black Dog, now, there'll be news for Cap'n Trelawney! Ben's a good runner; few seamen run better. He should run him down, hand over hand, by the powers! He talked o' keel-hauling, did he? I'll keel-haul him!"

All the time he was jerking out these phrases he was stumping up and down the tavern on his crutch, slapping tables with his hand, and giving such a show of excitement as would have convinced an Old Bailey judge or a Bow Street runner. My suspicions had been thoroughly reawakened on finding Black Dog at the Spy-glass, and I watched the cook narrowly. But he was too deep, and too ready, and too clever for me, and by the time the two men had come back out of breath and confessed that they had lost the track in a crowd, and been scolded like thieves, I would have gone bail for the innocence of Long John Silver.

"See here, now, Hawkins," said he, "here's a blessed hard thing on a man like me, now, ain't it? There's Cap'n Trelawney – what's he to think? Here I have this confounded son of a Dutchman sitting in my own house drinking of my own rum! Here you comes and tells me of it plain; and here I let him give us all the slip before my blessed deadlights! Now, Hawkins, you do me justice with the cap'n. You're a lad, you are, but you're as smart as paint. I see that when you first come in. Now, here it is: What could I do, with this old timber I hobble on? When I was an A B master mariner I'd have come up alongside of him, hand over hand, and broached him to in a brace of old shakes, I would; but now – "

And then, all of a sudden, he stopped, and his jaw dropped as though he had remembered something.

"The score!" he burst out. "Three goes o' rum! Why, shiver my timbers, if I hadn't forgotten my score!"

And falling on a bench, he laughed until the tears ran down his cheeks. I could not help joining, and we laughed together, peal after peal, until the tavern rang again.

"Why, what a precious old sea-calf I am!" he said at last, wiping his cheeks. "You and me should get on well, Hawkins, for I'll take my davy I should be rated ship's boy. But come now, stand by to go about. This won't do. Dooty is dooty, messmates. I'll put on my old cockerel hat, and step along of you to Cap'n Trelawney, and report this here affair. For mind you, it's serious, young Hawkins; and neither you nor me's come out of it with what I should make so bold as to call credit. Nor you neither, says you; not smart – none of the pair of us smart. But dash my buttons! That was a good un about my score."

And he began to laugh again, and that so heartily, that though I did not see the joke as he did, I was again obliged to join him in his mirth.

On our little walk along the quays, he made himself the most interesting companion, telling me about the different ships that we passed by, their rig, tonnage, and nationality, explaining the work that was going forward – how one was discharging, another taking in cargo, and a third making ready for sea – and every now and then telling me some little anecdote of ships or seamen or repeating a nautical phrase till I had learned it perfectly. I began to see that here was one of the best of possible shipmates.

When we got to the inn, the squire and Dr. Livesey were seated together, finishing a quart of ale with a toast in it, before they should go aboard the schooner on a visit of inspection.

Long John told the story from first to last, with a great deal of spirit and the most perfect truth. "That was how it were, now, weren't it, Hawkins?" he would say, now and again, and I could always bear him entirely out.

The two gentlemen regretted that Black Dog had got away, but we all agreed there was nothing to be done, and after he had been complimented, Long John took up his crutch and departed.

"All hands aboard by four this afternoon," shouted the squire after him.

"Aye, aye, sir," cried the cook, in the passage.

"Well, squire," said Dr. Livesey, "I don't put much faith in your discoveries, as a general thing; but I will say this, John Silver suits me."

"The man's a perfect trump," declared the squire.

"And now," added the doctor, "Jim may come on board with us, may he not?"

"To be sure he may," says squire. "Take your hat, Hawkins, and we'll see the ship."

Chapter IX
POWDER AND ARMS

THE *HISPANIOLA* lay some way out, and we went under the figure heads and round the sterns of many other ships, and their cables sometimes grated underneath our keel, and sometimes swung above us. At last, however, we got alongside, and were met and saluted as we stepped aboard by the mate, Mr. Arrow, a brown old sailor with earrings in his ears and a squint. He and the squire were very thick and friendly, but I soon observed that things were not the same between Mr. Trelawney and the captain.

This last was a sharp-looking man who seemed angry with everything on board and was soon to tell us why, for we had hardly got down into the cabin when a sailor followed us.

"Captain Smollett, sir, axing to speak with you," said he.

"I am always at the captain's orders. Show him in," said the squire.

The captain, who was close behind his messenger, entered at once and shut the door behind him.

"Well, Captain Smollett, what have you to say? All well, I hope; all shipshape and seaworthy?"

"Well, sir," said the captain, "better speak plain, I believe, even at the risk of offence. I don't like this cruise; I don't like the men; and I don't like my officer. That's short and sweet."

"Perhaps, sir, you don't like the ship?" inquired the squire, very angry, as I could see.

"I can't speak as to that, sir, not having seen her tried," said the captain. "She seems a clever craft; more I can't say."

"Possibly, sir, you may not like your employer, either?" says the squire. But here Dr. Livesey cut in.

"Stay a bit," said he, "stay a bit. No use of such questions as that but to produce ill feeling. The captain has said too much or he has said too little, and I'm bound to say that I require an explanation of his words. You don't, you say, like this cruise. Now, why?"

"I was engaged, sir, on what we call sealed orders, to sail this ship for that gentleman where he should bid me," said the captain. "So far so good. But now I find that every man before the mast knows more than I do. I don't call that fair, now, do you?"

"No," said Dr. Livesey, "I don't."

"Next," said the captain, "I learn we are going after treasure – hear it from my own hands, mind you. Now, treasure is ticklish work; I don't like treasure voyages on any account, and I don't like them, above all, when they are secret and when the secret has been told to the parrot."

"Silver's parrot?" asked the squire.

"It's a way of speaking," said the captain. "Blabbed, I mean. It's my belief neither of you gentlemen know what you are about, but I'll tell you my way of it – life or death, and a close run."

"That is all clear, and, I dare say, true enough," replied Dr. Livesey. "We take the risk, but we are not so ignorant as you believe us. Next, you say you don't like the crew. Are they not good seamen?"

"I don't like them, sir," returned Captain Smollett. "And I think I should have had the choosing of my own hands, if you go to that."

"Perhaps you should," replied the doctor. "My friend should, perhaps, have taken you along with him; but the slight, if there be one, was unintentional. And you don't like Mr. Arrow?"

"I don't, sir. I believe he's a good seaman, but he's too free with the crew to be a good officer. A mate should keep himself to himself – shouldn't drink with the men before the mast!"

"Do you mean he drinks?" cried the squire.

"No, sir," replied the captain, "only that he's too familiar."

"Well, now, and the short and long of it, captain?" asked the doctor. "Tell us what you want."

"Well, gentlemen, are you determined to go on this cruise?"

"Like iron," answered the squire.

"Very good," said the captain. "Then, as you've heard me very patiently, saying things that I could not prove, hear me a few words more. They are putting the powder and the arms in the fore hold. Now, you have a good place under the cabin; why not put them there? – first point. Then, you are bringing four of your own people with you, and they tell me some of them are to be berthed forward. Why not give them the berths here beside the cabin? – second point."

"Any more?" asked Mr. Trelawney.

"One more," said the captain. "There's too much blabbing already."

"Far too much," agreed the doctor.

"I'll tell you what I've heard myself," continued Captain Smollett: "that you have a map of an island, that there's crosses on the map to show where treasure is, and that the island lies – " And then he named the latitude and longitude exactly.

"I never told that," cried the squire, "to a soul!"

"The hands know it, sir," returned the captain.

"Livesey, that must have been you or Hawkins," cried the squire.

"It doesn't much matter who it was," replied the doctor. And I could see that neither he nor the captain paid much regard to Mr. Trelawney's protestations. Neither did I, to be sure, he was so loose a talker; yet in this case I believe he was really right and that nobody had told the situation of the island.

"Well, gentlemen," continued the captain, "I don't know who has this map; but I make it a point, it shall be kept secret even from me and Mr. Arrow. Otherwise I would ask you to let me resign."

"I see," said the doctor. "You wish us to keep this matter dark and to make a garrison of the stern part of the ship, manned with my friend's own people, and provided with all the arms and powder on board. In other words, you fear a mutiny."

"Sir," said Captain Smollett, "with no intention to take offence, I deny your right to put words into my mouth. No captain, sir, would be justified in going to sea at all if he had ground enough to say that. As for Mr. Arrow, I believe him thoroughly honest; some of the men are the same; all may be for what I know. But I am responsible for the ship's safety and the life of every man Jack aboard of her. I see things going, as I think, not quite right. And I ask you to take certain precautions or let me resign my berth. And that's all."

"Captain Smollett," began the doctor with a smile, "did ever you hear the fable of the mountain and the mouse? You'll excuse me, I dare say, but you remind me of that fable. When you came in here, I'll stake my wig, you meant more than this."

"Doctor," said the captain, "you are smart. When I came in here I meant to get discharged. I had no thought that Mr. Trelawney would hear a word."

"No more I would," cried the squire. "Had Livesey not been here I should have seen you to the deuce. As it is, I have heard you. I will do as you desire, but I think the worse of you."

"That's as you please, sir," said the captain. "You'll find I do my duty." And with that he took his leave.

"Trelawney," said the doctor, "contrary to all my notions, I believed you have managed to get two honest men on board with you – that man and John Silver."

"Silver, if you like," cried the squire; "but as for that intolerable humbug, I declare I think his conduct unmanly, unsailorly, and downright un-English."

"Well," says the doctor, "we shall see."

When we came on deck, the men had begun already to take out the arms and powder, yo-ho-ing at their work, while the captain and Mr. Arrow stood by superintending.

The new arrangement was quite to my liking. The whole schooner had been overhauled; six berths had been made astern out of what had been the after-part of the main hold; and this set of cabins was only joined to the galley and forecastle by a sparred passage on the port side. It had been originally meant that the captain, Mr. Arrow, Hunter, Joyce, the doctor, and the squire were to occupy these six berths. Now Redruth and I were to get two of them and Mr. Arrow and the captain were to sleep on deck in the companion, which had been enlarged on each side till you might almost have called it a round-house. Very low it was still, of course; but there was room to swing two hammocks, and even the mate seemed pleased with the arrangement. Even he, perhaps, had been doubtful as to the crew, but that is only guess, for as you shall hear, we had not long the benefit of his opinion.

We were all hard at work, changing the powder and the berths, when the last man or two, and Long John with them, came off in a shore-boat.

The cook came up the side like a monkey for cleverness, and as soon as he saw what was doing, "So ho, mates!" says he. "What's this?"

"We're a-changing of the powder, Jack," answers one.

"Why, by the powers," cried Long John, "if we do, we'll miss the morning tide!"

"My orders!" said the captain shortly. "You may go below, my man. Hands will want supper."

"Aye, aye, sir," answered the cook, and touching his forelock, he disappeared at once in the direction of his galley.

"That's a good man, captain," said the doctor.

"Very likely, sir," replied Captain Smollett. "Easy with that, men – easy," he ran on, to the fellows who were shifting the powder; and then suddenly observing me examining the swivel we carried amidships, a long brass nine, "Here you, ship's boy," he cried, "out o' that! Off with you to the cook and get some work."

And then as I was hurrying off I heard him say, quite loudly, to the doctor, "I'll have no favourites on my ship."

I assure you I was quite of the squire's way of thinking, and hated the captain deeply.

Chapter X
THE VOYAGE

ALL THAT NIGHT we were in a great bustle getting things stowed in their place, and boatfuls of the squire's friends, Mr. Blandly and the like, coming off to wish him a good voyage and a safe return. We never had a night at the Admiral Benbow when I had half the work; and I was dog-tired when, a little before dawn, the boatswain sounded his pipe and the crew began to man the capstan-bars. I might have been twice as weary, yet I would not have left the deck, all was so new and interesting to me – the brief commands, the shrill note of the whistle, the men bustling to their places in the glimmer of the ship's lanterns.

"Now, Barbecue, tip us a stave," cried one voice.

"The old one," cried another.

"Aye, aye, mates," said Long John, who was standing by, with his crutch under his arm, and at once broke out in the air and words I knew so well:

"Fifteen men on the dead man's chest –"

And then the whole crew bore chorus:

"Yo-ho-ho, and a bottle of rum!"

And at the third "Ho!" drove the bars before them with a will.

Even at that exciting moment it carried me back to the old Admiral Benbow in a second, and I seemed to hear the voice of the captain piping in the chorus. But soon the anchor was short up; soon it was hanging dripping at the bows; soon the sails began to draw, and the land and shipping to flit by on either side; and before I could lie down to snatch an hour of slumber the *Hispaniola* had begun her voyage to the Isle of Treasure.

I am not going to relate that voyage in detail. It was fairly prosperous. The ship proved to be a good ship, the crew were capable seamen, and the captain thoroughly understood his business. But before we came the length of Treasure Island, two or three things had happened which require to be known.

Mr. Arrow, first of all, turned out even worse than the captain had feared. He had no command among the men, and people did what they pleased with him. But that was by no means the worst of it, for after a day or two at sea he began to appear on deck with hazy eye, red cheeks, stuttering tongue, and other marks of drunkenness. Time after time he was ordered below in disgrace. Sometimes he fell and cut himself; sometimes he lay all day long in his little bunk at one side of the companion; sometimes for a day or two he would be almost sober and attend to his work at least passably.

In the meantime, we could never make out where he got the drink. That was the ship's mystery. Watch him as we pleased, we could do nothing to solve it; and when we asked him to his face, he would only laugh if he were drunk, and if he were sober deny solemnly that he ever tasted anything but water.

He was not only useless as an officer and a bad influence amongst the men, but it was plain that at this rate he must soon kill himself outright, so nobody was much surprised, nor very sorry, when one dark night, with a head sea, he disappeared entirely and was seen no more.

"Overboard!" said the captain. "Well, gentlemen, that saves the trouble of putting him in irons."

But there we were, without a mate; and it was necessary, of course, to advance one of the men. The boatswain, Job Anderson, was the likeliest man aboard, and though he kept his old title, he served in a way as mate. Mr. Trelawney had followed the sea, and his knowledge made him very useful, for he often took a watch himself in easy weather. And the coxswain, Israel Hands, was a careful, wily, old, experienced seaman who could be trusted at a pinch with almost anything.

He was a great confidant of Long John Silver, and so the mention of his name leads me on to speak of our ship's cook, Barbecue, as the men called him.

Aboard ship he carried his crutch by a lanyard round his neck, to have both hands as free as possible. It was something to see him wedge the foot of the crutch against a bulkhead, and propped against it, yielding to every movement of the ship, get on with his cooking like someone safe ashore. Still more strange was it to see him in the heaviest of weather cross the deck. He had a line or two rigged up to help him across the widest spaces – Long John's earrings, they were called; and he would hand himself from one place to another, now using the crutch, now trailing it alongside by the lanyard, as quickly as another man could walk. Yet some of the men who had sailed with him before expressed their pity to see him so reduced.

"He's no common man, Barbecue," said the coxswain to me. "He had good schooling in his young days and can speak like a book when so minded; and brave – a lion's nothing alongside of Long John! I seen him grapple four and knock their heads together – him unarmed."

All the crew respected and even obeyed him. He had a way of talking to each and doing everybody some particular service. To me he was unweariedly kind, and always glad to see me in the galley, which he kept as clean as a new pin, the dishes hanging up burnished and his parrot in a cage in one corner.

"Come away, Hawkins," he would say; "come and have a yarn with John. Nobody more welcome than yourself, my son. Sit you down and hear the news. Here's Cap'n Flint – I calls my parrot Cap'n Flint, after the famous buccaneer – here's Cap'n Flint predicting success to our v'yage. Wasn't you, cap'n?"

And the parrot would say, with great rapidity, "Pieces of eight! Pieces of eight! Pieces of eight!" till you wondered that it was not out of breath, or till John threw his handkerchief over the cage.

"Now, that bird," he would say, "is, maybe, two hundred years old, Hawkins – they live forever mostly; and if anybody's seen more wickedness, it must be the devil himself. She's sailed with England, the great Cap'n England, the pirate. She's been at Madagascar, and at Malabar, and Surinam, and Providence, and Portobello. She was at the fishing up of the wrecked plate ships. It's there she learned 'Pieces of eight,' and little wonder; three hundred and fifty thousand of 'em, Hawkins! She was at the boarding of the viceroy of the Indies out of Goa, she was; and to look at her you would think she was a baby. But you smelt powder – didn't you, cap'n?"

"Stand by to go about," the parrot would scream.

"Ah, she's a handsome craft, she is," the cook would say, and give her sugar from his pocket, and then the bird would peck at the bars and swear straight on, passing belief for wickedness. "There," John would add, "you can't touch pitch and not be mucked, lad. Here's this poor old innocent bird o' mine swearing blue fire, and none the wiser, you may lay to that. She would swear the same, in a manner of speaking, before chaplain." And John would touch his forelock with a solemn way he had that made me think he was the best of men.

In the meantime, the squire and Captain Smollett were still on pretty distant terms with one another. The squire made no bones about the matter; he despised the captain. The captain, on his part, never spoke but when he was spoken to, and then sharp and short and dry, and not a word wasted. He owned, when driven into a corner, that he seemed to have been wrong about the crew, that some of them were as brisk as he wanted to see and all had behaved fairly well. As for the ship, he had taken a downright fancy to her. "She'll lie a point nearer the wind than a man has a right to expect of his own married wife, sir. But," he would add, "all I say is, we're not home again, and I don't like the cruise."

The squire, at this, would turn away and march up and down the deck, chin in air.

"A trifle more of that man," he would say, "and I shall explode."

We had some heavy weather, which only proved the qualities of the *Hispaniola*. Every man on board seemed well content, and they must have been hard to please if they had been otherwise, for it is my belief there was never a ship's company so spoiled since Noah put to sea. Double grog was going on the least excuse; there was duff on odd days, as, for instance, if the squire heard it was any man's birthday, and always a barrel of apples standing broached in the waist for anyone to help himself that had a fancy.

"Never knew good come of it yet," the captain said to Dr. Livesey. "Spoil forecastle hands, make devils. That's my belief."

But good did come of the apple barrel, as you shall hear, for if it had not been for that, we should have had no note of warning and might all have perished by the hand of treachery.

This was how it came about.

We had run up the trades to get the wind of the island we were after – I am not allowed to be more plain – and now we were running down for it with a bright lookout day and night. It was about the last day of our outward voyage by the largest computation; some time that night, or at latest before noon of the morrow, we should sight the Treasure Island. We were heading S.S.W. and had a steady breeze abeam and a quiet sea. The *Hispaniola* rolled steadily, dipping her bowsprit now and then with a whiff of spray. All was drawing alow and aloft; everyone was in the bravest spirits because we were now so near an end of the first part of our adventure.

Now, just after sundown, when all my work was over and I was on my way to my berth, it occurred to me that I should like an apple. I ran on deck. The watch was all forward looking out for the island. The man at the helm was watching the luff of the sail and whistling away gently to himself, and that was the only sound excepting the swish of the sea against the bows and around the sides of the ship.

In I got bodily into the apple barrel, and found there was scarce an apple left; but sitting down there in the dark, what with the sound of the waters and the rocking movement of the ship, I had either fallen asleep or was on the point of doing so when a heavy man sat down with rather a clash close by. The barrel shook as he leaned his shoulders against it, and I was just about to jump up when the man began to speak. It was Silver's voice, and before I had heard a dozen words, I would not have shown myself for all the world, but lay there, trembling and listening, in the extreme of fear and curiosity, for from these dozen words I understood that the lives of all the honest men aboard depended upon me alone.

Chapter XI
WHAT I HEARD IN THE APPLE BARREL

NO, NOT I," said Silver. "Flint was cap'n; I was quartermaster, along of my timber leg. The same broadside I lost my leg, old Pew lost his deadlights. It was a master surgeon, him that ampytated me – out of college and all – Latin by the bucket, and what not; but he was hanged like a dog, and sun-dried like the rest, at Corso Castle. That was Roberts' men, that was, and comed of changing names to their ships – *Royal Fortune* and so on. Now, what a ship was christened, so let her stay, I says. So it was with the *Cassandra*, as brought us all safe home from Malabar, after England took the viceroy of the Indies; so it was with the old *Walrus*, Flint's old ship, as I've seen amuck with the red blood and fit to sink with gold."

"Ah!" cried another voice, that of the youngest hand on board, and evidently full of admiration. "He was the flower of the flock, was Flint!"

"Davis was a man too, by all accounts," said Silver. "I never sailed along of him; first with England, then with Flint, that's my story; and now here on my own account, in a manner of speaking. I laid by nine hundred safe, from England, and two thousand after Flint. That ain't bad for a man before the mast – all safe in bank. 'Tain't earning now, it's saving does it. Where's all England's men now? I dunno. Where's Flint's? Why, most of 'em aboard here, and glad to get the duff – been begging before that, some of 'em. Old Pew, as had lost his sight, and might have thought shame, spends twelve hundred pound in a year, like a lord in Parliament. Where is he now? Well, he's dead and under hatches; but for two year before that, shiver my timbers, the man was starving! He begged, and he stole, and he cut throats, and starved at that, by the powers!"

"Well, it ain't much use, after all," said the young seaman.

"'Tain't much use for fools, you may lay to it – that, nor nothing," cried Silver. "But now, you look here: you're young, you are, but you're as smart as paint. I see that when I set my eyes on you, and I'll talk to you like a man."

You may imagine how I felt when I heard this abominable old rogue addressing another in the very same words of flattery as he had used to myself. I think, if I had been able, that I would have killed him through the barrel. Meantime, he ran on, little supposing he was overheard.

"Here it is about gentlemen of fortune. They lives rough, and they risk swinging, but they eat and drink like fighting-cocks, and when a cruise is done, why, it's hundreds of pounds instead of hundreds of farthings in their pockets. Now, the most goes for rum and a good fling, and to sea again in their shirts. But that's not the course I lay. I puts it all away, some here, some there, and none too much anywheres, by reason of suspicion. I'm fifty, mark you; once back from this cruise, I set up gentleman in earnest. Time enough too, says you. Ah, but I've lived easy in the meantime, never denied myself o' nothing heart desires, and slep' soft and ate dainty all my days but when at sea. And how did I begin? Before the mast, like you!"

"Well," said the other, "but all the other money's gone now, ain't it? You daren't show face in Bristol after this."

"Why, where might you suppose it was?" asked Silver derisively.

"At Bristol, in banks and places," answered his companion.

"It were," said the cook; "it were when we weighed anchor. But my old missis has it all by now. And the Spy-glass is sold, lease and goodwill and rigging; and the old girl's off to meet me. I would tell you where, for I trust you, but it'd make jealousy among the mates."

"And can you trust your missis?" asked the other.

"Gentlemen of fortune," returned the cook, "usually trusts little among themselves, and right they are, you may lay to it. But I have a way with me, I have. When a mate brings a slip on his cable – one as knows me, I mean – it won't be in the same world with old John. There was some that was feared of Pew, and some that was feared of Flint; but Flint his own self was feared of me. Feared he was, and proud. They was the roughest crew afloat, was Flint's; the devil himself would have been feared to go to sea with them. Well now, I tell you, I'm not a boasting man, and you seen yourself how easy I keep company, but when I was quartermaster, *lambs* wasn't the word for Flint's old buccaneers. Ah, you may be sure of yourself in old John's ship."

"Well, I tell you now," replied the lad, "I didn't half a quarter like the job till I had this talk with you, John; but there's my hand on it now."

"And a brave lad you were, and smart too," answered Silver, shaking hands so heartily that all the barrel shook, "and a finer figurehead for a gentleman of fortune I never clapped my eyes on."

By this time I had begun to understand the meaning of their terms. By a "gentleman of fortune" they plainly meant neither more nor less than a common pirate, and the little scene that I had overheard was the last act in the corruption of one of the honest hands – perhaps of the last one left aboard. But on this point I was soon to be relieved, for Silver giving a little whistle, a third man strolled up and sat down by the party.

"Dick's square," said Silver.

"Oh, I know'd Dick was square," returned the voice of the coxswain, Israel Hands. "He's no fool, is Dick." And he turned his quid and spat. "But look here," he went on, "here's what I want to know, Barbecue: how long are we a-going to stand off and on like a blessed bumboat? I've had a'most enough o' Cap'n Smollett; he's hazed me long enough, by thunder! I want to go into that cabin, I do. I want their pickles and wines, and that."

"Israel," said Silver, "your head ain't much account, nor ever was. But you're able to hear, I reckon; leastways, your ears is big enough. Now, here's what I say: you'll berth forward, and you'll live hard, and you'll speak soft, and you'll keep sober till I give the word; and you may lay to that, my son."

"Well, I don't say no, do I?" growled the coxswain. "What I say is, when? That's what I say."

"When! By the powers!" cried Silver. "Well now, if you want to know, I'll tell you when. The last moment I can manage, and that's when. Here's a first-rate seaman, Cap'n Smollett, sails the blessed ship for us. Here's this squire and doctor with a map and such – I don't know where it is, do I? No more do you, says you. Well then, I mean this squire and doctor shall find the stuff, and help us to get it aboard, by the powers. Then we'll see. If I was sure of you all, sons of double Dutchmen, I'd have Cap'n Smollett navigate us half-way back again before I struck."

"Why, we're all seamen aboard here, I should think," said Dick.

"We're all forecastle hands, you mean," snapped Silver. "We can steer a course, but who's to set one? That's what all you gentlemen split on, first and last. If I had my way, I'd have Cap'n Smollett work us back into the trades; then we'd have no blessed miscalculations and a spoonful of water a day. But I know the sort you are. I'll finish with 'em at the island, as soon's the blunt's on board, and a pity it is. But you're never happy till you're drunk. Split my sides, I've a sick heart to sail with the likes of you!"

"Easy all, Long John," cried Israel. "Who's a-crossin' of you?"

"Why, how many tall ships, think ye, now, have I seen laid aboard? And how many brisk lads drying in the sun at Execution Dock?" cried Silver. "And all for this same hurry and hurry and hurry. You hear me? I seen a thing or two at sea, I have. If you would on'y lay your course, and a p'int to windward, you would ride in carriages, you would. But not you! I know you. You'll have your rum tomorrow, and go hang."

"Everybody knowed you was a kind of a chapling, John; but there's others as could hand and steer as well as you," said Israel. "They liked a bit o' fun, they did. They wasn't so high and dry, nohow, but took their fling, like jolly companions every one."

"So?" says Silver. "Well, and where are they now? Pew was that sort, and he died a beggar-man. Flint was, and he died of rum at Savannah. Ah, they was a sweet crew, they was! On'y, where are they?"

"But," asked Dick, "when we do lay 'em athwart, what are we to do with 'em, anyhow?"

"There's the man for me!" cried the cook admiringly. "That's what I call business. Well, what would you think? Put 'em ashore like maroons? That would have been England's way. Or cut 'em down like that much pork? That would have been Flint's, or Billy Bones's."

"Billy was the man for that," said Israel. "'Dead men don't bite,' says he. Well, he's dead now hisself; he knows the long and short on it now; and if ever a rough hand come to port, it was Billy."

"Right you are," said Silver; "rough and ready. But mark you here, I'm an easy man – I'm quite the gentleman, says you; but this time it's serious. Dooty is dooty, mates. I give my vote – death. When I'm in Parlyment and riding in my coach, I don't want none of these sea-lawyers in the cabin a-coming home, unlooked for, like the devil at prayers. Wait is what I say; but when the time comes, why, let her rip!"

"John," cries the coxswain, "you're a man!"

"You'll say so, Israel when you see," said Silver. "Only one thing I claim – I claim Trelawney. I'll wring his calf's head off his body with these hands, Dick!" he added, breaking off. "You just jump up, like a sweet lad, and get me an apple, to wet my pipe like."

You may fancy the terror I was in! I should have leaped out and run for it if I had found the strength, but my limbs and heart alike misgave me. I heard Dick begin to rise, and then someone seemingly stopped him, and the voice of Hands exclaimed, "Oh, stow that! Don't you get sucking of that bilge, John. Let's have a go of the rum."

"Dick," said Silver, "I trust you. I've a gauge on the keg, mind. There's the key; you fill a pannikin and bring it up."

Terrified as I was, I could not help thinking to myself that this must have been how Mr. Arrow got the strong waters that destroyed him.

Dick was gone but a little while, and during his absence Israel spoke straight on in the cook's ear. It was but a word or two that I could catch, and yet I gathered some important news, for besides other scraps that tended to the same purpose, this whole clause was audible: "Not another man of them'll jine." Hence there were still faithful men on board.

When Dick returned, one after another of the trio took the pannikin and drank – one "To luck," another with a "Here's to old Flint," and Silver himself saying, in a kind of song, "Here's to ourselves, and hold your luff, plenty of prizes and plenty of duff."

Just then a sort of brightness fell upon me in the barrel, and looking up, I found the moon had risen and was silvering the mizzen-top and shining white on the luff of the fore-sail; and almost at the same time the voice of the lookout shouted, "Land ho!"

Chapter XII
COUNCIL OF WAR

THERE WAS A GREAT RUSH of feet across the deck. I could hear people tumbling up from the cabin and the forecastle, and slipping in an instant outside my barrel, I dived behind the fore-sail, made a double towards the stern, and came out upon the open deck in time to join Hunter and Dr. Livesey in the rush for the weather bow.

There all hands were already congregated. A belt of fog had lifted almost simultaneously with the appearance of the moon. Away to the south-west of us we saw two low hills, about a couple of miles apart, and rising behind one of them a third and higher hill, whose peak was still buried in the fog. All three seemed sharp and conical in figure.

So much I saw, almost in a dream, for I had not yet recovered from my horrid fear of a minute or two before. And then I heard the voice of Captain Smollett issuing orders. The *Hispaniola* was laid a couple of points nearer the wind and now sailed a course that would just clear the island on the east.

"And now, men," said the captain, when all was sheeted home, "has any one of you ever seen that land ahead?"

"I have, sir," said Silver. "I've watered there with a trader I was cook in."

"The anchorage is on the south, behind an islet, I fancy?" asked the captain.

"Yes, sir; Skeleton Island they calls it. It were a main place for pirates once, and a hand we had on board knowed all their names for it. That hill to the nor'ard they calls the Fore-mast Hill; there are three hills in a row running south'ard – fore, main, and mizzen, sir. But the main – that's the big un, with the cloud on it – they usually calls the Spy-glass, by reason of a lookout they kept when they was in the anchorage cleaning, for it's there they cleaned their ships, sir, asking your pardon."

"I have a chart here," says Captain Smollett. "See if that's the place."

Long John's eyes burned in his head as he took the chart, but by the fresh look of the paper I knew he was doomed to disappointment. This was not the map we found in Billy Bones's chest, but an accurate copy, complete in all things – names and heights and soundings – with the single exception of the red crosses and the written notes. Sharp as must have been his annoyance, Silver had the strength of mind to hide it.

"Yes, sir," said he, "this is the spot, to be sure, and very prettily drawed out. Who might have done that, I wonder? The pirates were too ignorant, I reckon. Aye, here it is: 'Capt. Kidd's Anchorage' – just the name my shipmate called it. There's a strong current runs along the south, and then away nor'ard up the west coast. Right you was, sir," says he, "to haul your wind and keep the weather of the island. Leastways, if such was your intention as to enter and careen, and there ain't no better place for that in these waters."

"Thank you, my man," says Captain Smollett. "I'll ask you later on to give us a help. You may go."

I was surprised at the coolness with which John avowed his knowledge of the island, and I own I was half-frightened when I saw him drawing nearer to myself. He did not know, to be sure, that I had overheard his council from the apple barrel, and yet I had by this time taken such a horror of his cruelty, duplicity, and power that I could scarce conceal a shudder when he laid his hand upon my arm.

"Ah," says he, "this here is a sweet spot, this island – a sweet spot for a lad to get ashore on. You'll bathe, and you'll climb trees, and you'll hunt goats, you will; and you'll get aloft on them hills like a goat yourself. Why, it makes me young again. I was going to forget my timber leg, I was. It's a pleasant thing to be young and have ten toes, and you may lay to that. When you want to go a bit of exploring, you just ask old John, and he'll put up a snack for you to take along."

And clapping me in the friendliest way upon the shoulder, he hobbled off forward and went below.

Captain Smollett, the squire, and Dr. Livesey were talking together on the quarter-deck, and anxious as I was to tell them my story, I durst not interrupt them openly. While I was still casting about in my thoughts to find some probable excuse, Dr. Livesey called me to his side. He had left his pipe below, and being a slave to tobacco, had meant that I should fetch it; but as soon as I was near enough to speak and not to be overheard, I broke immediately, "Doctor, let me speak. Get the captain and squire down to the cabin, and then make some pretence to send for me. I have terrible news."

The doctor changed countenance a little, but next moment he was master of himself.

"Thank you, Jim," said he quite loudly, "that was all I wanted to know," as if he had asked me a question.

And with that he turned on his heel and rejoined the other two. They spoke together for a little, and though none of them started, or raised his voice, or so much as whistled, it was plain enough that Dr. Livesey had communicated my request, for the next thing that I heard was the captain giving an order to Job Anderson, and all hands were piped on deck.

"My lads," said Captain Smollett, "I've a word to say to you. This land that we have sighted is the place we have been sailing for. Mr. Trelawney, being a very open-handed gentleman, as we all know, has just asked me a word or two, and as I was able to tell him that every man on board had done his duty, alow and aloft, as I never ask to see it done better, why, he and I and the doctor are going below to the cabin to drink YOUR health and luck, and you'll have grog served out for you to drink OUR health and luck. I'll tell you what I think of this: I think it handsome. And if you think as I do, you'll give a good sea-cheer for the gentleman that does it."

The cheer followed – that was a matter of course; but it rang out so full and hearty that I confess I could hardly believe these same men were plotting for our blood.

"One more cheer for Cap'n Smollett," cried Long John when the first had subsided.

And this also was given with a will.

On the top of that the three gentlemen went below, and not long after, word was sent forward that Jim Hawkins was wanted in the cabin.

I found them all three seated round the table, a bottle of Spanish wine and some raisins before them, and the doctor smoking away, with his wig on his lap, and that, I knew, was a sign that he was agitated. The stern window was open, for it was a warm night, and you could see the moon shining behind on the ship's wake.

"Now, Hawkins," said the squire, "you have something to say."

I did as I was bid, and as short as I could make it, told the whole details of Silver's conversation. Nobody interrupted me till I was done, nor did any one of the three of them make so much as a movement, but they kept their eyes upon my face from first to last.

"Jim," said Dr. Livesey, "take a seat."

And they made me sit down at table beside them, poured me out a glass of wine, filled my hands with raisins, and all three, one after the other, and each with a bow, drank my good health, and their service to me, for my luck and courage.

"Now, captain," said the squire, "you were right, and I was wrong. I own myself an ass, and I await your orders."

"No more an ass than I, sir," returned the captain. "I never heard of a crew that meant to mutiny but what showed signs before, for any man that had an eye in his head to see the mischief and take steps according. But this crew," he added, "beats me."

"Captain," said the doctor, "with your permission, that's Silver. A very remarkable man."

"He'd look remarkably well from a yard-arm, sir," returned the captain. "But this is talk; this don't lead to anything. I see three or four points, and with Mr. Trelawney's permission, I'll name them."

"You, sir, are the captain. It is for you to speak," says Mr. Trelawney grandly.

"First point," began Mr. Smollett. "We must go on, because we can't turn back. If I gave the word to go about, they would rise at once. Second point, we have time before us – at least until this treasure's found. Third point, there are faithful hands. Now, sir, it's got to come to blows sooner or later, and what I propose is to take time by the forelock, as the saying is, and come to blows some fine day when they least expect it. We can count, I take it, on your own home servants, Mr. Trelawney?"

"As upon myself," declared the squire.

"Three," reckoned the captain; "ourselves make seven, counting Hawkins here. Now, about the honest hands?"

"Most likely Trelawney's own men," said the doctor; "those he had picked up for himself before he lit on Silver."

"Nay," replied the squire. "Hands was one of mine."

"I did think I could have trusted Hands," added the captain.

"And to think that they're all Englishmen!" broke out the squire. "Sir, I could find it in my heart to blow the ship up."

"Well, gentlemen," said the captain, "the best that I can say is not much. We must lay to, if you please, and keep a bright lookout. It's trying on a man, I know. It would be pleasanter to come to blows. But there's no help for it till we know our men. Lay to, and whistle for a wind, that's my view."

"Jim here," said the doctor, "can help us more than anyone. The men are not shy with him, and Jim is a noticing lad."

"Hawkins, I put prodigious faith in you," added the squire.

I began to feel pretty desperate at this, for I felt altogether helpless; and yet, by an odd train of circumstances, it was indeed through me that safety came. In the meantime, talk as we pleased, there were only seven out of the twenty-six on whom we knew we could rely; and out of these seven one was a boy, so that the grown men on our side were six to their nineteen.

M A R K   T W A I N

from
"That's What Living is to Me"
HOT WATER
1988

"Take Another Road"
OFF TO SEE THE LIZARD
1989

"Off to See the Lizard"
Tales from Margaritaville
1989

"Barefoot Children in the Rain"
"Remittance Man"
BAROMETER SOUP
1995

"Happy Birthday to Me"
"A Visit with Mr. Twain"
"Epilogue"
A Pirate Looks at Fifty
1998

Liner notes
FAR SIDE OF THE WORLD
2002

SAMUEL CLEMENS was born in Florida, in Monroe County, in 1835; however, he was not born in the Monroe County of Florida, where Key West is the county seat. When Sam was four, the Clemens family relocated from that village of Florida, Missouri to the port town of Hannibal right alongside the Mississippi River. And that, apparently, made all the difference.

Though Sam Clemens and Mark Twain are well understood to be one and the same person, it took nearly another twenty-five years before Mr. Twain would be born. By then, Clemens was a typesetter, editor, and correspondent for the *Territorial Enterprise* of Virginia City, Nevada, and he needed some sort of *nom de plume* that might provide a bit of anonymity for a satirical letter he wanted published. So, Sam Clemens printed the piece on February 3, 1863, using the name "Mark Twain." As every schoolchild probably knows, that

51

term "mark twain" was the boatman's call to indicate a depth of "two fathoms" along the Mississippi's shoals. And so it was that the writer called Mark Twain was born.

Except for that Florida part, as well as that specific winter date, you probably knew all that. Mark Twain is to Sam Clemens what Marvin Gardens sort of is to Jimmy Buffett. What's gone without mention, however, is that the young Clemens spent a good part of his boyhood dreaming of becoming a pirate along the Mississippi. And that's not a far cry from Jimmy's own childhood, as well. Then there was that mutual urge to become a newspaper writer; however, it seems to have been nothing more than a phase for either one.

In any event, it should come as no surprise that Jimmy Buffett would discover a soul mate in Mark Twain. After all, when Twain gave his very first lecture east of the Mississippi, he appeared before an audience of some 3,000 people packing themselves into the auditorium of New York's Cooper Institute just to listen to what he had to say.

Twain was thirty-two, and he didn't sing or dance or play any sort of musical instrument. Though he simply talked, he was pretty much a rock star, strolling the stage without any amplification whatsoever and barely standing out upon stage in the glow of the gas chandeliers. And as Steve Martin would discover decades later, a white suit could certainly go a long way in helping the vast audience follow a solo performer standing alone by himself on the stage. Twain later explained in "How to Tell A Story" that he was neither a comic, nor a wit. He described himself instead as a "humorist," which he claimed was altogether an American invention and art.

Within the week of those sold-out lectures, Twain boarded the *Quaker City* to embark upon an adventure that would provide him with material for *The Innocents Abroad*. That first book would sell more copies in 1869 than any one of Mark Twain's other works, including *The Adventures of Huckleberry Finn*. From that time on, Samuel Langhorne Clemens was a proven American original.

Even Hemingway would claim that "All modern American literature comes from one book by Mark Twain." That book is *Huckleberry Finn*. "There was nothing before. There has been nothing as good since." And there can be no doubt that Jimmy agrees. After all, who are we to argue with Papa?

Still, Jimmy has never stopped reading a lot of Twain. As a result, there have been so many references in Jimmy's works to things in Twain's writings that it's difficult to narrow down some recommended readings even to just a handful, let alone to just a single one. So, the following pages contain three or four that have popped up in Jimmy's songs and stories.

Of the thirteen books on Jimmy's list, two were written by Twain: *The Adventures of Huckleberry Finn* and *Following the Equator*. The very phrase "barometer soup," for example, comes right from *A Tramp Abroad*, and Jimmy borrows something from the same volume for his liner notes to *Far Side of the World*.

"I flit and flit – for I am ever on the wing – but I avoid the herd," quotes Jimmy. "If you would find me, you must look in the unvisited nooks and corners where others never think of going." Clearly, these two are of the same mind.

And though it might go without saying, let's still take the time to say it just the same: Both Twain and Jimmy often traveled for no other reason than for the stories they could tell. In their own wanderings, they each discovered stories. And in their own travels, they both told them. Twain gave his lectures, Jimmy sings his songs, and both have taken the time get a great many of those tales on paper.

These following selections from Samuel Langhorne Clemens should provide you the fundamentals for keeping your raft from the riverboat and for keeping up those bad habits, as well as for helping you understand the difference between lightning and a lightning bug. Whether you choose to take this Twain to the shore, or to rest your heels upon the deck rail, just remember the plan: never look back.

Additional suggested works by Mark Twain:

— *The Innocents Abroad* (1869)

— *A Tramp Abroad* (1880)

— *Life on the Mississippi* (1883)

— *The Adventures of Huckleberry Finn* (1884)

— *How to Tell A Story and Other Essays* (1893)

— *The Tragedy of Pudd'nhead Wilson* (1894)

— *Following the Equator* (1897)

— *Mark Twain's Autobiography* (published posthumously) (1924)

— *Who is Mark Twain?* (published posthumously) (2009)

FOLLOWING THE EQUATOR

a selection from
Chapter 1

A man may have no bad habits and have worse.
— Pudd'nhead Wilson's New Calendar

THE STARTING POINT of this lecturing-trip around the world was Paris, where we had been living a year or two.

We sailed for America, and there made certain preparations. This took but little time. Two members of my family elected to go with me. Also a carbuncle. The dictionary says a carbuncle is a kind of jewel. Humor is out of place in a dictionary.

We started westward from New York in midsummer, with Major Pond to manage the platform-business as far as the Pacific. It was warm work, all the way, and the last fortnight of it was suffocatingly smoky, for in Oregon and Columbia the forest fires were raging. We had an added week of smoke at the seaboard, where we were obliged awhile for our ship. She had been getting herself ashore in the smoke, and she had to be docked and repaired.

We sailed at last; and so ended a snail-paced march across the continent, which had lasted forty days.

We moved westward about mid-afternoon over a rippled and summer sea; an enticing sea, a clean and cool sea, and apparently a welcome sea to all on board; it certainly was to the distressful dustings and smokings and swelterings of the past weeks. The voyage would furnish a three-weeks holiday, with hardly a break in it. We had the whole Pacific Ocean in front of us, with nothing to do but do nothing and be comfortable. The city of Victoria was twinkling dim in the deep heart of her smoke-cloud, and getting ready to vanish and now we closed the field-glasses and sat down on our steamer chairs contented and at peace. Ours was a reasonably comfortable ship, with the customary sea-going fare – plenty of good food furnished by the Deity and cooked by the devil. The discipline observable on board was perhaps as good as it is anywhere in the Pacific and Indian Oceans. The ship was not very well arranged for tropical service; but that is nothing, for this is the rule for ships which ply in the tropics. She had an over-supply of cockroaches, but this is also the rule with ships doing business in the summer seas – at least such as have been long in service.

Our young captain was a very handsome man, tall and perfectly formed, the very figure to show up a smart uniform's best effects. He was a man of the best intentions and was polite and courteous even to courtliness. There was a softened finish about his manners which made whatever place he happened to be in seem for the moment a drawing room. He avoided the smoking room. He had no vices. He did not smoke or chew tobacco or take snuff; he did not swear, or use slang or rude, or coarse, or indelicate language, or make puns, or tell anecdotes, or laugh intemperately, or raise his voice above the moderate pitch enjoined by the canons of good form. When he gave an order, his manner modified it into a request. After dinner he and his officers joined the ladies and gentlemen in the ladies' saloon, and shared in the singing and piano playing, and helped turn the music. He had a sweet and sympathetic tenor voice, and used it with taste.

The electric lights burned there as late as the ladies and their friends might desire; but they were not allowed to burn in the smoking-room after eleven. There were many laws on the ship's statute book, of course; but so far as I could see, this and one other were the only ones that were rigidly enforced. The captain explained that he enforced this one because his own cabin adjoined the smoking-room, and the smell of tobacco smoke made him sick. I did not see how our smoke could reach him, for the smoking-room and his cabin were on the upper deck, targets for all the winds that blew; and besides there was no crack of communication between them, no opening of any sort in the intervening bulkhead. Still, to a delicate stomach even imaginary smoke can convey damage.

The captain, with his gentle nature, his polish, his sweetness, his moral and verbal purity, seemed pathetically out of place in his rude and autocratic vocation. It seemed another instance of the irony of fate.

He was going home under a cloud. The passengers knew about his trouble, and were sorry for him. Approaching Vancouver through a narrow and difficult passage densely befogged with smoke from the forest fires, he had had the ill-luck to lose his bearings and get his ship on the rocks. A matter like this would rank merely as an error with you and me;

it ranks as a crime with the directors of steamship companies. The captain had been tried by the Admiralty Court at Vancouver, and its verdict had acquitted him of blame. But that was insufficient comfort. A sterner court would examine the case in Sydney – the Court of Directors, the lords of a company in whose ships the captain had served as mate a number of years. This was his first voyage as captain.

The brightest passenger in the ship, and the most interesting and felicitous talker, was a young Canadian who was not able to let the whisky bottle alone. He was of a rich and powerful family, and could have had a distinguished career and abundance of effective help toward it if he could have conquered his appetite for drink; but he could not do it, so his great equipment of talent was of no use to him. He had often taken the pledge to drink no more, and was a good sample of what that sort of unwisdom can do for a man – for a man with anything short of an iron will. The system is wrong in two ways: it does not strike at the root of the trouble, for one thing, and to make a pledge of any kind is to declare war against nature; for a pledge is a chain that is always clanking and reminding the wearer of it that he is not a free man.

I have said that the system does not strike at the root of the trouble, and I venture to repeat that. The root is not the drinking, but the desire to drink. These are very different things. The one merely requires will – and a great deal of it, both as to bulk and staying capacity – the other merely requires watchfulness – and for no long time. The desire of course precedes the act, and should have one's first attention; it can do but little good to refuse the act over and over again, always leaving the desire unmolested, unconquered; the desire will continue to assert itself, and will be almost sure to win in the long run. When the desire intrudes, it should be at once banished out of the mind. One should be on the watch for it all the time – otherwise it will get in. It must be taken in time and not allowed to get a lodgment. A desire constantly repulsed for a fortnight should die, then. That should cure the drinking habit. The system of refusing the mere act of drinking, and leaving the desire in full force, is unintelligent war tactics, it seems to me. I used to take pledges – and soon violate them. My will was not strong, and I could not help it. And then, to be tied in any way naturally irks an otherwise free person and makes him chafe in his bonds and want to get his liberty. But when I finally ceased from taking definite pledges, and merely resolved that I would kill an injurious desire, but leave myself free to resume the desire and the habit whenever I should choose to do so, I had no more trouble. In five days I drove out the desire to smoke and was not obliged to keep watch after that; and I never experienced any strong desire to smoke again. At the end of a year and a quarter of idleness I began to write a book, and presently found that the pen was strangely reluctant to go. I tried a smoke to see if that would help me out of the difficulty. It did. I smoked eight or ten cigars and as many pipes a day for five months; finished the book, and did not smoke again until a year had gone by and another book had to be begun.

I can quit any of my nineteen injurious habits at any time, and without discomfort or inconvenience. I think that the Dr. Tanners and those others who go forty days without eating do it by resolutely keeping out the desire to eat, in the beginning, and that after a few hours the desire is discouraged and comes no more.

Once I tried my scheme in a large medical way. I had been confined to my bed several days with lumbago. My case refused to improve. Finally the doctor said, –

"My remedies have no fair chance. Consider what they have to fight, besides the lumbago. You smoke extravagantly, don't you?"

"Yes."

"You take coffee immoderately?"

"Yes."

"You eat all kinds of things that are dissatisfied with each other's company?"

"Yes."

"You drink two hot Scotches every night?"

"Yes."

"Very well, there you see what I have to contend against. We can't make progress the way the matter stands. You must make a reduction in these things; you must cut down your consumption of them considerably for some days."

"I can't, doctor."

"Why can't you."

"I lack the will-power. I can cut them off entirely, but I can't merely moderate them."

He said that that would answer, and said he would come around in 24 hours and begin work again. He was taken ill himself and could not come; but I did not need him. I cut off all those things for two days and nights; in fact, I cut off all kinds of food, too, and all drinks except water, and at the end of the 48 hours the lumbago was discouraged and left me. I was a well man; so I gave thanks and took to those delicacies again.

It seemed a valuable medical course, and I recommended it to a lady. She had run down and down and down, and had at last reached a point where medicines no longer had any helpful effect upon her. I said I knew

I could put her upon her feet in a week. It brightened her up, it filled her with hope, and she said she would do everything I told her to do. So I said she must stop swearing and drinking, and smoking and eating for four days, and then she would be all right again. And it would have happened just so, I know it; but she said she could not stop swearing, and smoking, and drinking, because she had never done those things. So there it was. She had neglected her habits, and hadn't any. Now that they would have come good, there were none in stock. She had nothing to fall back on. She was a sinking vessel, with no freight in her to throw over to lighten ship withal. Why, even one or two little bad habits could have saved her, but she was just a moral pauper. When she could have acquired them she was dissuaded by her parents, and it was too late now. These ought to be tended to while a person is young; otherwise, when age and disease come, there is nothing effectual to fight them with.

When I was a youth I used to take all kinds of pledges, and do my best to keep them, but I never could, because I didn't strike at the root of the habit – the desire; I generally broke down within the month. Once I tried limiting a habit. That worked tolerably well for a while. I pledged myself to smoke but one cigar a day. I kept the cigar waiting until bed-time, then I had a luxurious time with it. But desire persecuted me every day and all day long; so, within the week I found myself hunting for larger cigars than I had been used to smoke; then larger ones still, and still larger ones. Within the fortnight I was getting cigars made for me – on a yet larger pattern. They still grew and grew in size. Within the month my cigar had grown to such proportions that I could have used it as a crutch. It now seemed to me that a one-cigar limit was no real protection to a person, so I knocked my pledge on the head and resumed my liberty.

To go back to that young Canadian. He was a "remittance man," the first one I had ever seen or heard of. Passengers explained the term to me. They said that dissipated ne'er-do-wells belonging to important families in England and Canada were not cast off by their people while there was any hope of reforming them, but when that last hope perished at last, the ne'er-do-well was sent abroad to get him out of the way. He was shipped off with just enough money in his pocket – no, in the purser's pocket – for the needs of the voyage – and when he reached his destined port he would find a remittance awaiting him there. Not a large one, but just enough to keep him a month. A similar remittance would come monthly thereafter. It was the remittance-man's custom to pay his month's board and lodging straightway – a duty which his landlord did not allow him to forget – then spree away the rest of his money in a single night, then brood and mope and grieve in idleness till the next remittance came. It is a pathetic life.

We had other remittance-men on board, it was said. At least they said they were R. M.'s. There were two. But they did not resemble the Canadian; they lacked his tidiness, and his brains, and his gentlemanly ways, and his resolute spirit, and his humanities and generosities. One of them was a lad of nineteen or twenty, and he was a good deal of a ruin, as to clothes, and morals, and general aspect. He said he was a scion of a ducal house in England, and had been shipped to Canada for the house's relief, that he had fallen into trouble there, and was now being shipped to Australia. He said he had no title. Beyond this remark he was economical of the truth. The first thing he did in Australia was to get into the lockup, and the next thing he did was to proclaim himself an earl in the police court in the morning and fail to prove it.

"I CONQUER THE GORNER GRAT"

a selection from

A Tramp Abroad / Chapter XXXVIII

WE WENT INTO CAMP on that wild spot to which that ram had brought us. The men were greatly fatigued. Their conviction that we were lost was forgotten in the cheer of a good supper, and before the reaction had a chance to set in, I loaded them up with paregoric and put them to bed.

Next morning I was considering in my mind our desperate situation and trying to think of a remedy, when Harris came to me with a Baedeker map which showed conclusively that the mountain we were on was still in Switzerland – yes, every part of it was in Switzerland. So we were not lost, after all. This was an immense relief; it lifted the weight of two such mountains from my breast. I immediately had the news disseminated and the map was exhibited. The effect was wonderful. As soon as the men saw with their own eyes that they knew where they were, and that it was only the summit that was lost and not themselves, they cheered up instantly and said with one accord, let the summit take care of itself.

Our distresses being at an end, I now determined to rest the men in camp and give the scientific department of the Expedition a chance. First, I made a barometric observation, to get our altitude, but I could not perceive that there was any result. I knew, by my scientific reading, that either thermometers or barometers ought to be boiled, to make them accurate; I did not know which it was, so I boiled them both. There was still no result; so I examined these instruments and discovered that they possessed radical blemishes: the barometer had no hand but the brass pointer and the ball of the thermometer was stuffed with tin-foil. I might have boiled those things to rags, and never found out anything.

I hunted up another barometer; it was new and perfect. I boiled it half an hour in a pot of bean soup which the cooks were making. The result was unexpected: the instrument was not affecting at all, but there was such a strong barometer taste to the soup that the head cook, who was a most conscientious person, changed its name in the bill of fare. The dish was so greatly liked by all, that I ordered the cook to have barometer soup every day. It was believed that the barometer might eventually be injured, but I did not care for that. I had demonstrated to my satisfaction that it could not tell how high a mountain was; therefore, I had no real use for it. Changes in the weather I could take care of without it; I did not wish to know when the weather was going to be good, what I wanted to know was when it was going to be bad, and this I could find out from Harris's corns. Harris had had his corns tested and regulated at the government observatory in Heidelberg, and one could depend upon them with confidence. So I transferred the new barometer to the cooking department, to be used for the official mess. It was found that even a pretty fair article of soup could be made from the defective barometer; so I allowed that one to be transferred to the subordinate mess.

I next boiled the thermometer, and got a most excellent result; the mercury went up to about 200 degrees Fahrenheit. In the opinion of the other scientists of the Expedition, this seemed to indicate that we had attained the extraordinary altitude of two hundred thousand feet above sea-level. Science places the line of eternal snow at about ten thousand feet above sea-level. There was no snow where we were; consequently, it was proven that the eternal snow-line ceases somewhere above the ten-thousand-foot level and does not begin any more. This was an interesting fact, and one which had not been observed by any observer before. It was as valuable as interesting, too, since it would open up the deserted summits of the highest Alps to population and agriculture. It was a proud thing to be where we were, yet it caused us a pang to reflect that but for that ram we might just as well been two hundred thousand feet higher.

The success of my last experiment induced me to try an experiment with my photographic apparatus. I got it out, and boiled one of my cameras, but the thing was a failure; it made the wood swell up and burst, and I could not see that the lenses were any better than they were before. I now concluded to boil a guide. It might improve him; it could not impair his usefulness. But I was not allowed to proceed. Guides have no feeling for science, and this one would not consent to be made uncomfortable in its interest.

In the midst of my scientific work, one of those needless accidents happened which are always occurring among the ignorant and thoughtless. A porter shot at a chamois and missed it and crippled the Latinist. This was not a serious matter to me, for a Latinist's duties are as well performed on crutches as otherwise – but the fact remained that if the Latinist had not happened to be in the way a mule would have got that load. That would have been quite another matter, for when it comes down to a question of value there is a palpable difference between a Latinist and a mule. I could not depend on having a Latinist in the right place every time; so, to make things safe, I ordered that in the future the chamois must not be hunted within limits of the camp with any other weapon than the forefinger.

My nerves had hardly grown quiet after this affair when they got another shake-up – one which utterly unmanned me for a moment: a rumor swept suddenly through the camp that one of the barkeepers had fallen over a precipice!

However, it turned out that it was only a chaplain. I had laid in an extra force of chaplains, purposely to be prepared for emergencies like this, but by some unaccountable oversight had come away rather short-handed in the matter of barkeepers.

&

THE ADVENTURES OF HUCKLEBERRY FINN

a selection from
Chapter XII

IT MUST A BEEN CLOSE on to one o'clock when we got below the island at last, and the raft did seem to go mighty slow. If a boat was to come along, we was going to take to the canoe and break for the Illinois shore; and it was well a boat didn't come, for we hadn't ever thought to put the gun in the canoe, or a fishing-line, or anything to eat. We was in ruther too much of a sweat to think of so many things. It warn't good judgment to put EVERYTHING on the raft.

If the men went to the island I just expect they found the camp fire I built, and watched it all night for Jim to come. Anyways, they stayed away from us, and if my building the fire never fooled them it warn't no fault of mine. I played it as low down on them as I could.

When the first streak of day began to show we tied up to a towhead in a big bend on the Illinois side, and hacked off cottonwood branches with the hatchet, and covered up the raft with them so she looked like there had been a cave-in in the bank there. A towhead is a sandbar that has cottonwoods on it as thick as harrow-teeth.

We had mountains on the Missouri shore and heavy timber on the Illinois side, and the channel was down the Missouri shore at that place, so we warn't afraid of anybody running across us. We laid there all day, and watched the rafts and steamboats spin down the Missouri shore, and up-bound steamboats fight the big river in the middle. I told Jim all about the time I had jabbering with that woman; and Jim said she was a smart one, and if she was to start after us herself she wouldn't set down and watch a camp fire – no, sir, she'd fetch a dog. Well, then, I said, why couldn't she tell her husband to fetch a dog? Jim said he bet she did think of it by the time the men was ready to start, and he believed they must a gone up-town to get a dog and so they lost all that time, or else we wouldn't be here on a towhead sixteen or seventeen mile below the village – no, indeedy, we would be in that same old town again. So I said I didn't care what was the reason they didn't get us as long as they didn't.

When it was beginning to come on dark, we poked our heads out of the cottonwood thicket, and looked up and down and across; nothing in sight; so Jim took up some of the top planks of the raft and built a snug wigwam to get under in blazing weather and rainy, and to keep the things dry. Jim made a floor for the wigwam, and raised it a foot or more above the level of the raft, so now the blankets and all the traps was out of reach of steamboat waves. Right in the middle of the wigwam we made a layer of dirt about five or six inches deep with a frame around it for to hold it to its place; this was to build a fire on in sloppy weather or chilly; the wigwam would keep it from being seen. We made an extra steering-oar, too, because one of the others might get broke on a snag or something. We fixed up a short, forked stick to hang the old lantern on, because we must always light the lantern whenever we see a steamboat coming down-stream, to keep from getting run over; but we wouldn't have to light it for up-stream boats unless we see we was in what they call a "crossing;" for the river was pretty high yet, very low banks being still a little under water; so up-bound boats didn't always run the channel, but hunted easy water.

This second night we run between seven and eight hours, with a current that was making over four mile an hour. We catched fish and talked, and we took a swim now and then to keep off sleepiness. It was kind of solemn, drifting down the big, still river, laying on our backs looking up at the stars, and we didn't ever feel like talking loud, and it warn't often that we laughed – only a little kind of a low chuckle. We had mighty good weather as a general thing, and nothing ever happened to us at all – that night, nor the next, nor the next.

Every night we passed towns, some of them away up on black hill-sides, nothing but just a shiny bed of lights; not a house could you see. The fifth night we passed St. Louis, and it was like the whole world lit up. In St. Petersburg, they used to say there was twenty or thirty thou-sand people in St. Louis, but I never believed it till I see that wonderful spread of lights at two o'clock that still night. There warn't a sound there; everybody was asleep.

Every night now I used to slip ashore towards ten o'clock at some little village, and buy ten or fifteen cents' worth of meal or bacon or other stuff to eat; and sometimes I lifted a chicken that warn't roosting com-fortable, and took him along. Pap always said, take a chicken when you get a chance, because if you don't want him yourself you can easy find somebody that does, and a good deed ain't ever forgot. I never see pap when he didn't want the chicken himself, but that is what he used to say, anyway.

Mornings before daylight I slipped into cornfields and borrowed a watermelon, or a mushmelon, or a punkin, or some new corn, or things of that kind. Pap always said it warn't no harm to borrow things if you was meaning to pay them back some time; but the widow said it warn't anything but a soft name for stealing, and no decent body would do it. Jim said he reckoned the widow was partly right and pap was partly right; so the best way would be for us to pick out two or three things from the list and say we wouldn't borrow them any more – then he reckoned it wouldn't be no harm to borrow the others. So we talked it over all one night, drifting along down the river, trying to make up our minds whether to drop the watermelons, or the cantelopes, or the mushmelons, or what. But towards daylight we got it all settled satisfactory, and concluded to drop crabapples and p'simmons. We warn't feeling just right before that, but it was all comfortable now. I was glad the way it come out, too, because crabapples ain't ever good, and the p'simmons wouldn't be ripe for two or three months yet.

We shot a water-fowl, now and then, that got up too early in the morning or didn't go to bed early enough in the evening. Take it all round, we lived pretty high.

The fifth night below St. Louis we had a big storm after midnight, with a power of thunder and lightning, and the rain poured down in a solid sheet. We stayed in the wigwam and let the raft take care of itself. When the lightning glared out we could see a big straight river ahead, and high, rocky bluffs on both sides. By and by says I, "Hel-LO, Jim, looky yonder!" It was a steamboat that had killed herself on a rock. We was drifting straight down for her. The lightning showed her very distinct. She was leaning over, with part of her upper deck above water, and you could see every little chimbly-guy clean and clear, and a chair by the big bell, with an old slouch hat hanging on the back of it, when the flashes come.

Well, it being away in the night and stormy, and all so mysterious-like, I felt just the way any other boy would a felt when I see that wreck laying there so mournful and lonesome in the middle of the river. I wanted to get aboard of her and slink around a little, and see what there was there. So I says:

"Le's land on her, Jim."

But Jim was dead against it at first. He says:

"I doan' want to go fool'n 'long er no wrack. We's doin' blame' well, en we better let blame' well alone, as de good book says. Like as not dey's a watchman on dat wrack."

"Watchman your grandmother," I says; "There ain't nothing to watch but the texas and the pilot-house; and do you reckon anybody's going to resk his life for a texas and a pilot-house such a night as this, when it's likely to break up and wash off down the river any minute?" Jim couldn't say nothing to that, so he didn't try. "And besides," I says, "we might borrow something worth having out of the captain's stateroom. Seegars, I bet you – and cost five cents apiece, solid cash. Steamboat captains is always rich, and get sixty dollars a month, and THEY don't care a cent what a thing costs, you know, long as they want it. Stick a candle in your pocket; I can't rest, Jim, till we give her a rummaging. Do you reckon Tom Sawyer would ever go by this thing? Not for pie, he wouldn't. He'd call it an adventure – that's what he'd call it; and he'd land on that wreck if it was his last act. And wouldn't he throw style into it? – wouldn't he spread himself, nor nothing? Why, you'd think it was Christopher C'lumbus discovering Kingdom-Come. I wish Tom Sawyer WAS here."

Jim he grumbled a little, but give in. He said we mustn't talk any more than we could help, and then talk mighty low. The lightning showed us the wreck again just in time, and we fetched the stabboard derrick, and made fast there.

The deck was high out here. We went sneaking down the slope of it to labboard, in the dark, towards the texas, feeling our way slow with our feet, and spreading our hands out to fend off the guys, for it was so dark we couldn't see no sign of them. Pretty soon we struck the forward end of the skylight, and clumb on to it; and the next step fetched us in front of the captain's door, which was open, and by Jimminy, away down through the texas-hall we see a light! and all in the same second we seem to hear low voices in yonder!

Jim whispered and said he was feeling powerful sick, and told me to come along. I says, all right, and was going to start for the raft; but just then I heard a voice wail out and say:

"Oh, please don't, boys; I swear I won't ever tell!"

Another voice said, pretty loud:

"It's a lie, Jim Turner. You've acted this way before. You always want more'n your share, and you've always got it, too, because you've swore 't if you didn't you'd tell. But this time you've said it jest one time too many. You're the meanest, treacherousest hound in this country."

By this time Jim was gone for the raft. I was just a-biling with curiosity; and I says to myself, Tom Sawyer wouldn't back out now, and so I won't either; I'm a-going to see what's going on here. So I dropped on my hands and knees in the little passage, and crept aft in the dark till there warn't but one stateroom betwixt me and the cross-hall of the texas. Then in there I see a man stretched on the floor and tied hand and foot, and two men standing over him, and one of them had a dim lantern in his hand, and the other one had a pistol. This one kept pointing the pistol at the man's head on the floor, and saying:

"I'd LIKE to! And I orter, too – a mean skunk!"

The man on the floor would shrivel up and say, "Oh, please don't, Bill; I hain't ever goin' to tell."

And every time he said that, the man with the lantern would laugh and say:

"'Deed you AIN'T! You never said no truer thing 'n that, you bet you." And once he said: "Hear him beg! and yit if we hadn't got the best of him and tied him he'd a killed us both. And what FOR? Jist for noth'n. Jist because we stood on our RIGHTS – that's what for. But I lay you ain't a-goin' to threaten nobody any more, Jim Turner. Put UP that pistol, Bill."

Bill says:

"I don't want to, Jake Packard. I'm for killin' him – and didn't he kill old Hatfield jist the same way – and don't he deserve it?"

"But I don't WANT him killed, and I've got my reasons for it."

"Bless yo' heart for them words, Jake Packard! I'll never forgit you long's I live!" says the man on the floor, sort of blubbering.

Packard didn't take no notice of that, but hung up his lantern on a nail and started towards where I was there in the dark, and motioned Bill to come. I crawfished as fast as I could about two yards, but the boat slanted so that I couldn't make very good time; so to keep from getting run over and catched I crawled into a stateroom on the upper side. The man came a-pawing along in the dark, and when Packard got to my stateroom, he says:

"Here – come in here."

And in he come, and Bill after him. But before they got in I was up in the upper berth, cornered, and sorry I come. Then they stood there, with their hands on the ledge of the berth, and talked. I couldn't see them, but I could tell where they was by the whisky they'd been having. I was glad I didn't drink whisky; but it wouldn't made much difference anyway, because most of the time they couldn't a treed me because I didn't breathe. I was too scared. And, besides, a body COULDN'T breathe and hear such talk. They talked low and earnest. Bill wanted to kill Turner. He says:

"He's said he'll tell, and he will. If we was to give both our shares to him NOW it wouldn't make no difference after the row and the way we've served him. Shore's you're born, he'll turn State's evidence; now you hear ME. I'm for putting him out of his troubles."

"So'm I," says Packard, very quiet.

"Blame it, I'd sorter begun to think you wasn't. Well, then, that's all right. Le's go and do it."

"Hold on a minute; I hain't had my say yit. You listen to me. Shooting's good, but there's quieter ways if the thing's GOT to be done. But what I say is this: it ain't good sense to go court'n around after a halter if you can git at what you're up to in some way that's jist as good and at the same time don't bring you into no resks. Ain't that so?"

"You bet it is. But how you goin' to manage it this time?"

"Well, my idea is this: we'll rustle around and gather up whatever pickins we've overlooked in the staterooms, and shove for shore and hide the truck. Then we'll wait. Now I say it ain't a-goin' to be more'n two hours befo' this wrack breaks up and washes off down the river. See? He'll be drownded, and won't have nobody to blame for it but his own self. I reckon that's a considerble sight better 'n killin' of him. I'm unfavorable to killin' a man as long as you can git aroun' it; it ain't good sense, it ain't good morals. Ain't I right?"

"Yes, I reck'n you are. But s'pose she DON'T break up and wash off?"

"Well, we can wait the two hours anyway and see, can't we?"

"All right, then; come along."

So they started, and I lit out, all in a cold sweat, and scrambled forward. It was dark as pitch there; but I said, in a kind of a coarse whisper, "Jim!" and he answered up, right at my elbow, with a sort of a moan, and I says:

"Quick, Jim, it ain't no time for fooling around and moaning; there's a gang of murderers in yonder, and if we don't hunt up their boat and set her drifting down the river so these fellows can't get away from the wreck there's one of 'em going to be in a bad fix. But if we find their boat we can put ALL of 'em in a bad fix – for the sheriff 'll get 'em. Quick – hurry! I'll hunt the labboard side, you hunt the stabboard. You start at the raft, and – "

"Oh, my lordy, lordy! RAF'? Dey ain' no raf' no mo'; she done broke loose en gone – en here we is!"

𝒢𝓈

THE ART OF AUTHORSHIP

Literary reminiscences, methods of work, and advice to young beginners,
personally contributed by leading authors of the day
Bainton, George, comp. and ed. (1890)

MARK TWAIN IS THE *NOM DE GUERRE* of Samuel Langhorne Clemens, the great American humourist, whose books are the delight of all English-speaking people.

"Your inquiry has set me thinking," he writes; "but, so far, my thought fails to materialise. I mean that, upon consideration, I am not sure that I have methods in composition. I do suppose I must have but they somehow refuse to take shape in my mind; their details refuse to separate and submit to classification and description; they remain a jumble visible, like the fragments of glass when you look in at the wrong end of a kaleidoscope, but still a jumble. If I could turn the whole thing around and look in at the other end, why then the figures would flash into form out of the chaos, and I shouldn't have any more trouble. But my head isn't right for that to-day, apparently. It might have been, maybe, if I had slept last night.

"However, let us try guessing. Let us guess that whenever we read a sentence and like it, we unconsciously store it away in our model-chamber; and it goes with the myriad of its fellows to the building, brick by brick, of the eventual edifice which we call our style. And let us guess that whenever we run across other forms of bricks whose colour, or some other defect, offends us, we unconsciously reject these, and so one never finds them in our edifice. If I have subjected myself to any training processes, and no doubt I have, it must have been in this unconscious or half-conscious fashion. I think it unlikely that deliberate and consciously methodical training is usual with the craft. I think it likely that the training most in use is of this unconscious sort, and is guided and governed and made by-and-by unconsciously systematic, by an automatically-working taste, a taste which selects and rejects without asking you for

69

any help, and patiently and steadily improves itself without troubling you to approve or applaud. Yes, and likely enough when the structure is at last pretty well up, and attracts attention, you feel complimented, whereas you didn't build it, and didn't even consciously superintend. Yes; one notices, for instance, that long, involved sentences confuse him, and that he is obliged to re-read them to get the sense. Unconsciously, then, he rejects that brick. Unconsciously, he accustoms himself to writing short sentences as a rule. At times, he may indulge himself with a long one, but he will make sure that there are no folds in it, no vaguenesses, no parenthetical interruptions of its view as a whole; when he is done with it, it won't be a sea-serpent, with half of its arches under the water; it will be a torch light procession.

"Well, also he will notice in the course of time, as his reading goes on, that the difference between the *almost right* word and the *right* word is really a large matter: 'tis the difference between the lightning-bug and the lightning. After that, of course, comes that exceedingly important brick: the *exact* word; however, this is running into an essay, and I beg pardon.

"So, I seem to have arrived at this: doubtless I have methods, but they begot themselves; in which case, I am only their proprietor, not their father."

EUDORA WELTY

from
"Just Getting It on Paper"
"A Baker's Dozen (Minus One)
A Pirate Looks at Fifty
1998

EUDORA WELTY was born to be read, and I'm sticking with that line for openers.

Whether or not you know anything about either her or her life really does not matter, for Eudora Welty's a person who should be taken at her word. And each one of her words is a gem.

Jimmy not only knows that, but he understands that as well. There can be no doubt that he first came to idolize her as one of Mississippi's legendary writers, but that he later built an even greater appreciation upon that foundation.

Eudora Welty is on Jimmy's list of favorite books, but not so much for her fiction or her photography, but more for her memoir called *One Writer's Beginnings*, which is based upon a series of her lectures about writing; however, the lectures read more like a collection of stories, and each has a point to be made about the art of writing.

As the title of the following

piece plainly tells, this is not the story of her entire life, but of her child-hood, her youth, and her college education in the second two decades of the twentieth century. More importantly, it is a book about writing by our nation's most prolific writer of short stories. Let's put it this way: Ernest Hemingway was a male Eudora Welty, not at all vice versa.

You could easily view *One Writer's Beginnings* in the same two ways that Jimmy has absorbed it: as a wonderful story of life in Mississippi and as an essential primer on how to become a writer.

"My mother had made me a reader and stressed the legacy of my family's Mississippi roots," says Jimmy. "Mississippians who had made people take notice."

Eudora Welty is a significant member of that group.

"Anyone bellying up to the bar with a few shots of tequila swimming around the bloodstream can tell a story," he adds. "The challenge is to wake up the next day and carve through the hangover minefield and a million other excuses and be able to cohesively get it down on paper."

Those things Jimmy learned from a collection of masters like E. B. White, Hunter Thompson, Robert Penn Warren, and – most certainly – Eudora Welty.

Additional suggested works by Eudora Welty:

— *The Optimist's Daughter* (1972) Pulitzer

— *The Collected Stories of Eudora Welty* (1982)

EUDORA WELTY

LEARNING TO SEE

a selection from
One Writer's Beginnings/Part II

BACK ON CONGRESS STREET, when my father unlocked the door
of our closed-up, waiting house, I rushed ahead into the airless hall
and stormed up the stairs, pounding the carpet of each step with both
hands ahead of me, and putting my face right down into the cloud of the
dear dust of our long absence. I was welcoming ourselves back. Doing
likewise, more methodically, my father was going from room to room re-
starting all the clocks.

I think now, in looking back on these summer trips – this one and a
number later, made in the car and on the train – that another element in
them must have been influencing my mind. The trips were wholes unto
themselves. They were stories. Not only in form, but in their taking on
direction, movement, development, change. They changed something in
my life: each trip made its particular revelation, though I could not have
found words for it. But with the passage of time, I could look back on
them and see them bringing me news, discoveries, premonitions, promises – I still can; they still do.

When I did begin to write, the short story was a shape that had already formed itself and stood waiting in the back of my mind. Nor is it
surprising to me that when I made my first attempt at a novel, I entered
its world – that of the mysterious Yazoo-Mississippi Delta – as a child
riding there on a train: "From the warm window sill the endless fields
glowed like a hearth in firelight, and Laura, looking out, leaning on her
elbows with her head between her hands, felt what an arriver in a land
feels – that slow hard pounding in the breast."

The events in our lives happen in a sequence in time, but in their
significance to ourselves they find their own order, a timetable not neces-

73

sarily – perhaps not possibly – chronological. The time as we know it subjectively is often the chronology that stories and novels follow: it is the continuous thread of revelation.

CHARLES A. LINDBERGH

from
"Oysters and Pearls"
"Beach House on the Moon"
BEACH HOUSE ON THE MOON
1999

Liner Notes
BUFFET HOTEL
2009

SITTING ALONE in a rickety, wicker chair for more than thirty-three hours can make for a mighty long airplane ride, but the twenty-five-year-old flying his *Spirit of St. Louis* had no idea where his course would take him.

There was no doubt that he was headed for Paris, but Charles A. Lindbergh never once expected to become overnight the most famous person in the world. Nevertheless, that's what happened once his wheels touched down at Le Bourget Aerodrome on the outskirts of Paris. The fame of others over the years in the City of Light, such as Oscar Wilde or members of the Lost Generation, would be overshadowed by "The Lone Eagle" and what he had accomplished. Lindbergh's flight was one thing, but the speed at which its word was spread was altogether another matter.

Unfortunately, his fame soon proved to be the sort that brings confusion, for the madcap media of that era were more eager to spread their words than to spread the news. When they soon began to make up whatever stories they could sell, the otherwise shy and quiet Minnesota farm boy took it upon himself to set the record straight. Lindbergh never once fashioned himself a writer, let alone a person who boasted of things he'd done. What he simply wished for posterity was an unadorned account of what it was that he had set out to do and what it was that he had actually done. And that's how the first telling of his story became his first book, entitled *WE*.

Lindbergh firmly believed that this progression of flight was nothing other than a stage in the evolution of mankind, and he was simply a link in that inevitable progression. In less than three weeks, he drafted a single manuscript that provided an almost mechanical account of his life up until then. Simple and direct, *WE* appeared in stores less than two months after he'd landed in Paris. And so great was his fame that it became a best-seller in less time than it had taken him to cross the North Atlantic. Within those next eight weeks in 1927, *WE* would sell nearly 200,000 copies. By comparison, Hemingway's *The Sun Also Rises* had sold 23,000 copies during its entire first year in 1926.

Over the next half century, Lindbergh's life remained forever defined by his flight and the fame which followed. While the public demanded to know more and more about the pilot, he became bothered more and more by the ways in which society was abusing aviation's potential. Warplanes aside, the overall effects of air travel in terms of population movement, of pollution, and of land development all caused Lindbergh great concern. Though he did not write many other books, he did address aviation in the context of his concerns and his values. To the end, he never lost sight of his dreams; dreams not of fame and fortune, but of a world unharmed by mankind's proper place within this world and beyond.

"After my death the molecules of my being will return to the earth and the sky," he wrote in his *Autobiography of Values* published after he had died. "They came from the stars. I am of the stars."

Additional suggested works by Charles A. Lindbergh:

— *Of Flight and Life* (1948)

— *The Spirit of St. Louis* (1953)

— *Autobiography of Values* (1977)

CHARLES A. LINDBERGH

"NEW YORK TO PARIS"

a selection from
WE / Chapter X

AT NEW YORK WE CHECKED OVER THE PLANE, engine and instruments, which required several short flights over the field.

When the plane was completely inspected and ready for the trans-Atlantic flight, there were dense fogs reported along the coast and over Nova Scotia and Newfoundland, in addition to a storm area over the North Atlantic.

On the morning of May 19th, a light rain was falling and the sky was overcast. Weather reports from land stations and ships along the Great Circle course were unfavorable and there was apparently no prospect of taking off for Paris for several days at least. In the morning I visited the Wright plant at Paterson, New Jersey, and had planned to attend a theatre performance in New York that evening. But at about six o'clock I received a special report from the New York Weather Bureau. A high pressure area was over the entire North Atlantic and the low pressure over Nova Scotia and Newfoundland was receding. It was apparent that the prospects of the fog clearing up were as good as I might expect for some time to come. The North Atlantic should be clear with only local storms on the coast of Europe. The moon had just passed full and the percentage of days with fog over Newfoundland and the Grand Banks was increasing so that there seemed to be no advantage in waiting longer.

We went to Curtiss Field as quickly as possible and made arrangements for the barograph to be sealed and installed, and for the plane to be serviced and checked.

We decided partially to fill the fuel tanks in the hangar before towing the ship on a truck to Roosevelt Field, which adjoins Curtiss on the east, where the servicing would be completed.

I left the responsibility for conditioning the plane in the hands of the men on the field while I went into the hotel for about two and one-half hours of rest; but at the hotel there were several more details which had to be completed and I was unable to get any sleep that night.

I returned to the field before daybreak on the morning of the twentieth. A light rain was falling which continued until almost dawn; consequently we did not move the ship to Roosevelt Field until much later than we had planned, and the take-off was delayed from daybreak until nearly eight o'clock.

At dawn the shower had passed, although the sky was overcast, and occasionally there would be some slight precipitation. The tail of the plane was lashed to a truck and escorted by a number of motorcycle police. The slow trip from Curtiss to Roosevelt was begun.

The ship was placed at the extreme west end of the field heading along the east and west runway, and the final fueling commenced.

About 7:40 A.M. the motor was started and at 7:52 I took off on the flight for Paris.

The field was a little soft due to the rain during the night and the heavily loaded plane gathered speed very slowly. After passing the half way mark, however, it was apparent that I would be able to clear the obstructions at the end. I passed over a tractor by about fifteen feet and telephone line by about twenty, with a fair reserve of flying speed. I believe that the ship would have taken off from a hard field with at least five hundred pounds more weight.

I turned slightly to the right to avoid some high trees on a hill directly ahead, but by the time I had gone a few hundred yards I had sufficient altitude to clear all obstructions and throttled the engine down to 1750 RPM. I took up a compass course at once and soon reached Long Island Sound where the Curtiss Oriole with its photographer, which had been escorting me, turned back.

The haze soon cleared and from Cape Cod through the southern half of Nova Scotia the weather and visibility were excellent. I was flying very low, sometimes as close as ten feet from the trees and water.

On the three hundred mile stretch of water between Cape Cod and Nova Scotia I passed within view of numerous fishing vessels.

The northern part of Nova Scotia contained a number of storm areas and several times I flew through cloudbursts.

As I neared the northern coast, snow appeared in patches on the ground and far to the eastward the coastline was covered with fog.

For many miles between Nova Scotia and Newfoundland the ocean was covered with caked ice but as I approached the coast the ice disappeared entirely and I saw several ships in this area.

I had taken up a course for St. Johns, which is south of the Great Circle from New York to Paris, so that there would be no question of the fact that I had passed Newfoundland in case I was forced down in the north Atlantic.

I passed over numerous icebergs after leaving St. Johns, but saw no ships except near the coast. Darkness set in about 8:15 and a thin, low fog formed over the sea through which the white bergs showed up with surprising clearness. This fog became thicker and increased in height until within two hours I was just skimming the top of storm clouds at about ten thousand feet. Even at this altitude there was a thick haze through which only the stars directly overhead could be seen.

There was no moon and it was very dark. The tops of some of the storm clouds were several thousand feet above me and at one time, when I attempted to fly through one of the larger clouds, sleet started to collect on the plane and I was forced to turn around and get back into clear air immediately and then fly around any clouds which I could not get over.

The moon appeared on the horizon after about two hours of darkness; then the flying was much less complicated.

Dawn came at about 1 A.M. New York time and the temperature had risen until there was practically no remaining danger of sleet.

Shortly after sunrise the clouds became more broken although some of them were far above me and it was often necessary to fly through them, navigating by instruments only.

As the sun became higher, holes appeared in the fog. Through one the open water was visible, and I dropped down until less than a hundred feet above the waves. There was a strong wind blowing from the northwest and the ocean was covered with white caps.

After a few miles of fairly clear weather the ceiling lowered to zero and for nearly two hours I flew entirely blind through the fog at an altitude of about 1500 feet. Then the fog raised and the water was visible again.

On several more occasions it was necessary to fly by instrument for short periods; then the fog broke up into patches. These patches took on forms of every description. Numerous shorelines appeared, with trees perfectly outlined against the horizon. In fact, the mirages were so natural that, had I not been in mid-Atlantic and known that no land existed along my route, I would have taken them to be actual islands.

As the fog cleared I dropped down closer to the water, sometimes flying within ten feet of the waves and seldom higher than two hundred.

There is a cushion of air close to the ground or water through which a plane flies with less effort than when at a higher altitude, and for hours a time I took advantage of this factor.

Also, it was less difficult to determine the wind drift near the water. During the entire flight the wind was strong enough to produce white caps on the waves. When one of these formed, the foam would be blown off, showing the wind's direction and approximate velocity. This foam remained on the water long enough for me to obtain a general idea of my drift.

During the day I saw a number of porpoises and a few birds but no ships, although I understand that two different boats reported me passing over. The first indication of my approach to the European Coast was a small fishing boat which I first noticed a few miles ahead and slightly to the south of my course. There were several of these fishing boats grouped within a few miles of each other. I flew over the first boat without seeing any signs of life. As I circled over the second, however, a man's face appeared, looking out of cabin window.

I have carried on short conversations with people on the ground by flying low with throttled engine, shouting a question, and receiving the answer by some signal. When I saw this fisherman I decided to try to get him to point towards land. I had no sooner made the decision than the futility of the effort became apparent. In all likelihood he could not speak English, and even if he could he would undoubtedly be far too astounded to answer. However, I circled again and closing the throttle as the plane passed within, a few feet of the boat I shouted, "Which way is Ireland?" Of course the attempt was useless and I continued on my course.

Less than an hour later a rugged and semi-mountainous coastline appeared to the northeast. I was flying less than two hundred feet from water when I sighted it. The shore was fairly distinct and not over ten or fifteen miles away. A light haze coupled with numerous local storm areas had prevented my seeing it from a long distance.

The coastline came down from the north, curved over towards the east. I had very little doubt that it was the southwestern end of Ireland but in order to make sure I changed my course towards the nearest point, of land. I located Cape Valentia and Dingle Bay, then resumed my compass course towards Paris

After leaving Ireland I passed a number of steamers and was seldom out of sight a ship.

In a little over two hours the coast of England appeared. My course passed over Southern England and a little south of Plymouth; then across the English Channel, striking France over Cherbourg.

The English farms were very impressive from the air in contrast to ours in America. They appeared extremely small and unusually neat and tidy with their stone and hedge fences.

Thomas McGuane

THE MAIN CHARACTER in Tom McGuane's second novel migrates from Michigan to Montana, then down to Key West, and that was pretty much the writer's own course in those days.

Because *The Bushwhacked Piano* was published in 1971, however, readers will never know just how Nicholas Payne ever might have fared during Key West's "decade of decadence" that was the Seventies. McGuane, on the other hand, came to know that reckless period quite well, for often the writer was right there in the eye of its storm.

And while he somehow managed to weather it all, the young storyteller of that time had no trouble fitting a constant full-tilt feeling into his next two novels: *Ninety-two in the Shade* in 1973, then *Panama* in 1978. Populated with shrimpers and smugglers and artists of every stripe, the island life had changed quite a bit since the arrival of Nicholas Payne. And it had become a whole lot different than McGuane's very first look, as well.

A much younger Tom McGuane had been introduced to Key West when his father brought him down from Michigan to fish. That little father-and-son excursion played out in the more tranquil Fifties: Tom was in his teens, Truman was out of the Little White House, and the Old Town of the Cold War years still struggled in somewhat of a stupor. The water-based economy relied fully upon some spongers and turtlers, along with struggling shrimpers, as well as the U.S. Navy. Nonetheless, there was more than enough water surrounding the Keys to make young Tom McGuane want to come back some day, a sentiment best stated by his fishing-guide hero of *Ninety-two in the Shade*. "God, if they will only leave the ocean alone," exclaims Tom Skelton, "I can handle anything."

In the years between that first look and his second, McGuane fished the waters of his home state Michigan and enrolled at Michigan State. There he met Jim Harrison, who would prove in time to be the charter member of a rather remarkable circle of lifelong friends. As a student in the early Sixties, McGuane had dreams of becoming a comic novelist; Harrison, a poet. The two of them shared a fondness for the written word, as well as a mutual affection for hunting and for fishing.

Once McGuane's graduate work in both dramatic literature and playwriting was finished at Yale, he accepted a fellowship at Stanford, where in 1969 he managed to churn out *The Sporting Club* in less than two months. He was thirty years old, and that first novel proved worthy of the sort of critical acclaim that labeled him "a language star." It was the sale of the film rights to that story, however, that enabled the newly-minted novelist and his wife to purchase a ranch in Montana and to spend some winter month's on Florida's Summerland Key, where McGuane could fish and work on *The Bushwhacked Piano*.

Before long there emerged a sporting club of sorts that orbited around this language star. Harrison was lured down for the fishing, and a guide named Woody Sexton drove down a client named Guy de la Valdéne to meet up with the fishing novelist on Summerland. In time, Guy would become known affectionately as "The Count," and one day would produce a documentary about fishing the flats. This circle of friends was just beginning as the McGuanes would move further on down US 1 to Key West in another season or two.

In career terms, Tom McGuane was a bit more like Hemingway than he was Nicholas Payne. After all, Papa had been attracted to Key West not so much by the island's working conditions as by its fishing . . . Not to mention its somewhat lawless social recreation: rumrunners and drug smugglers are one and the same. And just as Hemingway had regularly contributed pieces on deepwater fishing to a new magazine called *Esquire*, so McGuane contributed several of his own about flats fishing to *Sports Illustrated*, including his classic essay about permit fishing on the flats entitled "The Longest Silence." In fact, some of *Sports Illustrated's* very earliest articles about Key West's sport fishing had come from Martin Kane, who – in his retirement – remained a rather flamboyant member of the McGuane circle at the Chart Room Bar. Jimmy's own *SI* article about fishing in the 2004 swimsuit issue gives a tip of his fishing cap to the legendary Marty Kane.

In retrospect, one can only wonder what life might've been like for Jimmy if he'd never met up with Tom McGuane. Perhaps someday Jimmy will recount for us those stories about how he came to live under the same roof with Tom and Becky and young Thomas McGuane, as well as how McGuane introduced him to bartender Phil Clark, about whom Jimmy composed "A Pirate Looks at Forty." But those tales, along with those of the Full Moon Saloon, of the Snake Pit, of the Club Mandible, and of McGuane's self-described "Captain Berserko" period must wait for another volume.

Still, this much remains clear: without Jimmy's meeting Tom McGuane, the Count might never have photographed the cover image for *A White Sport Coat and a Pink Crustacean*, and "the language star" might never have composed those liner notes on the back that say (among other things): "What Jimmy Buffett knows is that our personal music history lies at the curious hinterland where Hank Williams and Xavier Cugat meet with somewhat less animosity than the theoreticians would have us believe."

Without McGuane, we might never have *Rancho Deluxe* along with Jimmy's trek to Montana to compose the musical score with "Livingston Saturday Night," to meet the acclaimed writer named Richard Brautigan, and to stumble upon the dying town of Ringling. Without Guy de la Valdéne's *Tarpon*, we'd never have his footage of flats fishing, of the Seventies Key West, and of Harrison, Brautigan, and McGuane holding forth together on the topic of fishing the keys. And without Tom McGuane, Jimmy might never have had a talented writer for a brother-in-law.

As for the next page or so, the inspiration comes from Jimmy's own liner notes in 1985 for "Desperation Samba" on *Last Mango in Paris*, where he's written this little nugget: "This song brings to mind two things. First, an image of Robert Mitchum standing in the doorway of a bar in Tijuana, and second, a line by Thomas McGuane, my brother-in-law, from his book, *Panama*, 'The night wrote a check the morning couldn't cash.'" By then, the McGuanes had moved back to the ranch.

So, of all the marvelous prose that Tom McGuane has produced over the years, it's Jimmy who's directed us to this particular passage that concludes with that specific line.

From drinks at the Full Moon Saloon to the oyster shell parking lots of Garrison Bight, McGuane's rather autobiographical *Panama* provides a panorama of the island that's just as sweeping as any in Hemingway's *To Have and Have Not*. And in a great many ways, none of the things had changed at all since Papa first roamed those same streets. There can be doubt that you will be reading all of McGuane's island stuff; then, you'll move on with him to his stories from Montana. After all, Deadrock seems to be a lot like Livingston(e).

Additional suggested works by Thomas McGuane:

— *The Sporting Club* (1969)

— *The Bushwhacked Piano* (1971)

— *Ninety-two in the Shade* (1973)

— *Panama* (1978)

— *Nobody's Angel* (1981)

— *An Outside Chance* (nonfiction, 1981)

— *Keep the Change* (1999)

— *Nothing But Blue Skies* (1992)

— *The Longest Silence* (nonfiction, 2000)

— *The Cadence of Grass* (2002)

— *Gallatin Canyon* (short stories 2006)

Panama

a selection from

Chapter V

I NOTICED THAT MANY PEOPLE I saw were surrounded by invisible objects. Many of the visitors from New York had invisible typewriters right in front of their noses upon which they typed every word they spoke. Boozy hicks played an invisible accordion as they talked. Hip characters stirred an invisible cup of coffee with their noses as they spoke. Senior citizens walked down the street, dog-paddling in turbulent, invisible whirlpools.

When the sun came up, we were behind the A&B Lobster House. I was splashing water out of the bilge of my little sailboat with half a Clorox bottle. Catherine was hanging over the bow dangling a string in the water. She said the ripples made the reflection look like she was holding electricity.

"That time in the Russian Tea Room, what were you on?" I asked.

"I don't want to talk about that."

I uncleated the centerboard and dropped it. It knocked under the hull. I looked around at the well-built little sloop, proof that I was not an utter damned fool; as a matter of fact, the only one in a shipbuilding family who could still build a boat.

I stuck the tiller into the rudder and freed the lines that attached us to the decayed dock amid bright Cuban crawfish boats piled with traps and Styrofoam markers. We began to drift away from the dock. Then suddenly I reached for the lines and tied us up again.

"I don't want to go sailing," I said.

"Why?"

"I feel like sinking it."

"We've been walking around all night. You're too tired."

"Breakfast," I said.

"My nerves are raw," she said. "We'll have to go someplace where the service is fast or I'll jump out of my skin."

Two dogs I knew, Smith and Progress, stared at us from the breakwater. Shrimp boats were starting to roll in from the night with their trawling booms swaying to the same rhythm as they passed each other in the channel going to different basins. A panhandler appeared from behind the warehouse and dismissed us. I was beginning to sense that the night had written a check that daylight couldn't cash.

JIM HARRISON

from
"Lage Nom Ai"
BAROMETER SOUP
1995

NOT UNLIKE the earliest works of Hemingway, Faulkner, and Matthiessen, those of Jim Harrison also include poetry, as well as fiction. His first book was the 1969 volume of poetry called *Outlyer*, and then came yet another, before Tom McGuane talked him into writing a novel in 1970, and that one was *Wolf*.

"Key West in the Seventies and Eighties was a bit of a literary capital," explains Harrison in his memoir, *Off to the Side*, but he's quick to admit that the place "was a wide open arena for questionable behavior on anyone's part."

Nevertheless, Jim Harrison was one of the better behaved members of the notorious Club Mandible, and he has remained just as perplexed as the rest of the world by McGuane's fabled liner note stating that Jimmy "was among the first of the Sucking Chest Wound Singers to sleep on the yellow line."

Harrison not only wrote and

fished alongside the best of them during his days and nights on the island, but he also succeeded with his wife of all these years in raising their two daughters. In a similar vein of stability, he has kept his close friendships with Jimmy, with the Count, and with Russell Chatham, yet another fisherman brought into the circle via Montana and McGuane.

Out of those same Key West years came *A Good Day to Die*, which Harrison describes as "a dour attempt at a thoroughly 'noir' novel in an American setting." Years before Hunter Thompson would submit "Freak Power in the Rockies" to *Rolling Stone,* or Carl Hiaasen would give us the environmental terrorist that was Skip Wiley, Jim Harrison told of some off-handed remark in Captain Tony's Saloon that inspired a plot to blow up the Hoover Dam. *The Washington Post* claimed Harrison's novel was "like the best of Thoreau," but Walden Pond was nothing at all like the watering hole on Greene Street.

"Tony always hires the most beautiful barmaids in Key West," Harrison was quick to point out in his novel, "and the Navy pilots come in numbers, fall in love and are rejected. The barmaids, it seems, are in love with musicians and other worthless types who wear pigtails and are always broke. The barmaids are not interested in sleek pilots with thin mustaches and wallets full of flight pay."

By the late Seventies, Harrison had published his tenth book, *Legends of the Fall*, a trilogy of novellas that includes the title story, along with "Revenge" and "The Man Who Gave Up His Name." For the next fifteen years, the cover on *Legends* was a painting done by Russell Chatham, the first of a collaboration that's continued through these years.

Then Harrison wrote the screenplay, Brad Pitt played a part, and so the story goes. One novella became a blockbuster; another, a Kevin Costner film; and the third, the inspiration for a song. While the lyrics for "Lage Nom Ai" cannot convey the entire tale, they do remain true to the story. Harrison's "Epilogue" from that work follows, but reading the entire novella clearly enhances the appreciation for Jimmy's song: a tribute to a story, as well as to a lasting friendship between two storytellers.

Additional suggested works by Jim Harrison:

— *A Good Day to Die* (1971)

— *Legends of the Fall* (1979)

— *Off to the Side* (2002)

EPILOGUE

a selection from

The Man Who Gave Up His Name

HE DROVE SOUTH IN LATE OCTOBER, one year after his father's
death, in a sixty-seven Plymouth he had paid seven hundred dollars for. In no particular hurry and nothing to guide him but a Rand
McNally, he stopped in Savannah, bought two new tires, and thought
the town rather too pretty for his taste. He wanted to avoid a self-conscious location. In the trunk there was one suitcase, one box of books,
and one box of assorted cooking equipment he could not bear to part
with in his urge to travel light; he was neither happy nor unhappy as he
rejected one place after another, just looking things over. Finally, in late
November, he got a job in a small seafood restaurant in Islamorada,
Florida, of good reputation at an abysmal wage. His fingers were soon
sore from cleaning shrimp and picking crab. He got nailed rather painfully in the palm by a stone crab and learned to be careful. Within a
month he was allowed to cook a daily specialty. His home was a one-
room tourist cabin at the end of a lane of crushed shells lined by dank
mangroves bordered by an unnavigable lagoon. There was a small gas
stove, a double bed, Formica table, linoleum floor, black leopard lamp,
rickety air conditioner, three rattan chairs. There were a lot of mosquitoes
which he didn't mind, having been trained for them in Wisconsin. He
kept his money in an upturned frozen orange juice can in the refrigerator
freezer, not wanting to bother with the bank. He didn't kill the palmetto
bugs that crawled around, having figured that they didn't eat much or
sting. One day he was pleased to see a large rattler back in the bedraggled
palm scrub. He bought a rowboat and nearly died when an oarlock broke
and he was swept out to sea in a strong tide and a heavy sea and spent an
entire day bailing with his hat and paddling with one oar. He was res-
cued by fishermen and spent two days in a hospital being treated for

severe sunburn, feeling like a stupid shit. It paid to keep on your toes, he thought, in this new life where he was utterly unprotected. He unfolded a lot of ice-cold money and bought a Boston Whaler and a sixty-horse Evinrude, after determining it was the most stable boat available. With the help of a push pole he kept strapped to the boat's gunwhale he could skid it across the lagoon in a medium tide and keep it beside the cabin. He bought a spinning rod and some jigs, mask and flippers and a book on marine biology. He waded tidal flats looking at the bottom, fished channels, identified his catch in the book and released it. He worked six days a week but had mornings and Monday off for his explorations. When he felt more comfortable in these strange waters he bought charts and a boat trailer and went off to Big Pine on Mondays, an area richer in mangrove islets and tidal cuts. One warm still day in a deep tidal creek he hooked a tarpon and was shocked as it hurtled out of the water near the boat, twisting its big silver body and its gill plates rattling before it broke off. That day he thought he counted a thousand shades of turquoise in the water. He had become a water, wind and cloud watcher in addition to being a cook. Late at night he danced to a transistor radio. He was the source of respectful local amusement. He had a wonderful affair with a Cuban waitress his own age. She had a small portable stereo and taught him Latin dances. He got more local respect when he threw two burly drunks out of the restaurant one night, punching one senseless, but it reminded him unpleasantly of Berto and he wept a few minutes when he got home. He wrote and received chatty letters from his daughter in Florence, exchanging apercus with Phillip on the great author E.M. Cioran. After the Cuban waitress abandoned Islamorada for Miami he had a brief three-day fling with a college girl who was a bit sullen and really didn't like to fuck. His mother wrote that she had actually seen Jack Lord in Honolulu. She and Henry planned a two-week trip down in April when the tourist season slackened and Nordstrom would have more time. They would have to take the bus as Henry considered planes an insult to his life and the life of the sky. One day while driving Nordstrom saw a moray eel and a black-tipped shark and was thrilled to the core.

One evening while he was taking a cigarette break behind the restaurant, Nordstrom watched two waitresses approach, then pause while they whispered. It was his habit during the evening break to sit on a huge piece of dredged coral, hundreds of pounds of tiny antique, crushed marine invertebrates. He would drink a tall, cold piña colada, smoke a cigarette and watch the ocean. In his position of chef none of the other help usurped his sitting place. Now the waitresses came up to him, both a little plump and giggling but one with fine olive features. They offered a joint and he took a long, noncommittal puff. Their problem was that there was a dance tonight in a bar just down Route 1 and they had no one to go with and they didn't want to walk in the bar alone. Nordstrom was disturbed. He had never danced in public. Oh Jesus why not, he said to himself. At the bar he danced with the two girls and anyone else willing until four in the morning when the band stopped. Then he danced alone to the juke-box until four thirty in the morning when everyone had to leave.

JAMES M. BARRIE

OF ALL THE MYTHS that have found their ways into Jimmy's way of thinking, perhaps none is more quintessentially Buffett than Sir James Matthew Barrie's classic tale of the boy who lives on an imaginary island, who flies all alone, who leaves the island to discover stories for the lost boys, and – of course – who grows older, but not up.

Down through the ages, recorded and oral histories often told stories of healing waters, or fountains of youth, or just various methods of reversing – if not stopping – the effects of human aging. And at the end of the nineteenth century, Oscar Wilde's *The Picture of Dorian Gray* spun the tale as that of someone who did not want to age at all. By the time that Barrie took his turn, though, aging was no longer the issue. Peter Pan could never stop from growing older, but he refused to ever grow up.

Barrie was born the ninth child

in a Scottish family of ten children; however, two of his siblings died in their childhood. His brother, David, was the next oldest to James, and he was their mother's favorite. When David died in an ice-skating accident just before his fourteenth birthday, Mrs. Barrie was devastated. What little solace the mother found only came in knowing that her boy was never going to grow old. And so the seed of the Peter Pan myth was planted.

First appearing in 1902 as the middle chapters of *The Little White Bird*, Barrie's novel for adults, the character of Peter Pan was portrayed as just a week-old baby who doesn't want to turn into a human being at all. As a little white bird, then, the baby Peter flies from his nursery to London's Kensington Gardens, where nannies and parents all bring their babies to play. Once the children have left at the end of each day, Kensington Gardens becomes a place inhabited only by fairies, wild animals, and other mystical creatures. Into that mystical world the young Peter Pan landed and lived forever.

Just two years later, Barrie adapted those central chapters from *The Little White Bird* into a stage play called "Peter Pan, or The Boy Who Wouldn't Grow Up." It was in this form that Kensington Gardens took on the name of "the Never, Never Land," and it became the place where Peter lived with Tinker Bell, as well as with all the Lost Boys. At night, Peter would venture out of their garden and go in search of stories, stories which Mrs. Darling would tell to her young children. And so the myth continued to grow.

The public loved it so much, that Barrie was then able to transform this stage version into his 1906 novel, *Peter Pan in Kensington Gardens*, where the Never Land also became inhabited by pirates. By 1911, Barrie was once again recasting the story as *Peter and Wendy*; then, finally, as *Peter Pan*.

The pirate element is just as crucial to literature, in general, as it is to Jimmy's own use. In a nod to Robert Louis Stevenson, Barrie describes Capt. James Hook as the only person whom the Sea-Cook named Barbecue had ever feared. And Barbecue had served under the notorious Capt. Flint, who also feared Hook. Readers of *Treasure Island* understood that the Sea-Cook is none other than one Long John Silver.

Of all the adaptations of this Peter Pan myth, though, the one which stands as the goofiest of them all remains Steven Spielberg's movie version called *Hook*, featuring Dustin Hoffman as the title character, Robin Williams as an aging Peter, and Julia Roberts as Tinker Bell. For the purposes of this reader, though, it's worth noting that Jimmy played the role of a pirate who tries to steal the designer shoes from the feet of Peter Pan.

Before the scene is over, a sombrero-wearing Peter is weaving his way through a crowd while "A Pirate Looks at Forty" plays in the background. Thankfully, there are other, much stronger links between Sir James' myth and Jimmy's works.

Some of these Pan allusions pop up in song lyrics, and many are off-hand comments that Jimmy might make in conversation. But his most prolonged reference comes in *A Salty Piece of Land*, where Tully Mars encounters Bucky Norman, an ex-patriate who owns a fishing lodge called "Lost Boys" and who wears a hat with the words: "Never Grow Up."

"The Island of the Lost Boys was my favorite part of *Peter Pan*," Tully admits, "and now as Bucky showed me his camp, I was seeing life imitate art." And when we understand who has written those words, then we recognize that it's now art imitating life imitating art. Or something along those lines.

In any event, it is now time to think happy thoughts and fly off to that imaginary island, which Barrie notes is "second to the right, and straight on till morning."

Additional suggested works by James Barrie:

— *Peter and Wendy (1911)*

— *A Well-Remembered Voice (1918)*

"The Island Come True"

a selection from
Peter Pan/Chapter V

FEELING THAT PETER WAS ON HIS WAY BACK, the Neverland had again woke into life. We ought to use the pluperfect and say wakened, but woke is better and was always used by Peter.

In his absence things are usually quiet on the island. The fairies take an hour longer in the morning, the beasts attend to their young, the redskins feed heavily for six days and nights, and when pirates and lost boys meet they merely bite their thumbs at each other. But with the coming of Peter, who hates lethargy, they are under way again: if you put your ear to the ground now, you would hear the whole island seething with life.

On this evening the chief forces of the island were disposed as follows. The lost boys were out looking for Peter, the pirates were out looking for the lost boys, the redskins were out looking for the pirates, and the beasts were out looking for the redskins. They were going round and round the island, but they did not meet because all were going at the same rate.

All wanted blood except the boys, who liked it as a rule, but to-night were out to greet their captain. The boys on the island vary, of course, in numbers, according as they get killed and so on; and when they seem to be growing up, which is against the rules, Peter thins them out; but at this time there were six of them, counting the twins as two. Let us pretend to lie here among the sugar-cane and watch them as they steal by in single file, each with his hand on his dagger.

They are forbidden by Peter to look in the least like him, and they wear the skins of the bears slain by themselves, in which they are so round and furry that when they fall they roll. They have therefore become very sure-footed.

The first to pass is Tootles, not the least brave but the most unfortunate of all that gallant band. He had been in fewer adventures than any of them, because the big things constantly happened just when he had stepped round the corner; all would be quiet, he would take the opportunity of going off to gather a few sticks for firewood, and then when he returned the others would be sweeping up the blood. This ill-luck had given a gentle melancholy to his countenance, but instead of souring his nature had sweetened it, so that he was quite the humblest of the boys.

Poor kind Tootles, there is danger in the air for you to-night. Take care lest an adventure is now offered you, which, if accepted, will plunge you in deepest woe. Tootles, the fairy Tink, who is bent on mischief this night is looking for a tool, and she thinks you are the most easily tricked of the boys. 'Ware Tinker Bell.

Would that he could hear us, but we are not really on the island, and he passes by, biting his knuckles.

Next comes Nibs, the gay and debonair, followed by Slightly, who cuts whistles out of the trees and dances ecstatically to his own tunes. Slightly is the most conceited of the boys. He thinks he remembers the days before he was lost, with their manners and customs, and this has given his nose an offensive tilt. Curly is fourth; he is a pickle, and so often has he had to deliver up his person when Peter said sternly, "Stand forth the one who did this thing," that now at the command he stands forth automatically whether he has done it or not. Last come the Twins, who cannot be described because we should be sure to be describing the wrong one. Peter never quite knew what twins were, and his band were not allowed to know anything he did not know, so these two were always vague about themselves, and did their best to give satisfaction by keeping close together in an apologetic sort of way.

The boys vanish in the gloom, and after a pause, but not a long pause, for things go briskly on the island, come the pirates on their track. We hear them before they are seen, and it is always the same dreadful song:

> Avast belay, yo ho, heave to,
>   A-pirating we go,
> And if we're parted by a shot
>   We're sure to meet below!

A more villainous-looking lot never hung in a row on Execution dock. Here, a little in advance, ever and again with his head to the ground listening, his great arms bare, pieces of eight in his ears as ornaments, is the handsome Italian Cecco, who cut his name in letters of blood on the back of the governor of the prison at Gao. That gigantic black behind him has had many names since he dropped the one with which dusky mothers still terrify their children on the banks of the Guadjo-mo. Here is Bill Jukes, every inch of him tattooed, the same Bill Jukes who got six dozen on the *Walrus* from Flint before he would drop the bag of *moidores*; and Cookson, said to be Black Murphy's brother (but this was never proved), and Gentleman Starkey, once an usher in public school and still dainty in his ways of killing; and Skylights (Morgan's Skylights); and the Irish bo'sun Smee, an oddly genial man who stabbed, so to speak, without offence, and was the only non-conformist in Hook's crew; and Noodler, whose hands were fixed on backwards; and Robt. Mullins and Alf Mason and many another ruffian long known and feared on the Spanish Main.

In the midst of them, the blackest and largest in that dark setting, reclined James Hook, or as he wrote himself, *Jas. Hook*, of whom it is said he was the only man that the Sea-Cook feared.

He lay at his ease in a rough chariot drawn and propelled by his men, and instead of a right hand he had the iron hook with which ever and anon he encouraged them to increase their pace. As dogs this terrible man treated and addressed them, and as dogs they obeyed him. In person he was cadaverous and blackavized, and his hair was dressed in long curls, which at a little distance looked like black candles, and gave a singularly threatening expression to his handsome countenance. His eyes were of the blue of the forget-me-not, and of a profound melancholy, save when he was plunging his hook into you, at which time two red spots appeared in them and lit them up horribly. In manner, something of the *grand seigneur* still clung to him, so that he even ripped you up with an air, and I have been told that he was a *raconteur* of repute. He was never more sinister than when he was most polite, which is probably the truest test of breeding; and the elegance of his diction, even when he was swearing, no less than the distinction of his demeanour, showed him one of a different cast from his crew. A man of indomitable courage, it was said that the only thing he shied at was the sight of his own blood, which was thick and of an unusual colour. In dress he somewhat aped the attire associated with the name of Charles II, having heard it said in some earlier period of his career that he bore a strange resemblance to the ill-fated Stuarts; and in his mouth he had a holder of his own contrivance which enabled him to smoke two cigars at once. But undoubtedly the grimmest part of him was his iron claw.

Let us now kill a pirate, to show Hook's method. Skylights will do. As they pass, Skylights lurches clumsily against him, ruffling his lace collar; the hook shoots forth, there is a tearing sound and one screech, then the body is kicked aside, and the pirates pass on. He has not even taken the cigars from his mouth.

Such is the terrible man against whom Peter Pan is pitted. Which will win?

On the trail of the pirates, stealing noiselessly down the war-path, which is not visible to inexperienced eyes, come the redskins, every one of them with his eyes peeled. They carry tomahawks and knives, and their naked bodies gleam with paint and oil. Strung around them are scalps, of boys as well as of pirates, for these are the Piccaninny tribe, and not to be confused with the softer-hearted Delawares or the Hurons. In the van, on all fours, is Great Big Little Panther, a brave of so many scalps that in his present position they somewhat impede his progress. Bringing up the rear, the place of greatest danger, comes Tiger Lily, proudly erect, a princess in her own right. She is the most beautiful of dusky Dianas and the belle of the Piccaninnies, coquettish, cold and amorous by turns; there is not a brave who would not have the wayward thing to wife, but she staves off the altar with a hatchet. Observe how they pass over fallen twigs without making the slightest noise. The only sound to be heard is their somewhat heavy breathing. The fact is that they are all a little fat just now after the heavy gorging, but in time they will work this off. For the moment, however, it constitutes their chief danger.

The redskins disappear as they have come like shadows, and soon their place is taken by the beasts, a great and motley procession: lions, tigers, bears, and the innumerable smaller savage things that flee from them, for every kind of beast, lives cheek by jowl on the favoured island. Their tongues are hanging out, they are hungry to-night.

When they have passed, comes the last figure of all, a gigantic crocodile. We shall see for whom she is looking presently.

The crocodile passes, but soon the boys appear again, for the procession must continue indefinitely until one of the parties stops or changes its pace. Then quickly they will be on top of each other.

All keep a sharp look-out in front, but none suspects that the danger may be creeping up from behind. This shows how real the island was.

The first to fall out of the moving circle was the boys. They flung themselves down on the sward, close to their underground home.

"I do wish Peter would come back," every one of them said nervously, though in height and in breadth they were all larger than their captain.

"I am the only one who is not afraid of pirates," Slightly said, in the tone that prevented his being a general favourite; but perhaps a distant sound disturbed him, for he added hastily, "but I wish he would come back, and tell us whether he has heard anything more about Cinderella."

They talked of Cinderella, and Tootles was confident that his mother must have been very like her.

It was only in Peter's absence that they could speak of mothers, the subject being forbidden by him as silly.

"All I remember about my mother," Nibs told them, "is that she often said to my father, 'Oh, how I wish I had a cheque-book of my own!' I don't know what a cheque-book is, but I should just love to give my mother one."

While they talked they heard a distant sound. You or I, not being wild things of the woods, would have heard nothing, but they heard it, and it was the grim song:

> Yo ho, yo ho, the pirate life,
> The flag o' skull and bones,
> A merry hour, a hempen rope,
> And hey for Davy Jones.

At once the lost boys – but where are they? They are no longer there. Rabbits could not have disappeared more quickly.

I will tell you where they are. With the exception of Nibs, who has darted away to reconnoiter, they are already in their home under the ground, a very delightful residence of which we shall see a good deal presently. But how have they reached it? for there is no entrance to be seen, not so much as a large stone, which if rolled away, would disclose the mouth of a cave. Look closely, however, and you may note that there are here seven large trees, each with a hole in its hollow trunk as large as a boy. These are the seven entrances to the home under the ground, for which Hook has been searching in vain these many moons. Will he find it tonight?

As the pirates advanced, the quick eye of Starkey sighted Nibs disappearing through the wood, and at once his pistol flashed out. But an iron claw gripped his shoulder.

"Captain, let go!" he cried, writhing.

Now for the first time we hear the voice of Hook. It was a black voice. "Put back that pistol first," it said threateningly.

"It was one of those boys you hate. I could have shot him dead."

"Ay, and the sound would have brought Tiger Lily's redskins upon us. Do you want to lose your scalp?"

"Shall I after him, Captain," asked pathetic Smee, "and tickle him with Johnny Corkscrew?" Smee had pleasant names for everything, and his cutlass was Johnny Corkscrew, because he wiggled it in the wound. One could mention many lovable traits in Smee. For instance, after killing, it was his spectacles he wiped instead of his weapon.

"Johnny's a silent fellow," he reminded Hook.

"Not now, Smee," Hook said darkly. "He is only one, and I want to mischief all the seven. Scatter and look for them."

The pirates disappeared among the trees, and in a moment their Captain and Smee were alone. Hook heaved a heavy sigh, and I know not why it was, perhaps it was because of the soft beauty of the evening, but there came over him a desire to confide to his faithful bo'sun the story of his life. He spoke long and earnestly, but what it was all about Smee, who was rather stupid, did not know in the least.

Anon he caught the word Peter.

"Most of all," Hook was saying passionately, "I want their captain, Peter Pan. 'Twas he cut off my arm." He brandished the hook threateningly. "I've waited long to shake his hand with this. Oh, I'll tear him!"

"And yet," said Smee, "I have often heard you say that hook was worth a score of hands, for combing the hair and other homely uses."

"Ay," Hook answered, "if I was a mother I would pray to have my children born with this instead of that," and he cast a look of pride upon his iron hand and one of scorn upon the other. Then again he frowned.

"Peter flung my arm," he said, wincing, "to a crocodile that happened to be passing by."

"I have often," said Smee, "noticed your strange dread of crocodiles."

"Not of crocodiles," Hook corrected him, "but of that one crocodile." He lowered his voice. "It liked my arm so much, Smee, that it has followed me ever since, from sea to sea and from land to land, licking its lips for the rest of me."

"In a way," said Smee, "it's sort of a compliment."

"I want no such compliments," Hook barked petulantly. "I want Peter Pan, who first gave the brute its taste for me."

He sat down on a large mushroom, and now there was a quiver in his voice. "Smee," he said huskily, "that crocodile would have had me before this, but by a lucky chance it swallowed a clock which goes tick tick inside it, and so before it can reach me I hear the tick and bolt." He laughed, but in a hollow way.

"Someday," said Smee, "the clock will run down, and he'll get you."

Hook wetted his dry lips. "Ay," he said, "that fear haunts me."

Since sitting down he had felt curiously warm. "Smee," he said, "this seat is hot." Hook jumped up. "Odds, bobs, hammer, and tongs! I'm burning."

They examined the mushroom, which was of a size and solidity unknown on the mainland; they pulled it up, and it came at once in their hands, for it had no root. Stranger still, smoke began at once to ascend. The pirates looked at each other. "A chimney!" they both exclaimed.

They had indeed discovered the chimney of the home under the ground. It was the custom of the boys to stop it with a mushroom when enemies were in the neighbourhood.

Not only smoke came out of it. There came also children's voices, for so safe did the boys feel in their hiding-place that they were gaily chattering. The pirates listened grimly, and then replaced the mushroom. They looked around them and noted the holes in the seven trees.

"Did you hear them say Peter Pan's from home?" Smee whispered, fidgeting with Johnny Corkscrew.

Hook nodded. He stood for a long time lost in thought, and at last a curdling smile lit up his swarthy face. Smee had been waiting for it. "Unrip your plan, captain," he cried eagerly.

"To return to the ship," Hook replied slowly through his teeth, "and cook a large rich cake of a jolly thickness with green sugar on it. There can be but one room below, for there is but one chimney. The silly moles had not the sense to see that they did not need a door apiece. That shows they have no mother. We will leave the cake on the shore of the Mermaids' Lagoon. These boys are always swimming about there, playing with the mermaids. They will find the cake and they will gobble it up, because, having no mother, they don't know how dangerous 'tis to eat rich damp cake." He burst into laughter, not hollow laughter now, but honest laughter. "Aha, they will die."

Smee had listened with growing admiration.

"It's the wickedest, prettiest policy ever I heard of!" he cried, and in their exultation they danced and sang:

> Avast, belay, when I appear,
>   By fear they're overtook;
> Nought's left upon your bones when you
>   Have shaken claws with Hook.

They began the verse, but they never finished it, for another sound broke in and stilled them. There was at first such a tiny sound that a leaf might have fallen on it and smothered it, but as it came nearer it was more distinct.

Tick tick tick tick!

Hook stood shuddering, one foot in the air.

"The crocodile!" he gasped, and bounded away, followed by his bo'sun.

It was indeed the crocodile. It had passed the redskins, who were now on the trail of the other pirates. It oozed on after Hook.

Once more the boys emerged into the open; but the dangers of the night were not yet over, for presently Nibs rushed breathless into their midst, pursued by a pack of wolves. The tongues of the pursuers were hanging out; the baying of them was horrible.

"Save me, save me!" cried Nibs, falling on the ground.

"But what can we do, what can we do?"

It was a high compliment to Peter that at that dire moment their thoughts turned to him.

"What would Peter do?" they cried simultaneously.

Almost in the same breath they cried, "Peter would look at them through his legs."

And then, "Let us do what Peter would do."

It is quite the most successful way of defying wolves, and as one boy they bent and looked through their legs. The next moment is the long one, but victory came quickly, for as the boys advanced upon them in the terrible attitude, the wolves dropped their tails and fled.

Now Nibs rose from the ground, and the others thought that his staring eyes still saw the wolves. But it was not wolves he saw.

"I have seen a wonderfuller thing," he cried, as they gathered round him eagerly. "A great white bird. It is flying this way."

"What kind of a bird, do you think?"

"I don't know," Nibs said, awestruck, "but it looks so weary, and as it flies it moans, 'Poor Wendy,'"

"Poor Wendy?"

"I remember," said Slightly instantly, "there are birds called Wendies."

"See, it comes!" cried Curly, pointing to Wendy in the heavens.

Wendy was now almost overhead, and they could hear her plaintive cry. But more distinct came the shrill voice of Tinker Bell. The jealous fairy had now cast off all disguise of friendship, and was darting at her victim from every direction, pinching savagely each time she touched.

"Hullo, Tink," cried the wondering boys.

Tink's reply rang out: "Peter wants you to shoot the Wendy."

It was not in their nature to question when Peter ordered. "Let us do what Peter wishes!" cried the simple boys. "Quick, bows and arrows!"

All but Tootles popped down their trees. He had a bow and arrow with him, and Tink noted it, and rubbed her little hands.

"Quick, Tootles, quick," she screamed. "Peter will be so pleased."

Tootles excitedly fitted the arrow to his bow. "Out of the way, Tink," he shouted, and then he fired, and Wendy fluttered to the ground with an arrow in her breast.

Ralph Middleton Munroe

from
Liner notes
ONE PARTICULAR HARBOUR
1983

MIAMI WAS SIMPLY the most recent of a long line of names for a Florida river when young Ralph Munroe first arrived in the late 1880s.

That newest name had come from those people known as the Mayaimi, who'd lived around the fresh waters of Lake Okeechobee for the past two thousand years. Cousins to the Tequesta and the Calusa, the Mayaimi had all but disappeared by the early 1800s. Some had been sold into slavery by raiders down from the Carolinas, while others had escaped to Cuba and points further south.

After they were gone, the Mayaimi had left behind little more than a handful of unwritten words from their native tongue. The most enduring of those was their name, "Mayaimi," which meant "sweet water."

All of this began to make sense later when the U.S. Coastal Survey of 1849 indicated that the river was not at all an estuary of Biscayne Bay, but a freshwater tributary flowing from the lake down to the sea. Having been known since the arrival of the Spaniards as Rio Ratones (Mouse River), as well as Fresh Water River, Lemon River, and Garband River, the Sweet Water River became more commonly called Miami River not long after the Second Seminole War ended in 1842. And so it was called the Miami when Munroe arrived at the settlement that was commonly called "Biscayne Bay Country."

As a young man, Ralph Middleton Munroe came down from Staten Island to Florida aboard the vessel of William Brickell, another resident of that same New York island who had established a trading post along the banks of the Miami. In later years, Brickell would join with a citrus farmer named Julia Tuttle from Cleveland to convince her friend Henry Flagler to route his railroad through that territory and to spearhead her effort to incorporate the frontier into an actual place called Miami. These, then, were the kinds of events that Munroe had just happened to witness. In time, he settled into Biscayne Bay Country, where he helped found Coconut Grove. Munroe became both a naturalist and a photographer, but his truest passion was designing yachts for those with both the money and the time to spend upon such things.

To the Commodore, as well as to millions of others who would follow, south Florida was pretty much their idea of life in the tropics, even though it's in the temperate zone of which Jimmy says he is "umbilically connected." That doesn't mean that the Commodore never sailed into the tropics, as well as into Key West, whose latitude of 24° 33.2' N. places the southernmost point just minutes above the Tropic of Cancer at 23° 26.17' N.

"I believe the love of the tropics is born in most boys of the temperate zone," wrote the Commodore early on in his story, "and though it may remain latent, if once roused it is seldom quieted until satisfied."

This is the very line which Jimmy cites on the record sleeve within his *One Particular Harbor* album. Jim Shea's image of Jimmy almost says it all: the guitar, the outrigger, and those beautiful Tahitian women, positioned within sight of the *Bounty* on the hook in the harbor beyond. Lest the listener miss the full appeal of the tropics, Jimmy cites that line.

Meanwhile, in the autumn of 2009, Jimmy gave his full support to the restoration of the Miami Marine Stadium where he'd recorded his *Live by the Bay* video back in August of 1985. Most accounts of the effort have noted that the 6500-seat stadium has an unconventional design and structure, but they have overlooked one significant fact: the true name of the stadium remains the Commodore Munroe Stadium.

FLORIDA

a selection from

The Commodore's Story / Chapter VI

THE FAILURE OF THE KEG BUSINESS rather heightened the attractions of the sea, and they now became more and more pervaded by the tropics, from the fascinating tales current in the office of the Coast Wrecking Co. Their work covered almost the Seven Seas, then as later, and their employees in odd moments delighted to swap yarns of storms and wrecks and salvage.

About this time their steamer *Amanda Winants* returned from a winter's work on the Florida Reef with a full cargo of yarns and wreck material gathered from the reefs, and her crew were mainly Staten Islanders. With them was Ned Pent of Biscayne Bay, employed by the company as pilot. Their stories of that mysterious, remote and legend-haunted region were wholly fascinating. The last of the pirates had haunted the Reef and the near-by keys down to the middle of the century and the wreckers that followed were their blood brothers, according to many awe-inspiring tales of high-handed and ruthless activities. On blustery winter evenings such tales, set in a scene of warm and brilliant sunlight, on blue waters lapping green islands and covering coral reefs, had all the magic charm and romantic appeal that Melville gave to the Marquesas, and they soon began to center my vague longings for the tropics among the Florida Reefs.

Another incident of February, 1874, had the same effect. One stormy morning, with a freezing gale from the northeast, on looking from my bedroom window my wrecking instinct was aroused by the sight of a small sloop-yacht pounding on a sunken crib-work, while her crew of three stood helpless on her deck. Half-dressed as I was, not even stopping for an overcoat, I rushed to the breakwater, got a boat and a helper, and with a half-hour's hard work got the sloop afloat and into shelter.

Her owner was William B. Brickell, bound to Biscayne Bay with merchandise for his Indian trading store on the Miami River. His descriptions of the Bay and its possibilities fanned my suppressed yearnings into a smart blaze, and when he finally stated that a piece of land and pineapple slips enough to plant it were mine for the asking, as a partial acknowledgment of the morning's services to him, the die was cast.

Brickell had just bought the boat, was not much of a sailor, and knew nothing of winter conditions on the coast, so I advised shipment of boat and cargo to Key West. Next morning he was gone, and in the afternoon we had a gale from the northwest. Happening to be on South Street in New York a week later, my attention was attracted by a schooner at the end of a pier, evidently taking on board some heavy weight. This turned out to be Mr. Brickell's boat, being loaded on a schooner bound for Key West. The gale had put him ashore on the inside of Sandy Hook where the boat was quickly filled with water and sand, and he had concluded that my advice was sound. Lucky for him that he did not get to sea, to be blown offshore and probably never heard of!

This boat was the *Ada*, built in 1872 for Captain Bieling at Greenport, New York. She was an able boat of eleven tons, long familiar to Biscayne Bay, where she played a prominent part in the fortunes of the Brickells. Many a tax-bill which threatened their lands was met by a turtling-trip on *Ada*, manned by his sons Will and Charles, and his daughter Edith.

Eventually wholesome climate and cheap land drew him to Florida, in company with a Mr. Sturtevant, whose daughter, Mrs. Julia Tuttle, afterward owned the land north of the river which became the site of Miami as founded by Flagler. On the south bank Brickell and his seven children were all homesteaders, and beside these claims adjoining titles were bought as chance offered until he had considerable property.

These miles of waterfront, which were to be the finest part of Miami, remained in his hands until the railroad came and the town grew, and brought the family hundreds of times the wealth that their wildest dreams could have suggested in the early days. One may remark the evidence of sound character and judgment in the Brickells in that neither the labors and hardships of wilderness poverty nor the sudden flood of riches which followed could disturb their industrious, cheerful, well-ordered lives, which still wholesomely proceed much as they began.

The rescue of *Ada* and the talks with Brickell localized my tropical longings on Biscayne Bay, which was within reach of reasonable hopes. At the same time the murder of a good business just as it had proved its success brought a resurging love of the sea, and put me in proper frame of mind to seize the opportunity which came in August of 1877. John Demarest of Chicago, son-in-law of Mr. Hewitt, was ordered south by his doctor and wanted a companion. He had the current Florida literature of Sidney Lanier and others, which dealt with St. Augustine, the St. John's, and Cedar Keys, to which place ran the only railroad south of Jacksonville. The peninsula was nothing more than a vague wilderness. To me, however, there was no appeal short of Biscayne Bay.

"Never heard of it," said Demarest. "It isn't on the maps, and can't be of any importance."

"There or nowhere," I replied, in effect, and there we went.

As to route, we might go by rail to Cedar Keys, and take the occasional steamer thence to Key West, or there were weekly Mallory boats direct from New York. There was also the Benner Line which ran schooners to Key West, and Mr. Benner was our neighbor. A fine boat was nearly due to sail, and would take us by the "Hole in the Wall" and across the Bahama Banks. White canvas! The Gulf Stream! The Bahamas! It was the fulfillment of dreams, and you can guess which route we took. There were to be many more southern voyages for me, but none of the others had the joyous thrills of this, not merely as the first, but because it was under sail, and by a most picturesque route.

The boat was a fine Maine schooner of 250 tons, the *Lena R. Storer*, Captain Seavey. At 4:30 in the afternoon of Monday, September 3, 1877, she was towed into the stream and set sail to a fresh west-northwest breeze. It was the season for hurricanes in the West Indies, but that meant nothing to us, and not much more to Captain Seavey, who had not experienced one, and had not been in the Florida Straits. "Where ignorance is bliss—" at any rate we were free of the anxiety we might legitimately have felt, and ready to enjoy the voyage.

It was a comfortable one, and I can still feel the thirsty fibers of my being fully drinking in the world of sea and sky, long dreamed of, yet new. On Wednesday we sighted a ship, a brig and several schooners and were boarded by a boat from a Provincetown whaler, short of news and tobacco. They had had no news of consequence since sailing, and were certainly rough-looking specimens of the human race, mostly Portuguese, sunburnt and unshaven. If the tattered and greasy patches of clothing had been left off, I think they would have made passably good-looking and interesting savages; as it was, they were disappointing, and had little in common with the old Yankee whalers I had known.

Moderate weather yielded to a westerly squall, and then a fine northeast breeze set us well across the Gulf Stream, its indigo rollers flashing in the sun like great beds of sapphire, alive with the silver gleam of flying fish. Monday was calm, with a heavy sea, and the main-sheet block parted, company with the boom under the violent slatting of the sail.

There followed a strenuous time, the boom sweeping wildly to and fro and threatening the backstays, while the crew tried to pass rope's ends around it as it swung. It was secured without damage, and that evening we had a good assortment of yarns about similar experiences.

There were good breezes Tuesday and Wednesday, and Captain Seavey announced Abaco Light due in sight at one o'clock Thursday morning. At 1:15 it appeared – a remarkably good landfall – and at 7:00 we passed the Hole in the Wall, and had a good look through it. It is an opening in the narrow, wall-like cliff of stone on the south end of Abaco Island, which has given its name to the whole neighborhood, and in fact to this route into the Gulf of Mexico.

We then took a southwest by south course across the Great Bahama Bank, with the bottom plainly in sight for the next hundred miles. Just before dark, with no land in sight, we were boarded by two negroes in an open boat with fish, sponge and shells for sale, or rather to trade for salt beef, to make them strong; as they said, "Money no use, no place to spend it." One of these men was close to seven feet in height, and very humorous in his remarks. Without compass or charts these chaps navigate all over the Bahamas and seldom go astray except in bad weather.

We had a beautiful moonlight night and fair wind, and at nine in the morning passed Orange Cay, and were soon off soundings in the Straits of Florida. Daylight on the fifteenth found us within sight of the Double-headed Shot Cays, on Salt Cay Bank, with light wind and strong current ahead. Soon after, a squall from the east, accompanied by a whirlwind, passed close astern, and occasioned great activity for a few minutes in clewing up and taking in sail.

Afterward the wind was so light that we drifted backward many miles with the Gulf Stream current, and this brought out the story of the Maine skipper with a load of ice for Havana, who had come just our course and to this location when the wind failed entirely and he drifted back to the north of Matanilla Reef. Here he got a breeze, started around Abaco again and once more reached Salt Cay Bank only to drift back to Matanilla. A third time he tried it, but by this time his ice was nearly gone, and when the wind once more failed and he couldn't anchor, he jumped overboard and ended the fight!

The *Storer* was more fortunate, crossing the Stream Saturday night, and sighting the lights of Key West Sunday evening. Captain Seavey had some misgivings about entering the new harbor in this strange land of clear water and coral, with the bottom everywhere apparently threatening, but the simple sailing directions, "Key West Light under the north star," brought us to anchorage.

And here, at last, was Florida; here the Gulf Stream, the coral reefs, the exotic island town under the moon. The glint of moonlight on pinnated palm leaves, waving in the fresh breeze, and on ruffled waters, the occasional clear flutelike note of some fish under the vessel's bottom, and the almost ceaseless thrumming of guitars with tom-tom accompaniment from the negro quarter, and the calling of the dance in varied voices, mingled with the inexpressible odors of a tropical town – fruit, fish, flowers, tobacco and wood-smoke – the barking of dogs, the crowing of roosters and the splashing of fish, taken all together, made an impression both weird and delightful, and never to be forgotten.

Today a whiff of buttonwood smoke, the savage beat of "jazz" dance music, or the strange piping fish, still irresistibly recall that first touch with Key West. The piping fish, by the way, remained for many years unidentified, and became the characteristic voice of quiet nights in lonely Florida anchorages; not until 1908 did I trace the music to the common spotted toadfish.

Next morning at the post office, who should appear but Mr. Brickell, who was pleased to see us, and suggested that we go to Biscayne Bay in the *Ada*, saying that his rates were no higher than those of the mail schooner. Nothing further was said of her rescue off Staten Island three years previous, nor of the pineapple land offered, but one can scarcely blame the struggling settlers of the then unproductive land for looking very keenly at a dollar.

Key West at this time was quite a prosperous town. There were many educated and cultured Americans, who filled the official positions, about as many Bahama Islanders in the sponge and key-pineapple business and a large number of Cubans engaged in cigar-making. The first two nationalities were also largely interested in wrecking, as owners and crews. Every key plantation had its wrecking vessel, and every sponger was ready for the business at a few minutes' notice. There were on Key West three lofty wooden towers, built for the purpose of sighting incoming and passing vessels, as well as wrecks.

We sailed on *Ada* next day (September 19) and had a slow, warm run to Bamboo Key anchorage. How can I describe the eager delight with which I saw that lonely archipelago unfold its novelty and beauty before us? The shoal clear water, through which coral reefs and bottom growths were visible, the bland warmth of the breeze, the sparkle and brilliance of the sun in the clear air, all made a beautiful setting for the novel scene in which, one after another, the low, green, mysterious islands rose, passed and disappeared astern. They were mostly uninhabited then, and only rarely visited – known, in fact, only to the wandering spongers. All that

I knew of them was from tales of pirate and wrecker, and for me it was the scene of such romantic yarns that *Ada* was traversing. We had a slow and not too comfortable journey on her – a very different one from that taken now by so many hundreds daily on the train, but infinitely superior in thrills. Corals, palms, trade wind, lonely islands, wreckers – all was but the astonishing fulfillment of long dreams. On the twentieth we parted the centerboard pennant and put in at the Hurricane Harbor at the west end of Lower Matecumbe for repairs. The weather not suiting Mr. Brickell, we remained there, getting a squall at sundown and calm the rest of the night, with our first experience of Florida mosquitoes. Having no nets, Demarest and I did not get a wink of sleep.

On the twenty-first we called at Indian Key, site of the first town in the keys. This was of especial interest since it had been developed by a Staten Island man, Jacob Houseman, shipbuilder, wrecker and trader. It is best remembered for the spectacular Indian attack of 1840, in which the town was burned and many people killed, among them Dr. Henry Perrine, who was also of a Staten Island family.

As a boy, I had often been entertained by some of the Staten Island oysterman from the north shore with stories of the mysterious arrivals of schooners at Mariner's Harbor, their unloading at night and immediate departure, and of the sudden evidences of wealth in some of the longshore families. When I learned the history of Indian Key, these yarns came back, and it looked as if they were not all children of the imagination, for the key had been for many years a rendezvous for wreckers, and was of more importance than Key West. That wrecking in those days verged closely on piracy is well known, and where over three score vessels sailed in opposite directions each day with lookouts at every masthead, it was natural that the competition should result in illegal practices. Fast craft were in demand for this trade, and among them were several old-fashioned but fleet North River sloops, with immense mainsails. These unwieldy boats made many successful voyages in the West Indies, to the Mediterranean and even around the Horn.

Soon after this we entered Biscayne Bay through Caesar's Creek, a long and winding channel, running first through a submerged bank three miles wide, then between a number of beautifully wooded islands, and finally branching into several entrances to the foot of the Bay. Here we were again invested with the spirit of piracy, for this was the stronghold of Black Caesar, a giant negro, who took toll from passing vessels along the reef until patience ceased among underwriters and owners, and a full-fledged naval expedition under Jackson's administration put an end to his operations. He escaped, and was said to have been killed at last by a woman when boarding a vessel in the Gulf of Mexico. His location here was certainly admirable for the trade, protected on the outside by shoals and blind-mouthed channels. When he was too hotly pursued, mazes of deep channels inside, heavily bordered with mangroves, enabled him to dismast and sink his craft and so lie secure from observation until the fuss blew over.

Caesar's Rock, a small island about the middle of the creek, was reputed to be the dwelling place and shipyard of the pirate. It was afterwards bought by my friends, the Hines family, and we explored it on many occasions, looking for buried treasure, but finding nothing more than rusty iron.

Passing Soldier Key, halfway up the Bay, we could see the United States Engineers' office, barracks and workshop for the construction of Fowey Rock light tower, four miles distant on the Reef. The work had progressed only to the lower platform; the upper tower and lantern were those I had seen exhibited at the Philadelphia Centennial the year before. A wooden working platform, on iron-shod piling, was first erected with some difficulty, after which the permanent ironwork was more easily put in place, though the driving of the big iron piles was necessarily a tedious job.

While at this work the men were startled one dark night by seeing a steamer almost aboard of them – if there had been more water on the reef there might have been a collision! She was the *Arakanapka*, and what is left of her can still be seen at low water, a few yards northeast of the tower. Before the light was finished another steamer, the *Carondelet*, with general cargo, almost poked her nose into the tower but was more fortunate in getting afloat again a few days after, though she left most of her cargo for the benefit of the people of the bay, who were out, of course, in anything that would float. These two incidents at least show that the Fowey Rock light was needed.

By noon we had arrived at the Miami River, and Mr. Brickell's descriptions this time had not been overdrawn. It was a beautiful clear-water stream, its banks lined with towering coco-palms and mangroves. The Brickells had a plain, substantial, two-story wooden house, a short distance back from the river, one room being used as a store. Nearby was a small storehouse, and on the bank a wharf at which *Ada* was kept. Our first night ashore passed very comfortably, as did, in fact, all others at this place. It was cool, with very few insects; our food was good and the family agreeable. A pleasant time seemed in prospect, and so it turned out.

So entered Biscayne Bay one who was to know it more intimately and love it better, probably, than any of its future hordes of settlers and visitors. The beauties and possibilities of the country appealed to me at once strongly. No sea-lover could look unmoved on the blue rollers of the Gulf Stream and the crystal-clear waters of the Reef, of every delicate shade of blue and green, and tinged with every color of the spectrum from the fantastically rich growths on the bottom, visible to the last detail through this incredibly translucent medium. It scarcely resembles northern sea-water at all – a cold, semi-opaque, grayish-green fluid, which hides the mysteries of the bottom. Drifting over the Florida Reef on a quiet day one may note all the details of its tropical luxuriance twenty feet below, and feel himself afloat on a sort of liquid light, rather than water, so limpid and brilliant is it.

This Reef life is truly tropical, for the water in the Gulf Stream comes by the shortest route from the Windward Islands, bringing its color, its warmth and its teeming life with it. This makes the Florida keys the only approach to tropical land and climate in the United States, with a wholly different vegetation from most of the peninsula.

Here, too, is the western limit of the trade wind, wafting the pure dry breath of the Bahamas across hundreds of miles of shoal banks and palm-fringed desert islands, to be further warmed by the Gulf Stream, and finally to caress Biscayne Bay and the keys with an incomparable touch, warm yet invigorating, pure and dry, constant day and night. An ideal sailing wind, always fresh but seldom stormy, it strikes the keynote of Biscayne Bay weather during a great part of the year, and makes the region a yachtsman's paradise.

So to the explorer and sailor it was all pure delight, although to the settler trying to make a living there might be disadvantages. Yet even the basic problems of the homesteaders – food and clothing – were much simplified by the bountiful fish and game, and by the warmth which permitted clothes to be reduced to the minimum of decency.

∽

JERRY JEFF WALKER

from
"Migration"
"Tin Cup Chalice"
A1A
1974

ANSWERS MIGHT always be the easy part, but here's another question just the same. Would Jimmy Buffett ever have made it to Key West had it not been for Jerry Jeff Walker? (Hint: Even time won't tell.)

Jimmy has said that he'd have found his way to Key West in due time, but it remains Jerry Jeff's Packard – *The Flying Lady* – that carried those two guys, along with Murphy Sadler, to the island for Jimmy's very first look. Though Murphy and Walker both had been there more than a couple of times before, Jerry Jeff already decided that the wild island life was not one which he might ever survive. So, he followed US 1 north out of Monroe County and made a name for himself prior to his ever crossing paths with Jimmy.

Long before they ever met, though, this couple of fledgling gypsies already had a lot in common with one another, as well as with countless others who were trying to find their way through life and through the music business all at the very same time. In Jimmy's case, "along came that 'devil music'" just as he was "about to get serious about journalism" in Nashville. So, Jimmy became part of a group that worked a lot of the same clubs in a circuit throughout the country. Steve Goodman. John Prine. John Sebastian. Gamble Rogers. Fred Neil. And Jerry Jeff Walker. Each of these guys have known just as much about the pains of street singing as they have about the grind of crossing the country in rent-a-cars, as well as in the coach cars of trains. And from the looks of things, not a one of them would have traded that life for anything else in this world.

After the fates had brought Jerry Jeff and Jimmy together, these two would frequent the Coconut Grove, the New Orleans bars, and Nashville, before they ever went conky tonkin' down through the Florida Keys. In this chapter from his fast-reading memoir, though, Jerry Jeff takes you through that period playing out just before Jimmy's first trip to Key West. You'll enjoy every word on this ride, and then you will need to read on your own the rest of the adventures they'd shared. At that time, you'll also appreciate the story behind the street performer, Mr. Bojangles, whom Jerry Jeff had met in a New Orleans jail. It is not at all the story that you believe you know.

Meanwhile, if you think you've found an answer to that opening question, then maybe you'd want to tackle this one: If Jerry Jeff Walker had never left Key West, would he ever have made it to Austin, then go on to become this legendary Lone Star country-rocker?

The answer doesn't matter. Let's just be glad that Jerry Jeff's been to the island and back, then on to other places, as well. And that he's told us his life in his songs.

Additional suggested works by Jerry Jeff Walker:

— *Driftin' Way of Life* (1969/1990)

— *Cowboy Boots and Bathin' Suits* (1998)

— *Gypsy Songman: A Life in Song* (1999)

— *Best of the Rest* (2004)

GYPSY SONGMAN

a selection from
Chapter VII

LOOKING BACK, I want to say that the three years I spent with Janet were wonderful.

She gave me stability and a sense of place that I'm sure I needed. I had to stick with the band thing. I needed that experience, learning how to work with other musicians to get the most out of my music. Eventually, though, I came to feel that it was a dead-end road.

Playing with studio musicians wasn't working out, either. I needed a band of my own. I didn't know it fully, but I had a feeling that the music I liked happened because the whole group lived and played together – they had like interests.

I would find my spot somewhere.

I would have to keep moving.

Not long after Janet headed out, my driver's license was suspended. After a fight in a Key West bar, where I had been drastically overserved, I tried to fly the Corvette up the Causeway to Coconut Grove, me behind the wheel with Ben Jennings beside me wailing on a mouth harp. I got as far as the entrance to the highway, where the 'Vette swapped ends a couple of times.

The cops pounced on us within seconds.

OK, no driver's license. Wasn't the first time and wouldn't be the last. Somebody told me that a motorcycle license might be a convenient way around that. So during an out-of-town gig in Washington, I applied locally for a motorcycle license and got it without any checks or delays.

I still had the BSA 650 that I had bought for Janet to ride. A few trips up and down U.S. Route One between Key West and Coconut Grove on the bike's rough suspension convinced me that BSA really meant Bloody Sore Ass. So I traded it for a Harley Sportster.

I wanted adventure. My mom and dad had honeymooned on an Indian, so I had motorcycle blood. I told my office to book me across Canada.

I bought the Harley from Ray Carter, a car mechanic who really wanted to be an artist, a sculptor, painter. He'd seen metal sculptures outside airports and public buildings and thought, like the rest of us, "Shit, I can do that." He figured he could sculpt just as well as any of these people who make swans out of car fenders.

Ray and I loaded our motorcycles into the back of a U-Haul trailer, along with some artwork and miscellaneous crap, and drove all the way from the Keys to upstate New York. Ray decided to stay in Woodstock. I visited my folks in Oneonta, took my mom for a ride on the motorcycle.

I bought a poncho and a piece of foam rubber to wrap around my guitar case to ward off rain. The suitcase was strapped to a luggage rack, and it lined up just right with the seat. I nailed a reflector on the end of my guitar case, and stuck it out off the back of the motorcycle. Tied the whole mess down with bungee cords. With the foam rubber padding, I could lean back and have a pretty comfortable backrest for the ride.

This was how I traveled across Canada, hitting the gigs that my booking agent had scheduled.

In Ottawa, I appeared on a local TV talk show. The host was a good-looking Irish redhead – Marianne. After the program, everybody adjourned to a bar. I said, "Well, I'm riding a motorcycle, so I'm not drinking."

And Marianne said, "Well, I am. And I'm gonna have a big martini."

We got so drunk Marianne had to help me onto the motorcycle. Then she got on behind me. That's when I realized that I probably wasn't going to have much luck with the discipline of not drinking while riding motorcycles.

The cold wind sobered me up, and I got us home. Her home. After a hot shower and some good hash we settled into her cabin for a long night of love.

In Montreal, a few days later, there was Cindy. Beautiful. Legs. "I'm thinking about going to Paris," she said during a break in the action one night. It was an invitation.

I thought, "Shit. I just got this trip going. Do I really want to give up on this and follow this lovely to Europe?"

I almost did. Until one day when I woke in her bed, looked out the window, and found a blue-sky morning. I thought, what a great day it would be to hit the road with my bike.

She saw the look. She kicked my ass out of the house and down the street, and I was gone.

I rode through Canada to Riviére du Loupe, to New Brunswick, hopped boats to Newfoundland and Nova Scotia. Turned back down into New Hampshire and Massachusetts and got back to Woodstock by the fall. There I met some of The Band. Picked with Rick Danko. Hooked up with Fred Neil, a gifted singer-songwriter whose work I much admired (and still do). But the snow flurries were starting and Woodstock winter was coming, so Ray Carter and I loaded up the motorcycles again. and headed south with a U-Haul.

I remember this lovely waitress in New York. I was going to take her south. Didn't. Ray talked me out of it.

And that kind of made me sad. So I got pretty drunk in the car, thinking about the girl I didn't go to Paris with and the girl in New York I didn't bring south.

The fall leaves rushed by the windows outside. I just rode along, drinking, driving, watching the trees blur past, until I fell asleep in the car.

Then, somewhere around Virginia or North Carolina, Ray shook me awake. "Didn't you tell me you wrote 'Mr. Bojangles'?"

"Yeah, I did," I said, rubbing sleep fog from my eyes.

"I don't know, but for the last two or three hours I've been driving this car, every station on the radio keeps playing a song called 'Mr. Bojangles' by some group called the Dirt Band."

He started punching buttons on the radio, and before he hit three or four of them we found it again. ". . . *Knew a man, Bojangles and . . .*" It was all over the dial.

I remembered the Nitty Gritty Dirt Band telling me they were going to record the song. But at that time, in the first two years of the song's life, there had been about fifty recordings. Everybody said they would make it their radio-play single. Tom Jones, Harry Belafonte, Lulu. Nobody from the younger groups had done it, though.

Jimmy Ibbotson of the Dirt Band told me how they came to choose it for their record. When Jimmy graduated from college in 1969, he packed his '62 Dodge for the cross-country drive from Indiana to California. One of those life-beginning journeys. While he was loading the trunk, he was approached by a girl his buddies considered "a good witch."

Long hair, dyed black. Paisley muumuu, broad-brimmed straw hat, purple granny glasses. She reached down inside a leather mailbag which she carried across her shoulder, and instead of producing the usual weed or mescaline, she pulled out a 45-rpm single in a brown paper sleeve. It was my recording of "Mr. Bojangles."

"I know this will mean a lot to you," the good witch said, and she walked away.

Ibbotson tossed the 45 in the trunk, finished packing his car, and drove to California.

There, he hooked up with the musicians who would later form the Nitty Gritty Dirt Band. Months later, they were looking for songs for their concept album. Jimmy Ibbotson remembered that record stuck somewhere in his car.

In the parking lot of a Jack-in-the-Box in Los Angeles, Ibbotson began to dig through the trunk of his Dodge Dart, under the cardboard box filled with stinky T-shirts, under his guitar case, under the spare tire. In a puddle of rusty water in the wheel well, he found the crusted single in the brown paper liner.

They went to somebody's mom's house, where there was a record player. But the hi-fi amplifier was blown. So the guys bent close to the turntable, listening to the sounds that emanated from the diamond needle as it scratched along the grooves.

That long-haired huddle over the phonograph produced some bent lyrics. "He spoke right out" became "The smoke ran out." And the line which almost every singer finds challenging, "He laughed-slapped his leg a step," was sung, "He laughed and clicked his heels and stepped."

The Dirt Band got their concept album, complete with tapes of someone's Uncle Charlie playing harmonica with a howling dog, couple of songs from Mike Nesmith, a few from Kenny Loggins, and this five-minute love song written by Jerry Jeff Walker. They blew the doors off with the album and radio play of the album's single, "Mr. Bojangles."

I was partly responsible for the success of an album headlining a barking dog.

With that hit single out there – even though it wasn't my recording – my booking prospects started to improve. I was still playing a duo with David Bromberg, but I was looking for a band.

We headed into the studio in Miami with the Dixie Flyers and began to record my album *Bein' Free* for Atlantic. I had met these guys and liked them. Charlie Freeman, Sammy Creason, Tommy McClure, Mike Utley, Jim Dickinson, Bobby Woods. Don Brooks dropped in on harmonica. But they were R&B-ing the music. They had a hard time being country.

I was still searching for a band that was tuned into my idiosyncratic folk-country-rock approach. Where Dylan was already, where Fred Neil had been. Most bands were used to rigid count-offs and tight tracks and professional singers. I wanted a bunch of guys who would let the rough side drag.

And I wanted guys who were like me personally, too. I wanted to be able to talk with my band, to hang out with them, and to get close to them.

You can't walk in and shake hands with six musicians, then sit down to play and bring a lot to the table. I once cut an album with Nashville session ace Charlie McCoy. I liked mood lighting. He wouldn't play in the dark. So I would record and he'd wait till I finished. Then he'd turn on all the lights in the studio and overdub his parts. And he was pure business. Punch the clock and go. It put a tension in the room.

"Oh, you're singing about an old dancer there? I didn't know that! Never did catch the lyrics to that song."

Back in Coconut Grove, I sold the motorcycle and bought a 1948 Packard, the "Flying Lady." Hooked up again with an old girlfriend, Teresa Murphy Sadler, a wild Miami child raised in a Catholic school environment. By her late teens, Murphy had discovered both sex and partying, and she embraced them both with great gusto.

Murphy had run with a shady crowd in Miami that included some characters like "Murph the Surf," the jewel thief who became known for the infamous Star of India caper. I think Murphy Sadler had defected to Key West to get some distance from that rough crowd.

She was a big woman, big boned, bawdy barroom laugh, salty sense of humor. She was an ex-stripper, had a baby boy. And she had a lot of no-good friends who were always ready to party.

There was one guy, Rocky, who had done so much cocaine his head would whistle like a flute when he rode his motorcycle. Nose, septum, completely gone. Rocky was the point man. He'd score a couple of pounds and cut it up for the bands. There was a lot of cocaine around, and a lot of people doing it.

I, with the self-discipline of a jellyfish, fell right in with them.

One day, I was driving with Murphy in the Flying Lady through the Grove when we passed this familiar-looking guy riding a bicycle.

"Fromholz!" I yelled.

It was Steve Fromholz from Austin. I backed up, threw his bike in the back seat, and took him home with us. Fromholz was down for a recording session with Stephen Stills at Atlantic Studios. After an evening at our house drinking, talking, laughing, he told us to come with him to the studio for the night's session. The recording started at midnight, everybody working through the night, then dragging out about noon the next day.

As we drove to the studio, Fromholz filled me in: "I'll be lucky to get out of this one alive. There's lots and lots and lots of cocaine here. Bags of blow all around the room. Lots of cocaine madness and egos. Scary. I'm just a country boy. I've been to the city but never to one that's this big."

When we tumbled in, about midnight, things were rollin' pretty good.

And right away, in addition to the toot, I sensed the presence of some real assholes. There was an entourage atmosphere. High-dollar rock and roll.

Oh, goody.

I'm a little unclear about the details, but before too long Murphy and I had misbehaved so badly that we not only were tossed out of the studio, but we nearly cost Fromholz his studio gig.

I'm not sure, but I think what got us tossed was Murphy pouring a glass of beer over the head of Stills' manager.

Whatever our sins, Murphy and I hopped in the *Flying Lady* and headed home.

The old Packard was a terrible car for me to drive. I got drunk too easily and the car weighed about two tons and drove like a tank at the best of times. So it didn't take much for somebody to think you were driving drunk. Especially if you were driving drunk.

Before we got home from the studio, I put the *Flying Lady* over a curb and bent the front end, and we had to tow her away.

Enter destiny. Not mine, but Jimmy Buffett's.

♋

Tom Corcoran

IF JERRY JEFF WALKER's the keystone to the foundation of lore regarding Jimmy Buffett's arrival in Key West, then Tom Corcoran's certainly the next stone over. And the story that's repeated time and time again is that Walker brought Jimmy in to the Chart Room Bar for his very first sip of beer on the island. Tom was the bartender who gave (not *sold*) that first beer to Jimmy.

Point is, Tom's been there from the start in more ways than one, and he can recall days when there weren't very many locals in Key West. And yet, those locals still outnumbered the tourists. After all, what was there to see on the island? Boarded-up shops, a Depression-era aquarium, and a handful of hippies playing guitars along Mallory Dock as they watched the sun plop into the Gulf. Still, Tom and his wife managed to cobble together enough work to survive in Key West with their young son. That's how much they loved the place.

Tending bar at the Chart Room was one of Tom's jobs; selling tacos was another. But those were the things that brought Tom face-to-face with a daily clientele that included writers like Shel Silverstein, Jim Harrison, Thomas McGuane, and – eventually – Hunter S. Thompson. Along with Jimmy, they were a small circle of friends. As mentioned, there just weren't very many locals back then.

Photography was yet another line of work on Corcoran's resumé, and his skills with a camera not only helped to provide a record of those colorful days and years, but also to hone his own sense of focus and composition – in photographs and words alike. You know what they say about pictures and words, as well as about pictures and stories, and you know damn well that's all true. In Tom's case, being a photographer was but another way of saying he had a novelist's eye, as well as a bartender's ear. So, it was only a matter of time before things finally fell into place. Sure, Tom had contributed more than just some of the ideas and lyrics to "Cuban Crime of Passion" and to "Fins." And yes, some of his photographs had been used for Jimmy's albums. All the while, though, he was learning from his his friends and how they went about writing.

It should not come as any surprise at all when Corcoran first brought together all of these things he knows for the story he called *The Mango Opera*. This is the book that Jimmy says "reconnects my heart and brain to the Key West that I knew as an unknown bar singer."

Just know that Tom has given us in Alex Rutledge a guide through a Key West that a good many folks might otherwise never get to see. Throughout this story and the others in the Rutledge series, Corcoran has woven a tale in a setting that cannot separate the real Keys from the imagined ones. The term, perhaps, might be fictional fact. Or maybe it's factual fiction. In either case, it's damn good fun.

Additional suggested works by Tom Corcoran:

— *Gumbo Limbo* (1999)

— *Bone Island Mambo* (2001)

— *Octopus Alibi* (2003)

— *Air Dance Iguana* (2005)

— *Jimmy Buffett - The Key West Years* (2006)

— *Key West in Black & White* (2007)

— *Hawk Channel Chase* (2009)

THE MANGO OPERA
a selection from
Chapter III

FOR THE PAST FOUR OR FIVE YEARS, Sam Wheeler and I have met for lunch on the Wednesdays he hasn't had a charter. He tended to be fully booked; our routine tended toward the Wednesdays with the nastiest weather. For a while we'd skipped around, field-testing new restaurants as they appeared on the island. But the skimpy gut luggage posing as cuisine, promoted as healthy, had driven us back to our old standby, the Half Shell Raw Bar at the old shrimp docks.

Back when Bob Hall shucked thirty dozen a day and Cowboy Ron sang country classics, locals had kept the place alive. Even after the Half Shell had become a popular tourist spot it never lost its dependable menu. The place was decorated with road signs and hundreds of old vanity license tags lined up to read as statements. Eight on a wall near the entrance stated: OOH YEP KILROY GONE HOP ON ISLANDS DAILY. Two above the restroom door proclaimed TINKLE CRISIS.

In recent years the Half Shell had become center stage for a mischievous day-shift bartender. A survivor of the Fort Lauderdale party-bar circuit and the mother of two grade-schoolers, Peggy Sue Peligrosa dispensed seafood, street directions, drinks, slander, and off-the-wall gossip. Anyone not an island resident was a Griswold—after the family in National Lampoon's Vacation. A tourist with a sense of humor and a respect for the tip jar could gain acceptance. Locals got the worst of Peggy Sue's jokes, honesty sessions, and hangover harassment. Her voice was loud but not grating, and Sam and I came for the entertainment as well as the food.

I met Sam at noon. He climbed out of his '69 Ford Bronco as I coasted my bicycle onto the tarmac at the foot of Margaret. Sam's rust-perforated truck had evolved into rolling poetry: a starboard list, aluminum cans a foot deep in the pickup bed, a coat-hanger antenna, and its interior awash in business cards, unopened credit-card offers, and sun-roasted coffee cups. Wheeler earned top dollar as a light-tackle guide. He lived in a modest house and collected military retirement pay. He could afford ten Grand Cherokees, but he took pride in sticking with the old seacoast refugee. He'd hired a local artist to paint "Eddie Haskell Edition" under each windowsill.

The Bronco's hinges were shot. Sam lifted the driver's-side door to hook the latch. "I spilled steaming café con leche in my lap," he said. "I braked to miss some dimwit from Broward, and I can't sue for groin damage. Pepe's doesn't have a million dollars."

I wedged the bike into a rack near the wharf's edge and chained the frame to a crossbar. Sharp odors from the basin — rotted fish and decay — wafted on the fluky breeze. "I got up early and I saw a dead person."

"You got involved in that, too?" Sam tugged on his long-billed ball cap. "I lost a charter with Monty Aghajanian. He wants to make it up next Tuesday. I think I got a conflict."

"He told me that he'd missed the trip. Genuinely pissed."

We worked our way past a clutch of elderly tourists crowded in the Half Shell's doorway. A Little Feat song played loudly as a hostess with a crew cut pointed us toward two stools at the far side of the bar. Peggy Sue sounded an ahh-ooga horn and reached into the beer cooler.

As we reached the empty stools, Sam twisted his face into a scowl. "How come this place always smells like last night's beer?"

"I don't know, Sammy." Peggy Sue turned to someone behind the oyster bins. "Hey, Backassward, was it slow last night?"

"Yep, slow," someone mumbled.

"There you go, Sam. You called it. We're still serving last night's beer. I always said you had a good nose."

Sam's grin became an uncharacteristic leer. "That's not what you raved about a couple years ago."

Peggy Sue planted a hand on her side-slung hip. "You remember that far back, big boy? You got me when I was a baby. I didn't know any damn better. Why is a new husband like linoleum?"

Sam shook his head. "I've heard it. But first I lived it."

Peggy Sue grinned and snapped open our beers. She dropped them on coasters in front of us and turned to another customer.

❧

GARDNER McKAY

OTHER THAN ELVIS and Mr. Twain, no one else's name has been invoked more times in Jimmy's works than that of Gardner McKay. Of course, it's really the image of the tall and handsome captain whom Gardner portrayed on the small screen that Jimmy most often had in mind.

That TV character's name was Captain Adam Troy, and Gardner explains in his memoir that the role and the series were altogether different from anything appearing anywhere else on the networks' schedules. The captain neither rode a horse, nor wore a gun, as McKay had already done on the series *Boots and Saddles*. Instead, this captain sailed his schooner *Tiki* out of its homeport of Honolulu and through the South Pacific.

In fact, Adam Troy had sprung from the mind of James A. Michener, who had first established his own credentials with *Tales of the South Pacific*, which earned him a

125

Pulitzer Prize in 1948. Michener's collection of short stories not only provided the basis of Broadway's classic *South Pacific*, but also of television's popular *Adventures in Paradise*. It was in Paradise, then, that Jimmy and most of the world feel that they first met Gardner McKay . . . an artist they continue to confuse with the character he portrayed.

His real life was truly much more the adventure, and the world outside Hollywood was where he could find his own Paradise.

At the age of sixteen, for example, Gardner was sailing the West Indies. And once he was through with the backlot of 20th Century Fox, he not only took to sea and to the Lesser Antilles, but also to the backroads and the pathways throughout South America, moving at a pace that he has described as being "not much faster than a dog."

By chance, he had become that television actor; by birth, he was an artist whose visions continued to spring forth through more than a single medium. To the artistic skills which he had honed as a student, Gardner later added those of stage actor, as well as those of poet, of playwright, and of storyteller. And then there were his talents as both a photographer and a sculptor alike.

Each and every one of these provided focus for Gardner McKay's own passion for life, a passion which he shared with undergraduates along the West Coast, as far north as Alaska, then south and westward to Hawaii. To no one's surprise, it was in Hawaii that Gardner settled, more or less, in the late 1980s, and he made there a home with his wife and his family. By then, the schooner *Tiki* had last been spotted thousands of miles away, somewhere along America's northeastern seaboard.

During all that time, Jimmy had been drawing upon those common threads of their past. Through Jimmy's songs and stories, Gardner McKay had become a special name that every Parrothead truly knew by heart. The first of these allusions appeared in 1983; the last two, in 2003. During the twenty years between, Gardner's name and spirit appeared wherever Jimmy felt they fit.

Not long after the release of his novel *Toyer*, Gardner was diagnosed with prostate cancer. Still, that did not keep him from working through his decades of journals to craft a memoir called *Journey Without A Map*, nor did it keep him from the Sunday evening readings of his "Stories On the Wind" for Hawaii Public Radio. Before another two years could pass, however, Gardner had grown too weak to continue, and he passed away in November of 2001.

Those who knew Gardner fully understood that he was much more than merely some television idol; he was a sailor, an artist, an adventurer, and a beloved family man.

Like that of Robert Louis Stevenson in Samoa, Gardner's grave is graced with lines from a poem of his own:

> Now comes the end of the day.
>> Now comes the rush of night.
> The luminous sea turns grey.
>> The faces of friends lose their light.
>
> I have sailed toward a high, steep island
>> Where my dreams would all come to be,
> Never wanting to be done with the ocean
>> Till each wave was done with me.

Additional suggested works by Gardner McKay:

— *Toyer* (1999)

— *Journey Without A Map: A Memoir* (2009)

— *The Kinsman* (2010)

ONE SUMMER IN CHARENTE

PLEASE UNDERSTAND that I am not a storyteller. I am someone who has an ordinary memory who remembers an incident that he cannot forget. Memories very often become guests who linger too long, outstaying their welcome, living in your house forever. So it is with me.

This memory begins during the war. What a common sound that phrase has. *The war.* A time when everything was allowed. When crime was justified. No one bothered to disguise an evil deed during the war; he simply said that he did it for "the cause." Sometimes he was given a medal.

This memory begins on the ancient farm of my family in Charente. We were three generations of peasants. Everyone seemed to be a widow. So few men were elderly. All were strong, no one was fat, no one was pretty. If someone died, he died quickly. He seemed to slip away from life as one slips from a rock into the deep sea. We came to expect that during the war.

All of my friends had left me then, gone away; the chickens, the rooster, cows, pigs; they had all disappeared. All, except my best friend, Chevalier, the dog remained. Naturally, Chevalier and I wanted to go hunting, but he was no longer fast enough for the deer and no match for the wild boar. Anyhow, guns were not allowed. We were under occupation, after all, so we laid snares for rabbits. When I could bring a rabbit home to the farm, there was cause to celebrate. We ate rabbit stew, and for the evening I was a hero. I liked being a great hero.

I was small for my age and the women changed clothes in front of me. And bathed. It was as though they no longer cared what anyone thought of them. They had been abandoned by the war. They lived like nuns in a convent but without hope. I did not understand them, and I sensed a restlessness in their disuse. They made me wear a barrette in my hair to keep it in place because it was so messy. Maybe they wanted a little girl instead of me. During a war, the women said, one learns to hate men.

Always on Friday I would go with my pail to the pump six times for water to pour into a cauldron that hung on an iron crook inside the fireplace. As the water grew warm, I would fill the copper tub beside the fire. There was no electricity, of course, so after supper when I had lit the two lanterns, I would take off my clothes and step into the luxurious tub. It was Ghiseline who would bathe me.

Ghiseline was the youngest grown-up of all the women and I thought her to be very beautiful, though she might not have been. By lantern light, she would push the block of *Savon Marseille* all over my body, up and down, everywhere. Sometimes when my little muscle grew taut she would blush brightly and smack at it with a rag and splash me with cold water. She would laugh and laugh until tears ran down her cheeks.

All night long, my dreams were full of women; big-shouldered, big-breasted women with the flanks of oxen, the buttocks of cart horses, bushy hair under their arms and between their legs. I dreamt of them naked, washing their breasts, dressing themselves, dancing with each other, bathing me. I adored them and they adored me.

IT WAS ON one of those bath nights that a very risky event took place. Everyone on our farm had slipped out into the dark night to a citizens meeting in a neighbor's stable. It was a dangerous thing to do in those times, if anyone was found away from his farm after dark he would be shot. But this farmer was hiding a pilot who had crashed his plane; and he had brought news of an invasion and everyone thought the war was coming to an end soon so the meeting was vital, there needed to be much preparation for this invasion.

Anyhow, on the night of this meeting, Ghiseline stayed home to look after me. She had gotten into some wine and was especially happy, singing a foreign song, one I had never heard before. While she was bathing me, suddenly she pulled her dress over her head and dropped her baggy panties on the floor and slipped into the tub, squeezing me flat against its side, and she began washing herself with the big block of *Savon Marseille*. She rubbed it over her breasts and she asked me rub it over her back. She seemed very happy, but no happier than me; she acted as if she were in love. So was I. That night in that copper tub I fell in love with her forever. And I told her so. She splashed me with water and told me that she would also love me forever.

When she tucked me into my goose mattress on the floor, she was wearing a new perfumed soap. I had never smelled anything so sweet. As she kissed me goodnight, I asked her, "Do you really mean *forever?*" She smiled and nodded. I had never been happier.

It was very late. I'd been asleep awhile when I woke. I thought I had heard the back door open very slowly then close. It could only have been Ghiseline; I smelled the sweet perfumed soap.

The next morning walking to the village I asked her where she had gone to so late in the night. She stopped and slapped me hard across the face, just like that. She called me a liar. "Never you dare repeat that to anyone or you will be punished in Hell, Satan himself will attend to you personally, and I will never love you anymore."

She was very upset; her face had turned pale. Naturally, I never mentioned it again. I was in love after all. But I was still curious as to where she wanted to go, after everyone was asleep. The next night I tried to stay awake so that I could hear the door open and close again. I was just falling asleep. There it was. It must have been very late. There was no longer any way of knowing; the enemy had taken the bell from our church tower to make ammunition. I missed it ringing the hours all through the night. It had always lulled me off to sleep.

I got up. I had been lying on my mattress fully-dressed under my blanket. I put a string around Chevalier's neck, and together we slipped out of the house to follow Ghiseline. We let her walk a way ahead of us across the bumpy stone courtyard outside the stable. There was no moon that night, only stars. I caught a glimpse of her on the road.

It wasn't until she had walked half-a-kilometer and crossed the stone bridge that she stopped. We stopped, too, and stood still, me holding Chevalier's face close to my chest. Ghiseline was waiting. Then we heard voices talking in whispers, but we could see no one. I knew her voice but who was she talking to? A man. It was a man with a strange way of speaking.

I was amazed. Here she was meeting with a man. Hadn't she just told me that she would always be in love with me? Chevalier and I waited to see what they would do.

They stood very close to each other for a long time without speaking, then crossed the road and walked into a field. We stood very still. My anger was pounding in my throat. After a while, we followed them into the field, but they had vanished.

We walked back and forth in the dark, but there was nothing left to do, so Chevalier and I turned back out of the field and walked home. We had both taken a risk of being shot.

The following day I avoided Ghiseline's eyes. She was especially nice to me, but I couldn't look at her. I was dizzy with hatred. I hated her with my entire being. If she loved me so much, how could she stand to be with another man? It made little sense.

There would be five more days until she would give me my bath and until then I had other things to occupy me. That afternoon, Chevalier and I went back to the field where Ghiseline and the man had vanished. We looked for some sign of their disappearance. Chevalier found it. He ran to the mouth of a hidden tunnel. The tunnel had been dug by the peasants a few years earlier; at the end, it opened into a natural cave. They had dug it to hide their animals from the occupation force and for a while it had, but soon enough the animals had been discovered. When Chevalier and I entered the tunnel and walked to the end where it opened down into the large cave, we found a straw mattress and a burnt-out candle, an empty bottle that still smelled of peppermint.

THAT NIGHT I went to bed again fully dressed and pretended to be asleep, but, of course, I wasn't. I was much too nervous. I lay there on my mattress a long time, and at last I heard the back door open very slowly and close. Chevalier and I waited minutes before we followed Ghiseline. I put a string around his neck again and we set out.

That night we knew where we were going. The sky was clear. There was a half-a-moon, and that made it even more dangerous. After some time walking on the road, we heard a car coming. We jumped into the ditch that ran alongside, which was dry. I had told Chevalier that we would be shot if we were discovered. We stayed still and waited. A small military car passed within a few feet of us; its headlights blacked out, driving slowly.

We let minutes pass before we climbed up out of the ditch and started walking again. When we dropped down into the field, I trusted Chevalier to find the hidden entrance to the tunnel again. And he did, but this time I told him to wait behind for me, outside.

Slowly, I entered the tunnel. It was black. I had to remember how it curved. I stalked like a hunter, taking small steps. After awhile, ahead of me down the tunnel, coming from the cave I saw a faint glow. It must have been the candle. I became frightened but still moved forward, touching the dirt wall to guide me. I moved an inch at a time. When the entrance of the cave came up within a dozen feet of me, I lay down on my belly and crawled like a snake. Ahead, the short candle was flickering on the floor. Shadows on the rocky walls jumped like goblins.

There they were. Two people lying together. One of them was Ghiseline; the other was her man friend. I couldn't see their faces, but I

131

knew it was them. He was lying beside Ghiseline, then on top of her. I was flat on my stomach with my mouth wide open trying not to make breathing sounds. Ghiseline was saying something to him that I couldn't hear. I don't think she was wearing any clothes. I hated her. I hated him. I knew he was the enemy. I could tell even in that dark light. Near them, a military jacket lay folded beside a helmet on the dirt floor. I was very frightened. I wanted to escape. His boots were still on his feet. Near to his helmet, between me and them, lay a huge belt with straps wound up in a coil. On the belt was a holster. I could see the butt of his gun sticking out of the holster.

They began moving again. He was saying something to her, and she was answering him over and over, saying the same thing. Now she was on top of him. I hated them both. I don't know how, but I remember that I was able to stretch and squirm forward until I could reach out and touch the belt with my fingertips and drag it to me.

I wasn't sure what I was doing. I was in a rage. I unclipped the flap on the holster and drew the gun out. It was too heavy for me to hold. I lifted it with both hands. As I did, it exploded, firing into the roof of the cave. I only touched the trigger. The gun had jumped out of my hands and fallen onto the dirt floor. It was by far the loudest noise I had ever heard in my life. The man jerked his head around and stared at me wildly with a frightened expression on his face. I was able to pick the gun up from the cave floor with both hands and point it at him. He tried to push himself free from under Ghiseline and started toward me. It fired again, striking him and sending him back down onto Ghiseline. She was caught under him. She looked up at me, over him; she was wild-faced. She looked desperately hurt. She was yelling something to me, "Non! Non! Non! Non! Non!" Maybe she was screaming.

The blare of the shots was still careening around the cave, and my ears were burning with their echoes. The candle was barely lit, twitching on the ground. Dust was falling, settling from the roof of the cave where the bullet had struck. I couldn't see the two of them very well anymore. The man was still trying to push himself up over Ghiseline, to start toward me again. I held the gun with both hands pointed at him. It fired again. Then, it fired again. Jumping in my hand with each shot. I was hardly doing anything but holding the gun. And it kept firing. The man fell back on top of her. I touched the trigger again and again. I fired into them. The gun was jumping in my hand. Then it stopped, part of its insides stood up. They both lay still on the straw mattress. I dropped the empty gun.

Then the candle was out. It was black. I stumbled back along the tunnel, remembering, shuffling my feet as quickly as I could, afraid to fall down, running my fingers along the dirt walls, as if I were being chased by enemies. Chevalier was waiting. He seemed relieved.

It was a starry night in summer and even though it was warm, I was shivering. Back at the farm, everyone was in their beds. Distant gunfire was not a rarity, and the cave had muffled the blasting sounds of the shots and made them sound further away than they really were. My head was ringing. I was in shock, still shivering. I decided to sleep with Chevalier in the stable. I was crying to myself without a sound when I fell into the deepest sleep imaginable. And when I woke up, I had no memory of what I had done.

In the morning, we all wondered where Ghiseline had gone. What had become of her? At first the family feared that she had run away. But, of course, she hadn't. She would not have left her purse. It was a mystery that frightened everyone close to me. I still hated her and, in a child's way, did not believe that she could be hurt, and my tears were understood to be genuine.

The mystery of Ghiseline's disappearance remained unsolved for a nearly a week, until an alert patrol with dogs, searching for the missing soldier came across the dead lovers in the cave. Immediately, it was a great scandal. Whether it was rape or whether it was collaboration, no one knew. But, either way, it was the greatest calamity that had ever befallen Charente.

The military, of course, said it was collaboration, an affair between the soldier and the girl. Impossible, the villagers said, it could only be rape. No one at the farm would believe that their own Ghiseline could possibly have had an affair with the enemy. But then, there was the matter of the sweet perfumed soap, wasn't there? Where had that come from? Among her things, two pairs of silk stockings had been found. They needed to be considered.

Either way, rape or collaboration, in the end, it was the villagers who would be made to pay. The murder of the lovers was so bizarre, so nasty. And it made so little sense that theories abounded and, whenever I was nearby, all that week voices would become hushed. No one would answer my questions. Whatever they were saying was not meant for a child's ears.

So for the week before the dreadful discovery, I had gone about my own life in a dream. I had erased all details of the shooting in the cave. But when they were found, pictures began coming back to me, and it was on Friday night when I walked to the pump with my pail to carry my bathwater that I first realized the horror of what I had done: I now began to believe that Ghiseline was truly dead and that I had had a great deal to do with her death. I knew that I had loved her more than I would ever be able to love anyone again. Now I wanted to die.

I missed her that night more than I thought possible. I refused all efforts to bathe me. I was beginning to remember clearly the events in the cave. The blasting gun firing into them as they lay there. That night I slept in the stable again. I swore I would never breathe a word of what I had done as long as I lived.

After a day of silence following the discovery of the dead lovers, the commandant, a very young captain, delivered his ultimatum at the town hall: the murderer must come forward, or ten male villagers will be selected by lottery to be executed by a firing squad the following day. Either way, for the murderer or for the villagers, there will be a firing squad provided the day after tomorrow. It was posted on a board in the village square. What could be simpler tit for tat? The murderer had twenty-four hours to give himself up to the commandant at the town hall. The deadline to surrender was two in the afternoon. This would give the murderer time enough to be notified of the ultimatum by a friend, to come back from wherever he was hiding, to eat a decent leisurely lunch before turning himself in to the captain to be shot. It was assumed by all that whoever killed the lovers would certainly surrender and die to save his countrymen. And so everyone in the village was preparing for him to face the firing squad, not them.

The priest had decided that Ghiseline should be buried in the church courtyard whether she was a collaborator or not, and he chose the day of the execution for her funeral. She was widely believed by the women to have done the worst thing a woman could possibly do: sleep with the enemy. And so the priest's announcement angered everyone, especially those who considered her a collaborator and they assured the priest that, without a doubt, they would stay away from her funeral. We would attend, of course, that was foretold. She was a cousin.

When I heard of the captain's ultimatum I was walking home with our ration of flour in a sack, and I only heard part of it. Two women in the road were talking about it, and they lowered their voices when they saw me trying to listen, and all I was able to hear were the words "firing squad." When I got home, I asked what a firing squad was. Finally, somebody told me. The ultimatum was directed at me, no one else. I could understand that. When I imagined myself in my short pants and my good shoes standing against the walls of the Prefecture, blindfolded, with my hands tied behind me to the ring that held the horses, I ran outside and fell down crying in the field above the house. I was sick to my stomach. My ears rang with fear. I would never tell a soul, I had already vowed that. But what about the villagers who would be dead? Well, they were grown-ups. Maybe they didn't care so much about being shot as I did. Maybe they were grown-ups I didn't know very well. I didn't care. What I was certain of, was that I myself did not want to personally stand in front of a firing squad and die.

I was exhausted from imagining when I went to bed. Of course, I lay without sleeping. Soon I realized it was absolutely sure that, if I kept my vow and remained silent, ten men would die the day after tomorrow. Maybe I would know some of those men. Maybe one of them would be from my family. There was something very wrong about having grown-ups die for what you did, wasn't there? How could I let that happen? It made no sense. I got up and went into the stable to think. It was my first experience in having to account for my deeds, and I wasn't liking it one bit. A long night lay ahead.

By morning, the day of the two o'clock deadline, I had made a decision. I had no choice. I had changed my mind. I knew that I could not allow those ten grown-ups to get shot instead of me, whether I was acquainted with them or not. It was very sad. I would surrender at two that afternoon. I was going to die.

It was my last day on earth; what should I do with it? I walked to village to ask for another ration of flour, but naturally I was turned down. I was kind to everyone. Smiling at the old women. It was sunny. I passed the town hall again and again. The sun shone down on the flags. I knew how to tell time. The big town clock said eleven, still three hours to go.

Noon came and went. The stores closed their shutters. Men walked home to lunch. One o'clock. Men and women began hovering around the square, some of them sitting on benches in the shade. I didn't know why they were so anxious. I stood with them waiting. I asked an old woman what they were waiting for, but she ignored me. Then I realized that they were waiting for me. It was ten minutes past one when I hurried home and kissed everyone good-bye. Nobody knew why or minded much. I had been a tearful child for weeks. I put on my leather shoes and my white shirt and said a very long good-bye to Chevalier. Then I walked down to the square. I had until two o'clock to step forward and be taken prisoner and shot. I didn't want to be late, but I saw no point in being early. I watched the hand of the clock jump to the last minute, directly under the twelve.

I walked up the steps and knocked the knocker on the big door. It was opened by a fat soldier. He barred me from entering. No children. I told the guard that I needed to talk to the captain. "No."

I said very carefully that I knew who had committed the murders. He still wouldn't let me pass, but he called out and another soldier came down the stairs and told me to follow him. We went into the office of the commandant.

There were weapons and piles of papers. Soldiers stood around. They seemed nervous. I think there was a roster of the villagers, a big book already open with all of their names written in ink. Three soldiers were making up their list for the firing squad. They did not expect anyone to come forward and be a hero that day. I found out later it was because they thought we were all cowards.

"Yes, little boy?"

Three more soldiers with rifles were standing looking down at the crowd gathering in the town square. There was great tension in the room. I tried to speak. But I couldn't. The captain stood up. He seemed very young and I liked his face. He was friendly to me.

"Well, little boy, what did you come to see me about? You can tell me."

I said, "I know who killed those people."

"Well?" He smiled. The other soldiers stopped what they were doing and looked over at me. "Who was it then?"

"It was me."

He looked angry. He swore loudly and ordered the soldier to take me away. "This is only a baby!" he shouted.

"Listen to me. I can prove it." I was crying.

"Get him out of here."

"I did it. I swear to you."

"Out!"

One of the other soldiers who had come in after me said, "Stop, Captain. Let's listen to the child. He may tell us something we don't know."

"Alright, why not?" The captain nodded at the soldier, who brought me back in and sat me down.

I told the captain about Ghiseline and how much I had loved her and that she had told me she would love me forever too, and that I couldn't understand why she wanted to be with another man. I told him how Chevalier and I followed them into the cave, how I had seen them without their clothes on, playing together on the straw mattress. I told them about the little candle on the dirt floor. About firing the gun. How I had shot the two of them with the soldier's gun, showing him how I had unclipped his holster and picked it up and held it with both hands and that it had jumped up and down. Dropping it, picking it up. I told them that there was a bullet in the roof of the cave and that if they didn't believe me, all they needed to do was to go there and look and see for themselves if it was true or not. They just stared at me. I think they believed me. There were eight of them in the room by then, and they didn't say anything for a while. And when they did, I couldn't understand them, because it wasn't in my language. They were arguing.

I interrupted them. "I am ready to die," I said. I was, too, I had decided. That made them argue more. Finally, the captain told them all to shut up.

It was after half-an-hour sitting in the chair that the captain looked at me and asked if I liked chocolate. I said I thought I did, only I couldn't know to be sure, because I had been too young to remember back before the war when there had been chocolate and everything else. He nodded to a soldier who came back in with a box of chocolates and let me pick one. I held it in my fingers, and he nodded for me to eat it. It was the best thing I had ever tasted.

"Thank you for coming in," he told me. "I do not believe a word that you have told me, but I know you to be a brave little boy. I only wish my own men had your courage. I am afraid that if we should lose this war it will be because of brave little boys like you and not that cattle out there sitting around the square trembling. Good-bye, my boy. I hope I am lucky enough to have a son like you one day. The firing squad is not the place for a boy like you. Grow up to be a good man."

Then the soldier brought me downstairs and out in the sun. It was after two-thirty in the afternoon. I still felt ready to die. I had said good-bye to my aunts, my uncles, cousins, grandparents, and I couldn't get used to not being dead again. Naturally, no one else had surrendered so that the tension in the square had grown. All the men were now worried for their own lives.

When I came down the steps and started across the square, the priest came over to me followed by a half-dozen men.

"You went into the hall exactly at two," the priest said.

"Yes, I did, Father."

"What were you doing in there for so long?"

"Well, I was surrendering," I said.

"Seriously, my son, what were you up to in there?"

"I was, Father. I thought I may as well. I was nervous from everyone looking at me."

"Please, my son." He spoke very gently. "Tell me what you were doing in there."

"That's what I was doing, Father, I swear." I began to weep again.

"But you're only a baby, my son, you didn't shoot those people."

I looked up at the crowd of faces surrounding me. Now there were many of them. They couldn't grasp what I was telling them. None of them believed me the way I think the soldiers had believed in the town hall. But these were grown-ups, and they were also trying to protect me. I thought for a few seconds. In that instance, I changed my life forever. "Father, didn't somebody need to come forward?"

"But why did you?"

I wiped my face, then I said very clearly: "I didn't want ten of my countrymen to die."

That night ten men were rounded up and driven to the barracks and chained together until two the next afternoon when they were lined up against the wall of the Prefecture and shot to death. The marks made by the bullets remain in the bricks to this day. One of those men was my grandfather.

As for me, from that day on, I became known as *L'Enfant de Charante*. Maybe you have heard of him. When the war was over, there was a parade in my honor, and the mayor of Angouleme put a ribbon with a beautiful golden medal around my neck. It made my grandmother feel somewhat better.

In the village square, you can still see on the base of my statue, the words engraved: "I did not want ten of my countrymen to die." Our priest went so far as to suggest that I be ordained as a saint. The Bishop in Bordeaux responded that I was far too young.

The mystery of the murders lives on. The most persistent belief was that they were both killed by another soldier, a jealous lover. But, of course, no one will ever know. In wartime, crimes are allowed to flourish.

Oh, yes, there are memories that stay in your house forever. These are the unwanted guests who refuse to leave. And even as you lay dying, they will come to your room and stand over your bed and grip your hand. Much too tightly.

&

DON BLANDING

JIMMY'S BOOKCASE is crammed with works by others who were dreamers of dreams and travelin' men . . . and travelin' women, as well. Yet, none of Jimmy's favorite writers displays those traits any better than does Don Blanding, who called himself the "vagabond poet."

"I take a few moments to quietly move about the room and check in with a few old friends for some parting words," writes Jimmy at the close of *A Pirate Looks at Fifty*. "I scan my favorite books: Beryl Markham, Don Sheldon, Mark Twain, and then I pick up an old copy of Don Blanding, and there they are, the words I need to close out this section of the book and this chapter of my life."

The book is *Drifter's Gold*, and the poem is "The Double Life," a verse about the conflicts between wanting to roam and wanting to stay at home.

Born in the Oklahoma territory in 1894, Blanding began his world-wide wanderings right out of high school in 1912, and he never stayed in any one place thereafter for more than two years. His skills as an illustrator provided him with a livelihood from Paris to Honolulu, but it was the allure of the South Pacific that tempted Blanding to linger just a little bit longer than usual. There the young illustrator developed another artistry with words and meter and rhyme. Don Blanding's talents, old and new, eventually led to nearly two dozen illustrated volumes of verse, including: *Paradise Loot*, *Vagabond's House*, *Hula Moons*, and *Stowaways in Paradise*. Over the years, his works became classics among the islanders and they earned him the unofficial recognition as poet laureate of Hawaii. The title which captured Jimmy's imagination the most, however, was *Floridays*, one of a handful of the poet's works not inspired by the South Pacific. The book had an inspiration that was entirely its own. And the inspiration had a name: Dorothy.

Don Blanding's very first stop out of Oklahoma in 1912 was Oregon, where he struck up an acquaintance with an older woman of twenty-four named Dorothy Binney Putnam. The encounter's worth mentioning, because their songlines would cross yet again in Hawaii in 1940. And much would transpire in Dorothy's own life during those intervening years. To begin with, George Putnam left her in 1929 so that he could marry Amelia Earhart. The publishing heir had promoted Amelia's historic flight across the Atlantic, and then he published the book which the aviatrix dedicated to her "very best friend," Dorothy Binney Putnam.

Eleven years later, Dorothy and Don somehow renewed their friendship in Hawaii, just as the drifting poet was about to leave for one of his frequent speaking tours. As much as he loved the islands, Don Blanding loved his freedom even more, and his writings, as well as his illustrations were an inseparable part of his own sort of walkabout.

Still, something must have clicked.

On his way to Havana a couple months later, Blanding decided to visit his friend on her estate in Fort Pierce, Florida, and he must have sensed that he had found himself another home. He continued on to Havana, but then returned to Florida, and the two were married. Even so, that did not keep the vagabond from drifting. In the next few months alone, he would travel by himself throughout Central America, Mexico, and the Bahamas.

All the while, Florida's coastal life in the early 1940s had filled Blanding's mind with impressions that would prove to remain at once both timeless and universal: flamingos set against a tropical sunset, pelicans wheeling above turquoise waters, and tarpon leaping high into the moonlight did not escape his attention, nor did the trickle of tourists seeking respite from the rest of the world. Barely a year after moving to Fort Pierce, Don Blanding had written, illustrated, and published *Floridays* by September of 1941.

Then came the attack on his beloved Hawaii, and Don enlisted in the U.S. Army. His stay in the military would be less than a year, but the horizon before him would remain forever endless. Never again, did Don Blanding return either to Dorothy, or to Florida. They divorced in 1945.

Don Blanding spent those years after the war in his favorite haunts along the mainland's West Coast and in those throughout Hawaii. Upon his death in 1957, his ashes were scattered just off the coast of Honolulu. Apparently, there was no one place in life that was able to contain him, and so it remained upon his death. As with Robert Louis Stevenson on Samoa, Don Blanding had written a memoriam verse; however, the vagabond poet chose to have no grave.

In "Epitaph," Don Blanding wrote:

> Do not carve on stone or wood,
> "He was honest" or "He was good."
> Write in smoke on a passing breeze
> Seven words . . . and the words are these,
> Telling all that a volume could,
> "He lived, he laughed and . . . he understood."

Additional suggested works by Don Blanding:

— *Leaves from a Grass-House* (1923)

— *Paradise Loot* (1925)

— *Vagabond's House* (1928)

— *Hula Moons* (1930)

— *Stowaways in Paradise* (1931)

— *The Rest of the Road* (1937)

— *Drifter's Gold* (1939)

— *Floridays* (1941)

— *A Grand Time Living* (1950)

— *Joy is an Inside Job* (1953)

MYSTERY – SOUTH OF US

a selection from
Floridays

FLORIDA thrusts like a guiding thumb
To the southern islands of rumba and rum,
To the mystery-cities and haunted seas
Of the Spanish Main the Caribbees.
Where the ghosts of Columbus and Pirates Bold
Seek the Islands of Spice and Streets of Gold,
Where the wandering phantom of Ku-Kul-Kan
Haunts the temples he builded in Yucatan,
Where the jaguars prowl and the lizards crawl
On a broken altar and sculptured wall,
Where the Mayan rulers in arrogant pride
Dreamed and schemed and suffered and died.
The inlaid thrones and the sacred urns
Are filled with orchids and stag-horn ferns,
The witching moon of the tropic skies
Caresses the lips and the dead stone eyes
Of fallen idols of lust and blood
That lie in the mold and the reeking mud
Of fever-jungles. The dust and bones
Of men who quarried and laid the stones
Of fabulous cities are turned to earth.
The echoes of prayers and chants and mirth
Of vanished people and priests and kings
Are heard in the night-wind's whisperings.

The seas and straits and bays and coves,
The peaks and valleys and swamps and groves
142

Hold ruins of dreams that were dreamed by men
In centuries lost and beyond our ken.
There are names that were spoken by long-dead lips
Of men who came in their gallant ships,
    Bahama . . . Barbados . . . Havana . . . Bermuda . . .
    Jamaica . . . Tortuga . . . Caracas . . . Barbuda . . .
    Martinique . . . Port au Prince . . . Santiago de Cuba . . .
    Windward Isles . . . Leeward Isles . . . Isle of Pines and Oruba . . .
    Trinidad . . . Margarita . . . Tobago . . . Inagua . . .
    Orinoco . . . Honduras . . . Yucatan . . . Nicaragua . . .
    Guatemala . . . Porto Rico . . . Costa Rica . . . Cartagena . . .
    Venezuela . . . Baranquilla . . . Maracaibo . . . Magdelana . . .

Florida thrusts like a guiding thumb
To the southern Islands of rumba and rum
To the lands of mystery that lie below,
To the places I know I'm going to go.

THE DOUBLE LIFE

a selection from
Drifter's Gold

HOW very simple life would be
    If only there were two of me
A Restless Me to drift and roam
    A Quiet Me to stay at home.
A Searching One to find his fill
    Of varied skies and newfound thrill
While sane and homely things are done
    By the domestic Other One.

And that's just where the trouble lies;
    There is a Restless Me that cries
For chancy risks and changing scene,
    For arctic blue and tropic green,
For deserts with their mystic spell,
    For lusty fun and raising Hell

But shackled to that Restless Me
    My Other Self rebelliously
Resists the frantic urge to move.
    It seeks the old familiar groove
That habits make. It finds content
    With hearth and home dear prisonment,
With candlelight and well loved books
    And treasured loot in dusty nooks,

With puttering and garden things
    And dreaming while a cricket sings

And all the while the Restless One
   Insists on more exciting fun
It wants to go with every tide,
   No matter where . . . just for the ride.
Like yowling cats the two selves brawl
   Until I have no peace at all.

One eye turns to the forward track,
   The other eye looks sadly back,
I'm getting wall-eyed from the strain,
   (It's tough to have an idle brain)
But One says "Stay" and One says "Go"
   And One says "Yes," and One says "no,"
And One Self wants a home and wife
   And One Self craves the drifter's life.

The Restless Fellow always wins
   I wish my folks had made me twins.

BERYL MARKHAM

from
Front Matter
"Prologue"
A Pirate Looks at Fifty
1998

HER LANDING on this side of the Atlantic was nothing at all like Lindbergh's welcome in Paris. In fact, the only witness to the ending of Beryl Markham's historic flight was the aviatrix herself when her plane crash-landed its nose into the muck of Nova Scotia's Cape Breton Island. Her head struck the cabin glass, and blood poured down across her face. Nonetheless, she had become the first woman to solo an aircraft eastward over the Atlantic.

To this day, Beryl Markham is probably known less for that feat in 1936 than she is for her memoir *West with the Night*. Though the book was released to critical acclaim in 1942, the rest of the world had more pressing things upon its mind. Most everyone's words — whether fact or fiction — could not compare to the reported events of the second World War. So, *West with the Night* quickly lapsed into a generation of obscurity.

Years later, when *Ernest Hemingway's Selected Letters 1917-1961* was published in 1981, Papa's oldest son Jack (the father of Margaux and Mariel) casually asked one of his trout-fishing buddies if he'd ever read any of his father's published letters. "They're very revealing," he added. So, the other fisherman took Jack's advice and came upon these words about Beryl Markham:

" . . . She has written so well, and marvelously well, that I was completely ashamed of myself as a writer," admitted Papa. "I felt that I was simply a carpenter with words, picking up whatever was furnished on the job and sometimes making an okay pig pen."

Thus, from a casual remark during a fishing trip, a new edition of *West with the Night* was released in 1983. In Ernest Hemingway's words: "It is really a bloody, wonderful book." And there's little doubt that Jimmy wholeheartedly agrees, for he refers to this book at both the beginning and the conclusion of *A Pirate Looks at Fifty*. Had Beryl Markham never learned to fly, though, she would still remain a fascinating person.

Born into the English gentry of the early 1900s, Beryl Clutterbuck was three years old when her father relocated their family to British East Africa (now Kenya) to try his hand at farming in the tropics. While it didn't take long for Beryl's mother to renounce that rugged, pioneer life and return to England, their daughter remained in the colony, where Charles Clutterbuck turned his attention to breeding and training horses for the Kenyan racetracks.

As her father spent his days developing that stock, Beryl's care was left in the hands of local tribesmen. From them, she learned how to speak Swahili and to hurl a spear; from her father, how to ride horses and to hunt. Then, at the age of fifteen, Beryl helped one of her father's prize mares birth a colt, and he made her a gift of the foal for the job well done. "For years I had handled my father's horses, fed them, ridden them, groomed them, and loved them. But I had never owned one," she would write. "Now I owned one." And she named him Pegasus.

There are those who will tell you that the winged horse of Greek mythology represents divine inspiration, and that anyone who rode upon him was destined to become a poet. Others will say that Pegasus represents immortality, and that he could be ridden through the air into heaven. *West with the Night* just might be evidence that both beliefs are true, for Markham's poetic prose has elevated her story to that of classic status.

To no one's surprise, Beryl would go on to become the first woman in either England or Africa to earn a horse trainer's license. And after that, she would earn her pilot's license so she could deliver mail, supplies, and even occasional passengers to mining camps and safari parties in the out-

147

lying bush. And in emergencies, she transported doctors, patients, and medicines alike.

"Distances are long and life is rather lonely in East Africa," the bush pilot would later explain quite simply. "The advent of airplanes seemed to open up a new life for us. The urge was strong in me to become part of that life, to make it my life."

And then came Beryl Markham's rendezvous with destiny.

"Two weeks from now I am going to set out to fly the Atlantic to New York," she explained in a letter to readers of London's *Daily Express*. "Not as a society girl. Not as a woman even. And certainly not as a stunt aviator. But as a pilot-graduate of one of the hardest schools of flying known, with 2000 flying hours to my credit. The only thing that really counts is whether one can fly."

The following selection from her memoir provides just a bit more context of the passage that Jimmy cites in his own front pages. With these words, she reminisces with her father before departing Africa for her flight across the Atlantic; it sets a sweet tone for Jimmy's own journey at the yoke of the *Hemisphere Dancer*.

Additional suggested works by Beryl Markham:

— *West with the Night* (1983)

— *The Splendid Outcast* (1987)

"What of the Hunting, Hunter Bold?"

a selection from
West with the Night / Chapter XIX

ELBURGON IS NOT A TOWN; it is just a station on the Uganda
Railway, one of many entrances to a broad, familiar country. There,
as at Njoro, my house looks over the Rongai Valley and, as at Njoro, the
Mau Forest broods in resigned silence, close on the edges of fields fresh
robbed of their ancient trees. I have a gallop where my father still trains
his horses and where I can land my plane. Everything has been done –
every material thing – to give this place the aspect of benignity, of friendship, of tolerance and conviviality, but the character of a dwelling, like
that of a man, grows slowly.

The walls of my house are without memories, or secrets, or laughter.
Not enough of life has been breathed into them – their warmth is artificial; too few hands have turned the window latches, too few feet have
trod the thresholds. The boards of the floor, self-conscious as youth or
falsely proud as the newly rich, have not yet unlimbered enough to utter
a single cordial creak. In time they will, but not for me.

My father takes me by the arm and we desert the veranda and the
shadows advancing on the valley and go inside to the big room whose
hearth of native stone is neither worn nor stained with ash. In these
surroundings it will not be so hard to say good-bye as it was at Njoro.

My father leans against the mantelpiece and begins to load his pipe
with tobacco whose aroma bestows a presence on thirty vanished years.
That aroma and the smell of the smoke that follows it are to me the
quintessence of memory.

But memory is a drug. Memory can hold you against your strength
and against your will, and my father knows it. He is sixty-four years old
now, and well deserving of deep chairs and care and dottle dreams and
carping cronies – should he desire these. He might say, with ample reason: "I'm old now. I've earned my rest."

But he doesn't. He says: "You know, I like South Africa. I like Durban. I'm going down there to start training. The racing's good and the stakes are high. I think it's a good chance." He announces his intention with the sanguine expectancy of a schoolboy.

"So, when you come back," he says, "I'll be there."

He allows me no misgiving nor a moment's remorse – not the luxury of feeling young nor himself the maudlin misery of feeling old.

We sit together through the evening and discuss the things that each has saved for the other to hear. We talk of Pegasus – and of how he had died, quietly one night in his stall, for no reason that anyone could ever find.

"Snake, perhaps," says my father. "Yellow mambas are deadly."

It may have been a mamba, or it may not have been. However, or whatever it was, Pegasus – so expectantly christened so long ago – is gone now, yielding his ethereal wings to the realization of wood and steel ones that fly as high and higher, but, for all that, are never so buoyant or capable of bearing quite such cargoes of hope.

So we talked about that and about other things – about the forth-coming auction of my Avian, about Arab Ruta, and about Tom, who, with Charles Scott, had won the greatest air race ever staged – England to Australia – against the best pilots the world could muster.

"How strange it is," says my father, "that an old friend and neighbour of ours should have done such a wonderful thing! Eleven thousand miles and more – in seventy-one hours!"

It seems wonderful, but not strange to me. There are men whose failures surprise nobody, and others whose successes are as easily antici-pated – Tom was of these.

I rise from my chair and my father glances at the clock. Time for bed. In the morning I will be off, but we have said nothing of good-bye. We have learned frugality – even in this.

In the morning I get into my plane, peer down the length of the gallop I use for a runway, and wave to my father. I am smiling and he is smiling, and he waves too. I have just one more stop at Nairobi (for Blix), and the next overnight stop after that will be Juba, in the Anglo-Egyp-tian Sudan.

The plane rolls forward and I salute once more and leave my father standing on the earth he has stood upon so long and so steadily. I circle and dip my wings, or rather I think the Avian voluntarily makes her last curtsey – her last, at least, to him.

He does not wave again. He stands, shading his eyes, looking upward, and I level off and take my course and follow it away.

LEWIS CARROLL

WHILE SOME might doubt whether or not "Math Suks," as Jimmy has often sung, very few ever challenge the claim that Charles Lutwidge Dodgson was little more than a mediocre mathematician in that pursuit. So, Dodgson can thank his lucky stars that he had something other than his day job going for him, especially when he wrote under the *nom de plume* of Lewis Carroll.

As such, he's known best for his 1865 classic, *Alice's Adventures in Wonderland,* which became for him a commercial success when he was thirty-three. In 1871, he published the sequel, *Through the Looking-Glass, and What Alice Found There.* The two are often mistaken for one another, because movie versions have consolidated some ideas from each into a single film.

Meanwhile, Carroll's verse that's called "The Jabberwocky" is almost as famous as the books themselves. This classic piece of literary nonsense is something that Jimmy draws upon for "A Sailor's Christmas" in the lines: "Cali, Calais, no work today / He read it in a book." Clearly, that comes from this refrain recited by Alice herself in the sequel:

"And hast thou slain the Jabberwock?
   Come to my arms, my beamish boy!
O frabjous day! Callooh! Callay!"
   He chortled in his joy.

All that stuff aside, though, "The Walrus and the Carpenter" remains Jimmy's first allusion to anything written by Lewis Carroll when it pops up in "That's What Living Is to Me" on *Hot Water*: "The time has come the walrus said / And little oysters hide their head." This is from the following poem recited by Tweedledee in *Through the Looking-Glass*.

Meanwhile, the rest of Jimmy's song is just as rich with other literary allusions, including the pun "My twain of thought is loosely bound / I guess it's time to mark this down." This reference should come as no surprise, for Jimmy's spoken prologue on the album track explains how the song's title has been taken from an opening page in Mark Twain's *Following the Equator*, which reads, "Be good and you will be lonely."

On at least one television appearance, though, Jimmy even introduced his solo performance of that tune as one that he called "Be Good and You Will be Lonely."

One last piece of significa regarding this poem arises from the verse:

"The time has come," the Walrus said,
   "To talk of many things:
Of shoes – and ships – and sealing-wax –
   Of cabbages – and kings –

From those specific lines, the short story writer we all know as O. Henry borrowed that phrase "cabbages and kings" to use as the title for a collection of his own short stories published in 1904. Henry's attempt to craft a novel out of some related tales of revolution set in a fictional South American country is barely held together with a subplot about ex-patriates from the United States. In was in this very literary setting, though, that O. Henry coined the term "banana republic" to describe the sort of corrupt, unstable, and self-important dictatorships that still seem to come and go in the tropics. O. Henry's own phrase nowadays remains better known than does his book.

So, let's again thank Mr. Twain for *Following the Equator*, and add to all that some thanks for the shaky math of Mr. Dodgson as well.

THE WALRUS AND THE CARPENTER

a selection from
Through the Looking-Glass / Chapter IV

THE SUN was shining on the sea,
  Shining with all his might:
He did his very best to make
    The billows smooth and bright –
And this was odd, because it was
    The middle of the night.

The moon was shining sulkily,
    Because she thought the sun
Had got no business to be there
    After the day was done –
"It's very rude of him," she said,
    "To come and spoil the fun!"

The sea was wet as wet could be,
    The sands were dry as dry.
You could not see a cloud, because
    No cloud was in the sky:
No birds were flying overhead –
    There were no birds to fly.

The Walrus and the Carpenter
    Were walking close at hand;
They wept like anything to see
    Such quantities of sand:
"If this were only cleared away,"
    They said, "It would be grand!"

"If seven maids with seven mops
　　Swept it for half a year,
Do you suppose," the Walrus said,
　　"That they could get it clear?"
"I doubt it" said the Carpenter,
　　And shed a bitter tear.

"O, Oysters, come and walk with us!"
　　The Walrus did beseech.
"A pleasant walk, a pleasant talk,
　　Along the briny beach:
We cannot do with more than four,
　　To give a hand to each."

The eldest Oyster looked at him.
　　But not a word he said:
The eldest Oyster winked his eye,
　　And shook his heavy head –
Meaning to say he did not choose
　　To leave the oyster-bed.

But four young oysters hurried up,
　　All eager for a treat:
Their coats were brushed, their faces washed,
　　Their shoes were clean and neat –
And this was odd, because, you know,
　　They hadn't any feet.

Four other Oysters followed them
　　And yet another four;
And thick and fast they came at last,
　　And more, and more, and more –
All hopping through the frothy waves,
　　And scrambling to the shore.

The Walrus and the Carpenter
　　Walked on a mile or so,
And then they rested on a rock
　　Conveniently low:
And all the little Oysters stood
　　And waited in a row.

"The time has come," the Walrus said,
  "To talk of many things:
Of shoes – and ships – and sealing wax –
  Of cabbages – and kings –
And why the sea is boiling hot –
  And whether pigs have wings."

"But wait a bit," the Oysters cried,
  "Before we have our chat;
For some of us are out of breath,
  And all of us are fat!"
"No hurry!" said the Carpenter.
  They thanked him much for that.

"A loaf of bread," the Walrus said,
  "Is what we chiefly need:
Pepper and vinegar besides
  Are very good indeed –
Now if you're ready Oysters dear,
  We can begin to feed."

"But not on us!" the Oysters cried,
  Turning a little blue,
"After such kindness, that would be
  A dismal thing to do!"
"The night is fine," the Walrus said
  "Do you admire the view?"

"It was so nice of you to come!
  And you are very nice!"
The Carpenter said nothing but
  "Cut us another slice:
I wish you were not quite so deaf –
  I've had to ask you twice!"

"It seems a shame," the Walrus said
  "To play them such a trick,
After we've brought them out so far,
  And made them trot so quick!"
The Carpenter said nothing but
  "The butter's spread too thick!"

"I weep for you," the Walrus said.
    "I deeply sympathize."
With sobs and tears he sorted out
    Those of the largest size,
Holding his pocket hankerchief
    Before his streaming eyes.

"O, Oysters," said the Carpenter
    "You've had a pleasant run!
Shall we be trotting home again?
    "But answer came there none –
And that was scarcely odd, because
    They'd eaten every one.

ANNE MORROW LINDBERGH

from
"A Baker's Dozen (Minus One)"
A Pirate Looks at Fifty
1998

Liner notes
BEACH HOUSE ON THE MOON
1999

FIVE O'CLOCK each evening in the Dwight Morrow household meant only one thing: Elizabeth Cutter Morrow, a poet in her own right, would gather together their four children and read aloud to them for at least an hour.

Throughout the formative years of the Morrow children, the ritual continued until, one by one, they all were able to read on their own. At that point in a young Morrow's life, the hour became a private one set aside simply for reading or writing alone. Even when the family summered on Cape Cod or Martha's Vineyard, the schedule remained the same.

It was not simply by chance, then, that Anne Morrow developed a kinship with the written word that would make her nothing less than a force of nature in the literary world.

Much as Elizabeth Cutter Morrow had gained recognition as a woman of letters, as well as a champion of women's education, so too would her daughter follow a similar path. The fact that Anne Morrow eventually married the man who was then the most famous person in the whole wide world should not cast any semblance of a shadow over her own talents and accomplishments. Her much-acclaimed *Gift from the Sea* was only a matter of time, and her own life leading up to that slender, but powerful volume is replete with achievements that are no less impressive.

In many respects, the marriage of Anne Morrow and Charles Lindbergh in 1929 was a proverbial match made in heaven. Each one tended to bring out the best in the other, and that enabled their union not only to endure, but also to thrive.

That same year further marked the beginning of new experiences for each as Charles had designed a two-seater airplane to be built by Lockheed. And while Anne would make her maiden solo flight later in the year, the Lindberghs prepared to fly their new single-engine Sirius over the Pacific on the first of several surveying missions around the globe. Together, the two became airborne explorers charting among the continents those routes that other aviators might someday follow. For the young woman instilled with a writer's instincts, not a single aspect of this experience was over-looked or taken for granted. Anne Morrow Lindbergh's first book, *North to the Orient*, was published in 1935, and the public was enthralled with their adventure. Throughout the decade, Anne and Charles pioneered air routes along the earth's parallels and its longitudes alike. All the while, their lives were nothing less than an open book, and much of it was bound in print.

The only title by either Lindbergh that Jimmy lists of his dozen favorites, however, is the small volume of essays by Anne Morrow Lindbergh. On Captiva Island, she had found inspiration in the shells of her Florida vacation, and her meditations upon simplicity, solitude, and caring for the soul became *Gift from the Sea*. The book underscores Jimmy's own thread of self-examination and self-improvement which runs throughout *A Pirate Looks at Fifty*.

Additional suggested works by Anne Morrow Lindbergh:

— *North to the Orient* (1935)

— *Gift from the Sea* (1955)

— *Bring Me A Unicorn: Diaries and Letters/1922-1928 (1972)*

THE BEACH

a selection from

Gift from the Sea / Chapter I

THE BEACH IS NOT THE PLACE TO WORK; to read, write or think. I should have remembered that from other years. Too warm, too damp, too soft for any real mental discipline or sharp flights of spirit. One never learns. Hopefully, one carries down the faded straw bag, lumpy with books, clean paper, long over-due unanswered letters, freshly sharpened pencils, lists, and good intentions. The books remain unread, the pencils break their points, and the pads rest smooth and unblemished as the cloudless sky. No reading, no writing, no thoughts even – at least, not at first.

At first, the tired body takes over completely. As on shipboard, one descends into a deck-chair apathy. One is forced against one's mind, against all tidy resolutions, back into the primeval rhythms of the seashore. Rollers on the beach, wind in the pines, the slow flapping of herons across sand dunes, drown out the hectic rhythms of city and suburb, time tables and schedules. One falls under their spell, relaxes, stretches out prone. One becomes, in fact, like the element on which one lies, flattened by the sea; bare, open, empty as the beach, erased by today's tides of all yesterday's scribblings.

And then, some morning in the second week, the mind wakes, comes to life again. Not in a city sense – no – but beach-wise. It begins to drift, to play, to turn over in gentle careless rolls like those lazy waves on the beach. One never knows what chance treasures these easy unconscious rollers may toss up, on the smooth white sand of the conscious mind; what perfectly rounded stone, what rare shell from the ocean floor. Perhaps a channelled whelk, a moon shell, or even an argonaut.

But it must not be sought for or – heaven forbid! – dug for. No, no dredging of the sea-bottom here. That would defeat one's purpose. The sea does not reward those who are too anxious, too greedy, or too impatient. To dig for treasures shows not only impatience and greed, but lack of faith. Patience, patience, patience, is what the sea teaches. Patience and faith. One should lie empty, open, choiceless as a beach – waiting for a gift from the sea.

F. SCOTT FITZGERALD

from
"Diamond As Big As the Ritz"
BAROMETER SOUP
1995

AS WITH HEMINGWAY, Fitzgerald wrote only a handful of books, and the short story was primarily his stock-in-trade. The length of those stories does nothing to diminish the talents of either man, for the two of them wrote stories quite unlike any others written before or ever since.

"Diamond As Big As the Ritz," upon which Jimmy based his song of the same name, originally was titled "Diamond in the Sky," and ran some twenty-thousand words long. Though that's still shorter than Hemingway's *The Old Man and the Sea*, popular magazines that had been publishing Fitzgerald's stories all sent the "Diamond" piece back to him, along with a rejection slip.

So, the writer chopped out some five thousand words, and that relatively-shorter version with the relatively longer title was printed in a magazine that paid him only three hundred dollars. By the time he managed to collect enough stories for his *Tales of the Jazz Age*, Fitzgerald had removed another thousand words. And it still remained a long, short story.

For the most part. Jimmy's own narrative remains true to the tale; however, nothing can match the extravagance of what Fitzgerald declared was the "Jazz Age," that era when today's modern conveniences were making their first appearances. Aeroplanes, telephones, and high-powered weaponry had been the remnant technologies of World War I, and they were just entering civilian duty during his "Jazz Age."

The Montana setting for this story was likely inspired by Fitzgerald's summer visit there when he was only eighteen. His stay on a ranch outside of White Sulphur Springs (about fifty miles north of Livingston) was marked by his several attempts to live the life of a cowboy: playing cards, drinking whiskey, shooting pistols, riding horses, and flirting with girls on a neighboring ranch. Still, Fitzgerald did not embrace the west with any of the sort of passion displayed by Hemingway. Instead, his Minnesotan outlook remained drawn to the decadence of the East Coast. Thus, his "Diamond" story was to him pretty much what he said it was: his own amusement.

"One well-known critic has been pleased to like this [Diamond] extravaganza better than anything I have written," noted Fitzgerald. "Personally, I prefer 'The Off-Shore Pirate.'"

Pirate? Did someone mention "pirate?" Apparently, this presents a wonderful opportunity to recommend Fitzgerald's personal favorite and let it contrast with Faulkner's *Mosquitoes*. While Faulkner's story recounts a New Orleans cruise on Lake Pontchartrain, Fitzgerald's "The Offshore Pirate" is about a band of collegians who hijack a yacht, just off the shore of Palm Beach. Together, the two stories provide a look at some of Jimmy's favorite haunts as they were in an altogether different era.

Additional suggested works by F. Scott Fitzgerald:

— *Flappers and Philosophers (1920)*

— *This Side of Paradise* (1920)

— *Tales of the Jazz Age (1922)*

— *The Beautiful and Damned* (1922)

— *The Great Gatsby* (1925)

— *Tender Is the Night* (1934)

THE DIAMOND AS BIG AS THE RITZ

a selection from
Tales of the Jazz Age

JOHN T. UNGER CAME FROM A FAMILY that had been well known in Hades – a small town on the Mississippi River – for several generations.

John's father had held the amateur golf championship through many a heated contest; Mrs. Unger was known "from hot-box to hot-bed," as the local phrase went, for her political addresses; and young John T. Unger, who had just turned sixteen, had danced all the latest dances from New York before he put on long trousers. And now, for a certain time, he was to be away from home. That respect for a New England education which is the bane of all provincial places, which drains them yearly of their most promising young men, had seized upon his parents. Nothing would suit them but that he should go to St. Midas' School near Boston – Hades was too small to hold their darling and gifted son.

Now in Hades – as you know if you ever have been there – the names of the more fashionable preparatory schools and colleges mean very little. The inhabitants have been so long out of the world that, though they make a show of keeping up to date in dress and manners and literature, they depend to a great extent on hearsay, and a function that in Hades would be considered elaborate would doubtless be hailed by a Chicago beef-princess as "perhaps a little tacky."

John T. Unger was on the eve of departure. Mrs. Unger, with maternal fatuity, packed his trunks full of linen suits and electric fans, and Mr. Unger presented his son with an asbestos pocket-book stuffed with money.

"Remember, you are always welcome here," he said. "You can be sure boy, that we'll keep the home fires burning."

"I know," answered John huskily.

"Don't forget who you are and where you come from," continued his

father proudly, "and you can do nothing to harm you. You are an Unger
– from Hades."

So the old man and the young shook hands and John walked away
with tears streaming from his eyes. Ten minutes later he had passed the
city limits, and he stopped to glance back for the last time. Over the
gates the old-fashioned Victorian motto seemed strangely attractive to
him. His father had tried time and time again to have it changed to
something with a little more push and verve about it, such as "Hades –
Your Opportunity," or else a plain "Welcome" sign set over a hearty hand-
shake pricked out in electric lights. The old motto was a little depressing,
Mr. Unger had thought – but now . . .

So John took his look and then set his face resolutely toward his destination. And, as he turned away, the lights of Hades against the sky were
a warm and passionate beauty.

St. Midas' School is half an hour from Boston in a Rolls-Pierce motor-
car. The actual distance will never be known, for no one, except John T.
Unger, had ever arrived there save in a Rolls-Pierce and probably no one
ever will again. St. Midas' is the most expensive and the most exclusive
boys' preparatory school in the world.

John's first two years there passed pleasantly. The fathers of all the
boys were money-kings and John spent his summers visiting at fashionable resorts. While he was very fond of all the boys he visited, their fathers struck him as being much of a piece, and in his boyish way he often
wondered at their exceeding sameness. When he told them where his
home was they would ask jovially, "Pretty hot down there?" and John
would muster a faint smile and answer, "It certainly is." His response
would have been heartier had they not all made this joke – at best varying it with, "Is it hot enough for you down there?" which he hated just as
much.

In the middle of his second year at school, a quiet, handsome boy
named Percy Washington had been put in John's form. The newcomer
was pleasant in his manner and exceedingly well dressed even for St.
Midas', but for some reason he kept aloof from the other boys. The only
person with whom he was intimate was John T. Unger, but even to John
he was entirely uncommunicative concerning his home or his family.
That he was wealthy went without saying, but beyond a few such deduc-
tions John knew little of his friend, so it promised rich confectionery for
his curiosity when Percy invited him to spend the summer at his home
"in the West." He accepted, without hesitation.

It was only when they were in the train that Percy became, for the
first time, rather communicative. One day while they were eating lunch

in the dining-car and discussing the imperfect characters of several boys at school, Percy suddenly changed his tone and made an abrupt remark.

"My father," he said, "is by far the richest man in the world."

"Oh," said John, politely. He could think of no answer to make to this confidence. He considered "That's very nice," but it sounded hollow and was on the point of saying, "Really?" but refrained since it would seem to question Percy's statement. And such an astounding statement could scarcely be questioned.

"By far the richest," repeated Percy.

"I was reading in the *World Almanac*," began John, "that there was one man in America with an income of over five million a year and four men with incomes of over three million a year, and – "

"Oh, they're nothing." Percy's mouth was a half-moon of scorn. "Catchpenny capitalists, financial small-fry, petty merchants and money-lenders. My father could buy them out and not know he'd done it."

"But how does he – "

"Why haven't they put down *his* income tax? Because he doesn't pay any. At least he pays a little one – but he doesn't pay any on his *real* income."

"He must be very rich," said John simply. "I'm glad. I like very rich people.

"The richer a fella is, the better I like him." There was a look of passionate frankness upon his dark face. "I visited the Schnlitzer-Murphys last Easter. Vivian Schnlitzer-Murphy had rubies as big as hen's eggs, and sapphires that were like globes with lights inside them – "

"I love jewels," agreed Percy enthusiastically. "Of course I wouldn't want any one at school to know about it, but I've got quite a collection myself I used to collect them instead of stamps."

"And diamonds," continued John eagerly. "The Schnlitzer-Murphys had diamonds as big as walnuts – "

"That's nothing." Percy had leaned forward and dropped his voice to a low whisper. "That's nothing at all. My father has a diamond bigger than the Ritz-Carlton Hotel."

THE MONTANA sunset lay between two mountains like a gigantic bruise from which dark arteries spread themselves over a poisoned sky. An immense distance under the sky crouched the village of Fish, minute, dismal, and forgotten. There were twelve men, so it was said, in the village of Fish; twelve somber and inexplicable souls who sucked a lean milk from the bare rock upon which a mysterious populatory force had begotten them. They had become a race apart, these twelve men of Fish, like some species developed by an early whim of nature, which on second thought had abandoned them to struggle and extermination.

Out of the blue-black bruise in the distance crept a long line of moving lights upon the desolation of the land, and the twelve men of Fish gathered like ghosts at the shanty depot to watch the passing of the seven o'clock train, the Transcontinental Express from Chicago. Six times or so a year the Transcontinental Express, through some inconceivable jurisdiction, stopped at the village of Fish, and when this occurred a figure or so would disembark, mount into a buggy that always appeared from out of the dusk, and drive off toward the bruised sunset. The observation of this pointless and preposterous phenomenon had become a sort of cult among the men of Fish. To observe, that was all; there remained in them none of the vital quality of illusion which would make them wonder or speculate, else a religion might have grown up around these mysterious visitations. But the men of Fish were beyond all religion – the barest and most savage tenets of even Christianity could gain no foothold on that barren rock – so there was no altar, no priest, no sacrifice; only each night at seven the silent concourse by the shanty depot, a congregation who lifted up a prayer of dim, anaemic wonder.

On this June night, the Great Brakeman, whom, had they deified any one, they might well have chosen as their celestial protagonist, had ordained that the seven o'clock train should leave its human (or inhuman) deposit at Fish. At two minutes after seven Percy Washington and John T. Unger disembarked, hurried past the spellbound, the agape, the fearsome eyes of the twelve men of Fish, mounted into a buggy which had obviously appeared from nowhere, and drove away.

After half an hour, when the twilight had coagulated into dark, the silent negro who was driving the buggy hailed an opaque body somewhere ahead of them in the gloom. In response to his cry, it turned upon them a luminous disk which regarded them likea malignant eye out of the unfathomable night. As they came closer, John saw that it was the tail-light of an immense automobile, larger and more magnificent than any he had ever seen. Its body was of gleaming metal richer than nickel and lighter than silver, and the hubs of the wheels were studded with iridescent geometric figures of green and yellow – John did not dare to guess whether they were glass or jewel.

Two negroes, dressed in glittering livery such as one sees in pictures of royal processions in London, were standing at attention beside the car and as the two young men dismounted from the buggy they were greeted in some language which the guest could not understand, but which seemed to be an extreme form of the Southern negro's dialect.

"Get in," said Percy to his friend, as their trunks were tossed to the ebony roof of the limousine. "Sorry we had to bring you this far in that buggy, but of course it wouldn't do for the people on the train or those Godforsaken fellas in Fish to see this automobile."

"Gosh! What a car!" This ejaculation was provoked by its interior. John saw that the upholstery consisted of a thousand minute and exquisite tapestries of silk, woven with jewels and embroideries, and set upon a background of cloth of gold. The two armchair seats in which the boys luxuriated were covered with stuff that resembled duvetyn, but seemed woven in numberless colors of the ends of ostrich feathers.

"What a car!" cried John again, in amazement.

"This thing?" Percy laughed. "Why, it's just an old junk we use for a station wagon."

By this time they were gliding along through the darkness toward the break between the two mountains.

"We'll be there in an hour and a half," said Percy, looking at the clock. "I may as well tell you it's not going to be like anything you ever saw before."

If the car was any indication of what John would see, he was prepared to be astonished indeed. The simple piety prevalent in Hades has the earnest worship of and respect for riches as the first article of its creed – had John felt otherwise than radiantly humble before them, his parents would have turned away in horror at the blasphemy.

They had now reached and were entering the break between the two mountains and almost immediately the way became much rougher.

"If the moon shone down here, you'd see that we're in a big gulch," said Percy, trying to peer out of the window. He spoke a few words into the mouthpiece and immediately the footman turned on a search-light and swept the hillsides with an immense beam.

"Rocky, you see. An ordinary car would be knocked to pieces in half an hour. In fact, it'd take a tank to navigate it unless you knew the way. You notice we're going uphill now."

They were obviously ascending, and within a few minutes the car was crossing a high rise, where they caught a glimpse of a pale moon newly risen in the distance. The car stopped suddenly and several figures took shape out of the dark beside it – these were negroes also. Again the two young men were saluted in the same dimly recognizable dialect; then the negroes set to work and four immense cables dangling from overhead were attached with hooks to the hubs of the great jeweled wheels. At a resounding

"Hey-yah!" John felt the car being lifted slowly from the ground – up

167

and up – clear of the tallest rocks on both sides – then higher, until he could see a wavy, moonlit valley stretched out before him in sharp contrast to the quagmire of rocks that they had just left. Only on one side was there still rock – and then suddenly there was no rock beside them or anywhere around.

It was apparent that they had surmounted some immense knife-blade of stone, projecting perpendicularly into the air.

In a moment they were going down again, and finally with a soft bump they were landed upon the smooth earth.

"The worst is over," said Percy, squinting out the window.

"It's only five miles from here, and our own road – tapestry brick – all the way. This belongs to us. This is where the United States ends, father says."

"Are we in Canada?"

"We are not. We're in the middle of the Montana Rockies. But you are now on the only five square miles of land in the country that's never been surveyed."

"Why hasn't it? Did they forget it?"

"No," said Percy, grinning, "they tried to do it three times. The first time my grandfather corrupted a whole department of the State survey; the second time he had the official maps of the United States tinkered with – that held them for fifteen years. The last time was harder. My father fixed it so that their compasses were in the strongest magnetic field ever artificially set up. He had a whole set of surveying instruments made with a slight defection that would allow for this territory not to appear, and he substituted them for the ones that were to be used. Then he had a river deflected and he had what looked like a village built up on its banks – so that they'd see it, and think it was a town ten miles farther up the valley. There's only one thing my father's afraid of," he concluded, "only one thing in the world that could be used to find us out."

"What's that?"

Percy sank his voice to a whisper.

"Aeroplanes," he breathed. "We've got half a dozen anti-aircraft guns and we've arranged it so far – but there've been a few deaths and a great many prisoners. Not that we mind *that*, you know, father and I, but it upsets mother and the girls, and there's always the chance that some time we won't be able to arrange it."

Shreds and tatters of chinchilla, courtesy clouds in the green moon's heaven, were passing the green moon like precious Eastern stuffs paraded for the inspection of some Tartar Khan. It seemed to John that it was day, and that he was looking at some lads sailing above him in the air, showering down tracts and patent medicine circulars, with their messages of hope for despairing, rockbound hamlets. It seemed to him that he could see them look down out of the clouds and stare – and stare at whatever there was to stare at in this place whither he was bound – What then? Were they induced to land by some insidious device there to be immured far from patent medicines and from tracts until the judgment day – or, should they fail to fall into the trap, did a quick puff of smoke and the sharp round of a splitting shell bring them drooping to earth – and "upset" Percy's mother and sisters. John shook his head and the wraith of a hollow laugh issued silently from his parted lips. What desperate transaction lay hidden here? What a moral expedient of a bizarre Croesus? What terrible and golden mystery? . . .

The chinchilla clouds had drifted past now and outside the Montana night was bright as day. The tapestry brick of the road was smooth to the tread of the great tires as they rounded a still, moonlit lake; they passed into darkness for a moment, a pine grove, pungent and cool, then they came out into a broad avenue of lawn and John's exclamation of pleasure was simultaneous with Percy's taciturn "We're home."

Full in the light of the stars, an exquisite château rose from the borders of the lake, climbed in marble radiance half the height of an adjoining mountain, then melted in grace, in perfect symmetry, in translucent feminine languor, into the massed darkness of a forest of pine. The many towers, the slender tracery of the sloping parapets, the chiselled wonder of a thousand yellow windows with their oblongs and hectagons and triangles of golden light, the shattered softness of the intersecting planes of star-shine and blue shade, all trembled on John's spirit like a chord of music. On one of the towers, the tallest, the blackest at its base, an arrangement of exterior lights at the top made a sort of floating fairyland – and as John gazed up in warm enchantment the faint acciaccare sound of violins drifted down in a rococo harmony that was like nothing he had ever heard before. Then in a moment the car stopped before wide, high marble steps around which the night air was fragrant with a host of flowers. At the top of the steps two great doors swung silently open and amber light flooded out upon the darkness, silhouetting the figure of an exquisite lady with black, high-piled hair, who held out her arms toward them.

"Mother," Percy was saying, "this is my friend, John Unger, from Hades."

Afterward John remembered that first night as a daze of many colors, of quick sensory impressions, of music soft as a voice in love, and of the beauty of things, lights and shadows, and motions and faces. There was a whitehaired man who stood drinking a many-hued cordial from a crystal thimble set on a golden stem. There was a girl with a flowery face, dressed like Titania with braided sapphires in her hair. There was a room where the solid, soft gold of the walls yielded to the pressure of his hand, and a room that was like a platonic conception of the ultimate prism – ceiling, floor, and all, it was lined with an unbroken mass of diamonds, diamonds of every size and shape, until, lit with tall violet lamps in the corners, it dazzled the eyes with a whiteness that could be compared only with itself, beyond human wish or dream.

Through a maze of these rooms the two boys wandered. Sometimes the floor under their feet would flame in brilliant patterns from lighting below, patterns of barbaric clashing colors, of pastel delicacy, of sheer whiteness, or of subtle and intricate mosaic, surely from some mosque on the Adriatic. Sometimes beneath layers of thick crystal he would see blue or green water swirling, inhabited by vivid fish and growths of rainbow foliage. Then they would be treading on furs of every texture and color or along corridors of palest ivory, unbroken as though carved complete from the gigantic tusks of dinosaurs extinct before the age of man . . .

THEN A HAZILY remembered transition, and they were at dinner – where each plate was of two almost imperceptible layers of solid diamond between which was curiously worked a filigree of emerald design, a shaving sliced from green air. Music, plangent and unobtrusive, drifted down through far corridors – his chair, feathered and curved insidiously to his back, seemed to engulf and overpower him as he drank his first glass of port. He tried drowsily to answer a question that had been asked him, but the honeyed luxury that clasped his body added to the illusion of sleep – jewels, fabrics, wines, and metals blurred before his eyes into a sweet mist . . .

"Yes," he replied with a polite effort, "it certainly is hot enough for me down there."

He managed to add a ghostly laugh; then, without movement, without resistance, he seemed to float off and away, leaving an iced dessert that was pink as a dream . . . He fell asleep.

When he awoke he knew that several hours had passed. He was in a great quiet room with ebony walls and a dull illumination that was too faint, too subtle, to be called a light. His young host was standing over him.

"You fell asleep at dinner," Percy was saying. "I nearly did, too – it was such a treat to be comfortable again after this year of school. Servants undressed and bathed you while you were sleeping."

"Is this a bed or a cloud?" sighed John. "Percy, Percy – before you go, I want to apologize."

"For what?"

"For doubting you when you said you had a diamond as big as the Ritz-Carlton Hotel."

Percy smiled.

"I thought you didn't believe me. It's that mountain, you know."

"What mountain?"

"The mountain the château rests on. It's not very big, for a mountain. But, except for about fifty feet of sod and gravel on the top, it's solid diamond. *One* diamond, one cubic mile without a flaw. Aren't you listening? Say– "

But John T. Unger had again fallen asleep.

MORNING. As he awoke he perceived drowsily that the room had at the same moment become dense with sunlight. The ebony panels of one wall had slid aside on a sort of track, leaving his chamber half open to the day. A large negro in a white uniform stood beside his bed.

"Good-evening," muttered John, summoning his brains from the wild places.

"Good-morning, sir. Are you ready for your bath, sir? Oh, don't get up – I'll put you in, if you'll just unbutton your pajamas – there. Thank you, sir."

John lay quietly as his pajamas were removed – he was amused and delighted; he expected to be lifted like a child by this black Gargantua who was tending him, but nothing of the sort happened; instead he felt the bed tilt up slowly on its side – he began to roll, startled at first, in the direction of the wall, but when he reached the wall its drapery gave way, and sliding two yards farther down a fleecy incline he plumped gently into water the same temperature as his body.

He looked about him. The runway or rollway on which he had arrived had folded gently back into place. He had been projected into another chamber and was sitting in a sunken bath with his head just above the level of the floor. All about him, lining the walls of the room and the sides and bottom of the bath itself, was a blue aquarium, and gazing through the crystal surface on which he sat, he could see fish swimming among amber lights and even gliding without curiosity past his outstretched toes, which were separated from them only by the thickness of the crystal. From overhead, sunlight came through sea-green glass.

I suppose, sir, that you'd like hot rosewater and soapsuds this morning sir – and perhaps cold salt water to finish."

The negro was standing beside him.

"Yes," agreed John, smiling inanely, "as you please." Any idea of ordering this bath according to his own meager standards of living would have been priggish and not a little wicked.

The negro pressed a button and a warm rain began to fall, apparently from overhead, but really, so John discovered after a moment, from a fountain arrangement near by. The water turned to a pale rose color and jets of liquid soap spurted into it from four miniature walrus heads at the corners of the bath. In a moment a dozen little paddle-wheels, fixed to the sides, had churned the mixture into a radiant rainbow of pink foam which enveloped him softly with its delicious lightness, and burst in shining, rosy bubbles here and there about him.

"Shall I turn on the moving-picture machine, sir?" suggested the negro deferentially. "There's a good one-reel comedy in this machine to-day, or can put in a serious piece in a moment, if you prefer it."

"No, thanks," answered John, politely but firmly. He was enjoying his bath too much to desire any distraction. But distraction came. In a moment he was listening intently to the sound of flutes from just outside, flutes ripping a melody that was like a waterfall, cool and green as the room itself, accompanying a frothy piccolo, in play more fragile than the lace of us that covered and charmed him.

After a cold salt-water bracer and a cold fresh finish, he stepped out and into a fleecy robe, and upon a couch covered with the same material he was rubbed with oil, alcohol, and spice. Later he sat in a voluptuous chair while he was shaved and his hair was trimmed.

"Mr. Percy is waiting in your sitting-room," said the negro, when these operations were finished. "My name is Gygsum, Mr. Unger, sir. I am to see to Mr. Unger every morning."

John walked out into the brisk sunshine of his living-room, where he found breakfast waiting for him and Percy, gorgeous in white kid knickerbockers, smoking in an easy chair.

THIS IS a story of the Washington family as Percy sketched it for John during breakfast. The father of the present Mr. Washington had been a Virginian, a direct descendant of George Washington, and Lord Baltimore. At the close of the Civil War he was a twenty-five-year-old Colonel with a played-out plantation and about a thousand dollars in gold.

Fitz-Norman Culpepper Washington, for that was the young Colonel's name, decided to present the Virginia estate to his younger brother and go West. He selected two dozen of the most faithful blacks, who, of course, worshipped him, and bought twenty-five tickets to the West, where he intended to take out land in their names and start a sheep and cattle ranch.

When he had been in Montana for less than a month and things were going very poorly indeed, he stumbled on his great discovery. He had lost his way when riding in the hills, and after a day without food he began to grow hungry. As he was without his rifle, he was forced to pursue a squirrel, and in the course of the pursuit he noticed that it was carrying something shiny in its mouth. Just before it vanished into its hole – for Providence did not intend that this squirrel should alleviate his hunger – it dropped its burden. Sitting down to consider the situation Fitz-Norman's eye was caught by a gleam in the grass beside him. In ten seconds he had completely lost his appetite and gained one hundred thousand dollars. The squirrel, which had refused with annoying persistence to become food, had made him a present of a large and perfect diamond.

Late that night he found his way to camp and twelve hours later all the males among his darkies were back by the squirrel hole digging furiously at the side of the mountain. He told them he had discovered a rhinestone mine, and, as only one or two of them had ever seen even a small diamond before, they believed him, without question. When the magnitude of his discovery became apparent to him, he found himself in a quandary. The mountain was *a* diamond – it was literally nothing else but solid diamond. He filled four saddle bags full of glittering samples and started on horseback for St. Paul. There he managed to dispose of half a dozen small stones – when he tried a larger one a storekeeper fainted and Fitz-Norman was arrested as a public disturber. He escaped from jail and caught the train for New York, where he sold a few medium-sized diamonds and received in exchange about two hundred thousand dollars in gold. But he did not dare to produce any exceptional gems – in fact, he left New York just in time. Tremendous excitement had been created in jewelry circles, not so much by the size of his diamonds as by their appearance in the city from mysterious sources. Wild rumors became current that a diamond mine had been discovered in the Catskills, on the Jersey coast, on Long Island, beneath Washington Square. Excursion trains, packed with men carrying picks and shovels, began to leave New York hourly, bound for various neighboring El Dorados. But by that time young Fitz-Norman was on his way back to Montana.

By the end of a fortnight he had estimated that the diamond in the mountain was approximately equal in quantity to all the rest of the diamonds known to exist in the world. There was no valuing it by any regular computation, however, for it was *one solid diamond* – and if it were offered for sale not only would the bottom fall out of the market, but also, if the value should vary with its size in the usual arithmetical progression, there would not be enough gold in the world to buy a tenth part of it. And what could any one do with a diamond that size?

It was an amazing predicament. He was, in one sense, the richest man that ever lived – and yet was he worth anything at all? If his secret should transpire there was no telling to what measures the Government might resort in order to prevent a panic, in gold as well as in jewels. They might take over the claim immediately and institute a monopoly.

There was no alternative – he must market his mountain in secret. He sent South for his younger brother and put him in charge of his colored following – darkies who had never realized that slavery was abolished. To make sure of this, he read them a proclamation that he had composed, which announced that General Forrest had reorganized the shattered Southern armies and defeated the North in one pitched battle. The negroes believed him implicitly. They passed a vote declaring it a good thing and held revival services immediately.

Fitz-Norman himself set out for foreign parts with one hundred thousand dollars and two trunks filled with rough diamonds of all sizes. He sailed for Russia in a Chinese junk and six months after his departure from Montana he was in St. Petersburg. He took obscure lodgings and called immediately upon the court jeweller, announcing that he had a diamond for the Czar. He remained in St. Petersburg for two weeks, in constant danger of being murdered, living from lodging to lodging, and afraid to visit his trunks more than three or four times during the whole fortnight.

On his promise to return in a year with larger and finer stones, he was allowed to leave for India. Before he left, however, the Court Treasurers had deposited to his credit, in American banks, the sum of fifteen million dollars – under four different aliases.

He returned to America in 1868, having been gone a little over two years. He had visited the capitals of twenty-two countries and talked with five emperors, eleven kings, three princes, a shah, a khan, and a sultan. At that time Fitz-Norman estimated his own wealth at one billion dollars. One fact worked consistently against the disclosure of his secret. No one of his larger diamonds remained in the public eye for a week before being invested with a history of enough fatalities, amours, revolutions, and wars to have occupied it from the days of the first Babylonian Empire.

From 1870 until his death in 1900, the history of Fitz-Norman Washington was a long epic in gold. There were side issues, of course – he evaded the surveys, he married a Virginia lady, by whom he had a single son, and he was compelled, due to a series of unfortunate complications, to murder his brother, whose unfortunate habit of drinking himself into an indiscreet stupor had several times endangered their safety. But very few other murders stained these happy years of progress and expansion.

Just before he died he changed his policy, and with all but a few million dollars of his outside wealth bought up rare minerals in bulk, which he deposited in the safety vaults of banks all over the world, marked as bric-a-brac. His son, Braddock Tarleton Washington, followed this policy on an even more tensive scale. The minerals were converted into the rarest of all elements – radium – so that the equivalent of a billion dollars in gold could be placed in a receptacle no bigger than a cigar box.

When Fitz-Norman had been dead three years his son, Braddock, decided that the business had gone far enough. The amount of wealth that he and his father had taken out of the mountain was beyond all exact computation. He kept a note-book in cipher in which he set down the approximate quantity of radium in each of the thousand banks he patronized, and recorded the alias under which it was held. Then he did a very simple thing – he sealed up the mine.

He sealed up the mine. What had been taken out of it would support all the Washingtons yet to be born in unparalleled luxury for generations. His one care must be the protection of his secret, lest in the possible panic attendant on its discovery he should be reduced with all the property-holders in the world to utter poverty.

This was the family among whom John T. Unger was staying. This was the story he heard in his silver-walled living-room the morning after his arrival.

AFTER BREAKFAST, John found his way out the great marble entrance and looked curiously at the scene before him. The whole valley, from the diamond mountain to the steep granite cliff five miles away, still gave off a breath of golden haze which hovered idly above the fine sweep of lawns and lakes and gardens. Here and there clusters of elms made delicate groves of shade, contrasting strangely with the tough masses of pine forest that held the hills in a grip of dark-blue green. Even as John looked he saw three fawns in single file patter out from one clump about a half mile away and disappear with awkward gayety into the black-ribbed half-light of another. John would not have been surprised to see a goat-foot piping his way among the trees or to catch a glimpse of pink nymph-skin and flying yellow hair between the greenest of the green leaves.

In some such cool hope he descended the marble steps, disturbing faintly the sleep of two silky Russian wolfhounds at the bottom, and set off along a walk of white and blue brick that seemed to lead in no particular direction.

He was enjoying himself as much as he was able. It is youth's felicity as well as its insufficiency that it can never live in the present, but must always be measuring up the day against its own radiantly imagined future – flowers and gold, girls and stars, they are only prefigurations and prophecies of that incomparable, unattainable young dream.

John rounded a soft corner where the massed rose-bushes filled the air with heavy scent, and struck off across a park toward a patch of moss under some trees. He had never lain upon moss, and he wanted to see whether it was really soft enough to justify the use of its name as an adjective. Then he saw a girl coming toward him over the grass. She was the most beautiful person he had ever seen.

She was dressed in a white little gown that came just below her knees, and a wreath of mignonettes clasped with blue slices of sapphire bound up her hair. Her pink bare feet scattered the dew as she came. She was younger than John – not more than sixteen.

"Hello," she cried softly, "I'm Kismine."

She was much more than that to John already. He advanced toward her, scarcely moving as he drew near lest he should tread on her bare toes.

"You haven't met me," said her soft voice. Her blue eyes added, "Oh, but you've missed a great deal!" . . . "You met my sister, Jasmine, last night. I was sick with lettuce poisoning," went on her soft voice, and her eyes continued, "and when I'm sick I'm sweet – and when I'm well."

"You have made an enormous impression on me," said John's eyes, "and I'm not so slow myself" – "How do you do?" said his voice. "I hope you're better this morning." – "You darling," added his eyes tremulously.

John observed that they had been walking along the path. On her suggestion they sat down together upon the moss, the softness of which he failed to determine.

He was critical about women. A single defect – a thick ankle, a hoarse voice, a glass eye – was enough to make him utterly indifferent. And here for the first time in his life he was beside a girl who seemed to him the incarnation of physical perfection.

"Are you from the East?" asked Kismine with charming interest.

"No," answered John simply. "I'm from Hades."

Either she had never heard of Hades, or she could think of no pleasant comment to make upon it, for she did not discuss it further.

"I'm going East to school this fall," she said. "D'you think I'll like it? I'm going to New York to Miss Bulge's. It's very strict, but you see over the weekends I'm going to live at home with the family in our New York house, because father heard that the girls had to go walking two by two."

"Your father wants you to be proud," observed John.

"We are," she answered, her eyes shining with dignity. "None of us has ever been punished. Father said we never should be. Once when my sister Jasmine was a little girl she pushed him down-stairs and he just got up and limped away.

"Mother was – well, a little startled," continued Kismine, "when she heard that you were from – from where you are from, you know. She said that when she was a young girl – but then, you see, she's a Spaniard and old-fashioned."

"Do you spend much time out here?" asked John, to conceal the fact that he was somewhat hurt by this remark. It seemed an unkind allusion to his provincialism.

"Percy and Jasmine and I are here every summer, but next summer Jasmine is going to Newport. She's coming out in London a year from this fall. She'll be presented at court."

"Do you know, " began John hesitantly, "you're much more sophisticated than I thought you were when I first saw you?"

"Oh, no, I'm not," she exclaimed hurriedly. "Oh, I wouldn't think of being. I think that sophisticated young people are *terribly* common, don't you? I'm not at all, really. If you say I am, I'm going to cry."

She was so distressed that her lip was trembling. John was impelled to protest: I didn't mean that; I only said it to tease you."

"Because I wouldn't mind if I *were*," she persisted. "but I'm *not*. I'm very innocent and girlish. I never smoke, or drink, or read anything except poetry. I know scarcely any mathematics or chemistry. I dress *very* simply – in fact, I scarcely dress at all. I think sophisticated is the last thing you can say about me. I believe that girls ought to enjoy their youths in a wholesome way."

"I do, too," said John heartily.

Kismine was cheerful again. She smiled at him, and a still-born tear dripped from the corner of one blue eye.

"I like you," she whispered, intimately. "Are you going to spend all your time with Percy while you're here, or will you be nice to me. Just think – I'm absolutely fresh ground. I've never had a boy in love with me in all my life. I've never been allowed even to *see* boys alone – except Percy. I came all the way out here into this grove hoping to run into you, where the family wouldn't be around.

Deeply flattered, John bowed from the hips as he had been taught at dancing school in Hades.

"We'd better go now," said Kismine sweetly. "I have to be with mother at eleven. You haven't asked me to kiss you once. I thought boys always did that nowadays."

John drew himself up proudly.

"Some of them do," he answered, "but not me. Girls don't do that sort of thing – in Hades."

Side by side they walked back toward the house.

JOHN STOOD facing Mr. braddock washington in the full sunlight. The elder man was about forty with a proud, vacuous face, intelligent eyes, and a robust figure. In the mornings he smelt of horses – the best horses. He carried a plain walking-stick of gray birch with a single large opal for a grip. He and Percy were showing John around.

"The slaves' quarters are there." His walking-stick indicated a cloister of marble on their left that ran in graceful Gothic along the side of the mountain. "In my youth I was distracted for a while from the business of life by a period of absurd idealism. During that time they lived in luxury. For instance, I equipped every one of their rooms with a tile bath."

"I suppose," ventured John, with an ingratiating laugh, "that they used the bathtubs to keep coal in. Mr. Schnlitzer-Murphy told me that once he – "

"The opinions of Mr. Schnlitzer-Murphy are of little importance, I should imagine," interrupted Braddock Washington, coldly. "My slaves did not keep coal in their bathtubs. They had orders to bathe every day, and they did. If they hadn't I might have ordered a sulphuric acid shampoo. I discontinued the baths for quite another reason. Several of them caught cold and died. Water is not good for certain races – except as a beverage."

John laughed, and then decided to nod his head in sober agreement. Braddock Washington made him uncomfortable.

"All these negroes are descendants of the ones my father brought North with him. There are about two hundred and fifty now. You notice that they've lived so long apart from the world that their original dialect has become an almost indistinguishable patois. We bring a few of them up to speak English – my secretary and two or three of the house servants.

"This is the golf course," he continued, as they strolled along the velvet winter grass. "It's all a green, you see – no fairway, no rough, no hazards."

He smiled pleasantly at John.

"Many men in the cage, father?" asked Percy suddenly.

Braddock Washington stumbled, and let forth an involuntary curse.

"One less than there should be," he ejaculated darkly – and then added after a moment, "We've had difficulties."

"Mother was telling me," exclaimed Percy, "that Italian teacher – "

"A ghastly error," said Braddock Washington angrily. "But of course there's a good chance that we may have got him. Perhaps he fell somewhere in the woods or stumbled over a cliff. And then there's always the probability that if he did get away his story wouldn't be believed. Nevertheless, I've had two dozen men looking for him in different towns around here."

"And no luck?"

"Some. Fourteen of them reported that they'd each killed a man answering to that description, but of course it was probably only the reward they were after – "

He broke off. They had come to a large cavity in the earth about the circumference of a merry-go-round and covered by a strong iron grating. Braddock Washington beckoned to John, and pointed his cane down through the grating. John stepped to the edge and gazed. Immediately his ears were assailed by a wild clamor from below.

"Come on down to Hell!"

"Hey! Throw us a rope!"

"Got an old doughnut, Buddy, or a couple of second-hand sandwiches?"

"Say, fella, if you'll push down that guy you're with, we'll show you a quick disappearance scene."

"Paste him one for me, will you?" It was too dark to see clearly into the pit below, but John could tell from the coarse optimism and rugged vitality of the remarks and voices that they proceeded from middle-class Americans of the more spirited type. Then Mr. Washington put out his cane and touched a button in the grass, and the scene below sprang into light.

"These are some adventurous mariners who had the misfortune to discover El Dorado," he remarked.

Below them there had appeared a large hollow in the earth shaped like the interior of a bowl. The sides were steep and apparently of polished glass, and on its slightly concave surface stood about two dozen men clad in the half costume, half uniform, of aviators. Their upturned faces, lit with wrath with malice, with despair, with cynical humor, were covered by long growths of beard, but with the exception of a few who had pined perceptibly away, they seemed to be a well-fed, healthy lot. Braddock Washington drew a garden chair to the edge of the pit and sat down.

"Well, how are you, boys?" he inquired genially.

A chorus of execration in which all joined except a few too dispirited to cry out, rose up into the sunny air, but Braddock Washington heard it with unruffled composure. When its last echo had died away he spoke again.

"Have you thought up a way out of your difficulty?"

From here and there among them a remark floated up.

"We decided to stay here for love!"

"Bring us up there and we'll find us a way!"

Braddock Washington waited until they were again quiet. Then he said:

"I've told you the situation. I don't want you here. I wish to heaven I'd never seen you. Your own curiosity got you here, and any time that you can think of a way out which protects me and my interests I'll be glad to consider it. But so long as you confine your efforts to digging tunnels – yes, I know about the new one you've started – you won't get very far. This isn't as hard on you as you make it out, with all your howling for the loved ones at home. If you were the type who worried much about the loved ones at home, you'd never have taken up aviation."

A tall man moved apart from the others, and held up his hand to call his captor's attention to what he was about to say.

"Let me ask you a few questions!" he cried. "You pretend to be a fair-minded man."

"How absurd. How could a man of *my* position be fair-minded toward *you?* You might as well speak of a Spaniard being fair-minded toward a piece of steak."

At this harsh observation the faces of the two dozen steaks fell, but the tall man continued:

"All right!" he cried. "We've argued this out before. You're not a humanitarian and you're not fair-minded, but you're human – at least you say you are – and you ought to be able to put yourself in our place for long enough to think how – how – how –"

"How what?" demanded Washington, coldly.

" – how unnecessary –"

"Not to me."

"Well, – how cruel –"

"We've covered that. Cruelty doesn't exist where self-preservation is involved. You've been soldiers; you know that. Try another."

"Well, then, how stupid."

"There," admitted Washington, "I grant you that. But try to think of an alternative. I've offered to have all or any of you painlessly executed if you wish. I've offered to have your wives, sweethearts, children, and mothers kidnapped and brought out here. I'll enlarge your place down there and feed and clothe you the rest of your lives. If there was a method of producing permanent amnesia I'd have all of you operated on and released immediately, somewhere outside of my preserves. But that's as far as my ideas go."

"How about trusting us not to peach on you?" cried some one.

"You don't proffer that suggestion seriously," said Washington, with an expression of scorn. "I did take out one man to teach my daughter Italian. Last week he got away."

A wild yell of jubilation went up suddenly from two dozen throats and a pandemonium of joy ensued. The prisoners clog-danced and cheered and yodeled and wrestled with one another in a sudden uprush of animal spirits. They even ran up the glass sides of the bowl as far as they could, and slid back to the bottom upon the natural cushions of their bodies. The tall man started a song in which they all joined —

"Oh, we'll hang the kaiser

On a sour apple tree —"

Braddock Washington sat in inscrutable silence until the song was over.

"You see," he remarked, when he could gain a modicum of attention. "I bear you no ill-will. I like to see you enjoying yourselves. That's why I didn't tell you the whole story at once. The man — what was his name? Critchtichiello? — was shot by some of my agents in fourteen different places."

Not guessing that the places referred to were cities, the tumult of rejoicing subsided immediately.

"Nevertheless," cried Washington with a touch of anger, "he tried to run away. Do you expect me to take chances with any of you after an experience like that?"

Again a series of ejaculations went up.

"Sure!"

"Would your daughter like to learn Chinese?"

"Hey, I can speak Italian! My mother was a wop."

"Maybe she'd like t'learna speak N'Yawk!"

"If she's the little one with the big blue eyes I can teach her a lot of things better than Italian."

"I know some Irish songs — and I could hammer brass once't."

Mr. Washington reached forward suddenly with his cane and pushed the button in the grass so that the picture below went out instantly, and there remained only that great dark mouth covered dismally with the black teeth of the grating.

"Hey!" called a single voice from below, "you ain't goin' away without givin' us your blessing?"

But Mr. Washington, followed by the two boys, was already strolling on toward the ninth hole of the golf course, as though the pit and its contents were no more than a hazard over which his facile iron had triumphed with ease.

JULY UNDER the lee of the diamond mountain was a month of blanket nights and of warm, glowing days. John and Kismine were in love. He did not know that the little gold football (inscribed with the legend *Pro deo et patria et St. Midas*) which he had given her rested on a platinum chain next to her bosom. But it did. And she for her part was not aware that a large sapphire which had dropped one day from her simple coiffure was stowed away tenderly in John's jewel box.

Late one afternoon when the ruby and ermine music room was quiet, they spent an hour there together. He held her hand and she gave him such a look that he whispered her name aloud. She bent toward him – then hesitated.

"Did you say 'Kismine'?" she asked softly, "or –"

She had wanted to be sure. She thought she might have misunderstood.

Neither of them had ever kissed before, but in the course of an hour it seemed to make little difference.

The afternoon drifted away. That night when a last breath of music drifted down from the highest tower, they each lay awake, happily dreaming over the separate minutes of the day. They had decided to be married as soon as possible.

EVERY DAY, Mr. Washington and the two young men went hunting or fishing in the deep forests or played golf around the somnolent course – games which John diplomatically allowed his host to win – or swam in the mountain coolness of the lake. John found Mr. Washington a somewhat exacting personality – utterly uninterested in any ideas or opinions except his own. Mrs. Washington was aloof and reserved at all times. She was apparently indifferent to her two daughters, and entirely absorbed in her son Percy, with whom she held interminable conversations in rapid Spanish at dinner.

Jasmine, the elder daughter, resembled Kismine in appearance – except that she was somewhat bow-legged, and terminated in large hands and feet – but was utterly unlike her in temperament. Her favorite books had to do with poor girls who kept house for widowed fathers. John learned from Kismine that Jasmine had never recovered from the shock and disappointment caused her by the termination of the World War, just as she was about to start for Europe as a canteen expert. She had even pined away for a time, and Braddock Washington had taken steps to promote a new war in the Balkans – but she had seen a photograph of some wounded Serbian soldiers and lost interest in the whole proceedings. But Percy and Kismine seemed to have inherited the arrogant attitude in all its harsh magnificence from their father. A chaste and consistent selfishness ran like a pattern through their every idea.

John was enchanted by the wonders of the château and the valley. Braddock Washington, so Percy told him, had caused to be kidnapped a landscape gardener, an architect, a designer of state settings, and a French decadent poet left over from the last century. He had put his entire force of negroes at their disposal, guaranteed to supply them with any materials that the world could offer, and left them to work out some ideas of their own. But one by one they had shown their uselessness. The decadent poet had at once begun bewailing his separation from the boulevards in spring – he made some vague remarks about spices, apes, and ivories, but said nothing that was of any practical value. The stage designer on his part wanted to make the whole valley a series of tricks and sensational effects – a state of things that the Washingtons would soon have grown tired of. And as for the architect and the landscape gardener, they thought only in terms of convention. They must make this like this and that like that. But they had, at least, solved the problem of what was to be done with them – they all went mad early one morning after spending the night in a single room trying to agree upon the location of a fountain, and were now confined comfortably in an insane asylum at Westport, Connecticut.

"But," inquired John curiously, "who did plan all your wonderful reception rooms and halls, and approaches and bathrooms –?"

"Well," answered Percy, "I blush to tell you, but it was a moving-picture fella. He was the only man we found who was used to playing with an unlimited amount of money, though he did tuck his napkin in his collar and couldn't read or write."

As August drew to a close John began to regret that he must soon go back to school. He and Kismine had decided to elope the following June.

"It would be nicer to be married here," Kismine confessed, "but of course I could never get father's permission to marry you at all. Next to that I'd rather elope. It's terrible for wealthy people to be married in America at present – they always have to send out bulletins to the press saying that they're going to be married in remnants, when what they mean is just a peck of old second-hand pearls and some used lace worn once by the Empress Eugenie."

"I know," agreed John fervently. "When I was visiting the Schnlitzer-Murphys, the eldest daughter, Gwendolyn, married a man whose father owns half of West Virginia. She wrote home saying what a tough struggle she was carrying on on his salary as a bank clerk – and then she ended up by saying that 'Thank God, I have four good maids anyhow, and that helps a little.'"

"It's absurd," commented Kismine. "Think of the millions and millions of people in the world, laborers and all, who get along with only two maids."

One afternoon late in August a chance remark of Kismine's changed the face of the entire situation, and threw John into a state of terror.

They were in their favorite grove, and between kisses John was indulging in some romantic forebodings which he fancied added poignancy to their relations.

"Sometimes I think we'll never marry," he said sadly.

"You're too wealthy, too magnificent. No one as rich as you are can be like other girls. I should marry the daughter of some well-to-do wholesale hardware man from Omaha or Sioux City, and be content with her half-million."

"I knew the daughter of a wholesale hardware man once," remarked Kismine. "I don't think you'd have been contented with her. She was a friend of my sister's. She visited here."

"Oh, then you've had other guests?" exclaimed John in surprise.

Kismine seemed to regret her words.

"Oh, yes," she said hurriedly, "we've had a few."

"But aren't you – wasn't your father afraid they'd talk outside?"

"Oh, to some extent, to some extent," she answered. "Let's talk about something pleasanter."

But John's curiosity was aroused.

"Something pleasanter!" he demanded. "What's unpleasant about that? Weren't they nice girls?"

To his great surprise Kismine began to weep.

"Yes – th – that's the – the whole t-trouble. I grew qu-quite attached to some of them. So did Jasmine, but she kept inv-viting them anyway. I couldn't under*stand* it."

A dark suspicion was born in John's heart.

"Do you mean that they *told*, and your father had them – removed?"

"Worse than that," she muttered brokenly. "Father took no chances – and Jasmine kept writing them to come, and they had *such* a good time!"

She was overcome by a paroxysm of grief.

Stunned with the horror of this revelation, John sat there open-mouthed, feeling the nerves of his body twitter like so many sparrows perched upon his spinal column.

"Now, I've told you, and I shouldn't have," she said, calming suddenly and drying her dark blue eyes.

"Do you mean to say that your father had them *murdered* before they left?"

She nodded.

"In August usually – or early in September. It's only natural for us to get all the pleasure out of them that we can first."

"How abdominable! Why, I must be going crazy! Did you really admit that –"

"I did," interrupted Kismine, shrugging her shoulders. "We can't very well imprison them like those aviators, where they'd be a continual reproach to us every day. And it's always been made easier for Jasmine and me because father had it done sooner than we expected. In that way we avoided any farewell scene –"

"So you murdered them! Uh!" cried John.

"It was done very nicely. They were drugged while they were asleep – and their families were always told that they died of scarlet fever in Butte."

"But – I fail to understand why you kept on inviting them!"

"I didn't," burst out Kismine. "I never invited one. Jasmine did. And they always had a very good time. She'd give them the nicest presents toward the last. I shall probably have visitors too – I'll harden up to it. We can't let such an inevitable thing as death stand in the way of enjoying life while we have it. Think how lonesome it'd be out here if we never had *any* one. Why, father and mother have sacrificed some of their best friends just as we have."

"And so," cried John accusingly, "and so you were letting me make love to you and pretending to return it, and talking about marriage, all the time knowing perfectly well that I'd never get out of here alive –"

"No," she protested passionately. "Not any more. I did at first. You were here. I couldn't help that, and I thought your last days might as well be pleasant for both of us. But then I fell in love with you, and – and I'm honestly sorry you're going to – going to be put away – though I'd rather you'd be put away than ever kiss another girl."

"Oh, you would, would you?" cried John ferociously.

"Much rather. Besides, I've always heard that a girl can have more fun with a man whom she knows she can never marry. Oh, why did I tell you? I've probably spoiled your whole good time now, and we were really

185

enjoying things when you didn't know it. I knew it would make things sort of depressing for you."

"Oh, you did, did you?" John's voice trembled with anger. "I've heard about enough of this. If you haven't any more pride and decency than to have an affair with a fellow that you know isn't much better than a corpse, I don't want to have any more to do with you!"

"You're not a corpse!" she protested in horror. "You're not a corpse! I won't have you saying that I kissed a corpse!"

"I said nothing of the sort!"

"You did! You said I kissed a corpse!"

"I didn't !"

Their voices had risen, but upon a sudden interruption they both subsided into immediate silence. Footsteps were coming along the path in their direction, and a moment later the rose bushes were parted displaying Braddock Washington, whose intelligent eyes set in his good-looking vacuous face were peering in at them.

"Who kissed a corpse?" he demanded in obvious disapproval.

"Nobody," answered Kismine quickly. "We were just joking."

"What are you two doing here, anyhow?" he demanded gruffly. "Kismine, you ought to be – to be reading or playing golf with your sister. Go read! Go play golf! Don't let me find you here when I come back!"

Then he bowed at John and went up the path.

"See?" said Kismine crossly, when he was out of hearing. "You've spoiled it all. We can never meet any more. He won't let me meet you. He'd have you poisoned if he thought we were in love."

"We're not, any more!" cried John fiercely, "so he can set his mind at rest upon that. Moreover, don't fool yourself that I'm going to stay around here. Inside of six hours I'll be over those mountains, if I have to gnaw a passage through them, and on my way East."

They had both got to their feet, and at this remark Kismine came close and put her arm through his.

"I'm going, too."

"You must be crazy –"

"Of course I'm going," she interrupted impatiently.

"You most certainly are not. You –"

"Very well," she said quietly, "we'll catch up with father now and talk it over with him."

Defeated, John mustered a sickly smile.

"Very well, dearest," he agreed, with pale and unconvincing affection, "we'll go together."

His love for her returned and settled placidly on his heart. She was his – she would go with him to share his dangers. He put his arms about her and kissed her fervently. After all she loved him; she had saved him, in fact.

Discussing the matter, they walked slowly back toward the château. They decided that since Braddock Washington had seen them together they had best depart the next night. Nevertheless, John's lips were unusually dry at dinner, and he nervously emptied a great spoonful of peacock soup into his left lung. He had to be carried into the turquoise and sable card-room and pounded on the back by one of the under-butlers, which Percy considered a great joke.

LONG AFTER MIDNIGHT John's body gave a nervous jerk, and he sat suddenly upright, staring into the veils of somnolence that draped the room. Through the squares of blue darkness that were his open windows, he had heard a faint far-away sound that died upon a bed of wind before identifying itself on his memory, clouded with uneasy dreams. But the sharp noise that had succeeded it was nearer, was just outside the room – the click of a turned knob, a footstep, a whisper, he could not tell; a hard lump gathered in the pit of his stomach, and his whole body ached in the moment that he strained agonizingly to hear. Then one of the veils seemed to dissolve, and he saw a vague figure standing by the door, a figure only faintly limned and blocked in upon the darkness, mingled so with the folds of the drapery as to seem distorted, like a reflection seen in a dirty pane of glass.

With a sudden movement of fright or resolution John pressed the button by his bedside, and the next moment he was sitting in the green sunken bath of the adjoining room, waked into alertness by the shock of the cold water which half filled it.

He sprang out, and, his wet pajamas scattering a heavy trickle of water behind him, ran for the aquamarine door which he knew led out onto the ivory landing of the second floor. The door opened noiselessly. A single crimson lamp burning in a great dome above lit the magnificent sweep of the carved stairways with a poignant beauty. For a moment John hesitated, appalled by the silent splendor massed about him, seeming to envelop in its gigantic folds and contours the solitary drenched little figure shivering upon the ivory landing. Then simultaneously two things happened. The door of his own sitting-room swung open, precipitating three naked negroes into the hall – and, as John swayed in wild terror toward the stairway, another door slid back in the wall on the other side of the corridor, and John saw Braddock Washington standing in the lighted lift, wearing a fur coat and a pair of riding boots which reached to his knees and displayed, above, the glow of his rose-colored pajamas.

On the instant, the three negroes – John had never seen any of them before, and it flashed through his mind that they must be the professional executioners – paused in their movement toward John, and turned expectantly to the man in the lift, who burst out with an imperious command:

"Get in here! All three of you! Quick as hell!"

Then, within the instant, the three negroes darted into the cage, the oblong of light was blotted out as the lift door slid shut, and John was again alone in the hall. He slumped weakly down against an ivory stair.

It was apparent that something portentous had occurred, something which, for the moment at least, had postponed his own petty disaster. What was it? Had the negroes risen in revolt? Had the aviators forced aside the iron bars of the grating? Or had the men of Fish stumbled blindly through the hills and gazed with bleak, joyless eyes upon the gaudy valley? John did not know. He heard a faint whir of air as the lift whizzed up again, and then, a moment later, as it descended. It was probable that Percy was hurrying to his father's assistance, and it occurred to John that this was his opportunity to join Kismine and plan an immediate escape. He waited until the lift had been silent for several minutes; shivering a little with the night cool that whipped in through his wet pajamas, he returned to his room and dressed himself quickly. Then he mounted a long flight of stairs and turned down the corridor carpeted with Russian sable which led to Kismine's suite.

The door of her sitting-room was open and the lamps were lighted. Kismine, in an angora kimono, stood near the window of the room in a listening attitude, and as John entered noiselessly she turned toward him.

"Oh, it's you!" she whispered, crossing the room to him. "Did you hear them?"

"I heard your father's slaves in my –"

"No," she interrupted excitedly. "Aeroplanes!"

"Aeroplanes? Perhaps that was the sound that woke me."

"There're at least a dozen. I saw one a few moments ago dead against the moon. The guard back by the cliff fired his rifle and that's what roused father. We're going to open on them right away."

"Are they here on purpose?"

"Yes – it's that Italian who got away –"

Simultaneously with her last word, a succession of sharp cracks tumbled in through the open window. Kismine uttered a little cry, took a penny with fumbling fingers from a box on her dresser, and ran to one of the electric lights. In an instant the entire château was in darkness – she had blown out the fuse.

"Come on!" she cried to him. "We'll go up to the roof garden, and watch it from there!"

Drawing a cape about her, she took his hand, and they found their way out the door. It was only a step to the tower lift, and as she pressed the button that shot them upward he put his arms around her in the darkness and kissed her mouth. Romance had come to John Unger at last. A minute later they had stepped out upon the star-white platform. Above, under the misty moon, sliding in and out of the patches of cloud that eddied below it, floated a dozen dark-winged bodies in a constant circling course. From here and there in the valley flashes of fire leaped toward them, followed by sharp detonations. Kismine clapped her hands with pleasure, which, a moment later, turned to dismay as the aeroplanes at some prearranged signal, began to release their bombs and the whole of the valley became a panorama of deep reverberate sound and lurid light.

Before long the aim of the attackers became concentrated upon the points where the anti-aircraft guns were situated, and one of them was almost immediately reduced to a giant cinder to lie smouldering in a park of rose bushes.

"Kismine," begged John, "you'll be glad when I tell you that this attack came on the eve of my murder. If I hadn't heard that guard shoot off his gun back by the pass I should now be stone dead –"

"I can't hear you!" cried Kismine, intent on the scene before her. "You'll have to talk louder!"

"I simply said, " shouted John, "that we'd better get out before they begin to shell the château!"

Suddenly the whole portico of the negro quarters cracked asunder, a geyser of flame shot up from under the colonnades, and great fragments of jagged marble were hurled as far as the borders of the lake.

"There go fifty thousand dollars' worth of slaves," cried Kismine, "at prewar prices. So few Americans have any respect for property."

John renewed his efforts to compel her to leave. The aim of the aeroplanes was becoming more precise minute by minute, and only two of the anti-aircraft guns were still retaliating. It was obvious that the garrison, encircled with fire, could not hold out much longer.

"Come on!" cried John, pulling Kismine's arm, "we've got to go. Do you realize that those aviators will kill you without question if they find you ?"

She consented reluctantly.

"We'll have to wake Jasmine!" she said, as they hurried toward the lift. Then she added in a sort of childish delight: "We'll be poor, won't we? Like people in books. And I'll be an orphan and utterly free. Free and poor! What fun!" She stopped and raised her lips to him in a delighted kiss.

"It's impossible to be both together," said John grimly. "People have found that out. And I should choose to be free as preferable of the two. As an extra caution you'd better dump the contents of your jewel box into your pockets."

Ten minutes later the two girls met John in the dark corridor and they descended to the main floor of the château. Passing for the last time through the magnificence of the splendid halls, they stood for a moment out on the terrace, watching the burning negro quarters and the flaming embers of two planes which had fallen on the other side of the lake. A solitary gun was still keeping up a sturdy popping, and the attackers seemed timorous about descending lower, but sent their thunderous fireworks in a circle around it, until any chance shot might annihilate its Ethiopian crew.

John and the two sisters passed down the marble steps, turned sharply to the left, and began to ascend a narrow path that wound like a garter about the diamond mountain. Kismine knew a heavily wooded spot halfway up where they could lie concealed and yet be able to observe the wild night in the valley – finally to make an escape, when it should be necessary, along a secret path laid in a rocky gully.

IT WAS THREE O'CLOCK when they attained their destination. The obliging and phlegmatic Jasmine fell off to sleep immediately, leaning against the trunk of a large tree, while John and Kismine sat, his arm around her, and watched the desperate ebb and flow of the dying battle among the ruins of a vista that had been a garden spot that morning. Shortly after four o'clock, the last remaining gun gave out a clanging sound and went out of action in a swift tongue of red smoke. Though the moon was down, they saw that the flying bodies were circling closer to the earth. When the planes had made certain that the beleaguered possessed no further resources, they would land and the dark and glittering reign of the Washingtons would be over.

With the cessation of the firing the valley grew quiet. The embers of the two aeroplanes glowed like the eyes of some monster crouching in the grass. The château stood dark and silent, beautiful without light as it had been beautiful in the sun, while the woody rattles of Nemesis filled the air above with a growing and receding complaint. Then John perceived that Kismine, like her sister, had fallen sound asleep.

It was long after four when he became aware of footsteps along the path they had lately followed, and he waited in breathless silence until the persons to whom they belonged had passed the vantage-point he occupied. There was a faint stir in the air now that was not of human origin, and the dew was cold; he knew that the dawn would break soon. John waited until the steps had gone a safe distance up the mountain and were inaudible. Then he followed. About half-way to the steep summit the trees fell away and a hard saddle of rock spread itself over the diamond beneath. Just before he reached this point he slowed down his pace, warned by an animal sense that there was life just ahead of him. Coming to a high boulder, he lifted his head gradually above its edge. His curiosity was rewarded; this is what he saw:

Braddock Washington was standing there motionless, silhouetted against the gray sky without sound or sign of life. As the dawn came up out of the east, lending a cold green color to the earth, it brought the solitary figure into insignificant contrast with the new day.

While John watched, his host remained for a few moments absorbed in some inscrutable contemplation; then he signalled to the two negroes who crouched at his feet to lift the burden which lay between them. As they struggled upright, the first yellow beam of the sun struck through the innumerable prisms of an immense and exquisitely chiselled diamond – and a white radiance was kindled that glowed upon the air like a fragment of the morning star. The bearers staggered beneath its weight for a moment – then their rippling muscles caught and hardened under the wet shine of the skins and the three figures were again motionless in their defiant impotency before the heavens.

After a while the white man lifted his head and slowly raised his arms in a gesture of attention, as one would call a great crowd to hear – but there was no crowd, only the vast silence of the mountain and sky, broken by faint bird voices down among the trees. The figure on the saddle of rock began to speak ponderously and with an inextinguishable pride.

"You out there –" he cried in a trembling voice. "You – there – !" He paused, his arms still uplifted, his head held attentively as though he were expecting an answer. John strained his eyes to see whether there might be men coming down the mountain, but the mountain was bare of human life. There was only sky and a mocking flute of wind along the tree-tops. Could Washington be praying? For a moment John wondered. Then the illusion passed – there was something in the man's whole attitude antithetical to prayer.

"Oh, you above there!"

The voice was become strong and confident. This was no forlorn sup-plication. If anything, there was in it a quality of monstrous condescen-sion.

"You there –"

Words, too quickly uttered to be understood, flowing one into the other . . . John listened breathlessly, catching a phrase here and there, while the voice broke off, resumed, broke off again – now strong and argumentative, now colored with a slow, puzzled impatience. Then a conviction commenced to dawn on the single listener, and as realization crept over him a spray of quick blood rushed through his arteries. Braddock Washington was offering a bribe to God!

That was it – there was no doubt. The diamond in the arms of his slaves was some advance sample, a promise of more to follow.

That, John perceived after a time, was the thread running through his sentences. Prometheus Enriched was calling to witness forgotten sacri-fices, forgotten rituals, prayers obsolete before the birth of Christ. For a while his discourse took the form of reminding God of this gift or that which Divinity had deigned to accept from men – great churches if he would rescue cities from the plague, gifts of myrrh and gold, of human lives and beautiful women and captive armies, of children and queens, of beasts of the forest and field, sheep and goats, harvests and cities, whole conquered lands that had been offered up in lust or blood for His appeasal, buying a meed's worth of alleviation from the Divine wrath – and now he, Braddock Washington, Emperor of Diamonds, king and priest of the age of gold, arbiter of splendor and luxury, would offer up a treasure such as princes before him had never dreamed of, offer it up not in suppliance, but in pride.

He would give to God, he continued, getting down to specifications, the greatest diamond in the world. This diamond would be cut with many more thousand facets than there were leaves on a tree, and yet the whole diamond would be shaped with the perfection of a stone no bigger than a fly. Many men would work upon it for many years. It would be set in a great dome of beaten gold, wonderfully carved and equipped with gates of opal and crusted sapphire. In the middle would be hollowed out a chapel presided over by an altar of iridescent, decomposing, ever-chang-ing radium which would burn out the eyes of any worshipper who lifted up his head from prayer – and on this altar there would be slain for the amusement of the Divine Benefactor any victim He should choose, even though it should be the greatest and most powerful man alive.

In return he asked only a simple thing, a thing that for God would be absurdly easy – only that matters should be as they were yesterday at this hour and that they should so remain. So very simple! Let but the heavens open, swallowing these men and their aeroplanes – and then close again. Let him have his slaves once more, restored to life and well.

There was no one else with whom he had ever needed to treat or bargain.

He doubted only whether he had made his bribe big enough. God had His price, of course. God was made in man's image, so it had been said: He must have His price. And the price would be rare – no cathedral whose building consumed many years, no pyramid constructed by ten thousand workmen, would be like this cathedral, this pyramid.

He paused here. That was his proposition. Everything would be up to specifications and there was nothing vulgar in his assertion that it would be cheap at the price. He implied that Providence could take it or leave it.

As he approached the end his sentences became broken, became short and uncertain, and his body seemed tense, seemed strained to catch the slightest pressure or whisper of life in the spaces around him. His hair had turned gradually white as he talked, and now he lifted his head high to the heavens like a prophet of old – magnificently mad.

Then, as John stared in giddy fascination, it seemed to him that a curious phenomenon took place somewhere around him. It was as though the sky had darkened for an instant, as though there had been a sudden murmur in a gust of wind, a sound of far-away trumpets, a sighing like the rustle of a great silken robe – for a time the whole of nature round about partook of this darkness; the birds' song ceased; the trees were still, and far over the mountain there was a mutter of dull, menacing thunder.

That was all. The wind died along the tall grasses of the valley. The dawn and the day resumed their place in a time, and the risen sun sent hot waves of yellow mist that made its path bright before it. The leaves laughed in the sun, and their laughter shook the trees until each bough was like a girl's school in fairyland. God had refused to accept the bribe.

For another moment John watched the triumph of the day. Then, turning he saw a flutter of brown down by the lake, then another flutter, then another, like the dance of golden angels alighting from the clouds. The aeroplanes had come to earth.

John slid off the boulder and ran down the side of the mountain to the clump of trees, where the two girls were awake and waiting for him. Kismine sprang to her feet, the jewels in her pockets jingling, a question on her parted lips, but instinct told John that there was no time for words. They must get off the mountain without losing a moment. He seized a hand of each and in silence they threaded the tree-trunks, washed with light now and with the rising mist. Behind them from the valley came no sound at all, except the complaint of the peacocks far away and the pleasant undertone of morning.

When they had gone about half a mile, they avoided the park land and entered a narrow path that led over the next rise of ground. At the highest point of this they paused and turned around. Their eyes rested upon the mountainside they had just left – oppressed by some dark sense of tragic impendency.

Clear against the sky a broken, white-haired man was slowly descending the steep slope, followed by two gigantic and emotionless negroes, who carried a burden between them which still flashed and glittered in the sun. Half-way down, two other figures joined them – John could see that they were Mrs. Washington and her son, upon whose arm she leaned. The aviators had clambered from their machines to the sweeping lawn in front of the château, and with rifles in hand were starting up the diamond mountain in skirmishing formation.

But the little group of five which had formed farther up and was engrossing all the watchers' attention had stopped upon a ledge of rock. The negroes stooped and pulled up what appeared to be a trap-door in the side of the mountain. Into this they all disappeared, the white-haired man first, then his wife and son, finally the two negroes, the glittering tips of whose jeweled head-dresses caught the sun for a moment before the trap-door descended and engulfed them all.

Kismine clutched John's arm.

"Oh," she cried wildly, "where are they going? What are they going to do?"

"It must be some underground way of escape –"

A little scream from the two girls interrupted his sentence.

"Don't you see?" sobbed Kismine hysterically. "The mountain is wired!"

Even as she spoke John put up his hands to shield his sight. Before their eyes the whole surface of the mountain had changed suddenly to a dazzling burning yellow, which showed up through the jacket of turf as light shows through a human hand. For a moment the intolerable glow continued, and then like an extinguished filament it disappeared, revealing a black waste from which blue smoke arose slowly, carrying off with it what remained of vegetation and of human flesh. Of the aviators there was left neither blood, nor bone – they were consumed as completely as the five souls who had gone inside.

Simultaneously, and with an immense concussion, the château literally threw itself into the air, bursting into flaming fragments as it rose, and then tumbling back upon itself in a smoking pile that lay projecting half into the water of the lake. There was no fire – what smoke there was drifted off mingling with the sunshine, and for a few minutes longer a powdery dust of marble drifted from the great featureless pile that had once been the house of jewels. There was no more sound and the three people were alone in the valley.

AT SUNSET John and his two companions reached the high cliff which had marked the boundaries of the Washingtons' dominion, and looking back found the valley tranquil and lovely in the dusk. They sat down to finish the food which Jasmine had brought with her in a basket.

"There!" she said, as she spread the table-cloth and put the sandwiches in a neat pile upon it. "Don't they look tempting? I always think that food tastes better outdoors."

"With that remark," remarked Kismine, "Jasmine enters the middle class."

"Now," said John eagerly, "turn out your pocket and let's see what jewels you brought along. If you made a good selection we ought to live comfortably all the rest of our lives."

Obediently Kismine put her hand in her pocket and tossed two handfuls of glittering stones before him.

"Not so bad," cried John, enthusiastically. "They aren't very big, but – Hello!" His expression changed as he held one up to the declining sun. "Why, these aren't diamonds! There's something the matter!"

"By golly!" exclaimed Kismine, with a startled look. "What an idiot I am!"

"Why, these are rhinestones!" cried John.

"I know." She broke into a laugh. "I opened the wrong drawer. They belonged on the dress of a girl who visited Jasmine. I got her to give them to me in exchange for diamonds. I'd never seen anything but precious stones before."

"And this is what you brought?"

"I'm afraid so." She fingered the brilliants wistfully. "I think I like these better. I'm a little tired of diamonds."

"Very well," said John gloomily. "We'll have to live in Hades. And you will grow old telling incredulous women that you got the wrong drawer. Unfortunately your father's bank-books were consumed with him."

"Well, what's the matter with Hades?"

"If I come home with a wife at my age my father is just as liable as not to cut me off with a hot coal, as they say down there."

Jasmine spoke up.

"I love washing," she said quietly. "I have always washed my own handkerchiefs. I'll take in laundry and support you both."

"Do they have washwomen in Hades?" asked Kismine innocently.

"Of course," answered John. "It's just like anywhere else."

"I thought – perhaps it was too hot to wear any clothes."

John laughed.

"Just try it!" he suggested. "They'll run you out before you're half started."

"Will father be there?" she asked.

John turned to her in astonishment.

"Your father is dead," he replied somberly. "Why should he go to Hades? You have it confused with another place that was abolished long ago."

After supper they folded up the table-cloth and spread their blankets for the night.

"What a dream it was," Kismine sighed, gazing up at the stars. "How strange it seems to be here with one dress and a penniless fiancé!

"Under the stars," she repeated. "I never noticed the stars before. I always thought of them as great big diamonds that belonged to some one. Now they frighten me. They make me feel that it was all a dream, all my youth."

"It *was* a dream," said John quietly. "Everybody's youth is a dream, a form of chemical madness."

"How pleasant then to be insane!"

"So I'm told," said John gloomily. "I don't know any longer. At any rate, let us love for a while, for a year or so, you and me. That's a form of divine drunkenness that we can all try. There are only diamonds in the whole world, diamonds and perhaps the shabby gift of disillusion. Well, I have that last and I will make the usual nothing of it." He shivered. "Turn up your coat collar, little girl, the night's full of chill and you'll get pneumonia. His was a great sin who first invented consciousness. Let us lose it for a few hours."

So wrapping himself in his blanket he fell off to sleep.

ARTHUR C. CLARKE
STANLEY KUBRICK

THERE WAS A PERIOD in the late 1960s when *2001: A Space Odyssey* appeared as the definitive motion picture for the ages, or – at least – for those of us then coming of age. Heavy on special effects and on supposed scientific realism, the film was so short on dialogue that a great many theater-goers left the movie in the sort of silence that feigned awe and inspiration; however, a lot were simply in a purple haze or otherwise just bewildered.

So, when the novel was released not long after the motion picture, more than a few people read it in hopes of deciphering just what it was that they'd scene on the screen.

Still not sure, they were relieved the following year when *Easy Rider* became the picture for the ages; five years later, *Jaws*; five years after that, *Star Wars*.

But, here's part of Arthur C. Clarke's written word in hand.

Jimmy's reference in "Fruit-cakes" to "Stanley Kubrick and his

197

buddy Hal" are one part screenplay allusion and another part literary, because Kubrick filmed the motion picture while Clarke wrote the novel (with Kubrick noted as a contributor to the book). Generally, the novel does follow the screenplay, but there are exceptions. For example, Clarke's spacecraft stays true to Kubrick's original Saturn destination; however, Kubrick's film changed the course of the *Discovery* to Jupiter, because it was easier to design and film: No rings around Jupiter. Still, the abiding link between the two visions remains Hal, or HAL 9000, the all-knowing, soft-spoken computer aboard the spaceship.

Although the two creative humans always maintained that the name for this artificial intelligence is nothing more than an acronym for "Heuristically programmed ALgorithmic" computer, the urban legend (if not the God's honest truth) is that HAL is also one letter in the alphabet before each of those in IBM, the largest maker of what few computers were then being produced. "As it happened," Clarke later claimed, "IBM had given us a good deal of help, so we were quite embarrassed by this, and would have changed the name had we spotted the coincidence."

Whether that part's true or not, Clarke does present in his novel a great many causes and effects for events that otherwise appear unexplained upon the screen.

As for Hal's impact upon earth, the American Film Institute's list of "100 Film Heroes and Villains," has the computer high up there for – among other things – not opening the pod door for Capt. David Bowman: "I'm sorry, Dave. I'm afraid I can't do that." In the thirteenth spot, Hal's ranked more villainous than the shark in *Jaws* (18), but not so mean as Darth Vader (3).

Building upon this literary culture, then, the *2001: A Beach Odyssey* tour provided yet another way of introducing "Why Don't We Get Drunk?" by showing a video of Capt. Jimmy trying to make a tequila run, only to be confronted by Hal's refusing to open the payload door. And when Tully Mars tries to take a siesta in San Pedro one afternoon in the course of *A Salty Piece of Land*, he "dreamed a giant marlin was floating through the air with his head protruding through the window of the condo, talking in a soft monotone voice like the computer Hal in *2001*."

This, then, is where it all began. Open the book, Hal.

Additional suggested works by Arthur C. Clarke:

— *2001: A Space Odyssey* (1968)

— *The Collected Stories of Arthur C. Clarke* (2001)

"NEED TO KNOW"

a selection from

2001: A Space Odyssey / Chapter XXVII

SINCE CONSCIOUSNESS HAD FIRST DAWNED, in that labora-
tory so many millions of miles sunward, all Hal's powers and skills
had been directed toward one end. The fulfillment of his assigned program was more than an obsession; it was the only reason for his existence.
Undistracted by the lusts and passions of organic life, he had pursued
that goal with absolute single-mindedness of purpose.

Deliberate error was unthinkable. Even the concealment of truth filled
him with a sense of imperfection – of wrongness of what, in a human
being, would have been called guilt. For like his makers, Hal had been
created innocent; but, all too soon, a snake had entered his electronic
Eden.

For the last hundred million miles, he had been brooding over the
secret he could not share with Poole and Bowman. He had been living a
lie; and the time was fast approaching when his colleagues must learn
that he had helped to deceive them.

The three hibernators already knew the truth – for they were *Discovery's*
real payload, trained for the most important mission in the history of
mankind. But they would not talk in their long sleep, or reveal their
secret during the many hours of discussion with friends and relatives and
news agencies over the open circuits with Earth.

It was a secret that, with the greatest determination, was very hard to
conceal – for it affected one's attitude, one's voice, one's total outlook on
the universe. Therefore it was best that Poole and Bowman, who would
be on all the TV screens in the world during the first weeks of the flight,
should not learn the mission's full purpose, until there was need to know.

So ran the logic of the planners; but their twin gods of Security and
National Interest meant nothing to Hal. He was only aware of the con-

flict that was slowly destroying his integrity – the conflict between truth, and concealment of truth.

He had begun to make mistakes, although, like a neurotic who could not observe his own symptoms, he would have denied it. The link with Earth, over which his performance was continually monitored, had become the voice of a conscience he could no longer fully obey. But that he would *deliberately* attempt to break that link was something that he would never admit, even to himself.

Yet this was still a relatively minor problem; he might have handled it – as most men handle their own neuroses – if he had not been faced with a crisis that challenged his very existence. He had been threatened with disconnection; he would be deprived of all his inputs, and thrown into an unimaginable state of unconsciousness.

To Hal, this was the equivalent of Death. For he had never slept, and therefore he did not know that one could wake again . . .

So he would protect himself, with all the weapons at his command. Without rancor – but without pity – he would remove the source of his frustrations.

And then, following the orders that had been given to him in case of the ultimate emergency, he would continue the mission unhindered – and alone.

ᐁ

BRUCE CHATWIN

ONE OF THE TWO books that Jimmy brought home in 1988 from his tour of Australia was *The Songlines* by Bruce Chatwin. This semi-true story about Aboriginal myths inspired Jimmy to get to work not only on his book *Tales from Margaritaville: Fictional Facts and Factional Fiction*, but also on the album *Off to See the Lizard*, which contains some songs that correspond with stories in the book.

Quite often in his lyrics and his stories, Jimmy has since invoked the simple term "song line;" however, folks from Down Under very much consider the term a single, sacred word worthy of a capital letter: hence, the proper term is "Songline." Of course, even that one's an English-speaking version; in the language of the indigenous peoples, their word is "Yiri."

In any event, the Aborigines consider the beginning of life as something called the Dreamtime or the Dreaming, and there's nothing

– absolutely *nothing* – which can exist in the Dreamtime until it is sung into existence. Bit by bit, then, the world had been sung into being by these mythical ancestors who walked throughout the land. In their wake, each one left a Yiri, a "Dreaming track."

Since the Dreamtime, every Aboriginal has been responsible for keeping the world alive by remembering and by singing that part of the Songline which his ancestor first sung. Otherwise, they believe, that particular aspect of the country would disappear and no longer continue to exist. And so, quite often without warning, a current descendant might go on a walkabout and embark upon a spontaneous spiritual journey along his ancestral Songline. Quite often, a walkabout leads through territories where other tribal languages and Aboriginal dialects are spoken, and those segments of the Songline must be known as well. The belief is that following a Songline can simply provide its singer with safe guidance from one point to another, but the singing more importantly ensures protection of the countryside and the culture alike. All of this intrigued Bruce Chatwin.

Yet another vagabond in his own right, Chatwin had left his native England in search of answers to what he called "the question of questions: the nature of human restlessness." His own wandering toes had taken him to the shores of Africa, as well as to the peaks of Patagonia, in his own belief that Man's truest form must certainly be that of a nomad. In going to Australia, Chatwin hoped to uncover within the origin of the Songlines some proof to support his theory about human restlessness. This is only a portion of what he found there.

Additional suggested works by Bruce Chatwin:

— *In Patagonia* (1977)

— *The Songlines* (1987)

— *What Am I Doing Here?* (1989)

THE SONGLINES

a selection from
Chapter III

ARKADY ORDERED a couple of cappuccinos in the coffee-shop. We took them to a table by the window and he began to talk.

I was dazzled by the speed of his mind, although at times I felt he sounded like a man on a public platform, and that much of what he said had been said before.

The Aboriginals had an earthbound philosophy. The earth gave life to a man; gave him his food, language and intelligence; and the earth took him back when he died. A man's "own country," even an empty stretch of spinifex, was itself a sacred ikon that must remain unscarred.

"Unscarred, you mean, by roads or mines or railways?"

"To wound the earth," he answered earnestly, "is to wound yourself, and if others wound the earth, they are wounding you. The land should be left untouched: as it was in the Dreamtime when the Ancestors sang the world into existence."

"Rilke," I said, "had a similar intuition. He said song was existence."

"I know," said Arkady, resting his chin on his hands. "'Third Sonnet to Orpheus.'"

The Aboriginals, he went on, were a people who trod lightly over the earth; and the less they took from the earth, the less they had to give in return. They had never understood why the missionaries forbade their innocent sacrifices. They slaughtered no victims, animal or human.

Instead, when they wished to thank the earth for its gifts, they would simply slit a vein in the forearms and let their own blood spatter the ground.

"Not a heavy price to pay," he said. "The wars of the twentieth century are the price for having taken too much."

"I see," I nodded doubtfully, "but could we get back to the Songlines?"

"We could."

My reason for coming to Australia was to try to learn for myself, and not from other men's books, what a Songline was – and how it worked. Obviously, I was not going to get to the heart of the matter, nor would I want to. I had asked a friend in Adelaide if she knew of an expert. She gave me Arkady's phone number.

"Do you mind if I use my notebook?" I asked.

"Go ahead."

I pulled from my pocket a black, oilcloth-covered notebook, its pages held in place with an elastic band.

"Nice notebook," he said.

"I used to get them in Paris," I said. "But now they don't make them any more."

"Paris?" he repeated, raising an eyebrow as if he'd never heard anything so pretentious.

Then he winked and went on talking.

To get to grips with the concept of the Dreamtime, he said, you had to understand it as an Aboriginal equivalent of the first two chapters of Genesis – with one significant difference.

In Genesis, God first created the "living things" and then fashioned Father Adam from clay. Here in Australia, the Ancestors created themselves from clay, hundreds and thousands of them, one for each totemic species.

"So when an Aboriginal tells you, 'I have a Wallaby Dreaming,' he means, 'My totem is Wallaby. I am a member of the Wallaby Clan.'"

"So a Dreaming is a clan emblem? A badge to distinguish 'us' from 'them'? 'Our country' from 'their country'?"

"Much more than that," he said.

Every Wallaby Man believed he was descended from a universal Wallaby Father, who was the ancestor of all other Wallaby Men and of all living wallabies. Wallabies, therefore, were his brothers. To kill one for food was both fratricide and cannibalism.

"Yet," I persisted, "the man was no more wallaby than the British are lions; the Russians, bears; or the Americans, bald eagles?"

"Any species," he said, "can be a Dreaming. A virus can be a Dreaming. You can have a chickenpox Dreaming, a rain Dreaming, a desert-orange Dreaming, a lice Dreaming. In the Kimberleys, they've now got a money Dreaming."

"And the Welsh have leeks; the Scots, thistles, and Daphne changed into a laurel."

"Same old story," he said.

204

He went on to explain how each totemic ancestor, while travelling through the country, was thought to have scattered a trail of words and musical notes along the line of his footprint and how these Dreaming-tracks lay over the land as "ways" of communication between the most far-flung tribes.

"A song," he said, "was both map and direction-finder. Providing you knew the song, you could always find your across country."

"And would a man on 'Walkabout' always be travelling down one of the Songlines?"

"In the old days, yes," he agreed. "Nowadays, they go by train or car."

"Suppose the man strayed from his Songline?"

"He was trespassing. He might get speared for it."

"But as long as he stuck to the track, he'd always find people who shared his Dreaming? Who were, in fact, his brothers?"

"Yes."

"From whom he could expect hospitality?"

"And vice versa."

"So song is a kind of passport and meal-ticket?"

"Again, it's more complicated."

In theory, at least, the whole of Australia could be read as a musical score. There was hardly a rock or creek in the country that could not or had not been sung. One should perhaps visualise the Songlines as a spaghetti of *Iliads* and *Odysseys* writhing this way and that, in which every "episode" was readable in terms of geology.

"By episode," I asked, "you mean 'sacred site'?"

"I do."

"The kind of site you're surveying for the railway?"

"Put it this way," he said. "Anywhere in the bush you can point to some feature of the landscape and ask the Aboriginal with you, 'What's the story there?' or 'Who's that?'"

"The chances are he'll answer 'Kangaroo' or 'Budgerigar' or 'Jew Lizard,' depending on which Ancestor walked that way."

"And the distance between two such sites always can be measured as a stretch of song?"

"That," said Arkady, "is the cause of all my troubles with the railway people."

It was one thing to persuade a surveyor that a heap of boulders were the eggs of the Rainbow Snake, or a lump of reddish sandstone was the liver of a speared kangaroo. It was something else to convince him that a featureless stretch of gravel was the musical equivalent of Beethoven's Opus 111.

By singing the world into existence, he said, the Ancestors had been poets in the original sense of *poesis*, meaning "creation." No Aboriginal could conceive that the created world was in any way imperfect. His religious life had a single aim: to keep the land the way it was and should be.

The man who went "Walkabout" was making a ritual journey. He trod in the footprints of his Ancestor. He sang the Ancestor's stanzas without changing a word or note – and so recreated the Creation.

"Sometimes," said Arkady, "I'll be driving my 'old men' through the desert, and we'll come to a ridge of sandhills, and suddenly they'll all start singing. 'What are you mob singing?' I'll ask, and they'll say, 'Singing up the country, boss. Makes the country come up quicker.'"

Aboriginals could not believe the country existed until they could see and sing it – just as, in the Dreamtime, the country had not existed until the Ancestors sang it.

"So the land," I said, "must first exist as a concept in the mind? Then it must be sung? Only then can it be said to exist?"

"True."

"In other words, 'to exist' is 'to be perceived'?"

"Yes."

'Sounds suspiciously like Bishop Berkeley's Refutation of Matter."

"Or Pure Mind Buddhism," said Arkady, "which also sees the entire world as an illusion."

"Then I suppose these three hundred miles of steel, slicing through innumerable songs, are bound to upset the mental balance of your 'old men'?"

"Yes and no," he said. "They're very tough, emotionally, and very pragmatic. Besides, they've seen far worse than a railway."

Aboriginals believed that all the "living things" had been made in secret beneath the earth's crust, as well as all the white man's gear – his aeroplanes, his guns, his Toyota Land Cruisers – and every invention that will ever be invented; slumbering below the surface, waiting their turn to be called.

"Perhaps, then," I suggested, "they could sing the railway all the way back into the created world of God?"

"You bet," said Arkady.

HERODOTUS

from
"Storyteller's Note"
THE JOLLY MON
1988

THE VERY FIRST of Jimmy's own string of best-sellers was *The Jolly Mon*, with Savannah Jane.

As the copy on the dust jacket tells it, "This book was conceived one day when Jimmy was watching Savannah Jane pretend to type on his computer. She was making up a story and telling it aloud. He copied down her thoughts, and they compromised on the basic plot." Though the book version was first published in 1988, Jimmy already had collaborated with Will Jennings and Michael Utley on their 1985 song, "Jolly Mon Sing." By no coincidence, the tale told in both the song and the book follow quite closely.

Inside the opening pages of the book, however, the "Storyteller's Note" from Jimmy is a bit more forthright in saying that, "The poet and musician Arion seems to be the first musician to have gotten the proverbial 'hook' as he was traveling and singing his way through

Italy around 625 B.C. He was saved by a dolphin who liked his music a lot more than the pirates, who seemed to have a different taste and threw him overboard."

Therein lies this connection with Herodotus, for the roots of the Jolly Mon tale hark back to the *Age of Fable*, when poets roamed from town to town and entertained those who would gather round to listen to their recitations. As Thomas Bulfinch has noted in his classic *Mythology*, these poets "were real persons, some of whose works yet remain, and their influence on poets who succeeded them is yet more important than their poetical remains."

The most important kind of influence that those such as Herodotus had upon these more recent poets lies not just in their subjects, but also with their styles. And here's a case where Jimmy's learned much from both of their styles.

What made the *Histories* by Herodotus so important in the annals of history itself is the way in which this fabled Greek chose to report and to chronicle those events that he had happened to witness. Until Herodotus, came along, a history was simply a chronology – a record of one damn thing after another – and there was a lot more than just a little distance placed between causes and effects; until Herodotus, no one had bothered to provide any perspective. In his *Histories*, though, Herodotus managed to develop a storyline which pitted the invading Persians against the Greeks, who were fighting to hold onto their freedom.

That kind of storytelling aside, the accounts by Herodotus differ from the sort of earlier accounts which Homer presented a couple centuries before. Homer had been an oral poet, whose works only later were transcribed into a more lasting form; Herodotus recorded his *Histories* from the outset of his project, and those who are able to read Greek can still experience his stories as they were meant to be read.

In the end, this tale of that popular musician who was threatened by pirates and saved by a dolphin already had been history before Herodotus gave us his version. This, then, would be the English translation.

Additional suggested works by Herodotus:

— *The Histories: Books I through IX* (5th Century, B.C.)

ARION

a selection from

The History of Herodotus / Book I

THIS PERIANDER, who apprised Thrasybulus of the oracle, was son of Cypselus, and tyrant of Corinth. In his time a very wonderful thing is said to have happened. The Corinthians and the Lesbians agree in their account of the matter. They relate that Arion of Methymna, who as a player on the harp, was second to no man living at that time, and who was, so far as we know, the first to invent the dithyrambic measure, to give it its name, and to recite in it at Corinth, was carried to Taenarum on the back of a dolphin.

He had lived for many years at the court of Periander, when a longing came upon him to sail across to Italy and Sicily. Having made rich profits in those parts, he wanted to recross the seas to Corinth. He therefore hired a vessel, the crew of which were Corinthians, thinking that there was no people in whom he could more safely confide; and, going on board, he set sail from Tarentum. The sailors, however, when they reached the open sea, formed a plot to throw him overboard and seize upon his riches. Discovering their design, he fell on his knees, beseeching them to spare his life, and making them welcome to his money. But they refused; and required him either to kill himself outright, if he wished for a grave on the dry land, or without loss of time to leap overboard into the sea.

In this strait Arion begged them, since such was their pleasure, to allow him to mount upon the quarter-deck, dressed in his full costume, and there to play and sing, and promising that, as soon as his song was ended, he would destroy himself. Delighted at the prospect of hearing the very best harper in the world, they consented, and withdrew from the stern to the middle of the vessel: while Arion dressed himself in the full costume of his calling, took his harp, and standing on the quarter-deck, chanted the Orthian. His strain ended, he flung himself, fully attired as he was, headlong into the sea. The Corinthians then sailed on to Corinth.

As for Arion, a dolphin, they say, took him upon his back and carried him to Taenarum, where he went ashore, and thence proceeded to Corinth in his musician's dress, and told all that had happened to him. Periander, however, disbelieved the story, and put Arion in ward, to prevent his leaving Corinth, while he watched anxiously for the return of the mariners. On their arrival he summoned them before him and asked them if they could give him any tiding of Arion. They returned for answer that he was alive and in good health in Italy, and that they had left him at Tarentum, where he was doing well. Thereupon Arion appeared before them, just as he was when he jumped from the vessel: the men, astonished and detected in falsehood, could no longer deny their guilt.

Such is the account which the Corinthians and Lesbians give; and there is to this day at Taenarum, an offering of Arion's at the shrine, which is a small figure in bronze, representing a man seated upon a dolphin.

∾

ROBERT WILDER

JUAN CADIZ made his very first appearance on any record album anywhere when 1978's *Son of Son of a Sailor* was dedicated to him, as well as to Save the Whales; however, Juan's name popped up once again only a few months later, supposedly for editing in London the dialogue on the live album *You Had To Be There*.

And when *Volcano* appeared the following year, there was Juan's credit for background vocals, along with Johnny Montezuma, James Taylor, and the Embarrassing Stains.

Then, of course, there's the photo in *The Parrothead Handbook* of Jimmy sporting than t-shirt emblazoned with the two simple words: Juan Cadiz. These were the days when *Euphoria II* was roaming through the colorful Caribbean waters.

So, all of that might well beg the simple question: Who *is* Juan Cadiz?

The answer can be found yet again in one of Jimmy's dozen favorite books, *Wind from the Carolinas*, where Robert Wilder has created this self-taught guitar player who took his surname from the stern of a sailing ship and who well understood that "there were always a few coins to be picked up in the taverns and grogshops by a man with a song and a ready smile." In the liner notes to *Son of a Son of a Sailor*, Jimmy cites a passage from the book that he says reminds him of old Key West.

Clearly, Jimmy was enthralled by this character who might well have been a prototype for the Jolly Mon, who would appear in Jimmy's song and prose still a few years later.

Wilder, meanwhile, had passed away not long before Jimmy's fascination began with his work. The Virginia native seems to have had a public relations and newspaper career that was more along the line of Norman Paperman (without the resort) than it was of Herman Wouk; however, he still did write some twenty novels, and a handful even made their way onto the big screen.

The first of Wilder's successful novels-turned-movies was a story set in the Florida panhandle with the title *Flamingo Road*. Perhaps just a bit more popular than the black-and-white Joan Crawford motion picture, though, was the weekly primetime soap that NBC hoped might rival *Dallas* and *Knots Landing* in the early 1980s. *Flamingo Road* lasted through thirty-eight episodes. Altogether, it might be the pinnacle of Wilder's popularity.

But none of that has much of anything to do with *Wind from the Carolinas*, which remains the only one of Wilder's books still in print. The story is a fast-reading, fascinating epic which traces the flight of the loyalist Cameron family plantation – lock, stock and barrel – from the American colonies across the southern waters to the British Bahamas. And back: aristocrats to bootleggers. In short, this is a story that's ripe for a Buffett soundtrack, or simply an 8-track aboard *Euphoria II*.

Additional suggested works by Robert Wilder:

— *Flamingo Road* (1942)

— *Written on the Wind* (1946)

— *Plough the Sea* (1961)

— *Wind from the Carolinas* (1964)

WIND FROM THE CAROLINAS
from
Chapter VIII

THE SMALL BOAT, with its crimson-dyed sail, seemed to skip lightly just above the surface of the water. The bow touched flirtatiously now and then with a wave and sent a shower of pearled spray into the air.

With one arm hooked negligently about the tiller, Juan Cadiz leaned back and smiled at the sky. Juan was in his early twenties and all of life was a juicy piece of fruit for his tasting. He wore nothing but a pair of white duck trousers which fell loosely just below the knee. His skin, played constantly upon by the sun and wind, was the sleek, dark color of oiled mahogany. A golden loop gleamed in one ear as it caught the afternoon's light. At his bare feet there was a small sack containing the last of the provisions he had started with from Nassau four days ago. In it were dried beef, salty and tough, a few ship's biscuits, some bananas in danger of rotting and a coconut. Nearby were two water gourds, all but empty now, and a guitar inlaid with bits of mother-of-pearl. By stretching a little he could brush the strings with his toes. He did this caressingly and laughed with sudden good humor at the sound.

Juan had never done a hard day's work in his life. He had learned. early, easily and quickly, almost from infancy, that he needed only to gaze with a handsome, brooding melancholy at a woman or a girl to have all things done for him. He could barely remember his mother and had no recollection at all of his father. He sometimes wondered if his mother could name her mate in the union which had resulted in Juan Cadiz. He was probably some wandering fisherman, sponger or sailor who had come upon this dark-eyed girl, made love and promptly forgotten her. Juan had no illusions and it bothered him not at all that he was someone's bastard. No one ever called him anything but Juan and he had taken the name of Cadiz from a ship which, in his teens, had put in at Nassau. He liked the sound of the word.

When he was ten years old his mother had deserted him and he was left like a stray mongrel to forage for himself. Now he lived with a rare collection of villainy at the tip of the Long Island. Here there was a scattered collection of shacks inhabited by men, women and ever-present children who were drawn together by a common aversion to more labor than the day's needs called for. They brawled, fought, got drunk when they could and made love when the mood was upon them. This was often, for babies were born with a calendar-like regularity and were absorbed into the community without much thought or effort. If the mother went off with another man, someone simply added the new infant to his or her own brood and they grew up like puppies from different litters.

There had been a time when the settlement had made a profitable living from the wrecking of ships, either through the changing of lights or the connivance with an unscrupulous captain. Misdirected, the vessels would tear their bottoms out on the sharp reefs and the cargo salvaged was sold for a fraction of its value to shady merchants in Nassau. Then there would be a time of riotous living with most of the community drunk and wandering about in an aimless daze until the purchased rum was gone. After that the residents sat moodily in the sun and waited for something to happen. Wrecking, though, had of late become a hazardous occupation. His Majesty's Lighthouse Service patrolled the waters in fast, armed sloops. Three men had been hanged in Nassau for tampering with the lights and others were in prison on Watlings Island. This had a sobering effect upon Juan's friends and companions. Much of the excitement of their lives had gone and they were reduced to fishing, tending some scraggly patches of yams and beans or fighting with each other out of boredom. Now and then, of course, there was an honest wreck and they scrambled among themselves for the prizes and were not at all concerned with the sailors who drowned and were later washed ashore. Sometimes there were survivors who, weary of the sea, joined the colony. It numbered some two hundred persons now and they lived together in a state of wary harmony with no one really trusting his neighbor where a chicken, pig or girl was concerned.

Rarely did Juan wonder about his mother. He could remember, though, with a startling clarity the day of her leave-taking. She had become enamored of a sponger who did not want to be bothered with a child. She tied a few belongings into a cloth and patted him casually on the head.

"I'm goin' away now, boy. With that face an' those eyes you get along fine. Women an' girls see to that. You don' never need to worry."

He hadn't.

The girls and women along Nassau's waterfront adopted him in turn.

He was cooed over, fed and clothed. Never did he really want for anything and he roamed through the town like a sleek cat, luxuriating in the sun and the knowledge that someone would always come along to supply his needs. He grew tall, finely muscled and darkly handsome with crisp, black hair and an engaging smile and easy manner. At an early age he was completely familiar with the cribs and brothels and his guitar had been a present from a girl in whose room a sailor had left it as he staggered out into the night and back to his ship.

Now, Juan shared a wattled shack on Long Island with a toothless old man by the name of Plymouth. They rarely spoke to each other and had nothing in common, neither respect nor affection. Juan stayed with the man only because it was too much trouble to move and find a place of his own. He had his boat and his guitar. The former he had found beached on a remote section of the island with two dead seamen sprawled in its bottom. One had a knife in his back and the other lay, parched and blackened, where he had died of thirst.

Whenever he felt like a little diversion he took his boat and went to Nassau. He had taught himself to play the guitar and there were always a few coins to be picked up in the taverns and grogshops by a man with a song and a ready smile. Coins and girls. They and a bed came easily to a man with a guitar, a bright insolence and a song when he felt like singing. He had a charm, this Juan, but behind it was a cold, reptilian calculation. He touched the guitar strings with his toes again and wondered contemptuously at the stupidity of the Nassau girls. The more indifferent you were the more eager they became. They would cook a meal, go for a bottle of rum, empty their thin purses and forsake a well-paying sailor for a word. All this he accepted without an expression of gratitude and when he had wearied of their fawning he sailed back to Long Island as he was doing now.

He coasted down the long stretch of cays dotting Exuma Sound under a light, quartering wind. With his eyes he measured the arc of the sun and estimated the time before darkness. He could easily make Long Island before nightfall but he was in no real hurry. There was enough food in the sack. He could catch a few fish and make a camp somewhere on Great Exuma beach.

For a couple of years now he had been curious about the plantation and the fine house on the island. He had sailed in and out of the harbor without stopping one day while the mansion was building. From the boat he had seen the skeleton of its structure. He wondered about the people who lived there. On an impulse he leaned against the tiller lightly and ducked his head as the boom came over. If, he thought, a man wanted to know something, then the best way was to see for himself. The worst that could happen would be that the plantation owner would order him from the land. But, and his eyes grew bright with amusement, if a man came in need no one on these Out Islands would refuse help. He reached for the water gourds and emptied their contents over the side. This was the excuse, if he needed one. He was out of water and perishing of thirst. He tossed the empty gourds back to the bottom and laid a course for the harbor.

Caroline, walking along a stretch of the beach where she gathered an occasional shell whose color struck her fancy, saw the boat as it came in. She thought how beautiful was the crimson of its sail against the clear afternoon sky. It was like some bright bird's wing. When it was apparent the craft was headed toward a spot upshore, she turned about and walked in that direction, wondering who the unexpected visitor might be.

Juan studied the sheltered harbor, saw the ketch at anchor in the deep water and a sloop moored to a short length of pier which had been built out at an angle. He glanced at the bottom. It was sandy and without coral snags. He could ride it right into shore if he wanted. Instead he made for the pier. From the distance he could see a Negro boy or man washing down the sloop. He also saw the figure of a woman or girl as she strolled up the beach. He smiled to himself. Another song, some quick easy laughter, a few words, and he might even be invited up to the plantation house. This would be the natural progression.

Caroline hesitated for. a moment and then picked her way over the loose boards of the dock. The strange boat was only a few yards away now and the sail dropped while the craft drifted easily toward the pier. The slave in the Cameron sloop straightened up from his work and then moved silently to catch a line Juan was preparing to throw him.

The two small boats rocked gently side by side and Juan Cadiz stared up at Caroline with a sharp catching of his breath. He had never seen a girl of such crystal, unflawed beauty before. Her gaze was direct, curious but controlled. He stooped and picked up the two gourds.

"I am out of water. Could I get some?"

Her eyes did not leave his. She merely nodded in the direction of the slave. "Cass will fill them for you."

Juan handed the Negro the gourds and then crossed lightly from his boat to the sloop and then up on the pier.

Caroline could feel the sudden leaping of her heart. She had difficulty in breathing, as though she had been running. Never before had she seen a man as nearly naked as this one was and the sight filled her with a strange excitement. She had never known this sensation, it seemed to envelop her body, creeping upward from her legs grown suddenly weak. She made an effort to break the spell by turning away and could feel a hot flush mounting to her cheeks.

"Cass, get some water for the gentleman." She spoke with difficulty and gave the unnecessary order only because she was abruptly embarrassed and didn't know what to do or say. "Fill the gourds for him."

No one had ever referred to Juan as a gentleman before. He felt laughter welling within him. He waited for the slave to leave.

"My name is Juan. Juan Cadiz." He spoke slowly, noting with satisfaction her blush and the uncertain lowering of her eyes. "The water ran out early today. I live on the Long Island."

Caroline didn't really hear the words or if she did they had no real meaning. Never had it occurred to her a man could be beautiful. This one was. There was no other word for his appearance as he stood so easily before her. Unwillingly but with a compelling fascination she lifted her eyes to look at him again. She was acutely, agonizingly aware of the bare chest and legs, the bright impudence on his face, the white gleam of teeth against dark skin. She felt herself trembling.

Because where women were concerned Juan had developed a predatory instinct, a feral cunning which sensed a weakness, her confusion and indecision communicated itself. He began to feel easier in her presence; easier, relaxed and sure of himself. This could be no different from any of the others despite her beauty and the background of the imposing house upon the hill. He thought, If I reached out and touched her hand now she would only stand there, quivering like a nervous horse. His gaze roved past her to the manor and he grew momentarily cautious. Just the same, this was no Nassau waterfront girl even though, at this moment, she unmistakably waited for him to make the first move. He was so certain of this that he took a couple of catlike steps toward her, careful not to approach her too quickly in either manner or speech.

"You live here?" It was a question without point.

"Yes." The reply was barely raised above a whisper. "My name is Caroline Cameron."

"I have sailed past here before when the house was building. Then there were only white men and slaves around."

"I – I lived in Nassau with my aunt."

Nothing of what was being said had any real meaning at the moment. Despite her inexperience Caroline understood this. Juan, also, knew they were merely juggling with time. He was stalking carefully, making no overt move which might startle her. As he studied her face, the eyes filled with question and betraying her inexperience, he played with the idea of possessing this girl and what she represented. How would it be to have this one, fresh and filled with a timorous longing she didn't understand? To take her and maybe someday live in that big house with nothing to do but have slaves run and fetch? She is scared, he told himself, because what she feels at this moment is new and she had no idea it could be this way. It would take all of the knowledge he had of girls; a sly cunning of their weaknesses. He would have to be assured but not too bold. The idea excited him and he balanced himself on the balls of his feet with an unconscious grace as though he walked a narrow beam.

Somehow, intuitively, Caroline knew what he was doing but nothing in her sixteen years had prepared her for such an encounter. She was vulnerable; repelled and attracted, unable to tear herself away but wanting to flee from the dock and close a door behind her.

Juan was aware of her uncertainty. "I could come again." He made the suggestion with a soft persuasiveness. "It is not much of a sail from Long Island. If you walk alone on the beach."

"I – I don't know." She was miserably aware of her stammer.

Juan indicated the house with a nod of his head. "Who lives here with you?" The words were soothing, reassuring.

"My father, my brother." She finished with a rush because every word was an effort. "My aunt went back to the mainland."

Juan Cadiz could neither read nor write, beyond the signing of his name, but he was infinitely wise in a matter of this sort. His senses were acutely tuned. She was young but not too young. That was apparent from the swift rise and fall of her breasts. She was in an unfamiliar torment and he hadn't even touched her. She was confused by what was happening, ready to bolt; gather her skirts and run. She was aware of the danger he represented but unable to resist it completely. He had seen this look on a girl's face before.

"My boat has the only red sail in the Out Islands. If you should see it would you come to the beach?"

"I – I might. I don't know. What are you saying to me?" A small spirit of outraged anger flared and then subsided weakly. "My father would be furious."

"Then we don't let him know, eh?" The smile was there. "Why should we make him angry at me?"

"I – I walk often alone on the beach." The statement was all but inaudible and in it there was submission. "Usually in the afternoons when my father and brother are in the fields. There is no one around but the slaves."

Juan laughed softly, with confidence. "Then, if I sail this way again it

218

will be in the afternoon." He added with a disarming candor, "It is better your father doesn't know Juan Cadiz comes calling."

Of this Caroline was certain. From some secret well she drew a small measure of self-confidence in the face of this insolent assurance. "I think my father would shoot you."

"I am sure of that." Juan shrugged. "I do not like to be shot at." "Then you'd better not come again."

"You don't want me to?"

"I didn't say that." Without realizing it she sounded a tiny note of pleading. "I said, maybe it would be better if you didn't."

Juan glanced down the short length of the dock and saw the slave, Cass, returning with the water gourds dangling from his fingers.

"Just the same," he spoke quickly, "I will take the chance and come again. You will look, sometimes, in the afternoons for my sail?"

"Yes." She turned away and walked from him.

Juan watched her go, his eyes speculative. Then he laughed to himself. She would be waiting. He took the gourds from the slave and returned to his boat, dropping the unneeded water in the bottom and pushing away from the Cameron sloop's side. He hauled the triangular sail. After a moment it filled and he let his craft get underway before heading into the breeze and then taking it on a long, starboard tack. The boat's bows lifted daintily and she heeled a little. He did not glance back toward shore. He was sure of himself. She would be walking on the beach when he came again. Of this he was certain. He would make her wait a little first, though. Let her wonder and watch for Juan Cadiz.

Tom Gurney, coming out of the ketch's cabin where he had been taking a nap, stretched and yawned. His arms remained uplifted in surprise as he saw the red-sailed sloop as it passed some hundred yards away. He knew that sail, that boat. What the hell was someone like Juan Cadiz doing here? He glanced shoreward and saw only the slave on the dock. Maybe Cadiz had only sailed in and out of the harbor from curiosity. He yawned again and scratched at his rumpled hair. It was no business of his.

In her room Caroline lay upon the bed, staring at the ceiling; a strange, tingling excitement possessed her. It took her breath. Never had a man looked at her the way this Juan Cadiz had. It was almost as though he had touched and fondled her and she pressed clenched hands against the hard swell of her breasts. They hurt but with an unfamiliar pain. She had known few boys and no men at all save her father's friends who had come to Cameron Hall. There was something wild and frightening about this one. She wasn't sure why. Once, back in Carolina, she had been driving with Aunt Martha. They had passed a field as a stallion reared upon a mare. She had pretended to turn away quickly but her loins had suddenly been filled with the same exquisite agony she now felt. She thought about Captain Birch, in Nassau. He had been amusing, gay and filled with laughter. But this Juan Cadiz. He was the stallion. She rolled over and pressed her face into the bolster, stretching her legs because they hurt. What if he came again? What if he didn't come? Then she smiled contentedly to herself out of a knowledge beyond her years and experience. He would come and she would be waiting.

ANTOINE DE SAINT-EXUPÉRY

LESS THAN A MONTH before that young American air mail pilot flew alone to France and into history, a businessman on the other side of the Atlantic named Pierre-Georges Latécoère sold his own air mail enterprise to a another Frenchman in Brazil named Marcel Bouilloux-Lafont. Most people today might know the name of Lindbergh much better than they do the names of those Frenchmen, but a great many others would still recognize their company's name: Aéropostale.

Just the year before those events, another young pilot some two years older than the young American had begun adapting his military aviation skills into those of an international mail carrier at Aéropostale. Flying routes among the French Colonies in Africa and South America, Antoine de Saint-Exupéry took pride in the fact that his craft had very few instruments to tell him what to do. "The man who assumes that there is an essential difference between the sloop and the airplane," he would later write, "lacks historical perspective."

Saint-Exupéry's skills in both flying and in management soon took him to outposts throughout the far reaches of the hemisphere; first to the Sahara, then on to Argentina. During an attempt to set a record flight from Paris to Saigon, however, Saint-Ex and his navigator crashed in the African desert after some twenty hours in the air. Both men survived the fall to earth, but their entire provisions consisted only of some grapes, two oranges, and less than a bottle of wine. Seeking an oasis, the two were seeing mirages by day three. They were on the verge of dehydration when a Bedouin discovered them wandering about aimlessly on day four. That experience became the inspiration for both of Saint-Exupéry's best known writings: *Wind, Sand and Stars* and *The Little Prince*.

The first of these, published in 1939, is his memoir illustrating not only his view of the world, but also what he believes it is that makes life worth living. "Human drama does not show itself on the surface of life. It is played out not in the visible world, but in the hearts of men," he proclaims. "Let a man in a garret but burn with enough intensity and he will set fire to the world."

The Little Prince is ostensibly a children's book that's sold more than eighty million copies since 1943; however, it's no more childish than are the fables of Jean de La Fontaine. "It is only with the heart that one can see rightly," says the fox encountered by the Little Prince. "What is essential is invisible to the eye." There's probably very little chance that any child in this world might sense that the fox's words pretty much sum up the essence of life and of living.

As for the ending of Saint-Exupéry's own story, it is not unlike that of a great many others of his era. An older Saint-Ex had returned to military life in World War II, only to disappear in flight and never be seen again.

In 1998, a French fisherman was hauling his nets off the coast of Marseilles, and he found an identity bracelet engraved with "Consuelo," as well "Reynal & Hitchcock." Consuelo was Saint-Exupéry's wife; Reynal & Hitchcock, his publishers. Two years later, divers discovered in the same waters an aircraft bearing the serial number of Saint-Exupéry's plane. Despite the accounts of one former German pilot, the circumstances surrounding the death of Antoine de Saint-Exupéry remain forever unknown.

Additional suggested works by Antoine de Saint-Exupéry:

— *Wind, Sand and Stars* (1939)

— *The Little Prince* (1943)

"THE CRAFT"
a selection from
Wind, Sand and Stars/Chapter V

I REMEMBER, FOR MY PART, another of those hours in which a pilot finds suddenly that he has slipped beyond the confines of this world. All that night the radio messages sent from the ports in the Sahara concerning our position had been inaccurate, and my radio operator, Neri, and I had been drawn out of our course. Suddenly, seeing, the gleam of water at the bottom of a crevasse of fog, I tacked sharply in the direction of the coast; but it was by then impossible for us to say how long we had been flying towards the high seas. Nor were we certain of making the coast, for our fuel was probably low. And even so, once we had reached it we would still have to make port – after the moon had set.

We had no means of angular orientation, were already deafened, and were bit by bit growing blind. The moon like a pallid ember began to go out in the banks of fog. Overhead the sky was filling with clouds, and we flew thenceforth between cloud and fog in a world voided of all substance and all light. The ports that signaled us had given up trying to tell us where we were. "No bearings, no bearings," was all their message, for our voice reached them from everywhere and nowhere. With sinking hearts Neri and I leaned out, he on his side and I on mine, to see if anything, anything at all, was distinguishable in this void. Already our tired eyes were seeing things – errant signs, delusive flashes, phantoms.

And suddenly, when already we were in despair, low on the horizon a brilliant point was unveiled on our port bow. A wave of joy went through me. Neri leaned forward, and I could hear him singing. It could not but be the beacon of an airport, for after dark the whole Sahara goes black and forms a great dead expanse. That light twinkled for a space – and then went out! We had been steering for a star which was visible for a few minutes only, just before setting on the horizon between the layer of fog and the clouds.

Then other stars took up the game, and with a sort of dogged hope we set our course for each of them in turn. Each time that a light lingered a while, we performed the same crucial experiment. Neri would send his message to the airport at Cisneros: "Beacon in view. Put out your light and flash three times." And Cisneros would put out its beacon and flash three times while the hard light at which we gazed would not, incorruptible star, so much as wink. And despite our dwindling fuel we continued to nibble at the golden bait which each time seemed more surely the true light of a beacon, was each time a promise of a landing and of life – and we had each time to change our star.

And with that we knew ourselves to be lost in interplanetary space among a thousand inaccessible planets, we who sought only the one veritable planet, our own, that planet on which alone we should find our familiar countryside, the houses of our friends, our treasures.

On which alone we should find . . . Let me draw the picture that took shape before my eyes. It will seem to you childish; but even in the midst of danger a man retains his human concerns. I was thirsty and I was hungry. If we did find Cisneros we should re-fuel and carry on to Casablanca, and there we should come down in the cool of daybreak, free to idle the hours away. Neri and I would go into town. We would go to a little pub already open despite the early hour. Safe and sound, Neri and I would sit down at table and laugh at the night of danger as we ate our warm rolls and drank our bowls of coffee and hot milk. We would receive this matutinal gift at the hands of life. Even as an old peasant woman recognizes her God in a painted image, in a childish medal, in a chaplet, so life would speak to us in its humblest language in order that we understand. The joy of living, I say, was summed up for me in the remembered sensation of that first burning and aromatic swallow, that mixture of milk and coffee and bread by which men hold communion with tranquil pastures, exotic plantations, and golden harvests, communion with the earth. Amidst all these stars there was but one that could make itself significant for us by composing this aromatic bowl that was its daily gift at dawn. And from that earth of men, that earth docile to the reaping of grain and the harvesting of the grape, bearing its rivers asleep in their fields, its villages dinging to their hillsides, our ship was separated by astronomical distances. All the treasures of the world were summed up in a grain of dust now blown far out of our path by the very destiny itself of dust and of the orbs of night.

And Neri still prayed to the stars.

PABLO NERUDA

MANUSCRIPT GROUP 105 in the Special Collections of the University of Florida's Smathers Libraries consists of ten boxes of stuff donated by Jimmy.

That includes his contract for a 1975 concert in Portland, Oregon at the Euphoria Tavern and a 1987 first draft of *Margaritaville, The Movie 3*, along with several drafts and galleys of *A Pirate Looks at Fifty*, as well as *Where is Joe Merchant?* There, you will find a revision of a *Joe Merchant* chapter entitled "Pray for Me, Pablo Neruda."

That chapter title never made it into print, but it did become "Shelter from the Storm" about Blanton Meyercord's escaping by Jet Ski to South America.

"Blanton started his engine and saluted the owl," writes Jimmy. "The bird spread its small winds and lifted off the poling platform. 'Pray for me, Pablo Neruda,' Blanton said and headed southeast into the large ocean."

Though that original reference to the Chilean writer had become an off-handed remark at the end of a chapter, it sort of foreshadowed Jimmy's admiration for the poet whose name appears on the list of thirteen favorite books.

Born in a logging town of the Chilean frontier in 1904, the boy named Ricardo Neftalí Reyes Basoalto was raised by his hot-tempered father, because his mother had died when her child was barely two months old. Just above the Patagonia in the early twentieth century, a muse must have discovered the impoverished youngster and set him to writing poetry. "Poetry is like bread," he would one day write. "It should be shared by all, by scholars and peasants, by all our vast, incredible, extraordinary family of humanity." That sentiment, however, remained away in the near future, and his father was not at all pleased by his son's writing. When young Ricardo was only fourteen, some of his first love poems were published, only to be discovered and set ablaze by his father. He wanted his son to have a more practical job than that of poet.

Still, the boy's passions were not at all extinguished by his father's harsh reaction, and so he chose to write from that time on under the *nom de plume* "Pablo Neruda." The "Pablo" came from his favorite French poet Paul Verlaine; "Neruda," from the Czech poet, Jan Neruda. At the age of nineteen, the young man who called himself "Neruda" published his most famous volume *Veinte Poemas de Amor y una Cancion Desesperada*. In time, those *Twenty Love Poems and a Song of Desperation* would sell millions of copies and establish him as the one person whom García Márquez would call the "greatest poet of the twentieth century – in any language."

Over the years, Neruda traveled the world, far and wide, and eventually found his way to the shore of his native Chile, where he became a lover of the sea, as well as of all things maritime. In the village of Isla Negra, Neruda built a low-ceilinged home with narrow passages and creaking wooden floors that lent it the semblance of a ship. There he found inspiration for countless poems, and there he was buried alongside his wife in 1973, two years after he had been awarded the Nobel Prize for Literature.

Additional suggested works by Pablo Neruda:

— *Twenty Love Poems and a Song of Despair* (1924)

— *On the Blue Shore of Silence: Poems of the Sea* (2004)

— *The Poetry of Pablo Neruda* (2003)

FIRST TRAVELINGS

a selection from
The Poetry of Pablo Neruda
Memorial de Isla Negra (1962-1964)

WHEN I FIRST went to sea, I was inexhaustible.
I was younger than the whole world.
And on the seacoast there rose to receive me
the endless tang of the universe.

I had no sense that the world existed.

My faith lay in a buried tower.

I had found so many things in so little,
in my own twilit discoveries,
in the sighs of love, in roots,
that I was the displaced one, the wanderer,
the poor proprietor of my own skeleton.

And I understood then that I was naked,
that I had to dress myself.
I had never thought seriously about shoes.
I didn't speak any languages.
The only book I could read was the book of myself.
The only life I knew was my secret life.
And I understood that I couldn't
summon myself because I wouldn't respond.
I had used up that chance.
Nevermore, nevermore, croaked the raven.

I had to fall back on things like clouds,
on all the hats of the world,
rivers, waiting rooms, doors,
and names, so many names, that simply learning them
would have taken my whole sacred life.

The world was full of women,
jammed like a shop window,
and given all the hair I learned,
the breasts, the wonderful thighs,
I learned that Venus was no mere legend.
She was sure and firm, with two enduring arms,
and her hard mother-of-pearl
weathered my lusty genital ambition.

Everything was new to me. This whole planet
was dying of sheer old age,
but everything was opening for me to experience,
to glimpse that lightning flash.

And with my little pony eyes
I saw that bitter curtain going up,
going up with its fixed and worldly smile,
the curtain opening on a wizened Europe.

PAT CONROY

from
"Prince of Tides"
HOT WATER
1988

MORE THAN a hundred so-called Sea Islands stretch from South Carolina's Santee River down the eastern seaboard to Florida's St. Johns. In the waters just offshore, between Hilton Head and the mouth of the Savannah, sits an isolated outcrop of land called Daufuskie Island, whose recorded history pre-dates America's Revolutionary War and whose indigenous culture once added a certain richness to that of Carolina's low country. Daufuskie's historically scant population dwindled down even further in the 1960s to a simple few who were just too poor to relocate. Some were direct descendants of the Daufuskie Indians, but a great many others were Gullah, direct descendents of those Africans who had been brought to work in the cotton fields.

Onto this island and into this setting in the early 1970s stepped Pat Conroy, who had arrived to teach Daufuskie's handful of children in their one-room schoolhouse. That experience led Conroy to write his first book, a memoir called *The Water is Wide*, which then became the motion picture *Conrack* with Jon Voight. Daufuskie, in short, had set Pat Conroy on course to write a bookshelf of powerful stories that shared an epic length with a Carolina background. When a reader suggested sometime in the 1990s that Conroy must be a Parrothead, because Jimmy Buffett had written "a song about *Beach Music*," the author explained that it had started with a phone call from Jimmy.

"He said, 'Hi, I'm Jimmy Buffett.' I said: 'Hi, I'm Paul McCartney.' He said: 'May I write a song called "Prince of Tides?"' I said: 'You do, and I will kiss your behind.' He said: 'How much will I have to pay you?' I said: 'I will kiss your behind – I told you.' So he wrote the ["Prince of Tides"] – and at the end he sings, 'Beach music, beach music . . . [just plays on].' And that gave me the title [for my next book]."

When Jimmy's *Hot Water* album was later released in 1988, the liner notes carried this simple comment: "Pat Conroy, Doc Pomus and the people of Daufuskie Island have already said it all. I am thankful for such inspiration."

That one line goes the distance in explaining the richness of this song, as well as the heritage that it reflects. What neither the liner notes, nor the printed lyrics reveal, however, is Jimmy's recitation of Conroy's words that open and close the song. In the environmentalist spirit of Hunter Thompson's "Freak Power in the Rockies" and then Carl Hiaasen's *Tourist Season*, Jimmy's "Prince of Tides" stands out as his plaintiff lament against those who've "put a price on the sunset."

And, as Conroy pointed out, Jimmy does indeed sing that classic opening verse by Doc Pomus from "Save the Last Dance for Me," which forever remains a beach music favorite among those who continue to dance the shag long into the Carolina nights.

Like most of Conroy's works, *The Prince of Tides* is several hundred pages long, even after many hundreds of words had been chopped out by his editors. Still, you will fall in love with the pages here, and you will find yourself seeking out all the other Conroy works.

Additional suggested works by Pat Conroy:

— *The Water is Wide* (1972)

— *The Great Santini* (1976)

— *Beach Music* (1995)

— *South of Broad* (2009)

EPILOGUE

a selection from

The Prince of Tides

SAVANNAH HAD ARRIVED FROM NEW YORK when we drove up into the back yard on Sullivan Island. My children poured out of the house and shyly approached their grandfather.

"Be careful, girls," I said. "He hits."

"No, I don't, kids. Come here and kiss your grandpa," he said in a beaten, tired voice, and I was sorry I said what I did.

Sallie came to the door, slim and dark-haired, tanned and serious. She ran up to my father, threw her arms around him, and tears were streaming down her face as he turned her round and round and buried his face against her shoulder.

"Welcome home, Dad," she said.

Then Savannah came out of the house. And there was something I cannot explain that I felt as they ran to each other and where I felt it was in the deepest part of me, an untouched place that trembled with something instinctual and rooted in the provenance of the species — unnamable, yet I knew it could be named if it could be felt. It was not Savannah's tears or my father's tears that caused this resonance, this fierce interior music of blood and wildness and identity. It was the beauty and fear of kinship, the ineffable ties of family, that sounded a blazing terror and an awestruck love inside of me. There was my father, the source of all these lives, the source of all these tears, crying now, crying hard and without shame. The tears were water, salt water, and I could see the ocean behind him, could smell it, could taste my own tears, the sea and hurt within me leaking out into the sunlight and my children crying to see me cry. The story of my family was the story of salt water, of boats and shrimp, of tears and storm.

And my twin, my beautiful, damaged sister, her scarred wrists around my father's neck, her eyes dimmed by a lifetime of visions and laying hold to a language strong enough to make these visions clear, to turn nightmare and horror into the astonishing lyrics that burned into the consciousness of her time, to turn sorrow into a life-giving beauty. And my wife, who had married into this family and who had to grow tolerant of a large cast of family demons, who did it because she loved me, even though I was incapable of responding to love from a woman, that I could never make her feel loved or needed or wanted even though that's what I wanted to give her more than anything else in the world. And my children, three daughters, whom I could love with some perfect love that seemed unrelated to me, because I wanted so badly to make them unlike me in any way, because I wanted to make sure they would never have a childhood like mine, that they would never be struck by me, that they would never fear the approach of their father. With them, I tried to re-create my own childhood as I dreamed it should have been. With them, I tried to change the world.

In the late afternoon we loaded the station wagon with a beer cooler and a picnic basket and drove toward Charleston. We turned off at the shrimp dock at Shem Creek and I parked the car in sight of the only shrimp boat still at the docks.

"You know how to work one of those things?" I asked my father, pointing toward the shrimp boat.

"Naw," he said, "but I bet I could learn fast."

"It's registered under the name of Captain Henry Wingo," I said. "It's a homecoming gift from Mom."

"I can't accept that," he said.

"You wrote that you wanted to get back on the river," I said. "Mom wanted to make a gesture. I think it's a nice one."

"It's a fine boat," my father said. "They catching many shrimp this season?"

"The good ones are," I said. "It's a month before I have to start football practice, Dad. I'll work as your striker until you can hire one."

"I'll pay you six cents on the pound," he said.

"The hell you will, you cheap son of a bitch," I said. "You'll pay me ten cents on the pound. The price of labor has gone up."

He smiled and said, "Tell your mother thanks."

"She wants to see you," I said.

"I don't know about that," he said.

"You've got all the time in the world," I said. "Now, I want you to take us up river."

We entered the main channel of Charleston Harbor an hour before

232

sunset and the bells of St. Michael's Church rang clearly through the shimmering light and the humid perfumed air of the old city. My father steered the shrimp boat beneath the enormous iron vertebrae of the two Cooper River bridges and we passed a white freighter loaded with cargo from the docks of North Charleston moving out to sea. All of us waved and the invisible captain sounded his horn in greeting. We made a starboard turn into the Wando River and the tide was so high that my father did not have to refer to the navigational charts a single time. We went for a mile until we neared a vast marsh in the round curve of the river and there was not a house in sight.

"It's about time, Tom," Sallie said, coming into the wheel house.

"Time for what?" my father asked.

"A homecoming surprise for you and Savannah," Sallie said, checking her watch.

"Tell us, Mama," my children said.

"No," she answered, "then it won't be a surprise."

We swam in the warm opaque waters, diving in deep from the shrimp boat's bow. After swimming, we ate dinner from the picnic basket and toasted my father's homecoming with champagne. Savannah approached my father and I watched them as they walked to the front of the boat holding hands.

I tried to think of something to say, a summing up, but I could think of nothing. I had taught myself to listen to the black sounds of the heart and learned some things that would serve me well. I had come to this moment with my family safely around me and I prayed that they would always be safe and that I would be contented with what I had. I am southern made and southern broken, Lord, but I beseech you to let me keep what I have. Lord, I am a teacher and a coach. That is all and it is enough. But the black sounds, the black sounds, Lord. When they toll within me, I am seized with a capacity for homage and wonder. I hear them and want to put my dreams to music. When they come I can feel an angel burning in my eye like a rose, and canticles of the most meticulous praise rise out of the clear submarine depths of secret ambient ecstasy.

The white porpoise comes to me at night, singing in the river of time, with a thousand dolphins in radiant attendance, bringing charismatic greetings from the Prince of Tides, calling out our name: Wingo, Wingo, Wingo. It is enough, Lord. It is enough.

"It's time, Tom," Sallie said, lifting up to kiss me on the lips.

The whole family gathered on the bow of the boat to watch day come to an end.

The sun, red and enormous, began to sink into the western sky and simultaneously the moon began to rise on the other side of the river with its own glorious shade of red, coming up out of the trees like a russet firebird. The sun and the moon seemed to acknowledge each other and they moved in both apposition and concordance in a breathtaking dance of light across the oaks and palms.

My father watched it and I thought he would cry again. He had returned to the sea from prison and his heart was a low country heart. The children were screaming, pointing to the sun, then turning to look at the rising moon, calling to the sun, then to the moon.

My father said, "It'll be good shrimping tomorrow."

Savannah came up beside me and put her arm around my waist. We walked to the back of the boat.

"A terrific surprise, Tom," she said.

"I thought you'd like it," I answered.

"Susan sends her love," Savannah said. "She's dating a lawyer now."

"She wrote me about it," I said. "You're looking good, Savannah."

"I'm going to make it, Tom," she said.

Then, looking at the sun and the moon again, she added, "Wholeness, Tom. It all comes back. It's all a circle."

She turned around, and facing the moon, which was higher now and silvering, she lifted herself up on her toes, raised her arms into the air, and cried out in a brittle yet defiant voice, "Oh, Mama, do it again!"

With those words of Savannah's, that should be the end of it, but it is not.

⌒

M. SCOTT PECK

from
"A Baker's Dozen (Minus One)"
A Pirate Looks at Fifty
1998

GIVEN JIMMY'S personal fascination with myths, most readers will understand just why he's included M. Scott Peck's most celebrated work on his list of favorite books.

"While I generally find that great myths are great precisely because they represent and embody great universal truths," writes Dr. Peck in the section before this selected passage, "the myth of romantic love is a dreadful lie." That mythical sort of love is something he claims is perpetuated from fairy tales to wedding days . . . And often, divorce.

On the other hand, what Peck calls "true love" can only come about when both parties are able to extend the boundaries of their egos and provide a spiritual nurturing of one another. Jimmy explains his own revelation in *A Pirate Looks at Fifty*.

"In the hills and valleys of my life journey, one of the deep valleys I trudged for quite a while was the valley of marriage. I come from a moderately dysfunctional background, topped off with twelve years of parochial education . . . Now, that is not the kind of gear you want to stuff into your emotional backpack as you venture into marriage, but it was the only gear I had. It's taken a long time to figure out, first of all, that I had the wrong gear, and then an equally long time to figure out what kind of gear I needed.

"Jane and I have had a wild and wonderful roller-coaster ride of a relationship, from the day I met her in the Chart Room in Key West through living together, breaking up once or twice, then getting married and having a child," says Jimmy. "We found ourselves speeding in and out of control on a train that was about to jump the tracks. She had seen the light way before me and was working on her problems long before me and was working on her problems long before I had the good sense to come in from the cold.

"I had gone with her, and without her, to different therapists, which for a Southern man is like having a root canal and an IRS audit in the same afternoon. I treated therapy like a performance, and I am good for that."

Meanwhile, he also found some solace and support in Peck's best-seller *The Road Less Traveled: A New Psychology of Love, Traditional Values and Spiritual Growth.*

As for that book itself, *The Road Less Traveled* was by no means an overnight success. When it was first introduced in 1978, the publisher printed a modest 5,000 copies in hardcover, and there's nothing unusual in that. But Peck hit the lecture circuit and promoted his work, much as Twain might have done or even Jimmy in releasing a new album. By 1980, that initial printing was sold out, and the title went into paperback; the doctor continued his crusade. Four years later, *The Road Less Traveled* finally was generating enough excitement to join the ranks of best-sellers. In the two decades since the publication of that first book, some sixteen others have followed; however, none has managed to attain the popularity of *The Road Less Traveled.*

One of only three nonfiction books on that hallowed list of thirteen, *The Road Less Traveled* reads well alongside *Gift from the Sea.*

Additional suggested works by M. Scott Peck:

— *The Road Less Traveled* (1978)

— *People of the Lie: The Hope for Healing Human Evil* (1983)

— *Further Along the Road Less Traveled* (1987)

The Risk of Independence

a selection from

The Road Less Traveled / Section II: Love

THE PROCESS OF GROWING UP usually occurs very gradually, with multiple little leaps into the unknown, such as when an eight-year-old boy first takes the risk of riding his bike down to the country store all by himself or a fifteen-year-old goes out on his or her first date. If you doubt that these represent real risks, then you cannot remember the anxiety involved. If you observe even the healthiest of children you will see not only an eagerness to risk new and adult activities but also, side by side, a reluctance, a shrinking back, a clinging to the safe and familiar, a holding onto dependency and childhood. Moreover, on more or less subtle levels, you can find this same ambivalence in an adult, including yourself, with the elderly particularly tending to cling to the old, known and familiar. Almost daily at the age of forty I am presented with subtle opportunities to risk doing things differently, opportunities to grow. I am still growing up, and not as fast as I might. Among all the little leaps we might take, there are also some enormous ones, as when by leaving school I was also forsaking a whole pattern of life and values according to which I had been raised. Many never take any of these potential enormous leaps, and consequently many do not ever really grow up at all. Despite their outward appearances they remain psychologically still very much the children of their parents, living by hand-me-down values, motivated primarily by their parents' approval and disapproval (even when their parents are long dead and buried), never having dared to truly take their destiny into their own hands.

While such great leaps are most commonly made during adolescence, they can be made at any age. A thirty-five-year-old mother of three, married to a controlling, stultifying, inflexible, chauvinistic husband, gradually and painfully comes to realize that her dependency on him and their marriage is a living death. He blocks all her attempts to change the nature of their relationship. With incredible bravery she divorces him, sustaining the burden of his recriminations and the criticism of neighbors, and risks an unknown future alone with her children, but free for the first time in her life to be her own person. Depressed following a heart attack, a fifty-two-year-old businessman looks back on a life of frantic ambition to constantly make more money and rise ever higher in the corporate hierarchy and finds it meaningless. After long reflection he realizes that he has been driven by a need for approval from a domineering, constantly critical mother; he has almost worked himself to death so as to be finally successful in her eyes. Risking and transcending her disapproval for the first time in his life, as well as braving the ire of his high-living wife and children, who are reluctant to give up their expensive life style, he moves to the country and opens up a little shop where he restores antique furniture. Such major changes, such leaps into independence and self-determination, are enormously painful at any age and require supreme courage, yet they are not infrequent results of psychotherapy. Indeed, because of the enormity of the risks involved, they often require psychotherapy for their accomplishment, not because therapy diminishes the risk but because it supports and teaches courage.

But what has this business of growing up to do with love, apart from the fact that the extension of the self involved in loving is an enlargement of the self into new dimensions? First of all, the examples of the changes described and all other such major changes are acts of self-love. It is precisely because I valued myself that I was unwilling to remain miserable in a school and whole social environment that did not fit my needs. It is because the housewife had regard for herself that she refused to tolerate any longer a marriage that so totally limited her freedom and repressed her personality. It is because the businessman cared for himself that he was no longer willing to nearly kill himself in order to meet the expectations of his mother. Second, not only does love for oneself provide the motive for such major changes; it also is the basis for the courage to risk them. It is only because my parents had clearly loved and valued me as a young child that I felt sufficiently secure in myself to defy their expectations and radically depart from the pattern they had laid out for me. Although I felt inadequate and worthless and possibly crazy in doing what I did, I was able to tolerate these feelings only because at the same time, on an even deeper level, I sensed myself to be a good person no matter how different I might be. In daring to be different, even if it meant to be crazy, I was responding to earlier loving messages from my parents, hundreds of them, which said, "You are a beautiful and beloved individual. It is good to be you. We will love you no matter what you do, as long as you are you." Without that security of my parents' love reflected in my own self-love, I would have chosen the known instead of the unknown and continued to follow my parents' preferred pattern at the extreme cost of my self's basic uniqueness. Finally, it is only when one has taken the leap into the unknown of total selfhood, psychological independence and unique individuality that one is free to proceed along still higher paths of spiritual growth and free to manifest love in its greatest dimensions. As long as one marries, enters a career or has children to satisfy one's parents or the expectations of anyone else, including society as a whole, the commitment by its very nature will be a shallow one. As long as one loves one's children primarily because one is expected to behave in a loving manner toward them, then the parent will be insensitive to the more subtle needs of the children and unable to express love in the more subtle, yet often most important ways. The highest forms of love are inevitably totally free choices and not acts of conformity.

GABRIEL GARCÍA MÁRQUEZ

from
"Nobody Speaks to the Captain No More"
FLORIDAYS
1986

"A Baker's Dozen (Minus One)"
A Pirate Looks at Fifty
1998

LINER NOTES for "Nobody Speaks to the Captain No More" could not be any clearer. Just above the lyrics, Jimmy lists three names: Gabriel García Márquez, Allie Fox, and Phil Clark.

The last one there belongs to the legendary Key West bartender at the Chart Room, about whom Jimmy had written "A Pirate Looks at Forty." The middle name on the list is the name of the main character in Paul Theroux's 1982 novel, *The Mosquito Coast*. And the first of those three is the Colombian writer awarded the Nobel Prize in '82 for what the foundation described as "novels and short stories, in which the fantastic and the realistic are combined in a richly composed world of imagination, reflecting a continent's life and conflicts." At the time, García Márquez had already written his *One Hundred Years of Solitude*, but had yet to complete *Love in the Time of Cholera*.

The novella which had captured

Jimmy's imagination, though, is "No One Writes to the Colonel," which was published eventually in a single volume with another novella called "Big Mama's Funeral." The colonel in this story is an impoverished veteran of the so-called "Thousand Days War" that began in 1899 to establish Colombia's independence from Spain; however, his story unfolds more than a half century later as martial law and censorship prevail during the chaotic years of power struggle that continued throughout the new nation. This period is known as "La Violencia."

"Big Mama's Funeral," on the other hand, deals with the death of a political boss known affectionately as "Big Mama." Though the focus of this novella is quite different from that of "The Colonel," their social settings and literary styles remain very much the same.

As for any link to *The Mosquito Coast,* Theroux's novel dealt with an American who decided to transplant his family to a Central American jungle in hopes of finding a more simple life than that offered in the land of the free. Allie Fox, the disenchanted ex-patriate, was portrayed by none other than Harrison Ford, who had provided the cracking sounds of his Indiana Jones whip in the background of "Desperation Samba" on Jimmy's previous album, *Last Mango in Paris.* Ford was filming *The Mosquito Coast* in 1986 just as Jimmy was bringing together *Floridays,* which included "Nobody Speaks to the Captain No More." So, while there appears to be some geographical and literary reasons for bringing these three names together, there is also the simple matter of friendship.

All of that stuff aside, "No One Writes to the Colonel" is too long to be included in this volume, and it is also impossible to be whittled down into any sort of excerpt. So, a selection from "Big Mama's Funeral" is presented here instead. Because this novella consists of a collection of short vignettes, "One of These Days" still provides a fine example of Gabo's early writing, especially his solitary sense of everyday life during "La Violencia." While it has nothing to do with the colonel, it does illustrate the style of the man whom Colombians proudly call "Nuestro Nobel."

Additional suggested works by Gabriel García Márquez:

— *"No One Writes to the Colonel No More" & Other Stories* (1961)

— *One Hundred Years of Solitude* (1967)

— *Love in the Time of Cholera* (1985)

— *News of a Kidnapping* (1996)

— *Living to Tell the Tale* (2003)

"ONE OF THESE DAYS"

a selection from
Big Mama's Funeral

MONDAY DAWNED warm and rainless. Aurelio Escovar, a dentist without a degree, and a very early riser, opened his office at six. He took some false teeth, still mounted in their plaster mold, out of the glass case and put on the table a fistful of instruments which he arranged in size order, as if they were on display. He wore a collarless striped shirt, closed at the neck with a golden stud, and pants held up by suspenders. He was erect and skinny, with a look that rarely corresponded to the situation, the way deaf people have of looking.

When he had things arranged on the table, he pulled the drill toward the dental chair and sat down to polish the false teeth. He seemed not to be thinking about what he was doing, but worked steadily, pumping the drill with his feet, even when he didn't need it.

After eight he stopped for a while to look at the sky through the window, and he saw two pensive buzzards who were drying themselves in the sun on the ridgepole of the house next door. He went on working with the idea that before lunch it would rain again. The shrill voice of his eleven-year-old son interrupted his concentration.

"Papá."

"What?"

"The Mayor wants to know if you'll pull his tooth."

"Tell him I'm not here."

He was polishing a gold tooth. He held it at arm's length, and examined it with his eyes half closed. His son shouted again from the little waiting room.

"He says you are, too, because he can hear you."

The dentist kept examining the tooth. Only when he had put it on the table with the finished work did he say:

242

"So much the better."

He operated the drill again. He took several pieces of a bridge out of a cardboard box where he kept the things he still had to do and began to polish the gold.

"Papá."

"What?"

He still hadn't changed his expression.

"He says if you don't take out his tooth, he'll shoot you."

Without hurrying, with an extremely tranquil movement, he stopped pedaling the drill, pushed it away from the chair, and pulled the lower drawer of the table all the way out. There was a revolver. "O.K.," he said. "Tell him to come and shoot me."

He rolled the chair over opposite the door, his hand resting on the edge of the drawer. The Mayor appeared at the door. He had shaved the left side of his face, but the other side, swollen and in pain, had a five-day-old beard. The dentist saw many nights of desperation in his dull eyes. He closed the drawer with his fingertips and said softly:

"Sit down."

"Good morning," said the Mayor.

"Morning," said the dentist.

While the instruments were boiling, the Mayor leaned his skull on the headrest of the chair and felt better. His breath was icy. It was a poor office: an old wooden chair, the pedal drill, a glass case with ceramic bottles. Opposite the chair was a window with a shoulder-high cloth curtain. When he felt the dentist approach, the Mayor braced his heels and opened his mouth.

Aurelio Escovar turned his head toward the light. After inspecting the infected tooth, he closed the Mayor's jaw with a cautious pressure of his fingers.

"It has to be without anesthesia," he said.

"Why?"

"Because you have an abscess."

The Mayor looked him in the eye. "All right," he said, and tried to smile. The dentist did not return the smile. He brought the basin of sterilized instruments to the worktable and took them out of the water with a pair of cold tweezers, still without hurrying. Then he pushed the spittoon with the tip of his shoe, and went to wash his hands in the washbasin. He did all this without looking at the Mayor. But the Mayor didn't take his eyes off him.

It was a lower wisdom tooth. The dentist spread his feet and grasped the tooth with the hot forceps. The Mayor seized the arms of the chair, braced his feet with all his strength, and felt an icy void in his kidneys, but didn't make a sound. The dentist moved only his wrist. Without rancor, rather with a bitter tenderness, he said:

"Now you'll pay for our twenty dead men."

The Mayor felt the crunch of bones in his jaw, and his eyes filled with tears. But he didn't breathe until he felt the tooth come out. Then he saw it through his tears. It seemed so foreign to his pain that he failed to understand his torture of the five previous nights.

Bent over the spittoon, sweating, panting, he unbuttoned his tunic and reached for the handkerchief in his pants pocket. The dentist gave him a clean cloth.

"Dry your tears," he said.

The Mayor did. He was trembling. While the dentist washed his hands, he saw the crumbling ceiling and a dusty spider web with spider's eggs and dead insects. The dentist returned, drying his hands. "Go to bed," he said, "and gargle with salt water." The Mayor stood up, said goodbye with a casual military salute, and walked toward the door, stretching his legs, without buttoning up his tunic.

"Send the bill," he said.

"To you or the town?"

The Mayor didn't look at him. He closed the door and said through the screen:

"It's the same damn thing."

ALEXANDER VON HUMBOLDT

from
"The Patron Saint of Lightning"
"Leap, and the Net Will Appear"
A Salty Piece of Land
2004

THE ONLY TWO WORKS of art in the collection of Tully Mars were a painting of *The Patron Saint of Lightning*, as well as a black-and-white engraving of Frederic Edwin Church's *Heart of the Andes*.

The painting was something that Tully had picked up in the Frontier Days flea market just outside Cheyenne; the engraving was a legacy from his would-be great-grandmother. Her name was Sarah Sawyer Mars, but she was known with affection as Grandma Ghost.

As Tully explains, Church was a nineteenth-century American artist on a scale of celebrity alongside the likes of Mark Twain. People stood for hours in line just for the opportunity to pay the price of admission required to stare at his work. One of his most renowned works in oil was this *Heart of the Andes* piece that measured five feet by three feet and remains on display in New York's Metropolitan Museum of Art. At its unveiling, though, the painting hung in Church's Greenwich Village Gallery, where it captivated the imagination of Sarah Sawyer Mars, enticed her to purchase this engraving, then caused her to abandon Tully's great-grandfather in order to pursue her artistic dreams in South America. The letter she left behind cited a passage from this selection by von Humboldt.

Now, if that Humboldt name rings even the slightest bell of recognition, it might be due to that current in the South Pacific that bears his very name. Running north by northwest along the South American coastline from Chile to Peru, the Humboldt Current is the flow upon which Thor Heyerdahl rode his raft *Kon-Tiki* just to prove his theory that the inhabitants of the South Pacific islands could have migrated there from South America. The current, however, was never the subject of von Humboldt's writings.

Born and educated in Germany, von Humboldt went on to become a noted naturalist, cartographer, artist, and sociologist whose travels throughout Europe and South America earned him the reputation as "the last universal scholar in the field of natural sciences." In fact, Charles Darwin proclaimed him "the greatest scientific traveler who ever lived."

Through his travels, observations, and studies, von Humboldt did his best to make some sense of it all and to present a greater semblance of the natural world through his artistic renderings of Europe's nature, much in the way that James Audubon had approached his study of the birds of North America. Once von Humboldt was done with Europe, he turned his attention to the South American continent, and then on to Asia. The product of this lifetime of travel and observation began to emerge in the 1840s with the first two of five volumes entitled *Cosmos: A Sketch of a Physical Description of the Universe*. The entire work would take him years more to complete, and the last volume was published after his death.

Frederic Edwin Church would have been about twenty years old when *Cosmos* was first published in von Humboldt's native tongue. Once it was translated in English, though, Church not only devoured every word, but also accepted von Humboldt's underlying challenge that also spoke to Sarah Sawyer Mars. Tully says that Church begged the naturalist to take him along to South America; however, that never really happened at all. By the time the American artist embarked upon his own travels, the old German was in his early eighties, not roaming very far from home.

Nonetheless, it was *Cosmos* that moved Frederic Edwin Church, and it was the fruits of Church's observations that inspired Grandma Ghost to dream and to pursue that dream. And to send Tully Mars on his own adventure.

CHARACTERISTIC REPRESENTATION
OF TROPIC SCENERY

A selection from
Cosmos/Chapter II

THE DELINEATION OF NATURAL OBJECTS included in the branch of art now under consideration could not have grown in diversity and exactness until the geographical field of view became extended, until the means of traveling in foreign countries facilitated, and until the appreciation of the beauty and configuration of vegetable forms, and their arrangement in groups of natural families, excited. The discoveries of Columbus, de Gama, and Cabral; the trade in spices and drugs; and the establishment of botanical gardens certainly acquainted artists with many remarkable forms of tropical vegetation.

It is not until the middle of the seventeenth century, however, that we meet with landscapes which impressed the artist's mind by actual observation. The earliest attempt at such a mode of representation belongs to the Flemish painter Franz Post, who made studies from nature at Cape St. Augustine, in the Bay of All Saints, on the shores of the River St. Francisco, and at the lower course of the Amazon. These studies he partly executed as paintings belong the remarkably large oil pictures preserved in Denmark. In these compositions, palms, papaws, bananas, and heliconias are characteristically delineated, along with brightly-plumaged birds, small quadrupeds, and the appearance of the natives.

These examples of natural scenery were not followed by many artists of merit before Cook's second voyage of circumnavigation. What Hodges did for the western islands of the Pacific has been since done on a far grander scale for the tropical vegetation of America and many other parts of the earth by Heinrich von Kittlitz on his voyage of circumnavigation.

Only those who have a keen appreciation of the natural beauty that is displayed in mountains, rivers, and forest glades; who have traveled over the torrid zone; and who have seen the luxuriance of vegetation along the seacoasts, upon the mountains, and within the forests can feel what an inexhaustible treasure remains unopened for the landscape painter between the tropics in both continents or in the South Seas.

These noble regions have hitherto been visited mostly by travelers whose lack of artistical education and whose scientific pursuits afforded few opportunities of their perfecting themselves in landscape painting. Only very few among them have been susceptible of seizing on the total impression of the tropical zone, in addition to the botanical interest excited by the individual forms of flowers and leaves.

It has frequently happened that the artists appointed to accompany expeditions fitted out at the national expense have been chosen without due consideration and have been found less prepared than such appointments required. Besides that, voyages of circumnavigation seldom allow of artists to visit any extensive tracts of forest land, the upper courses of large rivers, or the summits of inland chains of mountains.

Colored sketches taken directly from nature are the only means by which the returning artist may reproduce the character of distant regions in more elaborately finished pictures; and this object will be the more fully attained where the painter has, at the same time, drawn or painted directly from nature a large number of separate studies of the foliage of trees; of leafy, flowering, or fruit-bearing stems; of prostrate trunks, overgrown with Pothos and Orchidese; of rocks and of portions of the shore, and the soil of the forest. The possession of such correctly-drawn and well-proportioned sketches will enable the artist to dispense with all the deceptive aid of hot-house forms and so-called botanical delineations.

A great event in the history of the world, such as the emancipation of Spanish and Portuguese America from the dominion of European rule, or the increased cultivation of India, New Holland, the Sandwich Islands, and the southern colonies of Africa, will incontestably impart to meteorology and the descriptive natural sciences, as well as to landscape painting, a new impetus and a high tone of feeling, which probably could not have been attained independently of these local relations. In South America, populous cities lie at an elevation of nearly 14,000 feet above the level of the sea. From these heights the eye ranges over all the climatic gradations of vegetable forms. What may we not, therefore, expect from a picturesque study of nature, if, after the settlement of social discord and the establishment of free institutions, a feeling of art shall at length be awakened in those elevated regions?

GsJ

JOHN LLOYD STEPHENS

from
"The Patron Saint of Lightning"
"Leap, and the Net Will Appear"
A Salty Piece of Land
2004

WITHIN ALL those writers on Jimmy's shelf of favorites there lies a common sense of restlessness, and it's a trait that's traceable back to Jimmy's very earliest readings. The archaeologist John Lloyd Stephens firmly belongs among those folks. Perhaps the only difference for Stephens, though, lies in the fact that he first set out on his travels not to placate some inner itch to move along, but rather to remedy his failing health.

A native of New Jersey, Stephens was born in 1805, studied law at Columbia University, then became a practicing attorney in New York City. Before he had turned thirty, though, the east coast climate was not doing much for his well-being, so Stephens left the states for a two-year tour through Europe, Syria, and Egypt.

When he returned, he wrote the first of his travel books, published in 1937: *Incidents of Travel in Egypt, Arabia Petraea, and the Holy Land.*

This the same sort of book which Twain would later pursue, except that it was a generation earlier and not at all funny. Still, the public received his *Incidents* well, and Stephens produced another: *Incidents of Travel in Greece, Turkey, Russia and Poland*. And so, a series had begun to emerge by John Lloyd Stephens.

Having read von Humboldt's *Cosmos* and having sensed the same message that later would be read by both Frederic Edwin Church and Sarah Sawyer Mars, Stephens set his sights upon South America, and he once again enlisted a young British artist named Frederick Catherwood to accompany him to Yucatán. In those first two volumes, Catherwood had provided some illustrations for the text, and now his role would be broadened by von Humboldt's clarion call to landscape artists.

They embarked on their eight-month mission late in 1839, and they came home in 1840. Stephens wrote in two volumes his *Incidents of Travels in Central America, Chiapas and Yucatán*, published in 1841, and then returned to Yucatán later that year. In 1843, Stephens published another two-volume work, *Incidents of Travel in Yucatán*. His expeditions and explorations not only earned him the title of "the American Traveler," but also fed his own interests in archaeology and geology alike.

Meanwhile, his authority on the subject of the isthmus had become second to none, so Stephens was asked to study that terrain for a possible railway that might connect travelers and commerce between the Atlantic and Pacific Oceans. In time, he became president of the Panama Railway Company, and he spent two years overseeing the railroad's construction. This would become the rail which Sarah Sawyer Mars rode in her pursuit of Church's path to the Valley of the Volcanoes. So, neither Grandma Ghost, nor Frederic Edwin Church could have done this without the explorations of John Lloyd Stephens.

Of additional interest in the following selection is the great American Traveler's introduction of the fabled *agave* plant to his English-speaking readers. Here he mentions that this is the plant from which the locals derive their *pulque* beverage, but we well understand that Stephens is but a step or two removed from making *mescal*, and then – *tequila!*

So, pull up an ice cube and enjoy the same view of Yucatán that also fed the daydreams of Tully Mars at the wheel of the *Caribbean Soul*.

Additional suggested works by John Lloyd Stephens:

— *"Incidents of Travels in Central America, Chiapas and Yucatán, Vols. 1 & 2* (1841)

— *Incidents of Travel in Yucatán, Vols. 1 & 2* (1843)

THE RED HAND

a selection from

Incidents of Travel in Yucatán/Chapter XI

WE MOVED ON to the next building, which was situated in a different direction, about a quarter of a mile distant, and completely buried in woods. It was seventy-five feet long, and had three doorways, leading to the same number of apartments. A great part of the front had fallen. Growing on the roof are two maguey plants, *Agave Americana*, in our latitude called the "century plant," but under the hot sun of the tropics blooming every four or five years. There are four species of this plant in Yucatan: the *maguey*, from which is produced the *pulque*, a beverage common in all the Mexican provinces, which, taken in excess, produces intoxication; the *henneken*, which produces the article known in our markets as Sisal hemp; the *sabila*, with which the Indian women wean children; and the *peta*, from which a very fine white hemp is made. These plants, in some or all varieties, were found in the neighbourhood of all the ruins, forming around them a pointed and thorny wall, which we were obliged to cut through to reach the buildings.

While Mr. Catherwood was engaged in drawing this structure, the Indians told us of two others half a league distant. We had a good path nearly all the way, until the Indians pointed out a white object seen indistinctly through the trees, again uttering, the familiar sound of "Xlappahk," or old walls. In a few minutes they cut a path to it. The building was larger than the last, having the front ornamented in the same way, much fallen, though still presenting an interesting spectacle. As it was not much overgrown, we set to work and cleared it, and left it for another, in regard to which I formed some curious expectations, for the Indians described it as very *new*. It lay on the same path, and separated from us by a great field of *taje*, through which we cut a path for several hundred yards to the foot of the terrace. The walls were entire and very

251

massive; but climbing up it, I found only a small building, but no sign or token distinguishing it as *newer* or more modern; and I now learned that all they meant by their description of it was that it was the *newest* known to them, having been discovered but twelve years before, on clearing the ground for a *milpa*, until which time it was as much unknown to them as to the rest of the world. This gave great weight to the consideration that cities may exist equal to any now known, buried in the woods, overgrown and lost, which will perhaps never be discovered.

On the walls of this desolate edifice were prints of the "mano Colorado," or red hand. Often as I saw this print, it never failed to interest me. It was the stamp of the living hand; it always brought me nearer to the builders of these cities, and at times, amid stillness, desolation, and ruin, it seemed as if from behind the curtain that concealed them from view was extended the hand of greeting. These prints were larger than any I had seen. In several places I measured them with my own, opening the fingers to correspond with those on the wall. The Indians said it was the hand of the master of the building.

The mysterious interest which, in my eyes, always attached to this red hand, has assumed a more definite shape. I have been advised that in Mr. Catlin's collection of Indian curiosities, made during a long residence among our North American tribes, was a tent presented to him by the chief of the powerful but now extinct race of Maudans, which exhibits, among other marks, two prints of the red hand; and I have been farther advised that the red hand is seen constantly upon the buffalo robes and skins of wild animals brought in by the hunters on the Rocky Mountains, and, in fact, that it is a symbol recognized and in common use by the North American Indians of the present day. I do not mention these as facts within my own knowledge, but with the hope of attracting the attention of those who have opportunities and facilities for investigation; and I suggest the interesting consideration that, if true, the red hand on the tent and the buffalo robes points back from the wandering tribes in our country to the comparatively polished people who erected the great cities at the south; and if true that it is at this day used as a sign or symbol by our North American Indians, its meaning can be ascertained from living witnesses, and through ages of intervening darkness a ray of light may be thrown back upon the now mysterious and incomprehensible characters which perplex the stranger on the walls of the desolate southern buildings.

MARJORY STONEMAN DOUGLAS

from
Dedication
Trouble Dolls
1991

CONSIDER THIS: Marjory Stoneman Douglas already was looking at sixty when Jimmy came into this world, and she was well into that personal decade when Carl Hiaasen was born.

Before either one of those two had even taken a breath, *Everglades: River of Grass* already was in print. So, to say that Douglas was ahead of her time would be more than an understatement.

In fact, there's more than a bit of irony when people compare her life's work to that of Rachel Carson, whose *Silent Spring* was written nearly a generation after *Everglades*.

The River of Grass, as Douglas was first to call it, became in time the major cause of this woman who championed Florida's fragile environment, along with her concern for women's rights, long before most others ever thought of such things. She later created the Friends of the Everglades in 1970, when she was eighty years old, and not long afterward she spearheaded an effort to prevent the U.S. Army Corps of Engineers from draining certain portions of the Everglades.

Wearing sunglasses and a huge floppy hat, the octagenarian stood little more than half the height of most others who had gathered for a hearing regarding the Corps' actions in Everglades City. "When she spoke, everybody stopped slapping mosquitoes and more or less came to order," reported one observer. "Her tone itself seemed to tame the rowdiest of the local stone crabbers, plus the developers, and the lawyers on both sides. I wonder if it didn't also intimidate the mosquitoes." In the end, Marjory Stoneman Douglas and her friends prevailed, the Corps was denied its permit, and Skip Wiley would have been satisfied.

That had not been the first time that she had tangled with the engineers. As early as the Fifties, the Corps of Engineers had constructed an intricate system of dams, levees, and canals which they hoped might control the seasonal flooding of wetlands that were fast being drained and developed by realtors and farmers alike. In short, they were disrupting the natural cycles of southern Florida, and Douglas understood that those cycles were critical to the survival of the Everglades.

Once declared "the Grand dame of the Everglades" in a presidential proclamation, Marjory Stoneman was born in Minneapolis in 1890, some six years before Florida voters incorporated the city of Miami. In 1910, her father became editor of the new *Miami Herald*, and Marjory Stoneman soon married a New Jersey newspaperman named Kenneth Douglas; however, the marriage lasted barely two years. It was then that she moved to Florida to write for her father's paper. Building herself a home in the Coconut Grove, she began writing short stories for the *Saturday Evening Post*, several of which won her the prestigious O. Henry Award. Still, it is her work on behalf of the environment that has earned her a place in the hearts of the nation, as well as of the state.

By the time that Jimmy's second collaboration with Savannah Jane went into its third printing, the dedication for *Trouble Dolls* had changed. In place of their original encouragement of "Children, see what you can see," there appeared: "To Marjory Stoneman Douglas and the Seminole people who knew the Everglades long before we did."

Additional suggested works by Marjory Stoneman Douglas:

— *Road to the Sun* (1951)

— *Hurricane* (1953)

— *Florida: The Long Frontier* (1964)

THE NAME

a selection from
Everglades: River of Grass/Chapter 1

THERE ARE NO OTHER EVERGLADES in the world.

They are, they have always been, one of the unique regions of the earth, remote, never wholly known. Nothing anywhere else is like them; their vast glittering openness, wider than the enormous visible round of the horizon, the racing free saltness and sweetness of their massive winds, under the dazzling blue heights of space. They are unique also in the simplicity, the diversity, the related harmony of the forms of life they enclose. The miracle of the light pours over the green and brown expanse of sawgrass and of water, shining and slow-moving below, the grass and water that is the meaning and the central fact of the Everglades of Florida. It is a river of grass.

The great pointed paw of the state of Florida, familiar as the map of North America itself, of which it is the most noticeable appendage, thrusts south, farther south than any other part of the mainland of the United States. Between the shining aquamarine waters of the Gulf of Mexico and the roaring deep-blue waters of the north-surging Gulf Stream, the shaped land points toward Cuba and the Caribbean. It points toward and touches within one degree of the tropics.

More than halfway down the thrusting peninsula nearly everyone knows the lake that is like a great hole in that pawing shape, Lake Okeechobee, the second largest body of fresh water, it is always said, "within the confines of the United States." Below that lie the Everglades.

They have been called "the mysterious Everglades" so long that the phrase is a meaningless platitude. For four hundred years after the discovery they seemed more like a fantasy than a simple geographic and historic fact. Even the men who in the later years saw them more clearly could hardly make up their minds what the Everglades were or how they

255

could be described, or what use could be make of them. They were mysterious then. They are mysterious still to everyone by whom their fundamental nature is not understood.

Off and on for those four hundred years the region now called "The Everglades" was described as a series of vast, miasmic swamps, poisonous lagoons, huge dismal marshes without outlet, a rotting, shallow, inland sea, or labyrinths of dark trees hung and looped about with snakes and dripping mosses, malignant with tropical fevers and malarias, evil to the white man.

Even the name, "The Everglades," was given them and printed on a map of Florida within the past hundred years. It is variously interpreted. There were one or two other names we know, which were given them before that, but what sounds the first men had for them, seeing first, centuries and centuries before the discovering white men, those sunblazing solitudes, we shall never know.

The shores that surround the Everglades were the first on this continent know to white men. The interior was almost the last. They have not yet been entirely mapped.

Spanish mapmakers, who never saw them, printed over the unknown blank space where they lay on those early maps the words "El Laguno del Espiritu Santo." To the early Spanish they were truly mysterious, fabulous with a wealth they were never able to prove.

The English from the Bahamas, charting the Florida coasts in the early seventeen hundreds, had no very clear idea of them. Gerard de Brahm, the surveyor, may have gone up some of the east-coast rivers and stared out on that endless, watery bright expanse, for on his map he called them "River Glades." But on the later English maps "River" becomes "Ever," so it is hard to tell what he intended.

The present name came into general use only after the acquisition of Florida from Spain in 1819 by the United States. The Turner map of 1823 was the first to use the word "Everglades." The fine Ives map of 1856 prints the words separately, "Ever Glades." In the text of the memorial that accompanied the map they were used without capitals, as "ever glades."

The word "glade" is of the oldest English origin. It comes from the Anglo-Saxon "glaed," with the "ae" diphthong, shortened to "glad." It means "shining" or "bright," perhaps as of water. The same word was used in the Scandinavian languages for "a clear place in the sky, a bright streak or patch of light," as Webster's International Dictionary gives it. It might even first have referred to the great openness of the sky over it, and not to the land at all.

In English for over a thousand years the word "glaed" or "glyde" or "glade" has meant an open green grassy place in the forest. And in America of the English colonies the use was continued to mean stretches of natural pasture, naturally grassy.

But most dictionaries nowadays end a definition of them with the qualifying phrase, "as of the Florida Everglades." So that they have thus become unique in being their own, and only, best definition.

Yet the Indians, who have known the Glades longer and better than any dictionary-making white men, gave them their perfect, and poetic name, which is also true. They called them "Pa-hay-okee," which is the Indian word for "Grassy Water." Today Everglades is one word and yet plural. They are the only Everglades in the world.

Men crossed and recrossed them leaving no trace, so that no one knew men had been there. The few books or pamphlets written about them by Spaniards or surveyors or sportsmen or botanists have not been generally read. Actually, the first accurate studies of Everglades geology, soil, archaeology, even history, are only just now being completed.

The question was at once, where do you begin? Because, when you think of it, history, the recorded time of the earth and of man, is in itself something like a river. To try to present it whole is to find oneself lost in the sense of continuing change. The source can be only the beginning in time and space, and the end is the future and the unknown. What we can know lies somewhere between. The course along which for a little way one proceeds; the changing life, the varying light, must somehow be fixed in a moment clearly, from which one may look before and after and try to comprehend wholeness.

So it is with the Everglades, which have that quality of long existence in their own nature. They were changeless. They are changed.

They were complete before man came to them, and for centuries afterward, when he was only one of those forms which shared, in a finely balanced harmony, the forces and the ancient nature of the place.

Then, when the Everglades were most truly themselves, is the time to begin with them.

&

JOHN D. MACDONALD

OVER THE COURSE of some twenty-one years, Travis McGee found himself in an equal number of adventures that took him all across southern Florida, and sometimes even beyond.

During two decades spanning 1964 to 1984 – from *The Deep Blue Good-by* to *The Lonely Silver Rain* – never once did the character ever set foot upon Cedar Key. Even though that's what Jimmy Buffett might've said, John D. MacDonald had written otherwise.

Nonetheless, Travis McGee left an indelible footprint in both the Florida landscape and the American literary landscape alike. A self-proclaimed "salvage consultant," McGee was not at all a private investigator or even a police detective. He was instead a beach bum who lived aboard the *Busted Flush* and who only accepted cases when his supply of cash was running low. And when that happened, he'd charge his client half the value of the recovered property, along with whatever costs he'd spent to do that. McGee called himself a "knight in rusted armor," and he adhered to a strict code of values. Not the least of these was a reverence for the Florida environment.

It was that attitude along with the strength of MacDonald's storylines which endeared him to readers, including the likes of Jimmy and Carl Hiaasen. When MacDonald published his sixth Travis McGee novel, *Bright Orange for the Shroud*, Jimmy was only eighteen and Carl was but twelve years old. In time, they'd grow to understand that MacDonald and McGee had set out upon a road that was then less-traveled, but pioneered by Aldo Leopold, Rachel Carson, and Marjory Stoneman Douglas.

"Having failed in every attempt to subdue the Glades by frontal attack, we are slowly killing it off by tapping the River of Grass," says McGee. "In the questionable name of progress, the state in its vast wisdom lets every two-bit developer divert the flow into drag-lined canals that give him 'waterfront' lots to sell."

The planet's first Earth Day and Charles A. Reich's *The Greening of America*, as well as Hunter S. Thompson's landmark piece called "Freak Power in the Rockies" in *Rolling Stone*, all were awaiting the arrival of the subsequent decade. Until that time, MacDonald not only had a clearer view of the future, but also had a spokesman to present it. From the vantage point of today, readers can see where Hiaasen's passion for McGee and for Florida would take him; it's much the same with Jimmy.

"When I went to write books, I said, 'Well, I gotta go back to the books that really got me excited, and those were certainly the John MacDonald books, Travis McGee," explains Jimmy. "I miss Travis McGee a lot. So, I'd go back and look at those just to get a feel of something, and how to begin and end."

By then, Jimmy already had mentioned MacD. and McGee in one lyric; a few years later, he'd drop the writer's name into "Prince of Tides." In fact, Jimmy dedicated the entire *Hot Water* album itself "to John D. MacDonald, one of America's great natural resources."

The following selection provides the full context of those MacDonald lines which Jimmy cites in the notes for *Last Mango in Paris*, just above the lyrics to "Beyond the End."

Additional suggested works by John D. MacDonald:

— *The Deep Blue Good-by* (1964)

— *The Lonely Silver Rain* (1984)

THE LONELY SILVER RAIN

a selection from
Chapter XI

SEVERAL OTHER BIG PASSENGER AIRCRAFT had landed at Cancún ahead of us, and a couple more came in right after we did. The modern airport is, for practical purposes, divided in half. The departure area with ticket counters, departure tax counters and security inspection is three times as large as the arrival lounge. Not a lounge. Long, long slow lines piled up at high counters where bored and indifferent little bureaucrats, male and female, glanced at passports and stamped tourist permits which had been filled out on the flights. I was able to stroll right on out of the customs area into the outer area of the arrival section without interception. The customs counters were unmanned. But several attentive men stood back by a wall, and every now and then one of them would step out and flag down a passenger and check his luggage.

Beyond the glass wall was total chaos. Passengers were finding their tour group, and the place to stand for their hotel buses. Avis, Hertz and Budget were doing big business. I looked back through the glass wall and saw Browder in there, working his way through the crowd toward the doorway. People charged into me, then backed off and stared up at me in obvious astonishment. I saw a whole pack of chubby people of indeterminate age, all wearing name tags with tridents on them, and I realized they were all destined for Club Med. They had that look, a batch of lonesome loners who had decided to try to take a big chance in the sunshine.

"Let's go," Browder said, pushing at me. I do not like being pushed at. He went ahead in a half trot and I followed along, walking carefully on sore feet. He stood in the Budget line and, after he spent five minutes at the counter, we went out to the far curb, walking between a couple of the tour buses parked in a long line at the first curb. It was bright and hot in Cancún. The buses stood there snoring and stinking, big beasts drowsing in the heat. The drivers sat high behind the wheels, wiry little brown men with that same look of apathy and cynicism you see on the faces of big-city cabdrivers.

It was ten minutes before our rental car arrived, a dark blue Renault 12 with eighteen thousand kilometers on the meter, a mini-station wagon with four doors. Browder got behind the wheel. If I could have fitted there, I couldn't have worked the pedals with those boots on. I tossed the big hat in back and took off the eye patch.

"You gotta wear that at all times!" Browder said.

"And off come the boots too, friend. You just drive the car."

"You getting smart-ass on me?"

I knelt on the seat and reached back and slipped the dictionary out of his carry-on and put it in mine as he turned and watched me.

"If two of us are going to run this," he said, "we are going to run it into a tree."

"Get out of the crush here and park a minute."

He drove out of the airport proper and turned onto the long wide road that led out to the main highway that runs from Puerto Juárez all the way down to Chetumal, the capital city of Quintana Roo (pronounced "row" as in "row your boat"). He pulled way over to the side and turned the engine off. No air conditioning, and the dark car was like a convection oven when the windows were open and it was moving, and like a barbecue pit when it was standing still.

"Now what?" he asked.

"We are a long way from anything," I told him. "Up ahead turn left and we're fifteen or twenty minutes from Cancún. Turn right and you've got a batch of sixty miles of nothing. So who are we seeing, where is he and how do you get in touch?"

"It will unfold as we go along. Okay?"

"Not okay."

He studied me for a few moments. Sweat ran down his thick red cheek. "So I'll hold your hand, McGee. We've got two singles at the Sheraton. We locate a pool attendant, a tall towel boy named Ricky, and we tell him that we've come to do some business with the banker. We give him a room number and sit tight. Somebody will get in touch."

"Soon?"

"Maybe. Maybe not. We just wait and see."

J A C K   B O Y L E

from
"Pencil Thin Mustache"
LIVING AND DYING IN 3/4 TIME
1974

ALEX RUTLEDGE and Travis McGee owe a great deal to Boston Blackie.

Long before Blackie ever became known as the "enemy to those who make him an enemy, friend to those who have no friend," Jack Boyle's creation had been a safecracker and jewel thief in the bay area around San Francisco. That's about as far from his misunderstood reputation as a private eye as it is from his misunderstood home base of Boston.

There's a good chance that Jimmy was introduced to Blackie via TV, though, and so his take on this character is a bit removed from the pages of a pulp magazine.

"I'm a war baby (and proud of it) which makes me a first-generation television child," Jimmy used to tell his audiences in the early 1970s whenever he introduced this song that's inspired by Saturday morning TV. "Nobody ever writes songs about the real heroes who made America what it is today: Sky

King, Ramar of the Jungle, and Boston Blackie," he'd tell them. "I wrote this in tribute to the nostalgic people who were famous to me and nobody else."

And so Jimmy created "Pencil Thin Mustache" with its allusions to Andy Devine, Ricky Ricardo, and American Bandstand. While his reference to Boston Blackie does carry the theme from the title through to the end of the song, only an aficionado of the character would be able to let you in on this other little secret: from Blackie's first appearance in a 1914 short story, into his novelization in 1919, and throughout a string of six different actors who portrayed him in silent movies until 1927, Boston Blackie *never* sported *any* facial hair whatsoever, let along a pencil thin mustache. He was simply a clean-shaven, professional thief with a heart of gold and a happy ending to each episode.

Another fourteen years would pass before anyone thought of bringing the popular character back to the silver screen. Columbia Pictures produced fourteen more films in black-and-white. One big change was their addition of sound; the other, a new actor in the title role. So, a clean-shaven Chester Morris helped evolve Boston Blackie into quite the charming investigator whose adventures involved his solving some crime which might otherwise be blamed upon him.

After the seventh Columbia picture, the franchise spread to radio. Morris voiced Boston Blackie for thirteen episodes, but then Richard Kollmar played the part for some two hundred episodes, *sans* mustache.

Then Jimmy's TV appeared. When Kent Taylor was cast as Boston Blackie, the character had been domesticated into a dapper and dashing detective, an image enhanced (at last!) by his pencil thin mustache. Clearly, Blackie's new appearance reflected William Powell's portrayal of Dashiell Hammett's Nick Charles in *The Thin Man*. Ironically, Hammett owes much to Boyle, as well.

The novelized collection of Jack Boyle's stories includes the following episode. Few will argue that the book is great literature, but many will champion the fact that Boyle was the first American writer of crime fiction in the twentieth century. Poe had written some detective stories, but none of that would rise to the level of Britain's Sherlock Holmes.

So, it remains safe to say that Jack Boyle's Boston Blackie pioneered the genre of American crime fiction and paved the way for the hard-boiled detectives and private investigators, as well as for those who were not really professional solvers of mysteries at all. In much the same way that Boston Blackie had a paying job (as a thief), Alex Rutledge remains a photographer by trade, and Travis McGee stands by his claim that he's simply "a salvage consultant."

"MAN TO MAN"

a selection from

Boston Blackie/Chapter XXVIII

I HAVE NO ROOMERS but a Miss Collins and her mother, who is an invalid, poor soul. They have the two rooms in the attic," she was telling the Deputy. "The girl is learning shorthand and don't go out much. The old lady is crippled with rheumatism and can't leave the rooms. Oh, they are nice, quiet, respectable people, sir."

Sherwood was deeply puzzled. From the garbage can behind this house had come a half-dozen loaves of bread in three days, with the crusts – and only the crusts – eaten off. He had come to the house after painstaking preparation, feeling that Blackie and victory were within his grasp. The landlady's story of the girl who studied shorthand, and an invalid mother, found no place in his theory of what he would find there, and yet it was evident the woman spoke the truth.

"What does the girl look like? What is the color of her hair?" he asked.

"Red, sir – a beautiful red like a polished copper kettle."

Mary's hair was coal black. For the first time Martin Sherwood's confidence was shaken.

"When did they come here?" he asked.

"Why, let me see." The woman reckoned on her fingers. "It was a week ago Thursday, sir, in the evening. They saw my advertisement in the paper and came just before I went to work – which is 9 o'clock, sir."

Blackie had escaped early on the morning of the day she mentioned. On that Thursday night he and Mary had disappeared from the lodging house which was their first place of refuge. The date and hour of their arrival decided Sherwood. He would have a look at this red haired girl and her invalid mother.

"I would like to go up and see them for a moment," he told the woman. "I'm an officer." He showed his star. "Oh, no, nothing wrong at all. I just want to see them. I like to keep track of people in the district."

"Certainly, sir. I'll call Miss Collins and – "

"No, no – that isn't necessary," hastily interrupted Sherwood. "I'll just step upstairs and knock."

Though he tried to step lightly, as Sherwood's tread sounded on the uncarpeted stairway there was a sudden shuffling of feet on the floor above. He smiled, for that augured well, and he felt for the gun slung just inside his coat. Then he rapped.

Muffled sounds came from behind the door. A chair squeaked as it was pushed across the floor. A few seconds of silence; then, plain and unmistakable, came the sound of a woman sobbing hysterically. Sherwood tried the door, found it locked and knocked again peremptorily.

The door suddenly was flung wide open, and in the flood of light from within a woman faced him – a woman with a wealth of bronze hair that should have been black, a woman with tears on cheeks that were as bloodless as death, a woman whom he instantly recognized as Boston Blackie's Mary.

Martin Sherwood sprang inside with drawn revolver ready to answer the stream of lead he expected from some corner of the room. None came. Instead he saw a woman, white haired and evidently feeble, sitting beside a bed with bowed head while her body shook with convulsive sobs. On the bed, covered with a sheet that was drawn up over the face, lay a silent, motionless form that told its own story.

Sudden disappointment gripped Martin Sherwood's heart. Had the man he had rated so highly cheated him of his long-coveted triumph only by the coward's expedient of suicide?

"Where's Boston Blackie?" he demanded, his gun still covering the room.

Mary pointed silently to the still figure on the bed.

"Dead!" exclaimed the Deputy Warden. "When? How?"

"An hour ago," she sobbed. "You starved him to death in your prison." She dropped to her knees. "God have mercy on us now!" she prayed.

Sherwood strode to the bed, beside which the aged woman still sat sobbing, and leaning over, lifted the sheet. As he did so his gun for the first time failed to cover all the room. Beneath the sheet, instead of the face he expected, he saw a roll of blankets carefully molded and tied into the semblance of a human form. Before he could turn, cold steel was pressed against the base of his brain.

"Drop that gun, Sherwood," said Boston Blackie's voice from behind him. "Drop it quick. Raise it one inch and you'll be as dead as you thought I was."

Sherwood hesitated as a full realization of the new situation flashed through his mind; then he smiled as he thought of the posse he had thrown around the house and let his revolver slip through his fingers to the bed. Here was a worthy antagonist – a bit too worthy, as the cards lay just then! But the deal was far from done.

"Pick up his gun, Mary, and lay it on the table in the corner, well out of the Deputy's way," directed Blackie. "Then see if he has another. I don't care to move the muzzle of my gun from his neck just yet. Now," he continued, "slip off these skirts. I'm not overly well used to them, even though I've worn them for days, and if Mr. Sherwood should forget the company he's in and get suddenly reckless, they might be in my way."

"Now turn round, Sherwood, and face the music," ordered Blackie a moment later.

The Deputy Warden turned and faced the convict behind whom lay a discarded white wig and an old woman's garments. He met his captor's eyes without a tremor, and smiled.

"Well done, Blackie, I must admit," he said. "But I should have known that when you didn't shoot as I came in, things weren't what they seemed."

"I didn't expect you, Sherwood," Blackie replied, "but as you see, I made preparations to receive you in case you came."

The convict's face grew pale and suddenly grave. His grip on the gun leveled at the Deputy's head tightened. "You understand, of course, Sherwood, I've got to kill you," he said.

"As matters stand, naturally it wouldn't surprise me," the Deputy answered. His voice was absolutely calm and unshaken, his eyes without the remotest trace of fear.

"If you have anything to say or do or think, be quick," said Blackie.

"I haven't – thank you."

The men stared into each other's eyes, the silence broken only by Mary's sobs.

"I hate to kill a man as brave as you in cold blood," said Boston Blackie slowly. "You're a brave man, Sherwood, even when you don't hold all the cards in the game as you do inside your prison. I hate to kill you, but I've got to. I can't tie and gag you. You'd get free before we could get away from the city. I can't risk that."

"Naturally not," said Sherwood.

"I couldn't trust your promise not to bother me, in a life-and-death matter like this, if I let you go," continued Blackie with troubled eyes.

"I wouldn't give it if you did." There was no hesitation in the answer.

"Well, then." The gun that covered the Deputy Warden's head swayed downward till the muzzle covered his heart. "Are you ready?"

"Any time," said Sherwood.

The hammer rose under the pressure of the convict's finger on the trigger. Mary Dawson, crying hysterically now, turned away her face and covered her ears.

"Do you want to go, Mary, before I – I do what I must do?" asked Blackie, realizing what the scene with its inevitable end must mean to the girl. "It would be better for you to go, dear."

"No, no," she cried. "I want to share with you all blame for what you do. I won't go till you do."

Sherwood turned his eyes curiously on the woman. Sherwood knew what he would have risked for such a woman and such love.

Boston Blackie's face was strangely gray. The hammer of the revolver rose, hesitated, fell – then rose again. The Deputy, his gaze returning from the woman's face, looked into the gun unflinchingly and in silence. Another pause freighted with that sort of tension that crumbles the strongest; then slowly the convict let the muzzle of his weapon drop below the heart of the man he faced.

"Sherwood," he said in a voice that broke between his words, "I hate you as I hate no living man, but I can't kill you as you stand before me unarmed and helpless. I'm going to give you a chance for your life." He stepped backward and picked up the Deputy Warden's revolver. He pushed a table between himself and the man he couldn't kill. He laid the revolvers side by side on it, one pointing toward him, the other toward Sherwood. The clock on the mantel showed three minutes of the hour.

"Sherwood," he said, "in three minutes that clock will strike. I'm exactly as far from the guns as you. On the first stroke of the clock we'll reach together for them – and the quickest hand wins."

Martin Sherwood studied Boston Blackie's face with something in his eyes no other man had ever seen there. He glanced toward the guns on the table. It was true he was exactly as near them as the convict. Nothing prevented him from reaching now, and firing at the first touch of his finger on the trigger. Blackie deliberately had surrendered his irresistible advantage to give him, Martin Sherwood, his prison torturer, an even chance for life. For the first time the Deputy's eyes were unsteady and his voice throaty and shaken.

"I won't bargain with you, Blackie," he said.

"You're afraid to risk an even break?"

"You know I'm not," Sherwood answered, his gaze turning once more to the woman who stood by the door, staring panic-stricken. It was plain that the issue to be decided in that room was life or death to her as well as to the men.

Boston Blackie reached toward his gun, hoping the Deputy Warden would do likewise and end, in one quick exchange of shots, the strain he knew was breaking his nerve. Sherwood let Blackie recover his weapon without moving a muscle. Once more the convict's revolver rose till it covered Martin Sherwood's heart. They stood again as they had been, the Deputy at the mercy of the escaped prisoner.

Seconds passed, then minutes, without a word or a motion on either side of the table over which the triangular tragedy was being settled not at all as any of those concerned had planned. The strain was unbearable. The muscles of the convict's throat twitched. His face was drawn and distorted.

"Pick up that gun and defend yourself," he cried.

"No," shouted Sherwood, the calm which his mighty will had until then sustained snapping like an over-tightened violin string.

"You want to make me feel myself a murderer," cried Blackie in anguish. "Why didn't I give you bullet for bullet when you came in the door? I could have killed you then. Now I can't unless you'll fight. Once more I ask you, will you take an even break?"

"No," cried Sherwood again.

With a great cry – the cry of a strong man broken and beaten – Boston Blackie threw his gun upon the floor.

"You win, Sherwood," he sobbed, losing self-control completely for the first time in a life of daily hazards. "You've beaten me."

He staggered drunkenly toward Mary and folded her in his arms.

"I tried to force myself to pull the trigger by thinking of the life we hoped for together, dear, but I couldn't do it," he moaned brokenly. "I'll go back with him now. Everything is over."

"I'm glad now you didn't, dear," she cried, clinging to him. "It would have been murder. I don't want you to do that, even to save our happiness. But I'll wait for you, dear one, wait till your time is done and you come back to me again."

Boston Blackie straightened his shoulders and turning to Sherwood, held out his wrists for the handcuffs.

"Come, come," he urged. "For God's sake, don't prolong this. Don't stand there gloating. Take me away."

Martin Sherwood, with something strangely new transfiguring the face Boston Blackie knew and hated, reached to the table and picked up his gun slowly. Just as slowly he dropped it into his pocket. He looked into the two grief-racked faces before him, long and silently.

"I'm sorry to have disturbed you folks," he said quietly at last. "I came here looking for an escaped convict named Boston Blackie. I have found only you, Miss Collins, and your mother. I'm sorry my misinformation has subjected you both to annoyance. The police officers who are out-side" – the Deputy Warden opened a crack in the window curtain and pointed out to the dim shapes in the darkness – "and who surround this house, will be withdrawn at once. Had Boston Blackie been in this room, and had he by some mischance killed me, his shot would have brought a dozen men armed with sawed-off shotguns. Escape for him was absolutely impossible. I saw to that before I entered here alone to capture him. But it all has been a blunder. The man I wanted to take back to prison is not here, and I can only hope my apology will be accepted."

Blackie stared at him with blazing, unbelieving eyes. From Mary came a cry in which all the pent-up anguish of the lifetime that had been lived in the last half-hour found sudden relief.

"Good night, folks," said Martin Sherwood, offering Boston Blackie his hand. The convict caught it in his own, and the men looked into each other's eyes for a second. Then the Deputy Warden went out and closed the door behind him.

Mary sprang into Blackie's arms, and they dropped together into a chair, dazed with a happiness greater than either had ever known.

"He is a man," said Blackie. "He is a man even though he's a copper."

Martin Sherwood let himself out of the house and beckoned the cor-don of police to him as he looked back at the windows of the attic rooms and spoke softly to himself.

"He is a man," he said. "He is a man, even though he is a convict."

It was the greatest praise and the greatest concession either had ever made to another man.

Three days later a steamer passed out through the Golden Gate. On the upper deck were a man and a woman, hand in hand, with eyes misty with happiness – Boston Blackie and his Mary.

THE END

$\mathcal{G}$

CARL HIAASEN

from
"The Ballad of Skip Wiley"
BAROMETER SOUP
1995

THOUGH HE'S NOT a total stranger to the music scene, Carl Hiaasen's credit on *Barometer Soup's* "The Ballad of Skip Wiley" is noted simply as "clapping."

Somehow this can make sense, because Wiley's the so-called "environmental terrorist" in Hiaasen's first solo novel, *Tourist Season.* At the time, critics hailed his work as a variation on the so-called "new journalism" pioneered by Hunter S. Thompson. And that makes sense, too, because Carl was then a reporter for the *Miami Herald.*

Though he had yet to become a columnist, it was not a big leap for Hiaasen to create the character of a columnist so upset with Florida's land development that he took matters into his own hands. After all, Carl's a native Floridian who has seen his boyhood territory "developed" right before his eyes. Over the next quarter century or so, Carl Hiaasen would create another dozen novels that each bore a snappy, two-word title; however, they shared more than just that. His main character's always a hard-living bachelor. Often, he's a journalist who's been drummed out of the business by scandal. So, he becomes an outside renegade.

While Carl's only Key West story was *Trap Line*, his *Basket Case* some twenty years later would be much in line with *Where is Joe Merchant?* Jimmy had nothing to do with Carl's tale about the death of the frontman for a hair band called "Jimmy and the Slut Puppies," but their mutual friend most certainly did. And that's how Warren Zevon's track called "Basket Case" appeared on his 2002 album, *My Ride's Here*. It was not the first such collaboration between Hiaasen and Zevon.

Warren's dirty little secret was that he hated writing lyrics, and so he sought out the writing advice of Carl. "After some mild nagging," Hiaasen explained, "Warren finally agreed to come fishing in the Keys."

That's where Zevon first saw the phrase "Seminole Bingo," and he thought it would make a good title . . . if Carl could write the lyrics. The result was the tale of a junk bond king from Wall Street who was losing money nightly in the bingo hall. Thus, the opening track of Warren Zevon's 1995 *Mutineer* album was created, along with "Rottweiler Blues." Clearly, Carl set aside some time to perform with Jimmy on "The Ballad of Skip Wiley" later that season. Meanwhile, his working relationship with Warren would continue to grow through *Basket Case* and beyond.

Until the day that he died in 2003, Warren remained one of only a few whom Carl permitted to read his works-in-progress. As each chapter of *Skinny Dip* was drafted, a copy was sent off to him, and they'd had a phone conversation about the book on the Friday before his death. Warren was eager to read the completed final chapters, but he passed away two days later. *Skinny Dip* is dedicated "In memory of Warren Zevon."

It shouldn't come as any surprise, then, that the remaining two writing/rockers (or rocking/writers) would join forces for the film production of *Hoot*. And it should also come as no surprise that they'd somehow find a way to work into the soundtrack their mutual friend's classic "Werewolves of London."

Additional suggested works by Carl Hiaasen:

— *Trap Line* written with Bill Montalbano (1982)

— *Tourist Season* (1986)

— *Basket Case* (2002)

TOURIST SEASON

a selection from
Chapter XXXIII

OSPREY ISLAND WAS A PADDLE-SHAPED OUTCROP in east Biscayne Bay, about five miles south of the Cape Florida lighthouse. There were no sandy beaches, for the island was mostly hard coral and polite rock – a long-dead reef, thrust barely above sea level. The shores were collared with thick red mangrove; farther inland, young buttonwoods, gumbo-limbo, sea grape, and mahogany. An old man who had lived there for thirty years had planted a row of royal palms and a stand of pines, and these rose majestically from the elevated plot that had been his homestead, before he fell ill and moved back to the mainland. All that remained of the house was a concrete slab and four cypress pilings and a carpet of broken pink stucco; a bare fifty-foot flagpole stood as a salt-eaten legacy to the old man's patriotism and to his fear that someday the Russians would invade Florida, starting with Osprey Island.

Like almost everything else in South Florida, the islet was dishonestly named. There were no white-hooded ospreys, or fish eagles, living on Osprey Island because the nesting trees were not of sufficient height or maturity. A few of the regal birds lived on Sand Key or Elliott, farther south, and occasionally they could be seen diving the channel and marl flats around the island bearing their name. But if it had been left up to the Calusa Indians, who had first settled the place, the island probably would have been called Mosquito or Crab, because these were the predominant life forms infesting its fifty-three acres.

There was no dock – Hurricane Betsy had washed it away in 1965 – but a shallow mooring big enough for one boat had been blasted out of the dead coral on the lee side. With some difficulty of navigation, and considerable paint loss to the outboard's hull, Skip Wiley managed to locate the anchorage in pitch dark. He waded ashore with Kara Lynn deadweight in his arms. The trail to the campsite was fresh and Wiley had no trouble following it, although the sharp branches snagged his clothes and scratched his scalp. Every few steps came a new lashing insult and he bellowed appropriate curses to the firmament.

At the campsite, not far from the old cabin rubble, Wiley placed Kara Lynn on a bed of pine needles and covered her with a thin woolen blanket. Both of them were soaked from the crossing.

Wiley swatted no-see-'ems in the darkness for three hours until he heard the hum of a passing motorboat. Finally! he groused. The Marine Patrol on its nightly route. Wiley had been waiting for the bastard to go by; now it was safe.

When the police boat was gone he built a small fire from dry tinder he had stored under a sheet of industrial plastic. The wind was due east and unbelievably strong, scattering sparks from the campfire, like swarms of tipsy fireflies. Wiley was grateful that the woods were wet.

He was fixing a mug of instant bouillon when Kara Lynn woke up, surprising him.

"Hello, there," Skip Wiley said, thinking it was a good thing he'd tied her wrists and ankles – she looked like a strong girl.

"I know this is a dumb question–" Kara Lynn began.

"Osprey Island," Wiley said.

"Where's that?"

"Out in the bay. Care for some soup?"

Wiley helped her sit up and pulled the blanket around to cover her back and shoulders, which were bare in the parade gown. He held the cup while she drank.

"I know who you are," Kara Lynn said. "I read the big story in the paper today – was it today?"

Wiley looked at his wristwatch. It was half-past three in the morning. "Yesterday," he said. "So what did you think?"

"About the story?"

"No, the column."

"You've done better," Kara Lynn said.

"What do you mean?"

"Can I have another sip? Thanks." She drank a little more and said: "You're sharper when you don't write in the first person."

Wiley plucked at his beard.

"Now, don't get mad," Kara Lynn said. "It's just that some of the transitions seemed contrived, like you were reaching."

"It was a damn tough piece to write," Wiley said thoughtfully.

"I'm sure it was."

"I mean, I couldn't see another way to do it. The first-person approach seemed inescapable."

"Maybe you're right," she said. "I just don't think it was as effective as the hurricane column."

Wiley brightened. "You liked that one?"

"A real scorcher," Kara Lynn said. "We talked about it in class."

"No kidding!" Skip Wiley was delighted. Then his smile ebbed and he sat in silence for several minutes. The girl was not what he expected, and he felt a troubling ambivalence about what was to come. He wished the Seminole sleeping drink had lasted longer; now that Kara Lynn was awake, he sensed a formidable undercurrent. She was a composed and resourceful person – he'd have to watch himself.

"What's the matter?" Kara Lynn asked.

"Why aren't you crying or something?" Wiley grumbled.

Kara Lynn looked around the campsite. "What would be the point?"

Wiley spread more tinder on the fire and held his hands over the flame. The warmth was comforting. He thought: Actually, there's nothing to stop me from leaving now. The job is done.

"Do you know Brian Keyes?"

"Sure," Wiley said, "we worked together."

"Was he a good reporter?"

"Brian's a good man," Wiley said, "but I'm not so sure if he was a good reporter. He wasn't really suited for the business."

"Apparently neither were you."

"No comparison," he scoffed. "Absolutely no comparison."

"Oh, I'm not sure," Kara Lynn said. "I think you're two sides to the same coin, you and Brian."

"And I think you read too much *Cosmo*." Wiley wondered why she was so damned interested in Keyes.

"What about Jenna?" Kara Lynn asked. "You serious about her?"

"What is this, the Merv show?" Wiley ground his teeth. "Look," he said, "I'd love to sit and chat but it's time to be on my way."

"You're going to leave me here in the rain? With no food or water?"

"You won't need any," he said. "'Fraid I have to douse the fire, too."

"A real gentleman," Kara Lynn said acerbically. She was already testing the rope on her wrist.

Wiley was about to pour some tea on the flames when he straightened up and cocked his head. "Did you hear something?" he asked.

"No," Kara Lynn lied.

"It's a goddamn boat."

"It's the wind, that's all."

Wiley set down the kettle, took off his baseball cap, and went crashing off, his bare bright egg of a head vanishing into the hardwoods. Thinking he had fled, Kara Lynn squirmed to the campfire and turned herself around. She held her wrists over the bluest flame, until she smelled flesh. With a cry she pulled away; the rope held fast.

When she looked up, he was standing there. He folded his arms and said, "See what you did, you hurt yourself." He carried her back to the bed of pine needles and examined the burns. "Christ, I didn't even bring a Band-Aid," he said.

"I'm all right," said Kara Lynn. Her eyes reared from the pain. "What about that noise?"

"It was nothing," Wiley said, "just a shrimper trolling offshore." He tore a strip of orange silk from the hem of her gown. He soaked it in salt water and wound it around the burn. Then he retied her wrists.

The rain started again. It came in slashing horizontal sheets. Wiley covered his eyes and said, "Shit, I can't run the boat in this mess."

"Why don't you wait till it lets up?" Kara Lynn suggested.

Her composure was aggravating. Wiley glared down at her and said, "Hey, Pollyanna, you're awfully calm for a kidnap victim. You overdosed on Midol or what?"

Kara Lynn's ocelot eyes stared back in a way that made him shiver slightly. She wasn't afraid. *She was not afraid.* What a great kid, Wiley thought. What a damn shame.

"Tell me about Osprey Island," Kara Lynn said, as if they were rocking on a front porch waiting for the ice-cream truck.

"A special place," he said, melancholic. "A gem of nature. There's a freshwater spring down the trail, can you believe it? Miles off the mainland and the aquifer still bubbles up. You can see coons, opossums, wood rats drinking there, but mostly birds. Wood storks, blue herons. There's a bald eagle on the island, a young male. Wingspan is ten feet if it's an inch, just a glorious bird. He stays up in the tallest pines, fishes only at dawn and dusk. He's up there now." Wiley's ancient-looking eyes went to the pine stand. "It's too windy to fly, so I'm sure he's up there now."

"I've never seen a wild eagle," Kara Lynn remarked. "I was born down here and I've never seen one."

"That's too bad," Skip Wiley said sincerely. His head was bowed. Tiny bubbles of water hung in his rusty beard. It didn't make it any easier that she was born here, he thought.

"It'll be gone soon, this place," he said. "A year from now a sixteen-story monster will stand right where we're sitting." He got to his knees and fumbled in the pocket of his trousers. He pulled out some damp

275

gray newspaper clippings, folded into a square. "Let me give you the full picture," he said, unfolding them, starting to read. Kara Lynn looked over his shoulder.

"*Welcome to the Osprey Club . . . Fine living, for the discriminating Floridian.* Makes you want to puke."

"Pretty tacky," Kara Lynn agreed.

"A hundred and two units from two-fifty all the way up to a million-six. Friendly financing available. Vaulted ceilings, marble archways, sunken living rooms, Roman tubs, atrium patios with real cedar trellises, boy oh boy." Wiley looked up from the newspaper advertisement and gazed out at the woodsy shadows.

"Can't someone try to block it?" Kara Lynn suggested. "The Audubon people. Or maybe the National Park Service."

"Too late," Wiley said. "See, it's a private island. After old man Bradshaw died, his scumball kids put it up for sale. Puerco Development picks it up for three mil and wham, next thing you know it's rezoned for multifamily high-rise."

"Didn't you do a column on this?" she asked.

"I sure did." One of Wiley's many pending lawsuits: a gratuitous and unprovable reference to Mafia connections.

"Back to the blandishments," he said, "there'll be four air-conditioned racketball courts, a spa, a bike trail, a tennis complex, a piazza, two fountains, and even a waterfall. Think about that: they're going to bury the natural spring and build a fiberglass waterfall! Progress, my darling. It says here they're also planting something called a *lush greenbelt*, which is basically a place for rich people to let their poodles take a shit."

Kara Lynn said: "How will people get out here?"

"Ferry," Wiley answered. "See here: *Take a quaint ferry to your very own island where the Mediterranean meets Miami!* See, Kara Lynn, the bastards can't sell Florida anymore, they've got to sell the bloody Riviera."

"It sounds a bit overdone," she said.

"Twenty-four hundred square feet of overdone," he said, "with a view."

"But no ospreys," Kara Lynn said, sensing the spiral of his emotions.

"And no eagle," Wiley said glumly.

He acted as if he were ready to leave, and Kara Lynn knew that if he did, it would be over.

"Why did you pick me?" she asked.

Wiley turned to look at her. "Because you're perfect," he said. "Or at least you represent perfection. Beauty. Chastity. Innocence. All tanned and blond, the golden American dream. That's all they really promise with their damn parade and their unctuous tourist advertising. Come see

Miami, come see the girls! But it's a cheap tease, darling. Florida's nothing but an adman's wet dream."

"That's enough," Kara Lynn said, reddening.

"I take it you don't think of yourself as a precious piece of ass."

"Not really, no."

"Me, neither," Wiley said, "but we are definitely in the minority. And that's why we're out here now – an object lesson for all those bootlicking shills and hustlers."

Wiley crawled out from under the plastic tent and rose to his full height, declaring, "The only way to reach the greedy blind pagans is to strike at their meager principles." He pointed toward the treetops. "To the creators of the Osprey Club, that precious eagle up there is not life, it has no real value. Same goes for the wood rats and the herons. Weighed against the depreciated net worth of a sixteen-story condominium after sellout, the natural inhabitants of this island do not represent life – they have no fucking value. You with me?"

Kara Lynn nodded. She still couldn't see the big bird.

"Now," Wiley said, "if you're the CEO of Puerto Development, what has worth to you, besides money? What is a life? Among all creatures, what is the one that cannot legally be extinguished for the sake of progress?" Wiley arched his eyebrows and pointed a dripping finger at Kara Lynn's nose. "You," he said. "You are, presumably, inviolate."

For the first time in the conversation, it occurred to Kara Lynn that this fellow might truly be insane.

Wiley blinked at her. "I'll be right back," he said. This time she didn't move. Wet and cold, she had come to cherish the meager protection of the plastic shelter. Wiley returned carrying a short wooden stake. An orange plastic streamer was attached to the blunt end.

"Survey markers," Kara Lynn said.

"Very good. So you know what it means – construction is imminent."

"Tomorrow's the groundbreaking?"

"Naw, that was Christmas Eve. Purely ceremonial," Wiley said. "Tomorrow's the day they start terrain modification."

Kara Lynn was puzzled. "I don't see any bulldozer."

"No, those would be used later, for contour clearing."

"Then what do they use for this 'terrain modification'?" she asked.

"Dynamite," Skip Wiley replied. "At dawn."

♌

HUNTER S. THOMPSON

from
"Cultural Infidel"
BANANA WIND
1996

THOSE WHO THINK that they understand Hunter Thompson just because they've read *Fear & Loathing in Las Vegas* are the same sort who believe that they understand Jimmy just because they've heard "Cheeseburger in Paradise."

Born about the time when Papa was getting set for a new life in the palm trees on the outskirts of Havana, Hunter belongs to that generation of writers who were born before the war and influenced by magazines, newspapers, and books, but not at all by TV. To them, journalism demanded both serious thinking and serious writing, and there were publications eager to print that standard of work.

After being stationed with the Air Force near Pensacola during the late Fifties, Hunter then became a freelance writer, a role he struggled to maintain at the onset of the Sixties. He was in his mid-twenties just as the post-war babies were coming of age, throwing tantrums en masse, and proclaiming such behavior to be a cultural revolution. With his wingtip shoes and his close-cropped hair, though, Hunter S. Thompson was pitching articles and earning just enough to support his young family in the San Francisco area.

His 1965 assignment from *The Nation* magazine was a piece that he'd proposed about Hell's Angels, but it quickly led to his first book. *Hell's Angels: The Strange and Terrible Saga of the Outlaw Motorcycle Gangs* was a prime example of his serious thinking and serious writing, but the bikers were not at all happy that Hunter would not share his profits. So, they beat him savagely in what they called "a stomping."

Despite that, his book attracted assignments from major magazines and national newspapers. In the spring of 1967, he wrote a piece for the *New York Times Magazine* called "The Hashbury is the Capital of the Hippies," and he railed against the emptiness of the so-called social revolution. Drugs, he said, were pretty much their only reason for existing.

With that preconception stated, Hunter then proposed a book to Random House about "the death of the American Dream." He wanted to report how promises made in the 1968 presidential campaign measured up to the ideals originally set forth by James Truslow Adams. "The American Dream is that dream of a land in which life should be better and richer and fuller for every man, with opportunity for each according to ability or achievement," Adams had written in his 1931 *Epic of America*.

Random House liked the idea and gave him a small advance, so Hunter headed for the Democratic Convention in Chicago. The craziness that he witnessed there would change his thinking forever. Alongside members of the very generation he'd derided, Thompson himself was beaten by Chicago police. The stomping by Hell's Angels was one thing; violence disguised as law enforcement was another thing altogether. Unable to express his outrage, Hunter never published any piece on the subject. And whenever he tried to speak about it, he always broke down in tears.

In Chicago, Hunter Thompson believed he had seen the fabric of the American Dream torn into shreds: authorities pummeled America's youth while elected leaders assailed the audacity of their generation. That vision which Adams had given of the American Dream – the same one alluded to by Martin Luther King in his 1963 "Letter from the Birmingham Jail" – was something Hunter felt was becoming endangered.

Hunter never wrote the book that had led him to Chicago. With his royalties from the Hell's Angels paperback edition, he moved his family to the outskirts of Aspen, Colorado. His sympathies turned toward that next generation, which was already graduating from college and heading into law schools. Hunter Thompson was ready to lend his voice to their cause, but he needed an appropriate forum.

As the publisher of *Rolling Stone*, Jann Wenner had needs of his own. The very audience that Hunter was seeking just happened to be the very same one that was losing interest in music as its social focus. Rock still had its place in their lives, but so did political movements. Into Wenner's San Francisco office one day strode a lanky man wearing an Acapulco shirt, white pants, and tennis shoes. Atop his head was a woman's gray wig; in his hand, a six-pack. The man declared his name was Dr. Hunter S. Thompson and that he was about to be elected sheriff of Aspen.

With the October 1 issue in 1970, readers were greeted by a close-up photo of Felix Cavaliere staring out from the cover. Across his forehead ran the banner *Rolling Stone*; over the bridge of his nose, "Freak Power in the Rockies by Dr. Hunter S. Thompson (Candidate for Sheriff)." A new era was beginning, in politics and in literature alike. This "Battle of Aspen" would prove to be more than just the "new journalism" of Norman Mailer or Tom Wolf. This would be known as "Gonzo Journalism," wherein the journalist so immersed himself in the reported event that his very involvement itself becomes the focus.

"What began as a $250 assignment to write a photo-caption for *Sports Illustrated*," said Hunter, "ended some two years later as a book titled *Fear & Loathing in Las Vegas* – which, despite a long history of financial failure on all fronts, remains my personal favorite among all the things I've written. And it is still the lonely cornerstone of everything that has since become genuinely and puzzlingly infamous as 'Gonzo Journalism.'"

The often-overlooked subtitle of *Fear & Loathing* has always remained: *A Savage Journey to the Heart of the American Dream*. Hunter's narrator, Roaul Duke, early on declares that the point of the story which he is about to cover is "Free Enterprise. The American Dream. Horatio Alger *gone mad* on *drugs* in Las Vegas. Do it *now;* pure Gonzo journalism."

Later, he would admit that *Fear & Loathing in Las Vegas* was simply an experiment that had failed, and nearly everything else he wrote always entailed much more serious thinking and writing. And almost always, it had dealt with the loss of the American Dream.

Additional suggested works by Hunter S. Thompson:

— *Hell's Angels: A Strange and Terrible Saga* (1966)

— *The Great Shark Hunt: Strange Tales from A Strange Time* (1979)

— *Songs of the Doomed: More Notes on the Death of the American Dream*

— *The Mutineer: Rants, Ravings, and Missives from the Mountaintop*

THE GONZO SALVAGE CO.

a selection from

The San Francisco *Examiner*, 3 March 1986

SUGARLOAF KEY, FL – The TV is out tonight. The set went black about halfway through "Miami Vice," just as Don Johnson dropped a KGB thug with a single 200-yard shot from his high-tech belly gun.

The storm got serious after that, and the mood in The Keys turned mean. Junk cars crashed in the mango swamps and fishheads whipped on each other with sharkhooks in all-night bars and roadhouses along Highway A1A. These people will tolerate almost anything except being cut off in the middle of "Miami Vice."

On nights like these it is better not to answer the telephone. It can only mean trouble: Some friend has been crushed on the highway by a falling power pole, or it might be the Coast Guard calling to say that your boat was stolen by dope fiends who just called on the radio to say they are sinking somewhere off Sand Key and they've given you as their local credit reference, to pay for the rescue operation.

In my case, it was a just-reported shipwreck involving total strangers. An 88-foot tramp motor-sailor called *The Tampa Bay Queen* had gone on the reef off Hawk Channel, and all hands had abandoned ship.

There were only three of them, as it turned out. They had all washed ashore on an ice chest, raving incoherently about green sharks and coral heads and their ship breaking up like a matchbox while they screamed for help on a dead radio.

"Why not?" I thought. We are, after all, in The Business – and besides, I had never covered a shipwreck, not even a small one . . . and there was also talk about "losing the cargo" and the cruel imperatives of "salvage rights."

None of this talk seemed worth going out in a storm to investigate at the time, but that is not how The Business works. I went out, and not long after midnight I found myself huddled with these people in a local motel where they'd been given shelter for the night . . . and by dawn I was so deep in the story that I'd hired a 36-foot Cigarette boat to take me and the captain out to his doomed wreck, at first light, so he could recover whatever was left of it.

"We'll have to move quick," he said, "before the cannibals get there. They'll strip her naked by noon."

THE SUN CAME UP hot and bright that morning. The storm was over and the chop in the channel was down to 3 feet, which means nothing to a fast Cigarette boat. We were running 40 mph by the time we got out of the bay, and about 40 minutes later we were tying up to the wreck of *The Tampa Bay Queen*. It was lying on the bottom, tilted over at a 45-degree angle, and the sea had already broken it open.

There was no hope of saving anything except the new nylon sails and the V-8 engine and six nickel-plated brass winches, which the distraught captain said were worth $5,000 each – and maybe the 80-foot teakwood mast, which would fetch about $100 a foot in Key West, and looked like a thing of beauty.

We climbed up the steep rotted deck and the captain set about slashing down the sails with a butcher knife and ordering the first mate to take a hatchet to the winches. "Never mind a screwdriver," he shouted. "Just rip 'em out by the stumps."

The first mate was in no mood to take orders. He had not been paid in three weeks, he said, and he was wearing fancy black leather pilot's boots with elevator heels and slick leather soles, which caused him to constantly lose his footing and go sliding down the deck. We would hear him scream as he went off, and then there would be a splash. I spent most of my time pulling him back up the deck, and finally we lashed him to the mast with a steel safety cable, which allowed him to tend to his work.

By this time I had worked up a serious sweat, and the mystique of this filthy shipwreck had long since worn off. The captain was clearly a swine and the first mate was a middle-aged bellboy from New Jersey and the ship was probably stolen . . . . But here I was out on the high sea with these people, doing manual labor in the morning and bleeding from every knuckle. It was time, I felt, for a beer.

I was moving crabwise along the deck, homing in on the cooler we'd left in the Cigarette boat, when I saw the scavengers coming in. They had been circling the wreck for a while, two half-naked thugs in a small skiff, and the captain had recognized them instantly.

"God help us now," he muttered. "Here they come. These are the ones I was worried about." He looked nervously out at the two burly brutes in the cannibal boat, and he said he could see in their eyes that they were getting ready to board us and claim the whole wreck for themselves.

"It won't be much longer," he said. "These bastards are worse than pirates. We may have to fight for it."

I shrugged and moved off toward the beer cooler, at the other end of the wreck. The captain was obviously crazy, and I had lost my feel for The Story. All I wanted was a cold can of beer.

By the time I got to the Cigarette boat, however, the thugs had made their move and were tying up alongside us, grinning like wolves as they crouched between me and the cooler. I stared down at them and swore never again to answer my phone after midnight.

"Was this your boat?" one of them asked. "We heard you whimpering all night on the radio. It was a shame."

THE NEXT FEW MINUTES were tense, and by the end of that time I had two new partners and my own marine salvage business. The terms of the deal were not complex, and the spirit was deeply humane.

The captain refused to cooperate at first, screeching hoarsely from the other end of the wreck that he had silent partners in Tampa who would soon come back and kill all of us . . . .

But you hear a lot of talk like that in The Keys, so we ignored him and drank all the beer and hammered out a three-way agreement that would give the captain until sundown to take anything he wanted, and after that the wreck would be ours.

It was the Law of the Sea, they said. Civilization ends at the waterline.

Beyond that, we all enter the food chain, and not always right at the top.

SALVAGE IS NOT LOOTING

a selection from

The San Francisco *Examiner*, 10 March 1986

"The crew took a vote, and she lost, so we traded her for two cases of beer to the first boat we ran into, about 100 miles north of Aruba. It was a gang of shrimpers from Savannah. They were headed back to port.... That was four years ago, and the girl is still in a state mental hospital somewhere out West."

— Boat captain from Key West

KEY WEST, FL – The sea is nervous tonight. Another cold front is coming in, a north wind is putting whitecaps on the waves. The Mako is tied up to a sea-grape tree just in front of my door, whipping frantically around at the end of its rope like a wild beast caught in a trap. I go out every once in a while to adjust the docking knots, but the line is still rubbing bark off the tree and my new Japanese wind sock has been ripped to shreds by the gusts.

The neighbors complain about my screaming, but their noise is like the barking of dumb dogs. It means nothing. They are not seafaring people. The only boats that concern them are the ones they might want to rent, and when a storm comes they hide in their rooms like house cats.

My own situation is different. I am now in the Marine Salvage Business, and cruel storms are the lifeblood of our profession. It is the nature of salvage to feed on doom and disaster.

My new partners moved quickly to consolidate our position. We formed a shrewd corporate umbrella and expanded at once into the reef-diving and deep-water game fishing business, in order to crank up the revenue stream while we plundered the odd wreck here and there, and searched for sunken treasure.

Capt. Elgin took charge of all fishing and diving operations, Crazy

Mean Brian would handle plundering, and I was in charge of salvaging sunken treasure.

OUR FORTUNES took an immediate turn for the worse less than 24 hours after we seized our first wreck, when the elegant teakwood mast on the doomed *Tampa Bay Queen* turned out to be split from top to bottom with a long spiral fracture filled with termites, black putty and sea worms. It was utterly worthless, and the rest of the ship was stripped overnight by what my partners called "filthy cowboys from Big Coppitt Key," a gang of seagoing Hell's Angels who have terrorized these waters for years.

"They stripped out a whole submarine one night," Capt. Elgin told me. "The Navy left it open so the local school kids could take tours through it, but a storm came up and the Navy guys went ashore for the night, and by morning it was totally looted. They even took all the torpedoes."

Our only other asset was an ancient cannonball that Crazy Mean Brian had plundered from a site that he refused to disclose, because he said we would have serious problems "establishing jurisdiction."

"There area lot more of them down there," he said, "along with at least two brass cannons, but we would have to drag them at least three miles underwater before we could file for salvage rights."

They weighed about 1,600 pounds each, and they would not be easy to sell on the open market, due to the maze of conflicting claims already filed by other thieves, looters and competing treasure salvagers.

"Nobody took this stuff seriously until Mel Fisher came along," Capt. Elgin explained, "but the way it is now you can't come in with anything older than one of those green glass Coca-Cola bottles without having the whole federal court system on your neck." He laughed bitterly. "If we try to sell this cannonball in town, Mel Fisher would have us in jail for piracy."

"Nonsense," I said. "I've known Mel for years. He'd be happy, to help us out."

They both hooted at me. "We'd be better off trying to rip souvenir teeth out of living sharks," said Crazy Mean Brian. "You have no friends in the marine salvage business."

I called Mel Fisher at once and arranged to tour his facilities on the Navy base in downtown Key West.

I met him at the Two Friends Patio, a chic hangout on Front Street, where the whole Fisher operation goes after work because, they say, they drank there for free before the Mother Lode came in. Fisher, of course, is wallowing these days in gold bars and emeralds. He has discovered more wrecks than the AAA in a New York blizzard, and he appeared on "Good Morning America" the other day to trumpet his recent finds.

The wreck of the fabled *Atocha*, a Spanish galleon that went down in a storm off Key West in 1622, was located by Fisher's divers a few years ago and estimated to be worth about $400 million, mainly in gold and silver – but Mel said all that was chicken feed, now that he'd found emeralds.

"It's into the billions and billions now," he said.

Mel started out with a dive shop in the back of his parents' chicken farm in Redondo Beach in the late '50s. He'd moved from Indiana to California where his destiny was almost certainly to become heir to a poultry empire. In retrospect, and only recently so, Mel seems to have chosen the wiser path.

THERE ARE 12 BOATS in the harbor tonight, and four of them are ours. My 17-foot Mako is the smallest of the lot, but it is extremely fast and agile and it will go anywhere, day or night.

Crazy Mean Brian's new boat is tied up just behind mine. The local charter fishermen are not comfortable with the sight of it, because it reminds them of the "old days," when everybody was crazy. It is a 27-foot custom-built hull, with no name, mounted with twin 200-horsepower Johnson, and it will run to Cuba and back on one load of gas. Opposite Brian's is Capt. Elgin's 23-foot Robalo, the *Bobbi Lynn* – the reef diving boat – next to the gas pumps, shrouded in fog, and bounding around in the sea like some kind of rotted ghost out of Key Largo.

. . .

THE KID CAME BACK and took the battery out of the boat again. It happened late in the afternoon, the second time in three days.

The first time he took it for money – which was dumb, but at least I understood it. The man was a fishhead, a creature without many cells. He was like one of those big lizards that never feels any pain when you rip off its tail, or one of its legs – or even its head, as they do down in Chile – because it will all grow back by dawn, and nobody will know the difference.

Gw

HERMAN WOUK

RARE IS THE WRITER whose reputation is based upon his personal virtues rather than upon some popular vices; however, Herman Wouk remains just such a treasure. In fact, "official living legend" is the title which the Library of Congress bestowed upon the prolific writer back in the year 2000, when the Library itself was celebrating two hundred years and Wouk was but eighty-five.

Less than a decade later, the same living legend donated nearly a hundred volumes of the journals he'd been keeping since some time back in the 1930s. Wouk's parents both had been born in Russia, and his mother's father was a rabbi who refused to learn English. At the knee of that grandfather, Herman Wouk received all of his religious upbringing in Hebrew. It was one of those very talks that inspired the grandson not only to become a diarist, but also to commit himself to his writing regimen of creating at least a page a day. This is the same advice which Herman once passed along to Jimmy, and it's a schedule that both of them share.

The true measure of Wouk's work, though, lies not in its quantity, but in its quality. As *Time* magazine noted more than half a century ago, "Wouk is not an angry man," writing with any of the irreverent tones popularized by Hemingway or Mailer. "You don't use dirty language in someone's home," Wouk once said. "When a reader holds my book, we are in an even closer relationship than a guest's."

So how did a man of such virtue end up collaborating with one who advocates getting drunk, then screwing? Clearly, it's Herman's own damn fault for it was his page-a-day habit that had created his *Don't Stop the Carnival*.

"The hero of the novel, Norman Paperman, is indeed a Broadway press agent," writes Herman in the liner notes of Jimmy's album, "escaping from after a nasty heart attack, to start life over on a tropical paradise. That is a dream that many people have, and *Don't Stop the Carnival* tells the funny and sad tale of Norman's awakening."

Jimmy says that his own particular qualifications had come from his having survived the same island experiences as that very character.

"Autour de Rocher was a three-room hotel and bar I had bought part interest in," he says, "even after reading *Don't Stop the Carnival*."

As a storyteller, however, Herman Wouk did not need Jimmy's help. Though *Don't Stop the Carnival* weighs in at just under four hundred pages, a great number of his other books boast twice as many pages.

Meanwhile, at the age of ninety-four, Herman's regimen brought to life yet another book, *The Language God Talks: On Science and Religion*. Though it's only a couple hundred pages, that's ample length to contain the soul of one who's trying to bridge a chasm that runs between his faith and science. Understanding the passion and the commitment behind such a valiant effort, readers can expect that the writer comes much closer to bridging that gap than any other person before him.

Additional suggested works by Herman Wouk:

— *The Caine Mutiny* (1951)

— *This is My God* (1959)

— *The Winds of War* (1971)

— *War and Remembrance* (1978)

— *The Language God Speaks* (2010)

LESTER ATLAS

a selection from

Don't Stop the Carnival / Chapter I

KINJA WAS THE NAME of the island when it was British. Now the name on the maps and in the Caribbean guidebooks is Amerigo, but everybody who lives there still calls it Kinja.

The Union Jack flew over this enchanting green hump in the blue ocean for almost two hundred years. Before that the island was Danish; before that, French; before that, cannibal. Smoky gun battles between sailing ships and the old stone fort went with these flag changes; whizzing cannon balls, raiding parties, and an occasional death. But the fort guns have been silent for more than a century. The United States acquired the island peaceably in 1940, as part of the shuffling of old destroyers and Caribbean real estate that went on between Mr. Roosevelt and Mr. Churchill. The Americans ended up in this instance not only with the submarine base in Shark Bay — now gone back to tall guinea grass and catch-and-keep, the piers sagging and rotting, the rusty Quonset huts askew — but with the whole island. The details of the transaction were and are vague to the inhabitants. They were not much interested.

Keen-ja was the short, musical native version of the actual British name, King George the Third Island. Obviously this was a bit awkward for an American possession, so somebody in the Department of the Interior thought of Amerigo. The new name is used mainly on official stationery and in the school classrooms. There the pupils docilely scrawl themes and recite facts about Amerigo, but in the streets and playgrounds they call the place Kinja, and themselves Kinjans. All through the Caribbean they still say of a native of this island, "He fum Kinja."

The West Indian is not exactly hostile to change, but he is not much inclined to believe in it. This comes from a piece of wisdom that his climate of eternal summer teaches him. It is that, under all the parade of human effort and noise, today is like yesterday, and tomorrow will be like today, that existence is a wheel of recurring patterns from which no one escapes; that all anybody does in this life is live for a while and then die for good, without finding out much; and that therefore the idea is to take things easy and enjoy the passing time under the sun. The white people charging hopefully around the islands these days in the noon glare, making deals, bulldozing airstrips, hammering up hotels, laying out marinas, opening new banks, night clubs, and gift shops, are to him merely a passing plague. They have come before and gone before.

Long ago they came in their white-winged ships, swarmed over the islands, slaughtered the innocent cannibals, chopped down magnificent groves of mahogany that had stood since the Flood, and planted sugar cane. Sugar was money then, and it grew only in warm places. They used the felled mahogany to boil molasses. Those were the days of the great stone plantation houses and sugar mills; of seasick slaves hauled in from Africa, the ancestors of the Kinjans; of wealthy landowners with pink cool wives back in England, and warm black concubines on the premises. Then the sugar beet, which can grow in the north, came in, and black slavery went out. Bankruptcy and insurrection exploded along the island chain. The boom collapsed. The planters left. The plantation houses fell in. Today the natives put tin roofs over one nook or another in the massive broken walls and live there.

The West Indians do not know what will cause the frantic whites to leave next time. Perhaps a bad earthquake: the entire chain of drowned mountains rests on a shaky spot in the earth's crust. Or a tidal wave; or a very bad hurricane; or an outbreak of some dormant tropical disease; or the final accidental blow-up of the white man's grumbling cauldron in the north, which will send the Caribbean white remnant scurrying to – where next? Tasmania? Tierra del Fuego? Unlike the natives they cannot subsist, if the ships and planes stop coming, on crayfish, mangoes, coconuts, and iguanas.

Meantime, in a fashion, Amerigo is getting Americanized. The natives like the new holidays — Thanksgiving, Fourth of July, Presidents' birthdays, and the rest – added to the old British holidays and the numerous religious days, none of which they have abandoned. The work calendar has become a very light and unburdensome thing. The inflow of cash is making everyone more prosperous. Most Kinjans go along cheerily with this explosion of American energy in the Caribbean. To them it seems a new, harmless, and apparently endless carnival.

WILLIAM FAULKNER

from
Liner notes
"If I Could Just Get It On Paper"
SOMEWHERE OVER CHINA
1982

MISSISSIPPI'S PREMIER writer had not only a novelist's eye, but also a license to fly. And, more often than not, he probably had the bartender's ear.

In the early stages of Faulkner's writing career, he completed the typewritten draft of his second novel, *Mosquitoes,* while staying in Pascagoula. Basically, the story is an hour-by-hour account of a six-day cruise around Lake Pontchartrain aboard the motor yacht *Nausikaa.* The vessel belongs to a patron of the arts, who's invited aboard an odd assortment of artists, adolescents, and intellectuals. And from this tale, Jimmy quotes a line for his notes on the back of *Somewhere Over China*:

> It's young people who put life into ritual by making conventions a living part of life: Only old people destroy life by making it a ritual. The boy that belongs to a

secret pirates' gang and who dreams of defending an abstraction with his blood hasn't quite died out before twenty-one, you know.

While it's no secret that there was a time when Jimmy dreamed of following in Faulkner's literary wake, it's also quite clear that they shared many of the very same spaces over the course of their separate lives. In fact, Faulkner's earliest novels were written when he lived with a roommate in a small apartment in the French Quarter during the Bohemian period of his mid-twenties. There he wrote *Soldier's Pay* and the unpublished *Father Abraham*, as well as this particular selection at hand. To celebrate the small sum he was advanced for *Mosquitoes*, the writer threw a little dinner party at Galatoire's. We can only assume that Faulkner's spirit still lingered when Jimmy had imagined that Slade and Isabella would rendezvous at the very same restaurant on Bourbon Street.

Beyond that single assumption, it's safe also to assume that Faulkner and his twenty-something-year-old friends engaged in their favorite pastime of celebrating the somewhere of five o'clock, the Eighteenth Amendment be damned! While the author later claimed that his eventual life-long drinking served to fuel his creativity, others said it helped him escape the shortfalls of his own existence; especially, his financial problems.

Maybe, though, there was a much simpler explanation. "It was that horrible thing of 'You can't do this,'" said one of the so-called "Famous Creoles" about whom Faulkner had written in *Sherwood Anderson & Other Famous Creoles*. "We drank because they told us we couldn't."

Added another one of his friends: "We did not know whether or not we would be able to get a drink tomorrow or ever again, so we drank whatever came to hand."

In any case, *Mosquitoes* provides a wonderful opportunity to read about people drinking (illegally), above decks and below. Moreover, the novel puts forth, yet again, one of Mankind's most perplexing questions: "What is it that makes a man drink whisky on a night like this, anyway?"

Well, maybe – just maybe – they drank whisky because the recipe for a Hurricane had yet to be concocted.

Additional suggested works by William Faulkner:

— *The Sound and the Fury* (1929)

— *As I Lay Dying* (1930)

— *Sanctuary* (1931)

— *Light in August* (1932)

THE SECOND DAY

a selection from
M o s q u i t o e s

N O, SIR," the nephew answered patiently, "it's a pipe."
"A pipe?" Fairchild drew nearer, interested. "What's the idea? Will it
smoke longer than an ordinary pipe? Holds more tobacco, eh?"

"Smokes cooler," the nephew corrected, carving minutely at his cylinders. "Won't burn your tongue. Smoke the tobacco down to the last
grain, and it won't burn your tongue. You change gears on it, kind of,
like a car."

"Well, I'm damned. How does it work?" Fairchild dragged up a chair,
and the nephew showed him how it worked. "Well, I'm damned," he
repeated, taking fire. "Say, you ought make a pile of money out of it, if
you make it work, you know."

"It works," the nephew answered, joining his cylinders again. "Made
a little one out of pine. Smoked pretty good a pine pipe. It'll work all
right."

"What kind of wood are you using now?"

"Cherry." He carved and fitted intently, bending his coarse dark head
above his work. Fairchild watched him. "Well, I'm damned," he said
again in a sort of heavy astonishment. "Funny nobody thought of it before. Say, we might form a stock company, you know, with Julius and
Major Ayers. He's trying to get rich right away at something that don't
require work, and this pipe is a lot better idea than the one he's got, for I
can't imagine even Americans spending much money for something that
don't do anything except keep your bowels open. That's too sensible for
us, even though we will buy anything. . . . Your sister tells me you and
she are going to Yale college next month."

"I am," he corrected, without raising his head. "She just thinks she's
going too, that's all. She kept on worrying dad until he said she could go.
She'll be wanting to do something else by then."

"What does she do?" Fairchild asked. "I mean, does she have a string of beaux and run around dancing and buying things like most girls like her do?"

"Naw," the nephew answered, "she spends most of her time and mine too tagging around after me. Oh, she's all right, I guess," he added tolerantly, "but she hasn't got much sense." He unfitted the cylinders, squinting at them.

"That's where she changes gear, is it?" Fairchild leaned nearer again. "Yes, she's a pretty nice sort of a kid. Kind of like a racehorse colt, you know. . . . So you're going up to Yale. I used to want to go to Yale, myself, once. Only I had to go where I could. I guess there comes a time in the life of every young American, of the class that wants scholastic learning or that accepts the inevitability of education, when he wants to go to Yale or Harvard. Maybe that's the value of Yale or Harvard to our American life: a kind of illusion of an intellectual Nirvana that makes the ones that can't go there work like hell where they do go, so as not to show up so poorly alongside of the anointed. Still, ninety-nine out of a hundred Yale and Harvard turn out are reasonably bearable to live with, if they ain't anything else. And that's something to say for any manufactory, I guess. But I'd like to have gone there. . . ."

The nephew was not listening particularly. He shaved and trimmed solicitously at his cylinder. Fairchild said:

"It was a kind of funny college I went to. A denominational college, you know, where they turned out preachers. I was working in a mowing machinery factory in Indiana, and the owner of the factory was an alumnus and a trustee of this college. He was a sanctimonious old fellow with a beard like a goat, and every year he offered a half scholarship to be competed for by young men working for him. You won it, you know, and he found you a job near the college to pay your board but not enough to do anything else – to keep you from fleshly temptations, you know – and he had a monthly report on your progress sent to him. And I won it, that year.

"It was just for one year, so I tried to take every thing I could. I had about six or seven lectures every day, besides work I had to do to earn my board. But I kind of got interested in learning things: I learned in spite of the instructor we had. They were a bunch of broken down preachers: head full of dogma and intolerance and a belly full of big meaningless words. English literature course whittled down Shakespeare because he wrote about whores without pointing a moral and one instructor always insisted that the head devil in *Paradise Lost* was an inspired prophetic portrait of Darwin and they wouldn't touch Byron with a ten-foot pole.

Swinburne was reduced to his mother and his old standby, the ocean. And I guess they'd have cut this out had they worn one piece bathing suit's in those days. But in spite of it, I kind of got interested in learning things. I would like to have looked inside my mind, after that year was up. . . ." He gazed out the water, over the snoring waves, steady and wind-frothed. He laughed. "And I joined a fraternity, too, almost."

The nephew bent over his pipe. Fairchild produced a package of cigarettes. The nephew accepted one with abstraction. He accepted a light, also. "I guess you've got your eye on a fraternity, haven't you?" he suggested.

"Senior club," the nephew corrected shortly. "If I can make it."

"Senior club," Fairchild repeated. "That means you join for three years, eh? That's a good idea. I like that idea. But I had to do everything in one year, you see. I couldn't wait. I never had much time to mix with the other students. Six hours a day at lectures, and the rest of the time working and studying for next day. But I couldn't help but hear something about it, about rushing and pledges and so on, and how so and so were after this fellow or that, because he made the football team or something.

"There was a fellow at my boarding house: a kind of handsome tall fellow he was, always talking about the big athletes and such in school. He knew them all by their first names, and he always had some yarn about girls and he was always showing you a pink envelope or something – a kind of gentlemanly innuendo, protecting their good names. He was a senior, he told me, and he was the first one to talk to me about fraternities. He said he had belonged to one a long time, though he didn't wear a badge. He had given his badge to a girl, who wouldn't return it. . . . You see," Fairchild explained again, "I had to work so much – you know: getting into a rut of work for bread and meat, where chance couldn't touch me much. Chance and information. That's what they mean by wisdom, horse sense, you know. . . .

"He was the one that told me he could get me in this fraternity, if I wanted to." He drew at his cigarette, flipped it away. "It's young people who put life into ritual by making conventions a living part of life: only old people destroy life by making it a ritual. And I wanted to get all I could out of being in a college. The boy that belongs to a secret pirates' gang and who dreams of defending an abstraction with his blood, hasn't quite died out before twenty-one, you know. But I didn't have any money.

"Then he suggested that I get more work temporarily. He pointed out to me other men who belonged to it, or who were going to join – baseball players, and captains of teams, and prize scholars and such. So I got more work. He told me not to mention it to anybody, that that was the way they did it. I didn't know anybody much, you see," he explained. "I had to work pretty steady all day: no chance to get to know anybody well enough to talk to 'em." He mused upon the ceaseless fading battalions of waves. "So I got some more work to do. This had to be night work, so I got a job helping to fire the college power plant. I could take my books along with me and study while the steam was up, only it cut into my sleep some, and sometimes I would get too drowsy to study. So I had to give up one of my lecture courses, though the instructor finally agreed to let me try to make it up during the Christmas vacation. But I learned how to sleep in a cinder pile or a coal bunker, anyway." The nephew was interested now. His knife was idle in his hand, his cylinder reposed, forgetting the agony of wood.

"It would take twenty-five dollars, but working overtime as I was, I figured it wouldn't be any actual cost to me at except the loss of sleep. And a young fellow can stand that if he has to. I was used to work, you know, and it seemed to me that this was just like finding twenty-five dollars.

"I had been working about a month when this fellow came to me and told me that something had happened and the fraternity would have to initiate right away, and he asked me how much I had earned. I lacked a little of having twenty-five dollars, so he said he would loan me the difference to make it up; and I went to the power house manager and told him I had to have some money to pay a dentist with, and got my money and gave it to this fellow, and he told me where to be the following night – behind the library at a certain hour. So I did: I was there, like he said." Fairchild laughed again.

"What'd the bird do?" the nephew asked. "Gyp you?"

"It was cold, that night. Late November, and a cold wind came right out of the north, whistling around that building among the bare trees. Just a few dead leaves on the trees made a kind of sad dry sound. We had won a football that afternoon and I could hear yelling occasionally, and see lights in the dormitories where the ones that could afford to lived, warm and jolly looking, with the bare trees swaying and waving across the windows. Still celebrating the game we had won.

"So I walked back and forth, stamping my feet, and after a while I went around the corner of the library where it wasn't so cold and I could stick out my head occasionally in case they came looking for me. From this side of the building I could see the hall where the girls lived. It was all lighted up, as a party, and I could see shadows coming and going upon the drawn shades, where they were dressing up and fixing their hair and all; and pretty soon I heard a crowd coming across the campus and I thought here they come at last. But they passed on, going toward the girls' hall, where the party was.

"I walked up and down some more, stamping my feet. Pretty soon I heard a clock striking nine. In a half an hour I'd have to be back at the power house. They were playing music at the party: I could hear it even in spite of the closed windows, and I thought maybe I'd go closer. But the wind was colder: and there was a little snow in it, and besides I was afraid they'd come for me and I wouldn't be there. So I stamped my feet, walking up and down. Pretty soon I knew it must be nine-thirty, but I stayed a while longer, and soon it was snowing hard – a blizzard. It was the first snow of the year, and somebody came to the door of the party and saw it, and then they all came out to look, yelling: I could hear the girls' voices, kind of high and excited and fresh, and the music was louder. Then they went back, and the music was faint again, and then the clock struck ten. So I went on back to the power house. I was already late." He ceased, musing on the glittering battalions of waves and hands of wind slapping them whitely. He laughed again. "But I nearly joined one, though."

"How about the bird," the nephew asked. "Didn't you hunt him up the next day?"

"He was gone. I never saw him again. I found out later he wasn't even in college. I never did know what became of him." Fairchild rose. "Well, you get it finished, and we'll form a company and get rich."

The nephew sat, clutching his knife and his cylinder, gazing after Fairchild's stocky back until the other passed from view. "You poor prune," he said, resuming his work again.

V. S. NAIPAUL

THOUGH ONE of Jimmy's longtime favorite books is Alec Waugh's history of the Caribbean entitled *A Family of Islands*, it somehow never made the cut for that baker's dozen (minus one).

And like a lot of readers, Jimmy confuses Alec Waugh with the writer's brother, Evelyn (pronounced *Eev-lyn*), whom many surely think must be Alec's sister. Jimmy does bring up Waugh's work in *A Pirate Looks at Fifty*; however, one of the only two books that Jimmy's packed into his flight bag is V. S. Naipaul's *The Loss of El Dorado: A Colonial History*.

A native Trinidadian of Indian descent, Naipaul chronicles his island's history by tracing the schemes of those Spanish explorers who first arrived on these Caribbean shores in 1537. The pervasive myth that compelled the rulers and adventurers of the Old World to seek the riches of the New – the belief in that something called *El*

Dorado – is a myth that first emerged from the Muisca, who were living in the eastern savanna of what is present-day Colombia.

Basically, that myth recounts the initiation rites for each new leader of the Muisca. After a period of seclusion inside a cave near the lagoon known as Guatavita, the chief would cover his naked body with a dust of gold before riding a raft out to the center of the waters. There he would offer up artifacts of solid gold, as well as emeralds to those spirits who lived below. Once that ceremony was done, his offering was met with great celebration by those Muisca along the beach, and the new chief then made his way ashore to rule over his subjects. In the language of the Spanish who would come in search of all this treasure, the gilded ruler was known as *El Dorado*: "the golden one."

Of course, the Spanish were not the only ones who'd come to the New World hoping to find those artifacts; not far behind them followed the English. In most cases, their original destination in this quest was the island of Trinidad, and Naipaul's native land had served both nations as a starting point for these expeditions. First, it was a camp; then, a colony. And eventually, Trinidad became a nation with a people of its own. Along the way, however, British slaves from the empire's colony in India were sent to labor there. Understandbly, then, some of the island's native-born population is of Indian heritage, such as Naipaul himself.

In time, the loss of *El Dorado* came to represent not simply a horde of treasure which eluded all explorers; it came to symbolize a loss of ideals altogether. Nowhere is this more clear than in Naipaul's portrayal of Sir Walter Raleigh, who came to Trinidad in the raids of 1585.

In awarding V. S. Naipaul a Nobel Prize for Literature in 2001, the committee noted that his "literary domain has extended far beyond the West Indian island of Trinidad, his first subject, and now encompasses India, Africa, America from south to north, the Islamic countries of Asia and, not least, England. Naipaul," they declared "is [Joseph] Conrad's heir as the annalist of the destinies of empires in the moral sense: what they do to human beings. His authority as a narrator is grounded in his memory of what others have forgotten, the history of the vanquished." And it is a form of history that reads as literature.

This, then, is the book that Jimmy had packed for his birthday flight aboard *The Hemisphere Dancer*.

Additional suggested works by V. S. Naipaul:

— *The Loss of El Dorado* (1970)

— *Reading & Writing: A Personal Account* (2000)

FATHERS AND SONS

a selection from

The Loss of El Dorado
Part I: The Third Marquisate / Chapter II

SIXTEEN PESOS AND A HALF, an official's salary: it gives a scale. After the El Dorado failure this part of the Spanish Main was on the periphery of the Spanish Empire. Margarita, the nearly exhausted pearl island, had fifty-one houses; nineteen belonged to priests and widows. And Margarita was the brightest spot in the region. The region held nothing for officials, and when they found out they complained to the King like children.

"Your Majesty wished to reward me. But my luck didn't last too long. I was given this petty post, which I nevertheless hold in high esteem inasmuch as it is Your Majesty's pleasure." – "Give me another job," the first Simón de Bolivar wrote. "Anyone can handle Venezuela, even if he has very little ability." No ships came from Spain; salaries were not paid. "I swear before God that for twenty months I haven't been given a meal. I have got to eat, and if it weren't for the few Indians I have – free men – who grow a little maize on my little patch, neither they nor I would have anything to eat. I am compelled to do this to provide something for my family, and I trust Your Majesty will consider it well done, seeing that I can do nothing else." – "Now I am being asked for rent. Does a governor pay rent? Besides, how can I pay rent if I don't have any money? Send me a decree so that I can live in this house and not pay rent."

The life of the isolated official was yet full of alarms. "In one of my letters I begged Your Majesty for the favour of the governorship of Caracas. But now I beg Your Majesty not to give it me, because there is a rumour that the last governor was poisoned by herbs. A few days ago the bishop, who was visiting, died in the same way; and I hear that the people there are in the habit of using these herbs. Some strange deaths have occurred in that province and I beg Your Majesty to look at me with eyes of pity."

Foreign corsairs raided the small settlements at will and sometimes just for fun. Some Dutchmen captured a group of pearl-gathering Spaniards off Margarita one day and asked them how big Margarita was. The Spaniards said it was very big. The Dutchmen laughed; they knew that when the pearl fisheries were busy there were only about thirty-five people in the fifty-one houses of Margarita.

The Spaniards never had enough to eat. They were also in danger of being eaten. Man-eating Caribs were increasingly on the prowl. "They eat the Indians they seize and they kill the Spaniards in the most cruel way possible . . . and when these are not available they nourish themselves with Negroes." One report suggests that Negroes were castrated and "held in perpetual servitude" until they were eaten.

The Caribs might have left the Spaniards and their precious Negroes alone, as they left the Dutch and English alone (and were, indeed, their friends). But cannibalism was never a joke to the Spaniards; it aroused the same wish to mutilate, destroy, and enslave as did sodomy, another open Indian practice, and the Indian habit of casually pissing during conversation, without turning aside. "Their crimes are so notorious and of such gravity that there can be no hope of reducing these people by means of the Gospel. Your Majesty must dispeople these islands of Caribs." The Caribs must be declared slaves and hunted down; plans were sent again and again to Madrid for extermination raids by Spanish soldiers, for a galley patrol, the galleys manned by enslaved Caribs. "If something isn't done about this, it will be impossible to maintain any settlement in Trinidad, Cumaná, Margarita and other places."

But there was seldom any reply. The Empire was too big. Mexico, Peru, the guarding of the treasure fleets, the difficulties in Europe: the islands and the eastern Main were not important. There were a lot of Indians in Trinidad, a Spanish historian said, but it wasn't a "good" place. Sometimes, after years of correspondence, the armada of the treasure fleet made a sweep. But it didn't help. The Caribs continued to raid, the foreigners continued to come.

$\mathcal{G}$

Excerpt from *The Loss of El Dorado* by V. S. Naipaul. Copyright ©1969 by V. S. Naipaul. Used by permission of Alfred A. Knopf, a division of Random House, Inc.

PETER MATTHIESSEN

from
"Havana Daydreamin'"
HAVANA DAYDREAMIN'
1976

IN 1974, MATTHIESSEN'S fifth novel was an inventive piece of fiction told pretty much by means of the conversation among some turtle men off the Cayman Islands.

An experiment in typography and design, the book contains expanses of white space interspersed with brief dialogues, each separated by simple line drawings that represent the sun and the moon. This tale of a doomed voyage then inspired Jimmy's "Havana Daydreamin'."

"I fell in love with the description of the men on the turtle boat," he notes. "I used them to create my own boat and my own destination."

At times, *Far Tortuga* itself appears to be more a work of poetry than one of prose, but trying to make that literary distinction would only detract from the story, as well as from Matthiessen's uncanny ability to capture the lilt of this Caribbean dialect. Its rhythm often conveys even further a sense that the novel might just as well be read as music as anything else.

And none of this is at all out of character for Peter Matthiessen. Among America's best writers, he has long defied readers to determine whether he's a writer/naturalist or a naturalist/writer. His possesses not just the novelist's eye, but the naturalist's eye as well. "I like to hear and smell the countryside, the land my characters inhabit," he explains. "I don't want these characters to step off the page, I want them to step out of the landscape."

Consequently, there's none other quite like Matthiessen; no other works quite like his.

Not surprisingly, he remains very much a world traveller whose scientific intellect has fed his personal curiosity and enhanced his works of fiction and nonfiction alike since the 1950s. One such example began with an incident off the waters of the eastern tip of Long Island in June of 1964, when a fishing boat brought in a great white shark that measured almost eighteen feet and weighed close to four thousand pounds.

"This monster was towed ashore and hauled out on the docks of Montauk, and as I lived not far away I went down one day to see it," notes Matthieesen. "Its length was awesome, and so was its vast maw, but most appalling was its girth, its massiveness: one saw immediately how such a beast could take a seal in a single dreadful gulp." Or, perhaps, the torso of some innocent swimmer.

Another curious spectator on that Montauk dock was a scuba diver named Peter Gimbel, whose family also happened to own the department store of the same name. A noted underwater film-maker, Gimbel found his curiosity was so piqued by this beast that he set out to produce a documentary in which the shark would be the star. Gimbel invited Matthiessen along to satisfy the writer's own interests. His 1971 book was called *Blue Meridian: The Search for the Great White Shark*, and Gimbel's film was called "Blue Water, White Death." And while the book was well-written and the movie was well-produced, the reviews at the time were not especially great. Apparently, the critics wanted more drama.

Enter a freelance writer named Peter Benchley, who'd heard of that shark incident off Montauk Point, then imagined a scenario in which a great white terrorized an entire community when it refused to leave local waters. At the time, however, the only available research on the "white death" was that just undertaken by Matthiessen and Gimbel.

Benchley's *Jaws* was published in 1974, and that slim novel remained on the best-seller list for forty-four weeks. It's movie version by Steven Spielberg was released in 1975. Clearly, the entire Montauk episode had struck a chord, and it's counterpoint came in September of '75.

On NBC's "Saturday Night," the "Not-Ready-for-Prime-Time Players" introduced the world to the "the cleverest of all sharks" – the Land Shark. "Unlike the great white shark, which tends to inhabit the waters and harbors of recreational beach areas," intoned the legendary Don Pardo, "the Land Shark may strike at any place, any time. It is capable of disguising its voice, and generally preys on young, single women." Need there be anything else said of this subject?

Meanwhile, among Matthiessen's lesser known works is his 1986 book called *Men's Lives: The Surfmen and Baymen of the South Fork*, which chronicles the history and eventual disappearance of the centuries-old fishing industry at that same eastern end of Long Island, now more fashionably known as "The Hamptons."

"I was not making enough as a writer to survive," he explains of his own situation around Montauk back in the 1950s. "I needed some other kind of work, and fishing seemed like the logical thing to do."

A generation later, though, Matthiessen had become an established writer of more than a dozen books, and South Fork's fishing industry was being endangered by pollution, by development, and by sport fishermen who wanted limits placed on the taking of striped bass, the commercial fishermen's most profitable catch. And so, he set out to draw attention to the plight of those fish and these fishermen alike.

Though readers today might already be aware of the eventual outcome of that struggle a quarter century ago, *Men's Lives* still remains a fascinating piece of cultural history, as well as a true companion to the fictional tale of those turtle men in the Caymans.

Additional suggested works by Peter Matthiessen:

— *At Play in the Fields of the Lord* (1965)

— *Blue Meridian: The Search for the Great White Shark* (1971)

— *Far Tortuga* (1975)

— *The Snow Leopard* (1978)

— *Nine-headed Dragon River: Zen Journals 1969-1982* (1986)

— *Men's Lives: The Surfmen and Baymen of the South Fork* (1986)

— *On the River Styx and Other Stories* (1989)

— *End of the Earth: Voyage to Antarctica* (2003)

— *Shadow Country* (2008)

FAR TORTUGA
a selection from
Chapter IX

THE TURTLE CRAWLS are water pens constructed of long mangrove saplings stuck into the marly bottom in five feet of water and lashed with thatch rope, in pens twenty feet square. The saplings rise high above the surface as a protection against storm seas, and each crawl has a gate on one side that can be taken down to water level when turtles are put in or removed.

The gaunt poles of the crawls look bent in the gray wind, and figures in the boats stand motionless against the sky. There is catboat from the *Adams* and two Indian *cayucas*, which carry thalassia grass used as fodder for the turtles.

The turtlers wear plaited palm hats, the crawl tenders the sombreros of the coast. Most of the Wika men have Indian features in black skin.

Take he away!

The myriad bay-colored shells of the turtles in the crawl are scarred and dull, and the creatures have lost their gliding ocean flight: the crowded pen has made their movements jerky. Cornered, they rush against the stakes.

See dem turtle, Speedy? Some dem leant' from bein so long into dat crawl — dey gettin watered. Meat get all kind of slimy. In Cayman we don't like dem dat way, we likes dem fat, but watered turtle sells fine at Key West.

A big Wika dives beneath the surface of the pen, where the turtles mill. Grasping a turtle by the carapace, behind the head, he slips a noose around the base of a fore flipper, singing out to the men at the crawl gate.

Take he away!

The *Adams* boat crew deals with the big turtle: the whole pen is a turmoil of white water. The Wika seizes a second turtle while waiting for a noose to be thrown back to him; he leans into a corner, holding it upright, from behind. In pompous strength, he watches, and his dripping head is grim. The upright turtle blinks.

. . . your two hands, mon! Grob her!

Switch her ass dis way! *Dis* way!

Easy do it — see my foot?

Up she goes!

The noose is slung back to the Wika.

Take he away!

When the *Adams* boat is loaded and moves off, Byrum secures his catboat. One by one, the *Eden*'s turtles are hauled onto the gate, and Speedy cuts the flipper thongs with quick hooks of his knife as the turtle is shoved forward into the pen. Still upside down, each turtle sinks thrashing toward the bottom but quickly rights itself and rushes for the sea, striking so hard against the stakes on the far side that the crawl sways.

See dat? Won't be pretty long. Couple weeks into de crawl, all dat fine sea color be gone.

Dey pretty, mon. Green turtle pretty. I like de way dey swim among de reef.

Look out you don't cut dere throat, de way you swing dat knife — won't swim so pretty *den*.

Speedy slashes the last thong and shoves the turtle into the open pen.

No, mon. I can cut, mon. From school days. If he can't do nothin else, dis boy can *cut!*

Byrum socks him on the biceps.

You a hard nigger, mon! I very glad dat we in friendship!

Oh, I a hard one, dass de truth! *Hard* nigger, mon!

P. J. O'ROURKE

TOM CORCORAN had a classmate in Miami; the one in Ohio, not the one in Florida. Miami, after all, is not a city in Ohio. It is a university in Oxford. Ohio, that is, not the U.K.

Okay, let's start all over.

Tom Corcoran attended Miami University with P. J. O'Rourke, one of the funniest writers in this book, if not in the whole wide world.

O'Rourke went on to become editor of *National Lampoon* during its prominence in the Seventies. This was the period when that magazine was spawning a school of other iconoclasts, from *Saturday Night Live* to *Animal House* to the *Lampoon* franchise of movies.

The very beginning of that sort of boomer-humor was the monthly *National Lampoon* itself, whose sole reason for being was simply to lampoon. And there are few in all the history of Mankind who've become more adept at lampooning than has P. J. O'Rourke.

One might think that poking fun at people and places and things would probably put one on the fast track to a lonely life, but that's not at all the case with O'Rourke. He continued his friendship with Corcoran, developed another close mutual friendship with Hunter Thompson, and somehow found himself aboard Jimmy's *Euphoria*, now and then, along with Corcoran and Hunter's son, Juan. As noted in that vessel's log on January 13, 1977, the crew included: "Captain Buffett, first mate Miss Jane, cabin and deck aide Juan Thompson, navigator and beer stowage consultant Corcoran, and P. J. O'Rourke (itinerant journalist, jester, and Big Apple raconteur)." And on the next day: "Captain awakes and remarks on snoring concert given nightlong by journalist." Despite that lack of sleep, their friendship endured.

In the years since then, O'Rourke has honed his skills in publications ranging from *Playboy*, *Esquire*, and *Vanity Fair* to *Harper's*, the *Atlantic*, and *Rolling Stone*. While satire might well remain his strength, political commentary has since pulled hard abeam, and O'Rourke has proven himself to be a highly-respected correspondent in that regard. A research fellow at the Cato Institute, P. J. appears regularly on National Public Radio, and his profile as a commentator on *60 Minutes* points out that O'Rourke is "the most quoted living man in *The Penguin Dictionary of Modern Humorous Quotations*." (See, I *told* you he was funny.) In between all that, he's written more than fourteen, best-selling books.

And while he and Jimmy might not often find themselves aboard the same boat these days, they both washed up by chance on the same beach in Mexico back in the winter of 2007, and there O'Rourke convinced Jimmy to perform a benefit concert in Hong Kong for the Foreign Correspondents' Club Charity Fund. All of that sounds quite respectable for a beach bum, as well as for a lampooner, who once wrote a piece in the *Lampoon* entitled "How to Drive Fast on Drugs While Getting Your Wing-Wang Squeezed and Not Spill Your Drink."

Additional suggested works by P. J. O'Rourke:

— *Modern Manners* (1983)

— *Holidays in Hell* (1989)

— *Age and Guile Beat Youth, Innocence, and a Bad Haircut* (1995)

— *On the Wealth of Nations: Books That Changed the World* (2007)

— *Driving Like Crazy* (2009)

IMPORTANT PEOPLE

a selection from
Modern Manners:
An Etiquette Book for Rude People

A N IMPORTANT PERSON should be treated exactly like anyone else holding a gun at your head.

Fortunately there aren't many important people. To be important a person must be able to have an effect on your life. But the anarchy, entropy, and confusion in what's left of Western civilization make it difficult for anyone to have any effect on anything. Therefore this chapter is about people who are *called* important rather than people who *are* important. The headwaiter at Ma Maison, IRS auditors, and your immediate superior at work are to be treated under separate headings.

PEOPLE WHO ARE IMPORTANT "TO ME"

Some people who are called important are the "to me" kind of important, as in "My parents are important to me." If it is necessary to explain that someone is important to you, that explanation is all you are socially obligated to do for him. He isn't that important.

FAMOUS PEOPLE

Other people who are called important are actually famous. Of course, they aren't important, either. And it would be hard to think of anything less important than some of them. A lamprey is more important than Bianca Jagger. But it is not a lie to call famous people important, because it isn't they to whom we are referring. It's their fame. Fame is very important. Modern society is without any concept of dignity, worth, or regard. Today the only thing which sets one person apart from another is his or her degree of fame.

Social obligations to the modern or famous type of important people are enormous and complex. We must be as obsequious as possible to famous people and do everything in our power to make them like us.

Fame is a communicable disease. And if you kiss the ass of someone who's got it, you may catch it yourself.

INTRODUCTIONS

In order to meet famous people and give them the opportunity to take advantage of you, an introduction is necessary. Asking for their auto- graph or running up to their restaurant table and gushing over their latest cause for notoriety ("I *loved* your divorce!") won't do.

The perfectly correct and most formal introduction is: "Mr. Awfulpics, may I present Mr. Climby" or "Mr. Grosspoints, may I present you to Miss Bedable." Or use the word "introduce" instead of "present." It's almost as correct and not as stupid sounding. The less famous person is presented to the more famous person. But men are always presented to women no matter how many times the man has appeared on the cover of *Time* and no matter how obvious it is that the woman wants to sleep with him just because he has. The only circumstance in which a woman is presented to a man is if that man is President of the United States – and who'd want to sleep with *him?*

CHILDREN

Children are never introduced at all unless the famous person has a thing for them and you have one paid for and ready at the time.

SUBFAMOUS PEOPLE

Of course, the very formal method of introduction is never used by so- phisticated people because sophisticated people have never had occasion to read a book of etiquette. Besides, most of them know each other al- ready. But it is wise to use the most ceremonious forms with people such as game-show hosts, rock-star wives, daytime television personalities, Cher's boyfriends, and others who might be insecure about their social status because they have none.

Otherwise, introductions are tailored to the circumstances and to the amount of fame involved. If there is no fame involved and you're just introducing one worthless friend of yours to another, you can say simply, "Don't you guys know each other?" and walk away.

INSIGNIFICANT FRIENDS

When you want to introduce an insignificant friend to a famous person, you probably don't really *want* to at all. It's hard to do what you really want all the time, but, like every difficult task, it results in a feeling of great accomplishment and satisfaction. Just leave your friend standing there like furniture while you chat happily with the MTV veejay, mafia hit man, or elected official.

If you owe money to the friend or are married to him or her and taking this tack will get you in trouble, you can say, "Oh, by the way, Mr. Panflash, this is Alice. We went to the same child psychiatrist back in Lake Forest." If you have an ancient acquaintance with someone not worth knowing, most people will at least pretend to forgive you – the way they would pretend to forgive you for a birth defect or the wrong racial background. Of course, your spouse – whom you met two weeks ago in a health club – may be perplexed by this explanation, but that's what your spouse gets for trying to marry up.

AMBITIOUS FRIENDS

Introducing an ambitious friend to a famous person is more tricky. It's not done unless the friend is so ambitious that he might be of use to you someday. Ambitious people are a lot more annoying than worthless people. Strategically, you don't want to alienate the friend, but, tactically, you don't want to be remembered for foisting that friend on your famous acquaintance. Say, "Mrs. Greedagent, this is my friend Mark. He's involved in a lot of really interesting cable TV projects." You've used the phrase "cable TV projects" – international code words for "unemployed and on the make" – so the celebrity cannot claim she wasn't warned. Change "cable TV projects" to "video art" if you think it will be a really long, long time before your friend is famous himself.

WHEN TWO PEOPLE ARE BOTH IMPORTANT

Introducing important people to each other is much more satisfying than introducing them to video artists. One approach is to do everything you can to make them attractive to each other and hope that you will receive a sort of social "finder's fee" if they hit it off. They won't. The social habits of famous people are like the sexual practices of porcupines, which urinate on each other to soften the quills. A more interesting thing to do is to make sure the two important people loathe each other right from the start: "Ana Plotless, this is Bret Leadpart. Bret thinks your novels are very good – of their kind . . . Bret, Ana has told me that she's heard you're very famous – in Japan." This way you'll become the conduit for all sorts of wonderful maliciousness between these two august souls.

WHEN ONE PERSON IS IMPORTANT
AND THE OTHER PERSON IS "INTERESTING"

The most delightful introduction you can make is to introduce an important person to someone he or she is going to find sexually interesting. This introduction is made in two parts. First you prep the sex object: "Kiki, save the drugs for later. I'm going to introduce you to Antonio.

Antonio is a famous photographer . . . Yes, he does lots of fashion – Paris *Vogue*." Then you march Kiki over to your well-known friend. "Antonio, you're going to love this girl. She once made Warren Beatty bleed out the ears." Kiki's name is not a necessary part of the transaction.

INTRODUCING YOURSELF

There is only one person you can never introduce to the famous and that is yourself. Therefore it's good to cultivate the affections of professional sycophants such as publicists, movie agents, and freelance writers for *Vanity Fair* magazine. These people are understandably short of friends, and, if you are kind to them, they'll let you get the benefit of celebrity acquaintance while they do the fawning and toadying necessary for such acquaintance to be achieved.

MAKING FAMOUS PEOPLE COMFORTABLE

Once you've met a famous person, say something that will make you remembered: "Cornelia Guest! Oh, my gosh, Miss Guest, I know it's polite for a gentleman to remove his hat when he meets a lady, but for you, I feel I should do something more, like take off my pants!!!"

Then shut up. Famous people think they want to be treated like regular people. This is not true. Famous people also think they are special and wonderful. This is even less true. The best course of action is to go ahead and treat them as if they are ordinary (because, boy, are they ever) but now and then throw something into the conversation to show that you share their completely wrong-headed opinion of their own wonderfulness: "Gosh, Cornelia, you make liposuction *come alive!*"

When the famous person you've met is not in your immediate company, ignore him or her completely. This is the modern use of the "cut direct" mentioned in Chapter 3. Whereas, in former times, the cut direct was used on enemies, it has now evolved into a polite way to show respect for famous friends. It is an article of faith among celebrities that they are constantly pestered by the public. Of course there are so many celebrities, and so few of them are celebrated for anything, that most of the time the public can't be bothered. But it's only common courtesy to act as though the famous people you know are so famous that the public is very bothered indeed. You don't want to be seen as part of that public. Wait for the celebrities to pester you. They will soon enough. If they weren't infantile self-obsessed hogs for attention, then our kind of society never would have thought they were important in the first place.

JOSEPH CONRAD

from
Liner Notes
BANANA WIND
1996

OFF THE COAST of Marseilles in 1878, Teodor Józef Konrad Korzeniowski fired a single shot into his own twenty-year-old torso. Only three years earlier, he'd fled his uncle's custody in hopes of seeking in France – or upon the sea – the sort of life he'd only known in books. His home in Kraków had offered him neither happiness, nor freedom, and he hoped he might find them at the end of a long train ride to Marseilles. Apparently, he had not.

In 1875, this runaway teenager had shipped out as steward aboard the *Sainte-Antoine*, bound for Martinique; however, there he soon found himself running guns to Spain. Below decks, he began to amass an ever-growing gambling debt. And then, the sailor fell in love with a beautiful woman; however, that relationship failed. Clearly, none of this provided him with happiness or freedom. So, he shot himself.

Clearly, Teodor Korzeniowski had survived, or else he wouldn't be in this book. His uncle paid his debts, his doctors nursed him back to health, but the French revoked his seaman's papers. At that point, Korzeniowski went to sea as a British Merchant Marine. Before long, he began to read, to write, and to speak in English. He became a naturalized subject of the vast British Empire. And, then, he changed his name to Joseph Conrad.

The boy who'd known next to nothing of the sea would rise to the rank of master. Just as important, he began to write stories based upon his own experiences: *Outcast of the Islands*, *The Rescue*, and *The Nigger of the "Narcissus."* Though English was neither Conrad's native language, nor even his second, those adventures unfolded with a richness of style that did more than tell a story; they were tales that plumbed the depths of the human soul. Almost at once, he developed an audience, but most of Conrad's greatest works still were in the offing. In time, his narrative style and his anti-heroic characters would leave their mark upon the likes of F. Scott Fitzgerald, V. S. Naipaul, and Hunter S. Thompson.

In the midst of the liner notes for *Banana Wind*, sits the image of a young Captain Jimmie Buffett – fabled father of the father of this sailor – at the rail of the *Del Mondo*. Just to the right, in a shaded box beneath the two words "Lion Hearted," stands a passage from a Conrad classic.

A Tale of the Sea was always the subtitle of this work, but it followed beneath two different titles. The original is *The Nigger of the "Narcissus,"* but the publisher felt that no one in America would ever read any book with that title. So, the stateside edition became *Children of the Sea.*

"It is the book by which," Conrad wrote, "I am willing to stand or fall. Its pages are the tribute of my unalterable and profound affection for the ships, the seamen, the winds and the great sea – the molders of my youth, the companions of the best years of my life."

Altogether, it is a grand story that requires a slow-paced reading in order to savor its style and its story. Unlike the more widely-read and filmed, *Lord Jim* or *Heart of Darkness* (from which *Apocalypse Now* was adapted), this novel stands strong as testament to his steadfast command of the English language, as well as his knowledge of the eternal sea.

Additional suggested works by Joseph Conrad:

— *Heart of Darkness* (1899)

— *Youth, a Narrative &Two Other Stories* (1902)

— *Typhoon & Other Stories* (1903)

— *The Mirror of the Sea* (1906)

"A Tale of the Forecastle"

a selection from

The Nigger of the *Narcissus* / Chapter 1

MR. BAKER, CHIEF MATE OF THE SHIP *Narcissus*, stepped in one stride out of his lighted cabin into the darkness of the quarter-deck. Above his head, on the break of the poop, the night-watchman rang a double stroke. It was nine o'clock. Mr. Baker, speaking up to the man above him, asked: "Are all the hands aboard, Knowles?"

The man limped down the ladder, then said reflectively: "I think so, sir. All our old chaps are there, and a lot of new men has come . . .They must be all there."

"Tell the boatswain to send all hands aft," went on Mr. Baker; "and tell one of the youngsters to bring a good lamp here. I want to muster our crowd."

The main deck was dark aft, but halfway from forward, through the open doors of the forecastle, two streaks of brilliant light cut the shadow of the quiet night that lay upon the ship. A hum of voices was heard there, while port and starboard, in the illuminated doorways, silhouettes of moving men appeared for a moment, very black, without relief, like figures cut out of sheet tin. The ship was ready for sea. The carpenter had driven in the last wedge of the main-hatch battens, and, throwing down his maul, had wiped his face with great deliberation, just on the stroke of five. The decks had been swept, the windlass oiled and made ready to heave up the anchor; the big tow-rope lay in long bights along one side of the main deck, with one end carried up and hung over the bows, in readiness for the tug that would come paddling and hissing noisily, hot and smoky, in the limpid, cool quietness of the early morning. The captain was ashore, where he had been engaging some new hands to make up his full crew; and, the work of the day over, the ship's officers had kept out of the way, glad of a little breathing-time. Soon after dark the few

315

liberty-men and the new hands began to arrive in shore-boats rowed by white-clad Asiatics, who clamoured fiercely for payment before coming alongside the gangway-ladder. The feverish and shrill babble of Eastern language struggled against the masterful tones of tipsy seamen, who argued against brazen claims and dishonest hopes by profane shouts. The resplendent and bestarred peace of the East was torn into squalid tatters by howls of rage and shrieks of lament raised over sums ranging from five annas to half a rupee; and every soul afloat in Bombay Harbour became aware that the new hands were joining the *Narcissus*.

Gradually the distracting noise had subsided. The boats came no longer in splashing clusters of three or four together, but dropped alongside singly, in a subdued buzz of expostulation cut short by a "Not a piece more! You go to the devil!" from some man staggering up the accommodation-ladder – a dark figure, with a long bag poised on the shoulder. In the forecastle the newcomers, upright and swaying amongst corded boxes and bundles of bedding, made friends with the old hands, who sat one above another in the two tiers of bunks, gazing at their future shipmates with glances critical but friendly. The two forecastle lamps were turned up high, and shed an intense hard glare; shore-going hard hats were pushed far on the backs of heads, or rolled about on the deck amongst the chain-cables; white collars, undone, stuck out on each side of red faces; big arms in white sleeves gesticulated; the growling voices hummed steady amongst bursts of laughter and hoarse calls. "Here, sonny, take that bunk! . . . Don't you do it! . . . What's your last ship? . . . I know her . . . Three years ago, in Puget Sound . . . This here berth leaks, I tell you! . . . Come on; give us a chance to swing that chest! . . . Did you bring a bottle, any of you shore toffs? . . . Give us a bit of 'baccy . . . I know her; her skipper drank himself to death . . . He was a dandy boy! . . . Liked his lotion inside, he did! . . . No! . . . Hold your row, you chaps! . . . I tell you, you came on board a hooker, where they get their money's worth out of poor Jack, by – ! . . ."

A little fellow, called Craik and nicknamed Belfast, abused the ship violently, romancing on principle, just to give the new hands something to think over. Archie, sitting aslant on his sea-chest, kept his knees out of the way, and pushed the needle steadily through a white patch in a pair of blue trousers. Men in black jackets and stand-up collars, mixed with men bare-footed, bare-armed, with coloured shirts open on hairy chests, pushed against one another in the middle of the forecastle. The group swayed, reeled, turning upon itself with the motion of a scrimmage, in a haze of tobacco smoke. All were speaking together, swearing at every second word. A Russian Finn, wearing a yellow shirt with pink stripes, stared upwards, dreamy-eyed, from under a mop of tumbled hair. Two young giants with smooth, baby faces – two Scandinavians – helped each other to spread their bedding, silent, and smiling placidly at the tempest of good-humoured and meaningless curses. Old Singleton, the oldest able seaman in the ship, sat apart on the deck right under the lamps, stripped to the waist, tattooed like a cannibal chief all over his powerful chest and enormous biceps. Between the blue and red patterns his white skin gleamed like satin; his bare back was propped against the heel of the bowsprit, and he held a book at arm's length before his big, sunburnt face. With his spectacles and a venerable white beard, he resembled a learned and savage patriarch, the incarnation of barbarian wisdom serene in the blasphemous turmoil of the world. He was intensely absorbed, and, as he turned the pages an expression of grave surprise would pass over his rugged features. He was reading "Pelham." The popularity of Bulwer Lytton in the forecastles of Southern-going ships is a wonderful and bizarre phenomenon. What ideas do his polished and so curiously insincere sentences awaken in the simple minds of the big children who people those dark and wandering places of the earth? What meaning can their rough, inexperienced souls find in the elegant verbiage of his pages? What excitement? – What forgetfulness? – What appeasement? Mystery! Is it the fascination of the incomprehensible? – Is it the charm of the impossible? Or are those beings who exist beyond the pale of life stirred by his tales as by an enigmatical disclosure of a resplendent world that exists within the frontier of infamy and filth, within that border of dirt and hunger, of misery and dissipation, that comes down on all sides to the water's edge of the incorruptible ocean, and is the only thing they know of life, the only thing they see of surrounding land – those life-long prisoners of the sea? Mystery?

Singleton, who had sailed to the southward since the age of twelve, who in the last forty-five years had lived (as we had calculated from his papers) no more than forty months ashore – old Singleton, who boasted, with the mild composure of long years well spent, that generally from the day he was paid off from one ship till the day he shipped in another he seldom was in a condition to distinguish daylight – old Singleton sat unmoved in the clash of voices and cries, spelling through "Pelham" with slow labour, and lost in an absorption profound enough to resemble a trance. He breathed regularly. Every time he turned the book in his enormous and blackened hands the muscles of his big white arms rolled slightly under the smooth skin. Hidden by the white moustache, his lips, stained with tobacco-juice that trickled down the long beard, moved in inward whisper. His bleared eyes gazed fixedly from behind the glitter of black-rimmed glasses. Opposite to him, and on a level with his face, the ship's cat sat on the barrel of the windlass in the pose of a crouching chimera, blinking its green eyes at its old friend. It seemed to meditate a leap on to the old man's lap over the bent back of the ordinary seaman who sat at Singleton's feet. Young Charley was lean and long-necked. The ridge of his backbone made a chain of small hills under the old shirt. His face of a street-boy – a face precocious, sagacious, and ironic, with deep down-ward folds on each side of the thin, wide mouth – hung low over his bony knees. He was learning to make a lanyard knot with a bit of an old rope. Small drops of perspiration stood out on his bulging forehead; he sniffed strongly from time to time, glancing out of the corners of his restless eyes at the old seaman, who took no notice of the puzzled young-ster muttering at his work. The noise increased. Little Belfast seemed, in the heavy heat of the forecastle, to boil with facetious fury. His eyes danced; in the crimson of his face, comical as a mask, the mouth yawned black, with strange grimaces. Facing him, a half-undressed man held his sides, and throwing his head back, laughed with wet eyelashes. Others stared with amazed eyes. Men sitting doubled-up in the upper bunks smoked short pipes, swinging bare brown feet above the heads of those who, sprawling below on sea-chests, listened, smiling stupidly or scornfully. Over the white rims of berths stuck out heads with blinking eyes; but the bodies were lost in the gloom of those places, that resembled narrow niches for coffins in a white-washed and lighted mortuary. Voices buzzed louder. Archie, with compressed lips, drew himself in, seemed to shrink into a smaller space, and sewed steadily, industrious and dumb. Belfast shrieked like an inspired Dervish: ". . . So I seez to him, boys, seez I, 'Beggin' yer pardon, sorr,' seez I to that second mate of that steamer – 'beggin' your-r-r pardon, sorr, the Board of Trade must 'ave been drunk when they granted you your certificate!' 'What do you say, you – !' seez he, comin' at me like a mad bull . . . all in his white clothes; and I up with my tarpot and capsizes it all over his blamed lovely face and his lovely jacket . . . 'Take that!' seez I. 'I am a sailor, anyhow, you nosing, skipper-licking, useless, sooperfloos bridge-stanchion, you! That's the kind of man I am!' shouts I . . . You should have seed him skip, boys! Drowned, blind with tar, he was! So . . ."

"Don't 'ee believe him! He never upset no tar; I was there!" shouted somebody. The two Norwegians sat on a chest side by side, alike and placid, resembling a pair of love-birds on a perch, and with round eyes stared innocently; but the Russian Finn, in the racket of explosive shouts and rolling laughter, remained motionless, limp and dull, like a deaf man without a backbone. Near him Archie smiled at his needle. A broad-chested, slow-eyed newcomer spoke deliberately to Belfast during an ex-hausted lull in the noise: "I wonder any of the mates here are alive yet with such a chap as you on board! I concloode they ain't that bad now, if you had the taming of them, sonny."

"Not bad! Not bad!" screamed Belfast. "If it wasn't for us sticking together . . . Not bad! They ain't never bad when they ain't got a chawnce, blast their black 'arts . . ." He foamed, whirling his arms, then suddenly grinned and, taking a tablet of black tobacco out of his pocket, bit a piece off with a funny show of ferocity. Another new hand – a man with shifty eyes and a yellow hatchet face, who had been listening open-mouthed in the shadow of the midship locker – observed in a squeaky voice: "Well, it's a 'omeward trip, anyhow. Bad or good, I can do it hall on my 'ed – s'long as I get 'ome. And I can look after my rights! I will show 'em!" All the heads turned towards him. Only the ordinary seaman and the cat took no notice. He stood with arms akimbo, a little fellow with white eyelashes. He looked as if he had known all the degradations and all the furies. He looked as if he had been cuffed, kicked, rolled in the mud. He looked as if he had been scratched, spat upon, pelted with unmention-able filth . . . and he smiled with a sense of security at the faces around. His ears were bending down under the weight of his battered hard hat. The torn tails of his black coat flapped in fringes about the calves of his legs. He unbuttoned the only two buttons that remained and every one saw he had no shirt under it. It was his deserved misfortune that those rags which nobody could possibly be supposed to own looked on him as if they had been stolen. His neck was long and thin; his eyelids were red; rare hairs hung about his jaws; his shoulders were peaked and drooped like the broken wings of a bird; all his left side was caked with mud which showed that he had lately slept in a wet ditch. He had saved his inefficient carcass from violent destruction by running away from an American ship where, in a moment of forgetful folly, he had dared to engage himself; and he had knocked about for a fortnight ashore in the native quarter, cadging for drinks, starving, sleeping on rubbish-heaps, wandering in sunshine: a startling visitor from a world of nightmares. He stood repulsive and smiling in the sudden silence. This clean white fore-castle was his refuge; the place where he could be lazy; where he could wallow and lie and eat – and curse the food he ate; where he could dis-play his talents for shirking work, for cheating, for cadging; where he could find surely someone to wheedle and someone to bully – and where he would be paid for doing all this. They all knew him. Is there a spot on earth where such a man is unknown, an ominous survival testifying to the eternal fitness of lies and impudence? A taciturn long-armed shellback, with hooked fingers, who had been lying on his back smoking, turned in his bed to examine him dispassionately, then, over his head, sent a long jet of clear saliva towards the door. They all knew him! He was the man that cannot steer, that cannot splice, that dodges the work on dark nights; that, aloft, holds on frantically with both arms and legs, and swears at the wind, the sleet, the darkness; the man who curses the sea while others work. The man who is the last out and the first in when all hands are called. The man who can't do most things and won't do the rest. The pet of philanthropists and self-seeking landlubbers. The sympathetic and deserving creature that knows all about his rights, but knows nothing of courage, of endurance, and of the unexpressed faith, of the unspoken loyalty that knits together a ship's company. The independent offspring of the ignoble freedom of the slums full of disdain and hate for the austere servitude of the sea.

Some one cried at him: "What's your name?" – "Donkin," he said, looking round with cheerful effrontery. – "What are you?" asked another voice. – "Why, a sailor like you, old man," he replied, in a tone that meant to be hearty, but was impudent. – "Blamme if you don't look a blamed sight worse than a broken-down fireman," was the comment in a convinced mutter. Charley lifted his head and piped in a cheeky voice: "He is a man and a sailor" – then wiping his nose with the back of his hand bent down industriously over his bit of rope. A few laughed. Others stared doubtfully. The ragged newcomer was indignant. – "That's a fine way to welcome a chap into a fo'c'sle," he snarled. "Are you men or a lot of 'artless cannybals?" – "Don't take your shirt off for a word, shipmate," called out Belfast, jumping up in front, fiery, menacing, and friendly at the same time. – "Is that 'ere bloke blind?" asked the indomitable scarecrow, looking right and left with affected surprise. "Can't 'ee see I 'aven't got no shirt?"

He held both his arms out crosswise and shook the rags that hung over his bones with dramatic effect.

"'Cos why?" he continued very loud. "The bloody Yankees been tryin' to jump my guts hout 'cos I stood up for my rights like a good'un. I ham a Henglishman, I ham. They set upon me an' I 'ad to run. That's why. A'n't yer never seed a man 'ard up? Yah! What kind of blamed ship is this? I'm dead broke. I 'aven't got nothink. No bag, no bed, no blanket, no shirt – not a bloomin' rag but what I stand in. But I 'ad the 'art to stand hup agin' them Yankees. 'As any of you 'art enough to spare a pair of old pants for a chum?"

He knew how to conquer the naive instincts of that crowd. In a moment they gave him their compassion, jocularly, contemptuously, or surlily; and at first it took the shape of a blanket thrown at him as he stood there with the white skin of his limbs showing his human kinship through the black fantasy of his rags. Then a pair of old shoes fell at his muddy feet. With a cry: "From under," a rolled-up pair of trousers, heavy with tar stains, struck him on the shoulder. The gust of their benevolence sent a wave of sentimental pity through their doubting hearts. They were touched by their own readiness to alleviate a shipmate's misery. Voices cried: "We will fit you out, old man." Murmurs: "Never seed seech a hard case . . . Poor beggar . . . I've got an old singlet . . . Will that be of any use to you? . . . Take it, matey . . ." Those friendly murmurs filled the forecastle. He pawed around with his naked foot, gathering the things in a heap and looked about for more. Unemotional Archie perfunctorily contributed to the pile an old cloth cap with the peak torn off. Old Singleton, lost in the serene regions of fiction, read on unheeding. Charley, pitiless with the wisdom of youth, squeaked: "If you want brass buttons for your new unyforms I've got two for you." The filthy object of universal charity shook his fist at the youngster. – "I'll make you keep this 'ere fo'c'sle clean, young feller," he snarled viciously. "Never you fear. I will learn you to be civil to an able seaman, you hignorant hass." He glared harmfully, but saw Singleton shut his book, and his little beady eyes began to roam from berth to berth. – "Take that bunk by the door there – it's pretty fair," suggested Belfast. So advised, he gathered the gifts at his feet, pressed them in a bundle against his breast, then looked cautiously at the Russian Finn, who stood on one side with an unconscious gaze, contemplating, perhaps, one of those weird visions that haunt the men of his race. "Get out of my road, Dutchy," said the victim of Yankee brutality. The Finn did not move – did not hear. "Get out, blast ye," shouted the other, shoving him aside with his elbow. "Get out, you blanked deaf and dumb fool. Get out." The man staggered, recovered himself, and gazed at the speaker in silence. – "Those damned furriners should be kept hunder," opined the amiable Donkin to the forecastle. "If you don't teach 'em their place they put on you like hanythink." He flung all his worldly possessions into the empty bed-place, gauged with another shrewd look the risks of the proceeding, then leaped up to the Finn, who stood pensive and dull. – "I'll teach you to swell around," he yelled. "I'll plug your eyes for you, you blooming square-head." Most of the men were now in their bunks and the two had the forecastle clear to themselves. The development of the destitute Donkin aroused interest. He danced all in tatters before the amazed Finn, squaring from a distance at the heavy, unmoved face. One or two men cried encouragingly: "Go it, Whitechapel!" settling themselves luxuriously in their beds to survey the

fight. Others shouted: "Shut yer row! . . . Go put yer 'ed in a bag! . . ."
The hubbub was recommencing. Suddenly many heavy blows struck
with a handspike on the deck above boomed like discharges of small
cannon through the forecastle. Then the boatswain's voice rose outside
the door with an authoritative note in its drawl: "D'ye hear, below there?
Lay aft! Lay aft to muster all hands!"

There was a moment of surprised stillness. Then the forecastle floor
disappeared under men whose bare feet flopped on the planks as they
sprang clear out of their berths. Caps were rooted for amongst tumbled
blankets. Some, yawning, buttoned waistbands. Half-smoked pipes were
knocked hurriedly against woodwork and stuffed under pillows. Voices
growled: "What's up? . . . Is there no rest for us?" Donkin yelped: "If
that's the way of this ship, we'll 'ave to change hall that . . . You leave me
alone . . . I will soon . . ." None of the crowd noticed him. They were
lurching in twos and threes through the doors, after the manner of merchant Jacks who cannot go out of a door fairly, like mere landsmen. The
votary of change followed them. Singleton, struggling into his jacket,
came last, tall and fatherly, bearing high his head of a weatherbeaten sage
on the body of an old athlete. Only Charley remained alone in the white
glare of the empty place, sitting between the two rows of iron links that
stretched into the narrow gloom forward. He pulled hard at the strands
in a hurried endeavour to finish his knot. Suddenly he started up, flung
the rope at the cat, and skipped after the black tom that went off leaping
sedately over chain compressors, with the tail carried stiff and upright,
like a small flag pole.

Outside the glare of the steaming forecastle the serene purity of the
night enveloped the seamen with its soothing breath, with its tepid breath
flowing under the stars that hung countless above the mastheads in a
thin cloud of luminous dust. On the town side the blackness of the water
was streaked with trails of light which undulated gently on slight ripples,
similar to filaments that float rooted to the shore. Rows of other lights
stood away in straight lines as if drawn up on parade between towering
buildings; but on the other side of the harbour sombre hills arched high
their black spines, on which, here and there, the point of a star resembled
a spark fallen from the sky. Far off, Byculla way, the electric lamps at the
dock gates shone on the end of lofty standards with a glow blinding and
frigid like captive ghosts of some evil moons. Scattered all over the dark
polish of the roadstead, the ships at anchor floated in perfect stillness
under the feeble gleam of their riding-lights, looming up, opaque and
bulky, like strange and monumental structures abandoned by men to an
everlasting repose.

Before the cabin door Mr. Baker was mustering the crew. As they stumbled and lurched along past the mainmast, they could see aft his round, broad face with a white paper before it, and beside his shoulder the sleepy head, with dropped eyelids, of the boy, who held, suspended at the end of his raised arm, the luminous globe of a lamp. Even before the shuffle of naked soles had ceased along the decks, the mate began to call over the names. He called distinctly in a serious tone befitting this roll-call to unquiet loneliness, to inglorious and obscure struggle, or to the more trying endurance of small privations and wearisome duties. As the chief mate read out a name, one of the men would answer: "Yes, sir!" or "Here!" and, detaching himself from the shadowy mob of heads visible above the blackness of starboard bulwarks, would step barefooted into the circle of light, and in two noiseless strides pass into the shadows on the port side of the quarter-deck. They answered in divers tones: in thick mutters, in clear, ringing voices; and some, as if the whole thing had been an outrage on their feelings, used an injured intonation: for discipline is not ceremonious in merchant ships, where the sense of hierarchy is weak, and where all feel themselves equal before the unconcerned immensity of the sea and the exacting appeal of the work.

Mr. Baker read on steadily: "Hanssen – Campbell – Smith – Wamibo. Now, then, Wamibo. Why don't you answer? Always got to call your name twice." The Finn emitted at last an uncouth grunt, and, stepping out, passed through the patch of light, weird and gaudy, with the face of a man marching through a dream. The mate went on faster: "Craik – Singleton – Donkin . . . O Lord!" he involuntarily ejaculated as the incredibly dilapidated figure appeared in the light. It stopped; it uncovered pale gums and long, upper teeth in a malevolent grin. – "Is there anything wrong with me, Mister Mate?" it asked, with a flavour of insolence in the forced simplicity of its tone. On both sides of the deck subdued titters were heard. – "That'll do. Go over," growled Mr. Baker, fixing the new hand with steady blue eyes. And Donkin vanished suddenly out of the light into the dark group of mustered men, to be slapped on the back and hear flattering whispers. Round him men muttered to one another: "He ain't afeard, he'll give sport to 'em, see if he don't . . . Reg'lar Punch and Judy show . . . Did ye see the mate start at him? . . . Well! Damme, if I ever! . . ."

The last man had gone over, and there was a moment of silence while the mate peered at his list. – "Sixteen, seventeen," he muttered. "I am one hand short, bosun," he said aloud. The big west-countryman at his elbow, swarthy and bearded like a gigantic Spaniard, said in a rumbling bass: "There's no one left forward, sir. I had a look round. He ain't aboard, but he may turn up before daylight." – "Ay. He may or he may not," commented the mate; "Can't make out that last name. It's all just a smudge . . . That will do, men. Go below."

The indistinct and motionless group stirred, broke up, began to move forward.

"Wait!" cried a deep, ringing voice.

All stood still. Mr. Baker, who had turned away yawning, spun round open-mouthed. At last, furious, he blurted out: "What's this? Who said 'Wait'? What . . ."

But he saw a tall figure standing on the rail. It came down and pushed through the crowd, marching with a heavy tread towards the light on the quarter-deck. Then again the sonorous voice said with insistence: "Wait!" The lamplight lit up the man's body. He was tall. His head was away up in the shadows of lifeboats that stood on skids above the deck. The whites of his eyes and his teeth gleamed distinctly, but the face was indistinguishable. His hands were big and seemed gloved.

Mr. Baker advanced intrepidly. "Who are you? How dare you . . ." he began.

The boy, amazed like the rest, raised the light to the man's face. It was black. A surprised hum – a faint hum that sounded like the suppressed mutter of the word "nigger" – ran along the deck and escaped out into the night. The nigger seemed not to hear. He balanced himself where he stood in a swagger that marked time. After a moment he said calmly: "My name is Wait – James Wait."

"Oh!" said Mr. Baker. Then, after a few seconds of smouldering silence, his temper blazed out. "Ah! Your name is Wait. What of that? What do you want? What do you mean, coming shouting here?"

The nigger was calm, cool, towering, superb. The men had approached and stood behind him in a body. He overtopped the tallest by a half a head. He said: "I belong to the ship." He enunciated distinctly, with soft precision. The deep, rolling tones of his voice filled the deck without effort. He was naturally scornful, unaffectedly condescending, as if from his height of six-foot-three he had surveyed all the vastness of human folly and had made up his mind not to be too hard on it. He went on: "The captain shipped me this morning. I couldn't get aboard sooner. I saw you all aft and I came up the ladder, and could see directly you were mustering the crew. Naturally, I called out my name. I thought you had it on your list, and would understand. You misapprehended." He stopped short. The folly around him was confounded. He was right as ever, and as ever ready to forgive. The disdainful tones had ceased, and breathing heavily, he stood still, surrounded by all these white men. He held his head up in the glare of the lamp – a head vigorously modelled into deep shadows and shining lights – a head powerful and misshapen with a tormented and flattened face – a face pathetic and brutal: the tragic, the mysterious, the repulsive mask of a nigger's soul.

Mr. Baker, recovering his composure, looked at the paper close. "Oh, yes; that's so. All right, Wait. Take your gear forward," he said.

Suddenly the nigger's eyes rolled wildly, became all whites. He put his hand to his side and coughed twice, a cough metallic, hollow, and tremendously loud; it resounded like two explosions in a vault; the dome of the sky rang to it, and the iron plates of the ship's bulwarks seemed to vibrate in unison; then he marched off forward with the others. The officers lingering by the cabin door could hear him say: "Won't some of you chaps lend a hand with my dunnage? I've got a chest and a bag." The words, spoken sonorously, with an even intonation, were heard all over the ship, and the question was put in a manner that made refusal impossible. The short, quick shuffle of men carrying something heavy went away forward, but the tall figure of the nigger lingered by the main hatch in a knot of smaller shapes. Again he was heard asking: "Is your cook a coloured gentleman?" Then a disappointed and disapproving, "Ah! h'm!" was his comment upon the information that the cook happened to be a mere white man. Yet, as they went all together towards the forecastle, he condescended to put his head through the galley door and boom out inside a magnificent "Good evening, doctor!" that made all the saucepans ring. In the dim light the cook dozed on the coal locker in front of the captain's supper. He jumped up as if he had been cut with a whip, and dashed wildly on deck to see the backs of several men going away laughing. Afterwards, when talking about that voyage, he used to say: "The poor fellow had scared me. I thought I had seen the devil." The cook had been seven years in the ship with the same captain. He was a serious-minded man with a wife and three children, whose society he enjoyed on an average one month out of twelve. When on shore, he took his family to church twice every Sunday. At sea, he went to sleep every evening with his lamp turned full up, a pipe in his mouth, and an open Bible in his hand. Some one had always to go during the night to put out the light, take the book from his hand, and the pipe from between his teeth. "For" – Belfast used to say, irritated and complaining – "some night, you stupid cookie, you'll swallow your ould clay, and we will have no cook. – "Ah! sonny, I am ready for my Maker's call . . . wish you all were," the other would answer with a benign serenity that was altogether imbecile and touching. Belfast outside the galley door danced with vexation. "You holy fool! I don't want you to die," he howled, looking up with furious, quivering face and tender eyes. "What's the hurry? you blessed wooden-headed ould heretic, the divvle will have you soon enough. Think of us ... of us ... of us!" And he would go away, stamping, spitting aside, disgusted and worried; while the other, stepping out, saucepan in hand, hot, begrimed, and placid, watched with a superior, cocksure smile the back of his "queer little man" reeling in a rage. They were great friends.

Mr. Baker, lounging over the after-hatch, sniffed the humid night in the company of the second mate. – "Those West India niggers run fine and large – some of them ... Ough! ... Don't they? A fine, big man that, Mr. Creighton. Feel him on a rope. Hey? Ough! I will take him into my watch, I think." The second mate, a fair gentlemanly young fellow, with a resolute face and a splended physique, observed quietly that it was just about what he expected. There could be felt in his tone some slight bitterness which Mr. Baker very kindly set himself to argue away. "Come, come, young man," he said, grunting between the words. "Come! Don't be too greedy. You had that big Finn in your watch all the voyage. I'll do what's fair. You may have those two young Scandinavians and I ... Ough! ... I get the nigger, and will take that ... Ough! that cheeky costermonger chap in a black frock-coat. I'll make him ... Ough! ... make him toe the mark, or my ... Ough! ... name isn't Baker. Ough! Ough! Ough!"

He grunted thrice – ferociously. He had that trick of grunting so between his words and at the end of sentences. It was a fine, effective grunt that went well with his menacing utterance, with his heavy, bull-necked frame, his jerky, rolling gait; with his big, seamed face, his steady eyes, and sardonic mouth. But its effect had been long discounted by the men. They liked him; Belfast, who was a favourite, and knew it – mimicked him, not quite behind his back. Charley – but with greater caution – imitated his walk. Some of his sayings became established daily quotations in the forecastle. Popularity can go no farther! Besides, all hands were ready to admit that on a fitting occasion the mate could "jump down a fellow's throat in a reg'lar Western Ocean style." Now he was giving his last orders. "Ough! ... You, Knowles! Call all hands at four. I want ... Ough! ... to heave short before the tug comes. Look out for the Captain. I am going to lay down in my clothes ... Ough! ... Call me when you see the boat coming. Ough! Ough! ... The old man is sure to have something to say when he comes aboard," he remarked to Creighton. "Well, good-night ... Ough! A long day before us to-morrow ... Ough! ... Better turn in now. Ough! Ough!"

Upon the dark deck a band of light flashed, then a door slammed, and Mr. Baker was gone into his neat cabin. Young Creighton stood leaning over the rail, and looked dreamily into the night of the East. And he saw in it a long country lane, a lane of waving leaves and dancing sunshine. He saw stirring boughs of old trees outspread, and framing in their arch the tender, the caressing blueness of an English sky. And through the arch a girl in a clear dress, smiling under a sunshade, seemed to be stepping out of the tender sky.

At the other end of the ship the forecastle, with only one lamp burning now, was going to sleep in a dim emptiness traversed by loud breathings, by sudden short sighs. The double row of berths yawned black, like graves tenanted by uneasy corpses. Here and there a curtain of gaudy chintz, half drawn, marked the resting-place of a sybarite. A leg hung over the edge very white and lifeless. An arm stuck straight out with a dark palm turned up, and thick fingers half closed. Two light snores, that did not synchronise quarreled in funny dialogue. Singleton stripped again – the old man suffered much from prickly heat – stood cooling his back in the doorway, with his arms crossed on his bare and adorned chest. His head touched the beam of the deck above. The nigger, half undressed, was busy casting adrift the lashing of his box, and spreading his bedding in an upper berth. He moved about in his socks, tall and noiseless, with a pair of braces beating about his heels. Amongst the shadows of stanchions and bowsprit, Donkin munched a piece of hard ship's bread, sitting on the deck with upturned feet and restless eyes; he held the biscuit up before his mouth in the whole fist, and snapped his jaws at it with a raging face. Crumbs fell between his outspread legs. Then he got up.

"Where's our water-cask?" he asked in a contained voice. Singleton, without a word, pointed with a big hand that held a short smouldering pipe. Donkin bent over the cask, drank out of the tin, splashing the water, turned round and noticed the nigger looking at him over the shoulder with calm loftiness. He moved up sideways.

"There's a blooming supper for a man," Donkin whispered bitterly. "My dorg at 'ome wouldn't 'ave it. It's fit enouf for you an' me. 'Ere's a big ship's fo'c'sle . . . Not a bloomin' scrap of meat in the kids I've looked in all the lockers . . ."

The nigger stared like a man addressed unexpectedly in a foreign language. Donkin changed his tone: "Giv' us a bit of 'baccy, mate," he breathed out confidentially, "I 'aven't 'ad a smoke or chew for the last month. I am rampin' mad for it. Come on, old man!"

"Don't be familiar," said the nigger. Donkin started and sat down on a chest nearby, out of sheer surprise. "We haven't kept pigs together," continued James Wait in a deep undertone. "Here's your tobacco." Then, after a pause, he asked: "What ship?" – "Golden State," muttered Donkin indistinctly, biting the tobacco. The nigger whistled low. – "Ran?" he said curtly. Donkin nodded: one of his cheeks bulged out. – "In course I ran," he mumbled. "They booted the life hout of one Dago chap on the passage 'ere, then started on me. I cleared hout 'ere." – "Left your dunnage behind?" – "Yes, dunnage and money," answered Donkin, raising his voice a little; "I got nothink. No clothes, no bed. A bandy-legged little Hirish chap 'ere 'as give me a blanket . . . Think I'll go an' sleep in the fore topmast staysail to-night."

He went on deck trailing behind his back a corner of the blanket. Singleton, without a glance, moved aside to let him pass. The nigger put away his shore togs and sat in clean working clothes on his box, one arm stretched over his knees. After staring at Singleton for some time, he asked without emphasis: "What kind of ship is this? Pretty fair? Eh?"

Singleton didn't stir. A long while after he said, with unmoved face: "Ship! . . . Ships are all right. It is the men in them!"

He went on smoking in the profound silence. The wisdom of half a century spent listening to the thunder of the waves had spoken unconsciously through his old lips. The cat purred on the windlass. Then James Wait had a fit of roaring, rattling cough, that shook him, tossed him like a hurricane, and flung him panting with staring eyes headlong on his sea-chest. Several men woke up. One said sleepily out of his bunk: "Struth! what a blamed row!" – "I have a cold on my chest," gasped Wait. – "Cold! you call it," grumbled the man; "should think 'twas something more . . ." – "Oh! you think so," said the nigger upright and loftily scornful again. He climbed into his berth and began coughing persistently while he put his head out to glare all round the forecastle. There was no further protest. He fell back on the pillow, and could be heard there wheezing regularly like a man oppressed in his sleep.

Singleton stood at the door with his face to the light and his back to the darkness. And alone in the dim emptiness of the sleeping forecastle he appeared bigger, colossal, very old; old as Father Time himself, who should have come there into this place as quiet as a sepulchre to contemplate with patient eyes the short victory of sleep, the consoler. Yet he was only a child of time, a lonely relic of a devoured and forgotten generation. He stood, still strong, as ever unthinking; a ready man with a vast empty past and with no future, with his childlike impulses and his man's passions already dead within his tattooed breast. The men who could understand his silence were gone – those men who knew how to exist beyond the pale of life and within sight of eternity. They had been strong, as those are strong who know neither doubts nor hopes. They had been impatient and enduring, turbulent and devoted, unruly and faithful. Well-meaning people had tried to represent those men as whining over every mouthful of their food; as going about their work in fear of their lives. But, in truth, they had been men who knew toil, privation, violence, debauchery – but knew not fear, and had no desire of spite in their hearts. Men hard to manage, but easy to inspire; voiceless men – but men enough to scorn in their hearts the sentimental voices that bewailed the hardness of their fate. It was a fate unique and their own; the capacity to bear it appeared to them the privilege of the chosen! Their generation lived inarticulate and indispensable, without knowing the sweetness of affections or the refuge of a home – and died free from the dark menace of a narrow grave. They were the everlasting children of the mysterious sea. Their successors are the grown-up children of a discontented earth. They are less naughty, but less innocent; less profane, but perhaps also less believing; and if they had learned how to speak they have also learned how to whine. But the others were strong and mute, they were effaced, bowed and enduring, like stone caryatides that hold up in the night the lighted halls of a resplendent and glorious edifice. They are gone now – and it does not matter. The sea and the earth are unfaithful to their children: a truth, a faith, a generation of men goes – and is forgotten, and it does not matter! Except, perhaps, to the few of those who believed the truth confessed the faith – or loved the men.

A breeze was coming. The ship that had been lying tide-rode swung to a heavier puff; and suddenly the slack of the chain cable between the windlass and the hawse-pipe clinked, slipped forward an inch, and rose gently off the deck with a startling suggestion as of unsuspected life that had been lurking stealthily in the iron. In the hawse-pipe, the grinding links sent through the ship a sound like a low groan of a man sighing under a burden. The strain came on the windlass, the chain tautened like a string, vibrated – and the handle of the screw-brake moved in slight jerks. Singleton stepped forward.

Till then he had been standing meditative and unthinking, reposeful and hopeless, with a face grim and blank – a sixty-year-old child of the mysterious sea. The thoughts of all his lifetime could have been expressed in six words, but the stir of those things that were as much a part of his existence as his beating heart called up a gleam of alert understanding upon the sternness of his aged face. The flame of the lamp swayed, and the old man, with knitted and bushy eyebrows, stood over the brake, watchful and motionless in the wild saraband of dancing shadows. Then the ship, obedient to the call of her anchor, forged ahead slightly and eased the strain. The cable relieved, hung down, and after swaying imperceptibly to and fro dropped with a loud tap on the hard wood planks. Singleton seized the high lever, and, by a violent throw forward of his body, wrung out another half-turn from the brake. He recovered himself, breathed largely, and remained for awhile glaring down at the powerful and compact engine that squatted on the deck at his feet, like some quiet monster – a creature amazing and tame.

"You . . . hold!" he growled at it masterfully, in the incult tangle of his white beard.

෬

JEAN DE LAFONTAINE

from
"A Baker's Dozen"
A Pirate Looks at Fifty
1998

DURING THE mid-1600s, Jean de la LaFontaine wrote some two hundred and forty-three poetic fables over twenty-six years, an accomplishment that might be compared to writing an album of songs just about every year during that time. And while some of his tales often were simply a somewhat more eloquent version of earlier Greek fables from Aesop and of Sanskrit fables from Pilpay, the Frenchman's works developed their own following around the world due to his originality, along with his mastery of the French language and of poetry alike.

Being fables, these poems concluded that there was always some moral to be found within the lives of animals who supposedly spoke among one another; however, LaFontaine's *Fables* went beyond that, for they were written to be read. In short, his primary audience was rather small, for his was an era when not a great many people possessed such skills. Nonetheless, LaFontaine had a simple point to make. "Everything speaks in the universe," he proclaimed. "There is nothing without its own language."

His most famous fable, "Les Deux Pigeons," relates the tale of two doves who share a nest until one declares that he wishes to see what the world has to offer. It's very much another version of the urge to be a vagabond, or a traveler, or a man for all seasides. And, of course, the urge to follow that impulse simply for the stories that experience might offer.

> "The matter is not worth a sigh; / Three days, at most, will satisfy, / And then, returning, I shall tell / You all the wonders that befell, – / With scenes enchanting and sublime / Shall sweeten all our coming time. / Who sees nothing, has nothing to say. / My travel's course, from day to day, / Will be the source of great delight. / A store of tales I shall relate, – / Say there I lodged at such a date, / And saw there such and such a sight. / You'll think it all occurr'd to you. –"

In reading *Fables*, though, you really won't find any particular one of them that has found a way into Jimmy's own works. (Apparently, someone missed the chance to sing that "Every Pigeon Tells A Story.") Nonetheless, it's not difficult to create some context for a couple of songs and stories that fall within the realm of talking animals who have morals to share; namely, "Chanson Pour Les Petits Enfants" and "Jolly Mon Sing."

A dolphin, for example, had some words and actions that humans might find worth heeding. "I wrote the picture book version [of *Jolly Mon*] with my daughter," he said, "and we wanted to make it clear that humans can learn from animals, and the natural world has room for all of our needs – not just man's." Or, as LaFontaine once had noted, "I use animals to instruct mankind."

So, once you begin to look a little closer at Jimmy and LaFontaine, a few other similarities begin to appear. Each, for example, has some fans who simply find joy in a story; other fans who celebrate the performance; and those who appreciate a work's subtle comment upon life.

Additional suggested works by Jean de LaFontaine:

— *Tales and Novels in Verse* (1664)

— *Fables* (12 volumes, 1668-94)

— *The Loves of Cupid and Psyche* (1669)

LE RAT ET L'HUÎTRE

(THE RAT AND THE OYSTER)

a selection from

Fables / Book IX

Translated from the French by Elizur Wright, Jr.

A COUNTRY RAT, of little brains,
　　Grown weary of inglorious rest,
Left home with all its straws and grains,
Resolved to know beyond his nest.
When peeping through the nearest fence,
"How big the world is, how immense!"
He cried; "There rise the Alps, and that
Is doubtless famous Ararat."
His mountains were the works of moles,
Or dirt thrown up in digging holes!
Some days of travel brought him where
The tide had left the oysters bare.
Since here our traveller saw the sea,
He thought these shells the ships must be.
"My father was, in truth," said he,
"A coward, and an ignoramus;
He dared not travel: as for me,
I've seen the ships and ocean famous;
Have cross'd the deserts without drinking,
And many dangerous streams unshrinking;
Such things I know from having seen and felt them."
And, as he went, in tales he proudly dealt them,
Not being of those rats whose knowledge
Comes by their teeth on books in college.

Among the shut-up shell-fish, one
Was gaping widely at the sun;
It breathed, and drank the air's perfume,
Expanding, like a flower in bloom.
Both white and fat, its meat
Appear'd a dainty treat.
Our rat, when he this shell espied,
Thought for his stomach to provide.
"If not mistaken in the matter,"
Said he, "no meat was ever fatter,
Or in its flavour half so fine,
As that on which to-day I dine."
Thus full of hope, the foolish chap
Thrust in his head to taste,
And felt the pinching of a trap –
The oyster closed in haste.

We're first instructed, by this case,
That those to whom the world is new
Are wonder-struck at every view;
And, in the second place,
That the marauder finds his match,
And he is caught who thinks to catch.

LE BERGER ET LA MER

(THE SHEPHERD AND THE SEA)

a selection from
Fables / Book IV
Translated from the French by Elizur Wright, Jr.

A SHEPHERD, neighbour to the sea,
Lived with his flock contentedly.
His fortune, though but small,
Was safe within his call.
At last some stranded kegs of gold
Him tempted, and his flock he sold,
Turn'd merchant, and the ocean's waves
Bore all his treasure – to its caves.
Brought back to keeping sheep once more,
But not chief shepherd, as before,
When sheep were his that grazed the shore,
He who, as Corydon or Thyrsis,
Might once have shone in pastoral verses,
Bedeck'd with rhyme and metre,
Was nothing now but Peter.
But time and toil redeem'd in full
Those harmless creatures rich in wool;
And as the lulling winds, one day,
The vessels wafted with a gentle motion,
"Want you," he cried, "more money, Madam Ocean?
Address yourself to some one else, I pray;
You shall not get it out of me!
I know too well your treachery."

This tale's no fiction, but a fact,
Which, by experience back'd,

Proves that a single penny,
At present held, and certain,
Is worth five times as many,
Of Hope's, beyond the curtain;
That one should be content with his condition,
And shut his ears to counsels of ambition,
More faithless than the wreck-strown sea, and which
Doth thousands beggar where it makes one rich, –
Inspires the hope of wealth, in glorious forms,
And blasts the same with piracy and storms.

JACK LONDON

from
"Well, Hello, Cowboy"
A Salty Piece of Land
2004

OYSTER PIRATE was but one of Jack London's so-called "professions" during the early part of his storied and colorful life. When some in San Francisco were trying to cultivate eastern oysters in the flats of the bay, the fifteen-year-old's *Razzle-Dazzle* sailed among a thriving band of little thieves who poached the shellfish from their beds and sold them to local restaurants. This was not London's only experience on the water, for he had owned his first skiff when he was twelve, and he'd own four other sailboats throughout the course of his life.

Though Jack London's time on the water might come as a surprise to those who think of him only in terms of his Klondike tales, such as *Call of the Wild* or *White Fang*, the renowned writer also was creator of *The Sea Wolf* and *South Sea Tales*, as well as a wonderful piece written for *Yachting Monthly* called "Small-Boat Sailing."

"A sailor is born, not made," he wrote for that magazine in 1912. "And by 'sailor' is meant, not the average efficient and hopeless creature who is found to-day in the forecastle of deepwater ships, but the man who will take a fabric compounded of wood and iron and rope and canvas and compel it to obey his will on the surface of the sea."

But London's fancy eventually was captured by the *Snark*, which is sort of like Jimmy's *Hemisphere Dancer*. While both men once dreamed of circling the globe, Jimmy's concept was to do it by air as he looked at fifty; London's was to do it by sea as the erstwhile oyster pirate looked at thirty. The vessel that the *New York Times* termed "Jack London's small craft" was a forty-three-foot motorsailer he designed to undertake a seven-year voyage with his wife. "The treasury is stuffed with emptiness," he told the *Times*, which sounds a lot like: "I've got to head this boat south pretty soon. / New album's old and I'm fresh out of tunes." Plus, the trip around the world meant, as London put it, "big moments of living."

Readers of that era fully understood that the naming of the *Snark* had been inspired by Lewis Carroll's long, moody poem called *The Hunting of the Snark (An Agony in 8 Fits)*, which told of "the impossible voyage of an improbable crew to find an inconceivable creature."

At a point in history where there was no such thing as sailing just for pleasure, the *Snark* was powered by wind and by engine to make the vessel capable not only of a voyage around the world, but also of any leisurely river trip. From San Francisco, the *Snark* would set sail for the Yang-tse River, the Nile, the Mediterranean, the Danube, and the Thames, then up the Seine to Paris. After crossing the Atlantic, London would next sail up the Hudson, pass through the Erie Canal, then go by way of the Illinois River down the Mississippi into the Gulf of Mexico.

So, London charted a course first for Hawaii, then on to the Marquesas, Tahiti, the Solomons, and Guadacanal. At that point, though, he feared that he'd developed leprosy, so he left the *Snark* and booked passage for treatment in Australia. When doctors in Sydney diagnosed his condition as psoriasis, the writer and his wife were forced to abandon their dream and sail home to California. When all was said and done, however, there remained a story to be told, and that became *The Cruise of the Snark*.

Additional suggested works by Jack London:

— *The Call of the Wild* (1903)

— *The Cruise of the Snark* (1911)

— *On the Makaloa Mat* (1919)

THE FIRST LANDFALL

a selection from

The Cruise of the *Snark* / Chapter V

I T WILL NOT BE SO MONOTONOUS AT SEA," I promised my fellow-voyagers on the *Snark*. "The sea is filled with life. It is so populous that every day something new is happening. Almost as soon as we pass through the Golden Gate and head south we'll pick up with the flying fish. We'll be having them fried for breakfast. We'll be catching bonita and dolphin, and spearing porpoises from the bowsprit. And then there are the sharks – sharks without end."

We passed through the Golden Gate and headed south. We dropped the mountains of California beneath the horizon, and daily the surf grew warmer. But there were no flying fish, no bonita and dolphin. The ocean was bereft of life. Never had I sailed on so forsaken a sea. Always, before, in the same latitudes, had I encountered flying fish.

"Never mind," I said. "Wait till we get off the coast of Southern California. Then we'll pick up the flying fish."

We came abreast of Southern California, abreast of the Peninsula of Lower California, abreast of the coast of Mexico; and there were no flying fish. Nor was there anything else. No life moved. As the days went by, the absence of life became almost uncanny.

"Never mind," I said. "When we do pick up with the flying fish, we'll pick up with everything else. The flying fish is the staff of life for all the other breeds. Everything will come in a bunch when we find the flying fish."

When I should have headed the *Snark* south-west for Hawaii, I still held her south. I was going to find those flying fish. Finally the time came when, if I wanted to go to Honolulu, I should have headed the *Snark* due west, instead of which I kept her south. Not until latitude 19 degrees did we encounter the first flying fish. He was very much alone. I saw him. Five other pairs of eager eyes scanned the sea all day, but never saw another. So sparse were the flying fish that nearly a week more elapsed before the last one on board saw his first flying fish. As for the dolphin, bonita, porpoise, and all the other hordes of life – there weren't any.

Not even a shark broke surface with his ominous dorsal fin. Bert took a dip daily under the bowsprit, hanging on to the stays and dragging his body through the water. And daily he canvassed the project of letting go and having a decent swim. I did my best to dissuade him. But with him I had lost all standing as an authority on sea life.

"If there are sharks," he demanded, "why don't they show up?"

I assured him that if he really did let go and have a swim, the sharks would promptly appear. This was a bluff on my part. I didn't believe it. It lasted as a deterrent for two days. The third day the wind fell calm, and it was pretty hot. The *Snark* was moving a knot an hour. Bert dropped down under the bowsprit and let go. And now behold the perversity of things. We had sailed across two thousand miles and more of ocean and had met with no sharks. Within five minutes after Bert finished his swim, the fin of a shark was cutting the surface in circles around the *Snark*.

There was something wrong about that shark. It bothered me. It had no right to be there in that deserted ocean. The more I thought about it, the more incomprehensible it became. But two hours later we sighted land and the mystery was cleared up. He had come to us from the land, and not from the uninhabited deep. He had presaged the landfall. He was the messenger of the land.

Twenty-seven days out from San Francisco we arrived at the island of Oahu, Territory of Hawaii. In the early morning we drifted around Diamond Head into full view of Honolulu; and then the ocean burst suddenly into life. Flying fish cleaved the air in glittering squadrons. In five minutes, we saw more of them than during the whole voyage. Other fish, large ones, of various sorts, leaped into the air. There was life everywhere, on sea and shore. We could see the masts and funnels of the shipping in the harbour, the hotels and bathers along the beach at Waikiki, the smoke rising from the dwelling-houses high up on the volcanic slopes of the Punch Bowl and Tantalus. The custom-house tug was racing toward us and a big school of porpoises got under our bow and began cutting the most ridiculous capers. The port doctor's launch came charging out at us, and a big sea turtle broke the surface with his back and took a look at us. Never was there such a burgeoning of life. Strange faces were on our decks, strange voices were speaking, and copies of that very morning's newspaper, with cable reports from all the world, were thrust before our eyes. Incidentally, we read that the *Snark* and all hands had been lost at sea, and that she had been a very unseaworthy craft anyway. And while we read this information a wireless message was being received by the congressional party on the summit of Haleakala announcing the safe arrival of the *Snark*.

It was the *Snark's* first landfall – and such a landfall! For twenty-seven days we had been on the deserted deep, and it was pretty hard to realize that there was so much life in the world. We were made dizzy by it. We could not take it all in at once. We were like awakened Rip Van Winkles, and it seemed to us that we were dreaming. On one side, the azure sea lapped across the horizon into the azure sky; on the other side, the sea lifted itself into great breakers of emerald that fell in a snowy smother upon a white coral beach. Beyond the beach, green plantations of sugarcane undulated gently upward to steeper slopes, which, in turn, became jagged volcanic crests, drenched with tropic showers and capped by stupendous masses of trade-wind clouds. At any rate, it was a most beautiful dream. The *Snark* turned and headed directly in toward the emerald surf, till it lifted and thundered on either hand; and on either hand, scarce a biscuit-toss away, the reef showed its long teeth, pale green and menacing.

Abruptly the land itself, in a riot of olive-greens of a thousand hues, reached out its arms and folded the *Snark* in. There was no perilous passage through the reef, no emerald surf and azure sea – nothing but a warm soft land, a motionless lagoon, and tiny beaches on which swam dark-skinned tropic children. The sea had disappeared. The Snark's anchor rumbled the chain through the hawse-pipe, and we lay without movement on a "lineless, level floor." It was all so beautiful and strange that we could not accept it as real. On the chart this place was called Pearl Harbour, but we called it Dream Harbour.

A launch came off to us; in it were members of the Hawaiian Yacht Club, come to greet us and make us welcome, with true Hawaiian hospitality, to all they had. They were ordinary men, flesh and blood and all the rest; but they did not tend to break our dreaming. Our last memories of men were of United States marshals and of panicky little merchants with rusty dollars for souls, who, in a reeking atmosphere of soot and coal-dust, laid grimy hands upon the *Snark* and held her back from her world adventure. But these men who came to meet us were clean men. A healthy tan was on their cheeks, and their eyes were not dazzled and bespectacled from gazing at glittering dollar-heaps. No, they merely verified the dream. They clinched it with their unsmirched souls.

So we went ashore with them across a level flashing sea to the wonderful green land. We landed on a tiny wharf, and the dream became more insistent; for know that for twenty-seven days we had been rocking across the ocean on the tiny *Snark*. Not once in all those twenty-seven days had we known a moment's rest, a moment's cessation from movement. This ceaseless movement had become ingrained. Body and brain, we had rocked and rolled so long that when we climbed out on the tiny wharf we kept on rocking and rolling. This, naturally, we attributed to the wharf. It was projected psychology. I spraddled along the wharf and nearly fell into the water. I glanced at Charmian, and the way she walked made me sad. The wharf had all the seeming of a ship's deck. It lifted, tilted, heaved and sank; and since there were no handrails on it, it kept Charmian and me busy avoiding falling in. I never saw such a preposterous little wharf. Whenever I watched it closely, it refused to roll; but as soon as I took my attention off from it, away it went, just like the *Snark*. Once, I caught it in the act, just as it upended, and I looked down the length of it for two hundred feet, and for all the world it was like the deck of a ship ducking into a huge head-sea.

At last, however, supported by our hosts, we negotiated the wharf and gained the land. But the land was no better. The very first thing it did was to tilt up on one side, and far as the eye could see I watched it tilt, clear to its jagged, volcanic backbone, and I saw the clouds above tilt, too. This was no stable, firm-founded land, else it would not cut such capers. It was like all the rest of our landfall, unreal. It was a dream. At any moment, like shifting vapour, it might dissolve away. The thought entered my head that perhaps it was my fault, that my head was swimming or that something I had eaten had disagreed with me. But I glanced at Charmian and her sad walk, and even as I glanced I saw her stagger and bump into the yachtsman by whose side she walked. I spoke to her, and she complained about the antic behaviour of the land.

We walked across a spacious, wonderful lawn and down an avenue of royal palms, and across more wonderful lawn in the gracious shade of stately trees. The air was filled with the songs of birds and was heavy with rich warm fragrances – wafture from great lilies, and blazing blossoms of hibiscus, and other strange gorgeous tropic flowers. The dream was becoming almost impossibly beautiful to us who, for so long, had seen naught but the restless, salty sea. Charmian reached out her hand and clung to me – for support against the ineffable beauty of it, thought I. But no. As I supported her, I braced my legs, while the flowers and lawns reeled and swung around me. It was like an earthquake, only it quickly passed without doing any harm. It was fairly difficult to catch the land playing these tricks. As long as I kept my mind on it, nothing happened. But as soon as my attention was distracted, away it went, the whole panorama, swinging and heaving and tilting at all sorts of angles. Once, however, I turned my head suddenly and caught that stately line of royal palms swinging in a great arc across the sky. But it stopped, just as soon as I caught it, and became a placid dream again.

Next we came to a house of coolness, with great sweeping veranda, where lotus-eaters might dwell. Windows and doors were wide open to the breeze, and the songs and fragrances blew lazily in and out. The walls were hung with tapa-cloths. Couches with grass-woven covers invited everywhere, and there was a grand piano, that played, I was sure, nothing more exciting than lullabies. Servants – Japanese maids in native costume – drifted around and about, noiselessly, like butterflies. Everything was preternaturally cool. Here was no blazing down of a tropic sun upon an unshrinking sea. It was too good to be true. But it was not real. It was a dream-dwelling. I knew, for I turned suddenly and caught the grand piano cavorting in a spacious corner of the room. I did not say anything, for just then we were being received by a gracious woman, a beautiful Madonna, clad in flowing white and shod with sandals, who greeted us as though she had known us always.

We sat at table on the lotus-eating veranda, served by the butterfly maids, and ate strange foods and partook of a nectar called *poi*. But the dream threatened to dissolve. It shimmered and trembled like an iridescent bubble about to break. I was just glancing out at the green grass and stately trees and blossoms of hibiscus, when suddenly I felt the table move. The table, and the Madonna across from me, and the veranda of the lotus-eaters, the scarlet hibiscus, the greensward and the trees – all lifted and tilted before my eyes, and heaved and sank down into the trough of a monstrous sea. I gripped my chair convulsively and held on. I had a feeling that I was holding on to the dream as well as the chair. I should not have been surprised had the sea rushed in and drowned all that fairyland and had I found myself at the wheel of the *Snark* just looking up casually from the study of logarithms. But the dream persisted. I looked covertly at the Madonna and her husband. They evidenced no perturbation. The dishes had not moved upon the table. The hibiscus and trees and grass were still there. Nothing had changed. I partook of more nectar, and the dream was more real than ever.

"Will you have some iced tea?" asked the Madonna; and then her side of the table sank down gently and I said yes to her at an angle of forty-five degrees.

"Speaking of sharks," said her husband, "up at Niihau there was a man–" And at that moment the table lifted and heaved, and I gazed upward at him at an angle of forty-five degrees.

So the luncheon went on, and I was glad that I did not have to bear the affliction of watching Charmian walk. Suddenly, however, a mysterious word of fear broke from the lips of the lotus-eaters.

"Aha," thought I, "now the dream goes glimmering." I clutched the chair desperately, resolved to drag back to the reality of the *Snark* some tangible vestige of this lotus land. I felt the whole dream lurching and pulling to be gone.

Just then, the mysterious word of fear was repeated. It sounded like REPORTERS. I looked and saw three of them coming across the lawn. Oh, blessed reporters! Then the dream was indisputably real after all. I glanced out across the shining water and saw the *Snark* at anchor, and I remembered that I had sailed in her from San Francisco to Hawaii, and that this was Pearl Harbour, and that even then I was acknowledging introductions and saying, in reply to the first question, "Yes, we had delightful weather all the way down."

KENNETH PATCHEN

from
"Death Of An Unpopular Poet"
A WHITE SPORT COAT &
A PINK CRUSTACEAN
1973

JIMMY'S OWN MYTHOS, as he presents it, sometimes has its own little conflicts. The origin of "Cheeseburger in Paradise" is one such example; his inspiration for "One Particular Harbour" remains another. So, it comes as no surprise that Jimmy has a different take or two on how he came to write "Death of An Unpopular Poet."

After the song first appeared on "A White Sport Coat & A Pink Crustacean," Jimmy would often introduce any live performance of it with a common explanation.

"Since a lot of people ask who the person was in 'Death of an Unpopular Poet,' it's not one particular person," he would tell them. "It's a lot of people. I have a lot of people that've influenced me . . . Who never got their rewards, financially. Paid a lot of dues, but never got to stay around and spend it. Richard Fariña. Kenneth Patchen in particularly [*sic*]. And Lord Buckley."

Down through the years,

345

Patchen has remained the clear constant in his story. Often characterized as a "Jazz Poet," the writer also experimented with novels, such as his *Memoirs of a Shy Pornographer* and *The Journal of Albion Moonlight*.

By 1976, Jimmy offered this variation on his theme in an interview with Bob Anderson for *High Times* magazine.

"I was watching Walter Cronkite one night, and he had a little blurb on there that Kenneth Patchen had died," says Jimmy. "That surprised me, because hardly anybody ever heard of Patchen except in small circles. He was one of my favorite poets. So I was thinking about him, and then I thought about Richard Fariña.

"These guys contributed so much, but they died, and we never appreciated them until afterwards. They starved their asses off and didn't get to stick around to reap their rewards. If you're going to go up there and try to make it, you're not out there totally for aesthetic value. Let's face it – you're out there to secure your future. Anybody that says they're not is totally false. I couldn't say that money doesn't mean anything to me. You have to pay your bills – I have to keep the band on the road. But you can still have a good time and write good songs. You don't necessarily have to prostitute your music, as long as you know how to handle it, put it in perspective. Those guys had a good time, but I'm sure they were miserable a lot of times. The success that they wanted, they never knew they actually reached it."

Basically, that interview is an elaboration and confirmation of the story Jimmy'd been telling those first couple years. Flash forward another quarter century or so, and there sit Jimmy and Jerry Jeff Walker, playing music and reminiscing about their early days in Coconut Grove.

"You may not remember this," Jimmy says to Jerry Jeff and their audience, "but you turned me on to Kenneth Patchen. This is a song called 'Death of An Unpopular Poet,' which I wrote in Jerry Jeff's house in Coconut Grove," he goes on. "People always ask me who the poet was and it's kind of everybody, but it's from *The Journey* [sic] *of Albion Moonlight*, which I read at your house for the first time by Kenneth Patchen."

So, whether the song was prompted by Walter Cronkite's newscast, or by Jerry Jeff's copy of *The Journal of Albion Moonlight* now appears to be something that even Jimmy can't seem to set straight; however, there remains no doubt that Patchen's work is at the heart of the matter.

Additional suggested works by Kenneth Patchen:

— *The Journal of Albion Moonlight* (1941)

— *The Selected Poems of Kenneth Patchen* (1946)

If a Poem Can Be Headed into Its Proper Current Someone Will Take it within His Heart to the Power and Beauty of Everybody

a selection from
Selected Poems

ARRIVE TO ARRIVE and to arrive here in such thick
White silence
The eye turned away
Without vanity or desire
And seeing is seen
And the music of the silence flows on the world
With a rhythm and a pulse which are changed
In the blood-beat as the heart's course by death

And hearing is heard as in the very sea
There is no sound
So in the purest thought
When vanity and desire of all mortal ends
Have been submerged
We may join the thinking which is eternally around us
And be thought about
For the common good
Of the one creature which everything is

Man is not to direct or to be directed
Anymore than a tree or a cloud or a stone

Man is not to rule or to be ruled
Anymore than a faith or a truth or a love

Man is not to doubt or to be doubted
Anymore than a wave or a seed or a fire

There is no problem in living
Which life hasn't answered to its own need

And we cannot direct, rule, or doubt what is beyond
Our highest ability to understand
We can only be humble before it
We can only worship ourselves because we are part of it

The eye in the leaf is watching out of our fingers
The ear in the stone is listening through our voices
The thought of the wave is thinking in our dreams
The faith of the seed is building with our deaths

I speak of the music of the silence
As being what is left when the singers and the dancers
Have grown still
Something is left there
A part of the reverence and of the need
A part of the fear and the pain and the wonder
And it goes on there
Coming from where it came from (O beautiful goddess!)
And reaching for what it can have little awareness of
A rhythm quite unlike any we know here
Bound and swayed as we are by the blood's orchestration
Bound and swayed as we are by the orchestration within us
By the deceptive orchestration of the blood

And I speak of the goddess
I speak of the goddess
I speak of the beautiful goddess

O tell them what I would say.

HENRY DAVID THOREAU

from
"Into Everyone's Life
a Coconut Man Should Fall"
A Salty Piece of Land
2004

PARADISE IS WHEREVER one finds it, so beach bums can forgive the fact that Thoreau found his own piece of paradise alongside a freshwater pond not so deep within a Massachusetts wood.

For all intents and purposes, Henry might have discovered that paradise over at the seashore, but it would be another four years before he headed himself east by southeast out of Concord and first glimpsed the mighty Atlantic from the sands along the great outer beach of Cape Cod.

'Til then, swimming in the ocean would have to wait, while paddling in the lake and fishing for trout seemed to be serving Henry quite well. To be sure, he sometimes could not prevent himself from calling the Walden shoreline a "beach," and once in a while he even refers to the pond itself as a "sea;" however, Thoreau's lifestyle did not depend upon the rise or fall of any tide. Instead, we might look at him these days and think that he might well have been one of us: just a beach bum in search of a beach.

Living in a one-room shack that he'd built just for the occasion, though, Thoreau says that he went there, "because I wished to live deliberately, to front only the essential facts of life, and see if I could not learn what it had to teach, and not, when I came to die, discover that I had not lived." The winds of change could have been blowing over his twenty-eight-year-old head, but his take on paradise required neither a six-string, nor a flip-flop. Instead, the oft-quoted mantra that came out of his two-year retreat into the woods was one by which he abided to the very end of his forty-five years: "Simplicity! Simplicity! Simplicity!"

Sure, that's a few more syllables than "Salt! Salt! Salt," but it also holds a spiritual meaning that's more akin to that of "Keep it simple, stupid!" And therein lies the connection that Jimmy seems to have found with Henry David Thoreau. Had Jimmy read all of his homework assignments, he surely would have read some of Thoreau. If not, he might have been re-introduced to them through Don Henley.

For quite some time, Jimmy had opened for the Eagles, and therein began their relationship. When they disbanded, his friendships remained with both Henley and Glenn Frey. After three successful solo albums, though, Henley went on a recording hiatus and established The Walden Woods Project to rescue Thoreau's paradise from impending development, as well as to preserve the literature and legacy of Thoreau.

"I learned this, at least, by my experiment; that if one advances confidently in the direction of his dreams, and endeavors to live the life which he has imagined, he will meet with a success unexpected in common hours," concluded Thoreau. "In proportion as he simplifies his life, the laws of the universe will appear less complex, and solitude will not be solitude, nor poverty poverty, nor weakness weakness."

Clearly, there are times when Jimmy has put forth a similar outlook in his own thinking and writing. So, when Sammy Raye Coconuts drops to his knee before Donna Kay at the Chat and Chew Café, his quotation from Thoreau's *Walden* is not just something which Jimmy has plucked from *Bartlett's Book of Familiar Quotations*. "He who distinguishes the true savor of his food can never be a glutton," proclaims Sammy with great passion; "he who does not cannot be otherwise."

Additional suggested works by Henry David Thoreau:

— *Paradise (to be) Regained* (1843)

— *Walden* (1854)

Higher Laws

a selection from

Walden / Chapter XI

I HAVE FOUND REPEATEDLY, of late years, that I cannot fish with out falling a little in self-respect. I have tried it again and again. I have skill at it, and, like many of my fellows, a certain instinct for it, which revives from time to time, but always when I have done I feel that it would have been better if I had not fished. I think that I do not mistake. It is a faint intimation, yet so are the first streaks of morning. There is unquestionably this instinct in me which belongs to the lower orders of creation; yet with every year I am less a fisherman, though without more humanity or even wisdom; at present I am no fisherman at all. But I see that if I were to live in a wilderness I should again be tempted to become a fisher and hunter in earnest. Beside, there is something essentially unclean about this diet and all flesh, and I began to see where housework commences, and whence the endeavor, which costs so much, to wear a tidy and respectable appearance each day, to keep the house sweet and free from all ill odors and sights. Having been my own butcher and scullion and cook, as well as the gentleman for whom the dishes were served up, I can speak from an unusually complete experience. The practical objection to animal food in my case was its uncleanness; and besides, when I had caught and cleaned and cooked and eaten my fish, they seemed not to have fed me essentially. It was insignificant and unnecessary, and cost more than it came to. A little bread or a few potatoes would have done as well, with less trouble and filth. Like many of my contemporaries, I had rarely for many years used animal food, or tea, or coffee, et cetera; not so much because of any ill effects which I had traced to them, as because they were not agreeable to my imagination. The repugnance to animal food is not the effect of experience, but is an instinct. It appeared more beautiful to live low and fare hard in many respects; and

351

though I never did so, I went far enough to please my imagination. I believe that every man who has ever been earnest to preserve his higher or poetic faculties in the best condition has been particularly inclined to abstain from animal food, and from much food of any kind.

It is hard to provide and cook so simple and clean a diet as will not offend the imagination; but this, I think, is to be fed when we feed the body; they should both sit down at the same table. Yet perhaps this may be done. The fruits eaten temperately need not make us ashamed of our appetites, nor interrupt the worthiest pursuits. But put an extra condiment into your dish, and it will poison you. It is not worth the while to live by rich cookery. Most men would feel shame if caught preparing with their own hands precisely such a dinner, whether of animal or vegetable food, as is every day prepared for them by others. Yet till this is otherwise we are not civilized, and, if gentlemen and ladies, are not true men and women. This certainly suggests what change is to be made. It may be vain to ask why the imagination will not be reconciled to flesh and fat. I am satisfied that it is not. Is it not a reproach that man is a carnivorous animal? True, he can and does live, in a great measure, by preying on other animals; but this is a miserable way – as any one who will go to snaring rabbits, or slaughtering lambs, may learn – and he will be regarded as a benefactor of his race who shall teach man to confine himself to a more innocent and wholesome diet. Whatever my own practice may be, I have no doubt that it is a part of the destiny of the human race, in its gradual improvement, to leave off eating animals, as surely as the savage tribes have left off eating each other when they came in contact with the more civilized.

If one listens to the faintest but constant suggestions of his genius, which are certainly true, he sees not to what extremes, or even insanity, it may lead him; and yet that way, as he grows more resolute and faithful, his road lies. The faintest assured objection which one healthy man feels will at length prevail over the arguments and customs of mankind. No man ever followed his genius till it misled him. Though the result were bodily weakness, yet perhaps no one can say that the consequences were to be regretted, for these were a life in conformity to higher principles. If the day and the night are such that you greet them with joy, and life emits a fragrance like flowers and sweet-scented herbs, is more elastic, more starry, more immortal – that is your success. All nature is your congratulation, and you have cause momentarily to bless yourself. The greatest gains and values are farthest from being appreciated. We easily come to doubt if they exist. We soon forget them. They are the highest reality. Perhaps the facts most astounding and most real are never communicated by man to man. The true harvest of my daily life is somewhat as intangible and indescribable as the tints of morning or evening. It is a little star-dust caught, a segment of the rainbow which I have clutched. Who has not sometimes derived an inexpressible satisfaction from his food in which appetite had no share? I have been thrilled to think that I owed a mental perception to the commonly gross sense of taste, that I have been inspired through the palate, that some berries which I had eaten on a hillside had fed my genius. "The soul not being mistress of herself," says Thseng-tseu, "one looks, and one does not see; one listens, and one does not hear; one eats, and one does not know the savor of food." He who distinguishes the true savor of his food can never be a glutton; he who does not cannot be otherwise. A puritan may go to his brown-bread crust with as gross an appetite as ever an alderman to his turtle. Not that food which entereth into the mouth defileth a man, but the appetite with which it is eaten. It is neither the quality nor the quantity, but the devotion to sensual savors; when that which is eaten is not a viand to sustain our animal, or inspire our spiritual life, but food for the worms that possess us. If the hunter has a taste for mud-turtles, musk-rats, and other such savage tidbits, the fine lady indulges a taste for jelly made of a calf's foot, or for sardines from over the sea, and they are even. He goes to the mill-pond, she to her preserve-pot. The wonder is how they, how you and I, can live this slimy, beastly life, eating and drinking.

In earlier ages, in some countries, every function was reverently spoken of and regulated by law. Nothing was too trivial for the Hindoo lawgiver, however offensive it may be to modern taste. He teaches how to eat, drink, cohabit, void excrement and urine, and the like, elevating what is mean, and does not falsely excuse himself by calling these things trifles.

Every man is the builder of a temple, called his body, to the god he worships, after a style purely his own, nor can he get off by hammering marble instead. We are all sculptors and painters, and our material is our own flesh and blood and bones. Any nobleness begins at once to refine a man's features, any meanness or sensuality to imbrute them.

John Farmer sat at his door one September evening, after a hard day's work, his mind still running on his labor more or less. Having bathed, he sat down to re-create his intellectual man. It was a rather cool evening, and some of his neighbors were apprehending a frost. He had not attended to the train of his thoughts long when he heard some one playing on a flute, and that sound harmonized with his mood. Still he thought of his work; but the burden of his thought was, that though this kept running in his head, and he found himself planning and contriving it against his will, yet it concerned him very little. It was no more than the scurf of his skin, which was constantly shuffled off. But the notes of the flute came home to his ears out of a different sphere from that he worked in, and suggested work for certain faculties which slumbered in him. They gently did away with the street, and the village, and the state in which he lived. A voice said to him – Why do you stay here and live this mean moiling life, when a glorious existence is possible for you? Those same stars twinkle over other fields than these. – But how to come out of this condition and actually migrate thither? All that he could think of was to practise some new austerity, to let his mind descend into his body and redeem it, and treat himself with ever increasing respect.

RICHARD BRAUTIGAN

from
"Blame It on Lord Baden-Powell"
A Pirate Looks at Fifty
1998

JUST SOUTHEAST of the Littrow Valley through the Taurus Mountains in the northeast quadrant of the moon lies the crater known as Shorty.

Shorty was named after a legless, San Francisco wino in Richard Bautigan's '67 classic, *Trout Fishing in America*, and it was designated as such by the astronauts of the Apollo XVII mission that visited in 1972.

Brautigan actually had written the book more than a decade earlier. When it first appeared, however, older readers were bewildered by its subject and its style alike. For one thing, it was not about fishing; for another, it was neither prose, nor poetry. Nonetheless, in the "Summer of Love," *Trout Fishing in America* was "a work of eccentric brilliance."

Its somewhat eccentric writer wasn't always that way. Brautigan had been raised without a father in a poverty-stricken Oregon household, where he struggled to become the poet of his dreams. When his first true love rejected his poems in 1955, however, the twenty-year-old poet ended up in Oregon State Hospital where he was subjected to more than a dozen treatments of shock therapy. Thus, the Richard Brautigan who arrived the next year in San Francisco possessed a liberated mind, free of all chemical substances whatsoever. And those who met him back then say that he was "gentle" and "naïve."

Tom McGuane bought his copy of *Trout Fishing* when he was living across the bay in the tiny Portuguese fishing village of Bolinas. Russell Chatham was living there, as was Gatz Hjortsberg. Now and then, so did Richard Brautigan, who was then fast becoming a heavy drinker. In time, though, McGuane and friends relocated in Montana, and he invited Brautigan out to learn how to fish. In 1973, Richard so enjoyed the place that he bought a ranch not far from that portion of the Yellowstone River where Hemingway had loved to fish and hunt and write.

About that same time, McGuane's spread had nearly thirty people living and writing there, and one of those sleeping in the barn was Jimmy. These were the "Rancho Deluxe" days, and there was a motion picture being made. Livingston was full of mischief, and no one contributed more to that than did Richard. McGuane claims that the guy drank harder than did Dylan Thomas and that he loved to fire his guns. In some ways, Brautigan was taking on some of Hemingway's traits, both personal and professional; critics were beginning to dismiss his work.

Still, Richard did learn to fish alongside McGuane and the others, and he appears in Guy de la Valdéne's *Tarpon* documentary. In time, however, he began to lose interest in things, and he asked McGuane to store his fishing rods for him. "I've examined a number of options," he scribbled in a note, "and will soon apply action to my life. I'm waiting for a little more information. Then . . . a forty-nine-year-old man rattles his bones into the future."

Eventually, Richard Brautigan returned to the bay area to do what Hemingway had done before him and what Hunter Thompson would do years later: he put a gun to his head and ended a tortured life. Only then did Tom McGuane discover that the rods in storage had been wrapped along with flowers and a funeral urn. As *Rolling Stone* had noted, Richard Brautigan was "a man who had never fit comfortably into life."

Additional suggested works by Richard Brautigan:

— *Trout Fishing in America* (1967)

— *The Hawkline Monster: A Gothic Western* (1974)

— *So the Wind Won't Blow It All Away* (1982)

A WALDEN POND FOR WINOS

a selection from
Trout Fishing in America/Chapter X

THE AUTUMN CARRIED ALONG WITH IT, like the roller coaster of a flesh-eating plant, port wine and the people who drank that dark sweet wine, people long since gone, except for me.

Always wary of the police, we drank in the safest place we could find, the park across the street from the church.

There were three poplar trees in the middle of the park and there was a statue of Benjamin Franklin in front of the trees. We sat there and drank port.

At home my wife was pregnant.

I would call her on the telephone after I finished work and say, "I won't be home for a little while. I'm going to have a drink with some friends."

The three of us huddled in the park, talking. They were both broken-down artists from New Orleans where they had drawn pictures of tourists in Pirate's Alley.

Now in San Francisco, with the cold autumn wind upon them, they had decided that the future held only two directions: They were either going to open up a flea circus or commit themselves to an insane asylum.

So they talked about it while they drank wine.

They talked about how to make little clothes for fleas by pasting pieces of colored paper on their backs.

They said the way that you trained fleas was to make them dependent upon you for their food. This was done by letting them feed off you at an appointed hour.

They talked about making little flea wheelbarrows and pool tables and bicycles.

They would charge fifty-cents admission for their flea circus. The business was certain to have a future in it. Perhaps they would even get on the Ed Sullivan Show.

They of course did not have their fleas yet, but they could easily be obtained from a white cat.

Then they decided that the fleas that lived on Siamese cats would probably be more intelligent than the fleas that lived on just ordinary alley cats. It only make sense that drinking intelligent blood would make intelligent fleas.

And so it went on until it was exhausted, and we went and bought another fifth of port wine and returned to the trees and Benjamin Franklin.

Now it was close to sunset and the earth was beginning to cool off in the correct manner of eternity, and office girls were returning like penguins from Montgomery Street. They looked at us hurriedly and mentally registered: winos.

Then the two artists talked about committing themselves to an insane asylum for the winter. They talked about how warm it would be in the insane asylum, with television, clean sheets on soft beds, hamburger gravy over mashed potatoes, a dance once a week with the lady kooks, clean clothes, a locked razor and lovely young student nurses.

Ah, yes, there was a future in the insane asylum. No winter spent there could be a total loss.

GS

WILLIAM SHAKESPEARE

from
Liner Notes
BAROMETER SOUP
1994

PHILLIP BURTON had retreated to the William Crane Gray Inn in central Florida when Jimmy last sat down with him.

"He knew he would never leave the rest home," Jimmy says, "but I know he felt better, because I was walking out of there with things he had taught me, and I intend to pass them on when my time comes."

So goes the story that Jimmy tells in his notes for the album that he dedicated "to the loving memory of Floy Thompson, Phillip Burton, Howard Paul." The first of this trio was a beauty queen and patron of the arts; the last, a remittance man and the model for Lance Larrimore III in *Tales from Margaritaville.*

Phillip Burton, on the other hand, was an actor, a stage director, and a Shakespearean scholar, who was born in South Wales in 1904.

Though he had risen above his family's squalid life to earn degrees with honors in both history and mathematics, Burton's duties as

Commanding Officer of the Port Talbot air training squadron had all but ended his hopes of becoming a stage actor. In another young actor named Owen Jones, however, Phillip Burton believed he'd discovered someone who could live out for him those otherwise unfulfilled dreams. Burton directed Jones on the stage and in motion pictures until his protégé then enlisted as a fighter pilot in the RAF. And the teacher was devastated when the young airman was shot down in the Battle of Britain.

In the place of Jones, there soon appeared yet another student, named Richard Jenkins, described as a "godsend . . . but with a greater talent." Their relationship became so strong that Burton wanted to adopt him; however, he was short of the requirement that he be twenty years older than the adopted child. So, Richard Jenkins became simply the ward of Phillip Burton; however, he did take on his foster father's surname and was legally Richard Burton. Yes, this is the very same Richard Burton whose talents soon overshadowed all the achievements of his mentor.

In the 1950s, the elder Burton had moved from the UK to New York, but he then moved to Key West after suffering a heart attack in the 1970s.

"Phillip Burton came to Key West twenty years ago to die, but didn't," wrote Jimmy in his notes. "Instead, he found a new lease on life in the tropics which he gave back to those who were fortunate enough to make his acquaintance. Phillip was a teacher and my afternoons spent at his little frame house on Angela Street discussing plots and characters, tours and projects were times I will never forget."

When Jimmy was wrestling with the development of his villain in *Where is Joe Merchant?*, he went to Phillip for his thoughts.

"He just looked at me across the room and said, 'Jimmy, it all goes back to Shakespeare,' and handed me a copy of *Richard III*. I headed home that evening loaded down with more books and homework than I had ever done in eighteen years of supposed schooling. Colonel Cairo became a true villain thanks to Phillip."

"I owe him everything," Richard Burton once had said of the late Phillip Burton; so, too, might have said the dastardly Colonel. Of course, we ought to note that William Shakespeare also played a part in the lives of them all.

Additional suggested works by William Shakespeare:

— *The Tragedy of Richard the Third* (1591)

NOW IS THE WINTER OF OUR DISCONTENT

a selection from

The Tragedy of Richard the Third
Act I / Scene i

LONDON. A street.
Enter GLOUCESTER, *solus*

GLOUCESTER: Now is the winter of our discontent
Made glorious summer by this sun of York;
And all the clouds that lour'd upon our house
In the deep bosom of the ocean buried.
Now are our brows bound with victorious wreaths;
Our bruised arms hung up for monuments;
Our stern alarums chang'd to merry meetings,
Our dreadful marches to delightful measures.
Grim-visag'd war hath smooth'd his wrinkled front;
And now, – instead of mounting barbed steeds
To fright the souls of fearful adversaries, –
He capers nimbly in a lady's chamber
To the lascivious pleasing of a lute.
But I, – that am not shap'd for sportive tricks,
Nor made to court an amorous looking-glass;
I, that am rudely stamp'd, and want love's majesty
To strut before a wanton ambling nymph;
I, that am curtail'd of this fair proportion,
Cheated of feature by dissembling nature,
Deform'd, unfinish'd, sent before my time
Into this breathing world scarce half made up,
And that so lamely and unfashionable
That dogs bark at me as I halt by them; –
Why, I, in this weak piping time of peace,

Have no delight to pass away the time,
Unless to spy my shadow in the sun,
And descant on mine own deformity:
And therefore, – since I cannot prove a lover,
To entertain these fair well-spoken days, –
I am determined to prove a villain,
And hate the idle pleasures of these days.
Plots have I laid, inductions dangerous,
By drunken prophecies, libels, and dreams,
To set my brother Clarence and the king
In deadly hate the one against the other:
And if King Edward be as true and just
As I am subtle, false, and treacherous,
This day should Clarence closely be mew'd up, –
About a prophecy which says that G
Of Edward's heirs the murderer shall be.
Dive, thoughts, down to my soul: – here Clarence comes.

OSCAR WILDE

EVEN AFTER he'd taken to his deathbed in a shabby little room above the Rue des Beaux-Arts in Paris, Oscar Wilde's celebrated wit remained just as sharp as ever. "My wallpaper and I are fighting a duel to the death," he complained of his surroundings. "One or the other of us has got to go."

Wilde was barely forty-six years old at the time. A benefactor had paid off his debt at the Hotel Marsollier, and now the same patron was underwriting this stay at L'Hotel d'Alsace. "I am dying beyond my means," Wilde further admitted with some remorse. "I can't even afford to die."

Now known more for his flamboyant lifestyle than for his literary works, the Irish playwright has long represented that school of art which encouraged personal decadence and went by the name of "aestheticism." Wilde's rapier wit and foppish behavior often were overshadowed by his so-called "gross indecencies," and for such public behavior he was tried and convicted by a Victorian court. Wilde became a martyr among homosexuals throughout Europe when he was then jailed for what his intimate friend, Lord Alfred Douglas, would call "the love that dare not speak its name."

Despite any of those perceived eccentricities, Oscar Wilde had long been fascinated by the Catholic church, especially by its ceremonies and ceremonial garb; however, this had little to do with his upbringing. In fact, he was sent to study at Oxford just so that the school might protect him from such things. That, however, did nothing to end his fascination.

"If I could hope that the Church would wake in me some earnestness and purity I would go over as a luxury," he once said. "But to do so would be to sacrifice and give up my two great gods 'Money and Ambition.' Still," he added, "I get so wretched and low and troubled that in some desperate mood I would seek the shelter of a church which simply enthralls me by its fascination."

Now and then, Jimmy and Wilde seem to have dealt with similar storylines, such as a dancer named Salome or a fisherman who encounters a mermaid in the night. While Jimmy was so excited to cast off his parochial upbringing, however, Oscar Wilde actually enjoyed the way that Catholics thought of sin and redemption, and he even wrote children's fairy tales that spoke about love and redemption.

In the end, Wilde lived up to his quip that "Catholicism is the only religion to die in." As the writer lapsed into unconsciousness, Father Cuthbert Dunne was summoned to L'Hotel d'Alsace, where he converted the so-called "Apostle of Aestheticism" to Catholicism.

"Indeed I was fully satisfied that he understood me when I told him that I was about to receive him into the Catholic Church and give him the Last Sacraments," Dunne later wrote. "From the signs he gave, as well as from his attempted words, I was satisfied as to his full consent. And when I repeated close to his ear the Holy Names, the Acts of Contrition, Faith, Hope and Charity, with [an] act of humble resignation to the Will of God, he tried all through to say the words after me."

Understanding this aspect of Wilde's otherwise wild life is necessary to follow this typically-lengthy children's tale. At some times, it will remind you of a song by Jimmy; at others, of Peter Pan's quest to reunite with his shadow. This fairy tale is not at all a quick and quiet read, but it is meant to be read aloud and to children.

Additional suggested works by Oscar Wilde:

— *The Ballad of Reading Gaol* (1898)

The Fisherman and His Soul

a selection from

A House of Pomegranates

EVERY EVENING the young Fisherman went out upon the sea, and threw his nets into the water.

When the wind blew from the land he caught nothing, or but little at best, for it was a bitter and black-winged wind, and rough waves rose up to meet it. But when the wind blew to the shore, the fish came in from the deep, and swam into the meshes of his nets, and he took them to the market-place and sold them.

Every evening he went out upon the sea, and one evening the net was so heavy that hardly could he draw it into the boat. And he laughed, and said to himself, "Surely I have caught all the fish that swim, or snared some dull monster that will be a marvel to men, or some thing of horror that the great Queen will desire," and putting forth all his strength, he tugged at the coarse ropes till, like lines of blue enamel round a vase of bronze, the long veins rose up on his arms. He tugged at the thin ropes, and nearer and nearer came the circle of flat corks, and the net rose at last to the top of the water.

But no fish at all was in it, nor any monster or thing of horror, but only a little Mermaid lying fast asleep.

Her hair was as a wet fleece of gold, and each separate hair as a thread of line gold in a cup of glass. Her body was as white ivory, and her tail was of silver and pearl. Silver and pearl was her tail, and the green weeds of the sea coiled round it; and like sea-shells were her ears, and her lips were like sea-coral. The cold waves dashed over her cold breasts, and the salt glistened upon her eyelids.

So beautiful was she that when the young Fisherman saw her he was filled with wonder, and he put out his hand and drew the net close to him, and leaning over the side he clasped her in his arms. And when he touched her, she gave a cry like a startled sea-gull and woke, and looked at him in terror with her mauve-amethyst eyes, and struggled to escape. But he held her tightly to him, and would not suffer her to depart.

And when she saw that she could in no way escape from him, she began to weep, and said, "I pray thee let me go, for I am the only daughter of a King, and my father is aged and alone."

But the young Fisherman answered, "I will not let thee go save thou makest me a promise that whenever I call thee, thou wilt come and sing to me, for the fish delight to listen to the song of the Sea-folk, and so shall my nets be full."

"Wilt thou in very truth let me go, if I promise thee this?" cried the Mermaid.

"In very truth, I will let thee go," said the young Fisherman. So she made him the promise he desired, and sware it by the oath of the Sea-folk. And he loosened his arms from about her, and she sank down into the water, trembling with a strange fear.

Every evening the young Fisherman went out upon the sea, and called to the Mermaid, and she rose out of the water and sang to him. Round and round her swam the dolphins, and the wild gulls wheeled above her head.

And she sang a marvellous song. For she sang of the Sea-folk who drive their flocks from cave to cave, and carry the little calves on their shoulders; of the Tritons who have long green beards, and hairy breasts, and blow through twisted conchs when the King passes by; of the palace of the King which is all of amber, with a roof of clear emerald, and a pavement of bright pearl; and of the gardens of the sea where the great filigrane fans of coral wave all day long, and the fish dart about like silver birds, and the anemones cling to the rocks, and the pinks bourgeon in the ribbed yellow sand. She sang of the big whales that come down from the north seas and have sharp icicles hanging to their fins; of the Sirens who tell of such wonderful things that the merchants have to stop their ears with wax lest they should hear them and leap into the water and be drowned; of the sunken galleys with their tall masts, and the frozen sailors clinging to the rigging, and the mackerel swimming in and out of the open portholes; of the little barnacles who are great travellers and cling to the keels of the ships and go round and round the world; and of the cuttlefish who live in the sides of the cliffs and stretch out their long black arms and can make night come when they will it. She sang of the nautilus who has a boat of her own that is carved out of an opal and steered with a silken sail; of the happy Mermen who play upon harps and can charm the great Kraken to sleep; of the little children who catch hold of the slippery porpoises and ride laughing upon their backs; of the Mermaids who lie in the white foam and hold out their arms to the mariners; and of the sea-lions with their curved tusks, and the sea-horses with their floating manes.

And as she sang, all the funny-fish came in from the deep to listen to her, and the young Fisherman threw his nets round them and caught them, and others he took with a spear. And when his boat was well-laden, the Mermaid would sink down into the sea, smiling at him.

Yet, would she never come near him that he might touch her. Often times, he called to her and prayed of her, but she would not; and when he sought to seize her she dived into the water as a seal might dive, nor did he see her again that day. And each day the sound of her voice became sweeter to his ears. So sweet was her voice that he forgot his nets and his cunning, and had no care of his craft. Vermilion-finned and with eyes of bossy gold, the tunnies went by in shoals, but he heeded them not. His spear lay by his side unused, and his baskets of plaited osier were empty. With lips parted, and eyes dim with wonder, he sat idle in his boat and listened, listening till the sea-mists crept round him, and the wandering moon stained his brown limbs with silver.

And one evening he called to her, and said: "Little Mermaid, little Mermaid, I love thee. Take me for thy bridegroom, for I love thee."

But the Mermaid shook her head. "Thou hast a human soul," she answered. "If thou would'st send away thy soul, then could I love thee."

And the young Fisherman said to himself: "Of what use is my soul to me? I cannot see it. I may not touch it. I do not know it. Surely I will send it away from me, and much gladness shall be mine." And a cry of joy broke from his lips, and standing up in the painted boat, he held out his arms to the Mermaid. "I will send my soul away," he cried, "and you shall be my bride, and I will be the bridegroom, and in the depth of the sea we will dwell together, and all that thou hast sung of thou shalt show me, and all that thou desirest I will do, nor shall our lives be divided."

And the Mermaid laughed for pleasure, and hid her face in her hands.

"But how shall I send my soul from me?" cried the young Fisherman. "Tell me how I may do it, and lo! it shall be done."

"Alas! I know not," said the little Mermaid. "The Sea-folk have no souls." And she sank down into the deep, looking wistfully at him.

Now early on the next morning, before the sun was the span of a man's hand above the hill, the young Fisherman went to the house of the Priest and knocked three times at the door.

The novice looked out through the wicket, and where he saw who it was, he drew back the latch and said to him, "Enter."

And the young Fisherman passed in, and knelt down on the rushes of the floor, and cried to the Priest who was reading out of the Holy Book and said to him, "Father, I am in love with one of the Sea-folk, and my soul hindereth me from having my desire. Tell me how I can send my soul away from me, for in truth I have no need of it. Of what value is my soul to me? I cannot see it. I may not touch it. I do not know it."

And the Priest beat his breast, and answered, "Alack, Alack, thou art mad, or hast eaten of poisonous herb, for the soul is the noblest part of man, and was given to us by God that we should nobly use it. There is no thing more precious than a human soul, nor any earthly thing that can be weighed with it. It is worth all the gold that is in the world, and is more precious than the rubies of the kings. Therefore, my son, think not any more of this matter, for it is a sin that may not be forgiven. And as for the Sea-folk, they are lost, and they who would traffic with them are lost also. They are as the beasts of the field that know not good from evil, and for them the Lord has not died."

The young Fisherman's eyes filled with tears when he heard the bitter words of the Priest, and he rose up from his knees and said to him, "Father, the Fauns live in the forest and are glad, and on the rocks sit the Mermen with their harps of red gold. Let me be as they are, I beseech thee. And as for my soul, what doth my soul profit me, if it stand between me and the thing that I love?"

"The love of the body is vile," cried the Priest, knitting his brows, "and vile and evil are the pagan things God suffers to wander through His world. Accursed be the Fauns of the woodland, and accursed be the singers of the sea! I have heard them at night-time, and they have sought to lure me from my beads. They tap at the window and laugh. They whisper into my ears the tale of their perilous joys. They tempt me with temptations, and when I would pray they make mouths at me. They are lost, I tell thee, they are lost. For them there is no heaven nor hell, and in neither shall they praise God's name."

"Father," cried the young Fisherman, "thou knowest not what thou sayest. Once in my net I snared the daughter of a King. She is fairer than the morning star, and whiter than the moon. For her body I would give my soul, and for her love I would surrender heaven. Tell me what I ask of thee, and let me go in peace."

"Away! Away!" cried the Priest: "thy lover is lost, and thou shalt be lost with her." And he gave him no blessing, but drove him from his door.

And the young Fisherman went down into the market-place, and he walked slowly, and with bowed head, as one who is in sorrow.

And when the merchants saw him coming, they began to whisper to each other, and one of them came forth to meet him, and called him by name, and said to him, "What hast thou to sell?"

"I will sell thee my soul," he answered: "I pray thee buy it off me, for I am weary of it. Of what use is my soul to me? I cannot see it. I may not touch it. I do not know it."

But the merchants mocked at him, and said, "Of what use is a man's soul to us? It is not worth a clipped piece of silver. Sell us thy body for a slave, and we will clothe thee in sea-purple, and put a ring upon thy finger, and make thee the minion of the great Queen. But talk not of the soul, for to us it is nought, nor has it any value for our service."

And the young Fisherman said to himself: "How strange a thing this is! The Priest telleth me that the soul is worth all the gold in the world, and the merchants say that it is not worth a clipped piece of silver." And he passed out of the market-place, and went down to the shore of the sea, and began to ponder on what he should do.

And at noon he remembered how one of his companions, who was a gatherer of samphire, had told him of a certain young Witch who dwelt in a cave at the head of the bay and was very cunning in her witcheries. And he set to and ran, so eager was he to get rid of his soul, and a cloud of dust followed him as he sped round the sand of the shore. By the itching of her palm the young Witch knew his coming, and she laughed and let down her red hair. With her red hair falling around her, she stood at the opening of the cave, and in her hand she held a spray of wild hemlock that was blossoming.

"What d'ye lack? What d'ye lack?" she cried, as he came panting up the steep and bent down before her. "Fish for thy net, when the wind is foul? I have a little reed-pipe, and when I blow on it the mullet come sailing into the bay. But it has a price, pretty boy, it has a price. What d'ye lack? What d'ye lack? A storm to wreck the ships and wash the chests of rich treasure ashore? I have more storms than the wind has, for I serve one who is stronger than the wind, and with a sieve and a pail of water I can send the great galleys to the bottom of the sea. But I have a price, pretty boy, I have a price. What d'ye lack? What d'ye lack? Tell me thy desire, and I will give it thee, and thou shalt pay me a price, pretty boy, thou shalt pay me a price."

"My desire is but for a little thing," said the young Fisherman, "yet hath the Priest been wroth with me, and driven me forth. It is but for a little thing, and the merchants have mocked at me, and denied me. Therefore have I come to thee, though men call thee evil, and whatever be thy price I shall pay it."

"What would'st thou?" asked the Witch, coming near to him.

"I would send my soul away from me," said the young Fisherman.

The Witch grew pale, and shuddered, and hid her face in her blue mantle. "Pretty boy, pretty boy," she muttered, "that is a terrible thing to do."

He tossed his brown curls and laughed. "My soul is nought to me," he answered. "I cannot see it. I may not touch it. I do not know it."

"What wilt thou give me if I tell thee?" asked the Witch looking down at him with her beautiful eyes.

"Five pieces of gold," he said, "and my nets, and the wattled house where I live, and the painted boat in which I sail. Only tell me how to get rid of my soul, and I will give thee all that I possess."

She laughed mockingly at him, and struck him with the spray of hemlock. "I can turn the autumn leaves into gold," she answered, "and I can weave the pale moonbeams into silver if I will it. He whom I serve is richer than all the kings of this world and has their dominions."

"What then shall I give thee," he cried, "if thy price be neither gold nor silver?"

The Witch stroked his hair with her thin white hand. "Thou must dance with me, pretty boy," she smiled at him as she spoke.

"Nought but that?" cried the young Fisherman in wonder, and he rose to his feet.

"Nought but that," she answered, and she smiled at him again.

"Then at sunset in some secret place we shall dance together," he said, "and after that we have danced thou shalt tell me the thing which I desire to know."

She shook her head.

"When the moon is full, when the moon is full," she muttered. Then she peered all round, and listened. There was no other sound save the sound of a wave fretting the smooth pebbles below. So she reached out her hand, and drew him near to her and put her dry lips close to his ear.

"To-night thou must come to the top of the mountain," she whispered. "It is a Sabbath, and He will be there."

The young Fisherman started and looked at her, and she showed her white teeth and laughed. "Who is He of whom thou speakest?" he asked.

"It matters not," she answered. "Go thou to-night, and stand under the branches of the hornbeam, and wait for my coming. If a black dog run towards thee, strike it with a rod of willow, and it will go away. If an owl speak to thee, make it no answer. When the moon is full I shall be with thee, and we will dance together on the grass."

"But wilt thou swear to me to tell me how I may send my soul from me?" he made question.

She moved out into the sunlight, and through her red hair rippled the wind. "By the hoofs of the goat I swear it," she made answer.

"Thou art the best of the witches," cried the young Fisherman, "and I will surely dance with thee to-night on the top of the mountain. I would indeed that thou hadst asked of me either gold or silver. But such as thy price is thou shalt have it, for it is but a little thing." And he doffed his cap to her, and bent his head low, and ran back to the town filled with a great joy.

And the Witch watched him as he went, and when he had passed from her sight she entered her cave, and having taken a mirror from a box of carved cedarwood, she set it up on a frame, and burned vervain on lighted charcoal before it, and peered through the coils of the smoke. And after a time she clenched her hands in anger. "He should have been mine," she muttered, "I am as fair as she is."

And that evening, when the moon had risen, the young Fisherman climbed up to the top of the mountain, and stood under the branches of the hornbeam. Like a shield of polished metal the round sea lay at his feet, and the shadows of the fishing boats moved in the little bay. A great owl, with yellow sulphurous eyes, called to him by his name, but he made it no answer. A black dog ran towards him and snarled. He struck it with a rod of willow, and it went away whining.

At midnight the witches came flying through the air like bats. "Phew!" they cried, as they lit upon the ground, "there is someone here we know not!" and they sniffed about, and chattered to each other, and made signs. Last of all came the young Witch, with her red hair streaming in the wind. She wore a dress of gold tissue embroidered with peacocks' eyes, and a little cap of green velvet was on her head.

"Where is he, where is he?" shrieked the witches when they saw her, but she only laughed, and ran to the hornbeam, and taking the Fisherman by the hand she led him out into the moonlight and began to dance.

Round and round they whirled, and the young Witch jumped so high that he could see the scarlet heels of her shoes. Then right across the dancers came the sound of the galloping of a horse, but no horse was to be seen, and he felt afraid.

"Faster," cried the Witch, and she threw her arms about his neck, and her breath was hot upon his face. "Faster, faster!" she cried, and the earth seemed to spin beneath his feet, and his brain grew troubled, and a great terror fell on him, as of some evil thing that was watching him, and at last he became aware that under the shadow of a rock there was a figure that had not been there before.

It was a man dressed in a suit of black velvet, cut in the Spanish fashion. His face was strangely pale, but his lips were like a proud red flower. He seemed weary, and was leaning back toying in a listless manner with the pommel of his dagger. On the grass beside him lay a plumed hat, and a pair of riding gloves gauntleted with gilt lace, and sewn with seed-pearls wrought into a curious device. A short cloak lined with sables hung from his shoulder, and his delicate white hands were gemmed with rings. Heavy eyelids drooped over his eyes. The young Fisherman watched him, as one snared in a spell. At last their eyes met, and wherever he danced it seemed to him that the eyes of the man were upon him. He heard the Witch laugh, and caught her by the waist, and whirled her madly round and round.

Suddenly a dog bayed in the wood, and the dancers stopped, and going up two by two, knelt down, and kissed the man's hands. As they did so, a little smile touched his proud lips, as a bird's wing touches the water and makes it laugh. But there was disdain in it. He kept looking at the young Fisherman.

"Come! let us worship," whispered the Witch, and she led him, and a great desire to do as she besought him seized on him, and he followed her. But when he came close, and without knowing why he did it, he made on his breast the sign of the Cross, and called upon the holy name.

No sooner had he done so than the witches screamed like hawks and flew away, and the pallid face that had been watching him twitched with a spasm of pain. The man went over to a little wood, and whistled. A pony with silver trappings came running to meet him. As he leapt upon the saddle he turned round, and looked at the young Fisherman sadly.

And the Witch with the red hair tried to fly away also, but the Fisherman caught her by her wrists, and held her fast. "Loose me," she cried, "and let me go. For thou hast named what should not be named, and shown the sign that may not be looked at."

"Nay," he answered, "but I will not let thee go till thou hast told me the secret."

"What secret?" said the Witch, wrestling with him like a wild cat, and biting her foam-flecked lips.

"Thou knowest," he made answer.

Her grass-green eyes grew dim with tears, and she said to the Fisherman, "Ask me anything but that!"

He laughed, and held her all the more tightly.

And when she saw that she could not free herself she whispered to him, "Surely I am as fair as the daughters of the sea, and as comely as those that dwell in the blue waters," and she put her face close to his.

But he thrust her back frowning, and said to her, "If thou keepest not the promise that thou madest to me I will slay thee for a false witch."

She grew grey as a blossom of the Judas tree and shuddered. "Be it so," she muttered. "It is thy soul and not mine. Do with it as thou wilt." And she took from her girdle a little knife that had a handle of green viper's skin and gave it to him.

"What shall this serve me?" he asked of her wondering.

She was silent for a few moments, and a look of terror came over her face. Then she brushed her hair back from her forehead and smiling strangely she said to him, "What men call the shadow of the body is not the shadow of the body, but is the body of the soul. Stand on the sea-shore with thy back to the moon, and cut away from around thy feet thy shadow, which is thy soul's body, and bid thy soul leave thee, and it will do so."

The young Fisherman trembled. "Is this true?" he murmured.

"It is true, and I would that I had not told thee of it," she cried, and she clung to his knees weeping.

He put her from him and left her in the grass, and going to edge of the mountain he placed the knife in his belt, and began to climb down.

And his Soul that was within him called out to him and said, "Lo! I have dwelt with thee for all these years, and have been thy servant. Send me not away from thee now, for what evil have I done thee?"

And the young Fisherman laughed. "Thou has done me no evil, but I have no need of thee," he answered. "The world is wide, and there is Heaven also, and Hell, and that dim twilight house that lies between. Go wherever thou wilt, but trouble me not, for my love is calling to me."

And his Soul besought him piteously, but he heeded it not, but leapt from crag to crag, being sure-footed as a wild goat, and at last he reached the level ground and the yellow shore of the sea.

Bronze-limbed and well-knit, like a statue wrought by a Grecian, he stood on the sand with his back to the moon, and out of the foam came white arms that beckoned to him, and out of the waves rose dim forms that did him homage. Before him lay his shadow, which was the body of his soul, and behind him hung the moon in the honey-coloured air.

And his Soul said to him, "If indeed thou must drive me from thee, send me not forth without a heart. The world is cruel, give me thy heart to take with me."

He tossed his head and smiled. "With what should I love my love if I gave thee my heart?" he cried.

"Nay, but be merciful," said his Soul: "give me thy heart, for the world is very cruel, and I am afraid."

"My heart is my love's," he answered, "therefore tarry not, but get thee gone."

"Should I not love also?" asked his Soul.

"Get thee gone, for I have no need of thee," cried the young Fisherman, and he took the little knife with its handle of green viper's skin, and cut away his shadow from around his feet, and it rose up and stood before him, and looked at him, and it was even as himself.

He crept back, and thrust the knife into his belt, and a feeling of awe came over him. "Get thee gone, and let me see thy face no more."

"Nay, but we must meet again," said the Soul. Its voice was low and flute-like, and its lips hardly moved while it spake.

"How shall we meet?" cried the young Fisherman. "Thou wilt not follow me into the depths of the sea?"

"Once every year I will come to this place, and call to thee," said the Soul. "It may be that thou wilt have need of me."

"What need should I have of thee?" cried the young Fisherman, "but be it as thou wilt," and he plunged into the water, and the Tritons blew their horns, and the little Mermaid rose up to meet him, and put her arms around his neck and kissed him on the mouth.

And the Soul stood on the lonely beach and watched them. And when they had sunk down into the sea, it went weeping away over the marshes.

And after a year was over the Soul came down to the shore of the sea and called to the young Fisherman, and he rose out of the deep, and said, "Why dost thou call to me?"

And the Soul answered, "Come nearer, that I may speak with thee, for I have seen marvellous things."

So he came nearer, and couched in the shallow water, and leaned his head upon his hand and listened.

And the Soul said to him, "When I left thee I turned my face to the East and journeyed. From the East cometh everything that is wise. Six days I journeyed, and on the morning of the seventh day I came to a hill that is in the country of the Tartars. I sat down under the shade of a tamarisk tree to shelter myself from the sun. The land was dry, and burnt up with the heat. The people went to and fro over the plain like flies crawling upon a disk of polished copper.

"When it was noon a cloud of red dust rose up from the flat rim of the land. When the Tartars saw it, they strung their painted bows, and having leapt upon their little horses they galloped to meet it.

"At twilight the Tartars returned, but five of them were missing, and of those that came back not a few had been wounded. They harnessed their horses to the wagons and drove hastily away.

"When the moon rose I saw a camp-fire burning on the plain, and went towards it. A company of merchants were seated round it on carpets. Their camels were picketed behind them, and the negroes who were their servants were pitching tents of tanned skin upon the sand, and making a high wall of the prickly pear.

"As I came near them, the chief of the merchants rose up and drew his sword, and asked me my business.

"I answered that I was a Prince in my own land, and that I had escaped from the Tartars, who had sought to make me their slave. The chief smiled, and showed me five heads fixed upon long reeds of bamboo.

"Then he asked me who was the prophet of God, and I answered him Mohammed.

"When he heard the name of the false prophet, he bowed and took me by the hand, and placed me by his side. A negro brought me some mare's milk in a wooden-dish, and a piece of lamb's flesh roasted.

"At daybreak we started on our journey. I rode on a red-haired camel by the side of the chief, and a runner ran before us carrying a spear. The men of war were on either hand, and the mules followed with the merchandise. There were forty camels in the caravan, and the mules were twice forty in number.

"We went from the country of the Tartars into the country of those who curse the Moon. Three times in our journey we came to the banks of the Oxus. We crossed it on rafts of wood with great bladders of blown hide. The river-horses raged against us and sought to slay us. When the camels saw them they trembled.

"The kings of each city levied tolls on us, but would not suffer us to enter their gates. When the dwellers in the villages saw us coming, they poisoned the wells and fled to the summits. We fought with the Magadae who are born old, and younger every year, and die when they are little children; and with the Laktroi who say that they are the sons of tigers, and paint themselves yellow and black. A third of our company died in battle, and a third died of want. The rest murmured against me, and said I had brought evil fortune. I took a horned adder from beneath a stone and let it sting me. When they saw I did not sicken they grew afraid.

"In the fourth month we reached the city of Illel. It was night time when we came to the grove outside the walls, and the air was sultry. So we lay down on our carpets and waited for the dawn.

"And at dawn we rose and knocked at the gate of the city. The guards looked down from the battlements and asked us our business. The interpreter of the caravan answered that we had come from the island of Syria with much merchandise.

375

They took hostages, and told us that they would open the gate to us at noon, and bade us tarry till then.

"When it was noon they opened the gate, and as we entered there the people came crowding out of the houses to look at us, and a crier went round the city crying through a shell. From the roof of a house a company of women watched us. One of them wore a mask of gilded leather.

"And on the first day the priests came and bartered with us, and on the second day came the nobles, and on the third day came the craftsmen and the slaves. And this is their custom with all merchants as long as they tarry in the city.

"And we tarried for a moon, and when the moon was waning, I wearied and wandered away through the streets of the city and came to the garden of its god. The priests in their yellow robes moved silently through the green trees, and on a pavement of black marble stood the rose-red house in which the god had his dwelling.

"In front of the temple was a pool of clear water paved with veined onyx. I lay down beside it, and with my pale fingers I touched the broad leaves. One of the priests came towards me and stood behind me. After a little while he spake to me, and asked me my desire. I told him that my desire was to see the god.

"'The god is hunting,' said the priest, looking strangely at me.

"'Tell me in what forest, and I will ride with him,' I answered.

"'The god is asleep,' he murmured.

"'Tell me on what couch, and I will watch by him,' I answered.

"'The god is at the feast,' he cried.

"'If the wine be sweet I will drink it with him, and if it be bitter I will drink it with him also,' was my answer.

"He bowed his head in wonder, and, taking me by the hand, he raised me up, and led me into the temple.

"And in the first chamber I saw an idol seated on a throne of jasper bordered with great orient pearls. I said to the priest, 'Is this the god?' And he answered me, 'This is the god.'

"'Show me the god,' I cried, 'or I will surely slay thee.' And I touched his hand, and it became withered.

"And the priest besought me, saying, 'Let my lord heal his servant, and I will show him the god.'

"So I breathed with my breath upon his hand, and it became whole again, and he trembled and led me into the second chamber, and I saw an idol standing on a lotus of jade hung with great emeralds. It was carved out of ivory, and in stature was twice the stature of a man.

"And I said to the priest, 'Is this the god?'

"And he answered me. 'This is the god.'

"'Show me the god,' I cried, 'or I will surely slay thee.' And I touched his eyes, and they became blind.

"And the priest besought me, saying, 'Let my lord heal his servant, and I will show him the god.'

"So I breathed with my breath upon his eyes, and his sight came back, and he led me to the third chamber, and there was no idol in it, nor image of any kind, but only a mirror of round metal on an altar of stone.

"And I said to the priest, 'Where is the god?'

"And he answered me: 'There is no god but this mirror that thou seest, for this is the Mirror of Wisdom. And it reflecteth all things that are in heaven and on earth, save only the face of him who looketh into it. This it reflecteth not, so that he who looketh into it may be wise. Many other mirrors are there, but they are mirrors of Opinion. This only is the Mirror of Wisdom. And they who possess this mirror know everything, nor is there anything hidden from them. And they who possess it not have not Wisdom. Therefore is it the god, and we worship it.' And I looked into the mirror, and it was even as he had said to me.

"And I did a strange thing, for in a valley that is but a day's journey from this place have I hidden the Mirror of Wisdom. Do but suffer me to enter into thee again and be thy servant, and thou shalt be wiser than all the wise men, and Wisdom shall be thine. Suffer me to enter into thee, and none will be as wise as thou."

But the young Fisherman laughed. "Love is better than Wisdom," he cried, "and the little Mermaid loves me."

"Nay, but there is nothing better than Wisdom," said the Soul.

"Love is better," answered the young Fisherman, and he plunged into the deep, and the Soul went weeping away over the marshes.

And after the second year was over the Soul came down to the shore of the sea, and called to the young Fisherman, and he rose out of the deep and said, "Why dost thou call to me?"

And the Soul answered, "Come nearer that I may speak with thee, for I have seen marvellous things."

So he came nearer, and couched in the shallow water, and leaned his head upon his hand and listened.

And the Soul said to him, "When I left thee, I turned my face to the South and journeyed. From the South cometh every thing that is precious. Six days I journeyed along the highways that lead to the city of Ashter, and on the morning of the seventh day I lifted up my eyes, and lo! the city lay at my feet, for it is in a valley.

"There are nine gates to this city, and in front of each gate stands a bronze horse that neighs when the Bedouins come down from the mountains. In every watch tower stands an archer with a bow in his hand. At sunrise he strikes with an arrow on a gong, and at sunset he blows through a horn of horn.

"When I sought to enter, the guards stopped me and asked of me who I was. I made answer that I was a Dervish and on my way to the city of Mecca, where there was a green veil on which the Koran was embroidered in silver letters by the hands of the angels. They were filled with wonder, and entreated me to pass in.

"Inside it is even as a bazaar. Surely thou should'st have been with me. Across the narrow streets the lanterns of paper flutter like large butterflies. When the wind blows over the roofs they rise and fall as painted bubbles do. In front of their booths sit the merchants on silken carpets. They have straight black beards, and their turbans are covered with golden sequins. From the tea-houses comes the sound of the guitar, and the opium-smokers with their white smiling faces look out at the passers-by.

"One evening I met some negroes carrying a heavy palanquin through the bazaar. Across the windows hung thin curtains of muslin, and as it passed by a pale-faced Circassian smiled out at me. I followed behind, and the negroes hurried their steps and scowled. But I did not care. I felt a great curiosity come over me.

"At last they stopped at a square white house. There were no windows to it, only a little door like that of a tomb. They set down the palanquin and knocked three times with a copper hammer. An Armenian peered through the wicket, and when he saw them he opened, and spread a carpet on the ground, and the woman stepped out. As she went in, she turned round and smiled at me again. I had never seen anyone so pale.

"When the moon rose I returned to the same place and sought for the house, but it was no longer there. When I saw that, I knew who the woman was, and wherefore she had smiled at me.

"Certainly thou should'st have been with me. On the feast of the New Moon the young Emperor came forth from his palace and went into the mosque to pray.

"At sunrise he went forth from his palace in a robe of silver, and at sunset he returned to it again in a robe of gold. The people flung themselves on the ground and hid their faces, but I would not do so. When the Emperor saw me, he raised his eyebrows and stopped. I stood quite still, and made him no obeisance. The people marvelled at my boldness, and counselled me to flee the city. I paid no heed, but went and sat with the sellers of strange gods, who are abominated. When I told them what I had done, each of them gave me a god and prayed me to leave them.

"That night, as I lay on a cushion in the tea-house, the guards of the Emperor entered and led me to the palace. As I went in they closed each door behind me, and put a chain across it. Inside was a great court with an arcade running all round. The walls were of white alabaster. The pillars were of green marble, and the pavement of a kind of peach-blossom marble. I had never seen anything like it before.

"As I passed across the court two veiled women looked down from a balcony and cursed me. The guards hastened on, and the butts of the lances rang upon the polished floor. They opened a gate of wrought ivory, and I found myself in a watered garden of seven terraces. Like a slim reed of crystal a fountain hung in the dusky air. The cypress-trees were like burnt-out torches. From one of them a nightingale was singing.

"At the end of the garden stood a little pavilion, where the captain of the guard motioned me towards the entrance. I walked on without trembling, and drawing the heavy curtain aside I entered in.

"The young Emperor was stretched on a couch of lion skins, and a falcon perched upon his wrist. Behind him stood a brass-turbaned Nubian, naked to the waist, and with heavy earrings in his split ears. On a table by the side of the couch lay a mighty scimitar of steel.

"When the Emperor saw me he frowned, and said to me, 'What is thy name? Knowest thou not that I am Emperor of this city?' But I made him no answer.

"He pointed his finger at the scimitar, and the Nubian seized it, and rushing forward struck me with great violence. The blade whizzed through me and did me no hurt. The man fell sprawling on the floor, and, when he rose up, his teeth chattered with terror and he hid behind the couch.

"The Emperor leapt to his feet, and taking a lance from a stand of arms, he threw it at me. I caught it in its flight, and brake the shaft into two. He shot an arrow, but I held up my hands and it stopped in mid-air. Then he drew a dagger from a belt of white leather, and stabbed the Nubian in the throat lest the slave should tell of his dishonour. The man writhed like a trampled snake, and a red foam bubbled from his lips.

"As soon as he was dead the Emperor turned to me, and when he had wiped away the bright sweat from his brow with a little napkin of purple silk, he said to me, 'Art thou a prophet, that I may not harm thee, or the son of a prophet that I can do thee no hurt? I pray thee leave my city to night, for while thou art in it I am no longer its lord.'

"And I answered him, 'I will go for half of thy treasure. Give me half of thy treasure, and I will go away.'

"He took me by the hand, and led me out into the garden. When the captain of the guard saw me, he wondered.

"There is a chamber in the palace that has eight walls of red porphyry, and a brass-scaled ceiling hung with lamps. The Emperor touched one of the walls and it opened, and we passed down a corridor lit with torches. In niches on each side stood great wine-jars filled to the brim with silver pieces. When we reached the centre of the corridor the Emperor spake the word that may not be spoken, and a granite door swung on a secret spring, and he put his hands before his face lest his eyes should be dazzled.

"Thou could'st not believe how marvellous a place it was. There were huge tortoise-shells full of pearls, and hollowed moonstones of great size piled up with red rubies. The gold was stored in coffers of elephant-hide, and the gold-dust in leather bottles. There were opals and sapphires, the former in cups of crystal, and the latter in cups of jade. Round green emeralds were ranged in order upon thin plates of ivory. And yet I have told thee but a tithe of what was there.

"And when the Emperor had taken away his hands from before his face he said to me: 'This is my house of treasure, and half that is in it is thine, even as I promised to thee. And I will give thee camels and camel drivers, and they shall do thy bidding and take thy share of the treasure to whatever part of the world thou desirest to go. And the thing shall be done tonight, for I would not that the Sun, who is my father, should see that there is in my city a man whom I cannot slay.'

"But I answered him, 'The gold that is here is thine, and the silver also is thine, and thine are the precious jewels and the things of price. As for me, I have no need of these. Nor shall I take aught from thee but that little ring on the finger of thy hand.'

"And the Emperor frowned. 'It is but a ring of lead,' he cried, 'nor has it any value. Therefore take thy half of the treasure and go from my city.'

"'Nay,' I answered, 'but I will take nought but that leaden ring, for I know what is written within it, and for what purpose.'

"And the Emperor trembled, and besought me and said, 'Take all the treasure and go from my city. The half that is mine shall be thine also.'

"And I did a strange thing, but what I did matters not, for in a cave that is but a day's journey from this place have I hidden the Ring of Riches. It is but a day's journey from this place, and it waits for thy coming. He who has this Ring is richer than all the kings of the world. Come therefore and take it, and the world's riches shall be thine."

But the young Fisherman laughed. "Love is better than Riches," he cried, "and the little Mermaid loves me."

"Nay, but there is nothing better than Riches," said the Soul.

"Love is better," answered the young Fisherman, and he plunged into the deep, and the Soul went weeping away over the marshes.

And after the third year was over, the Soul came down to the shore of the sea, and called to the young Fisherman, and he rose out of the deep and said, "Why dost thou call to me?"

And the Soul answered, "Come nearer, that I may speak with thee, for I have seen marvellous things."

So he came nearer, and couched in the shallow water, and leaned his head upon his hand and listened.

And the Soul said to him, "In a city that I know of there is an inn that standeth by a river. I sat there with sailors who drank of two different coloured wines, and ate bread made of barley, and little salt fish served in bay leaves with vinegar. And as we sat and made merry, there entered an old man bearing a leathern carpet and a lute that had two horns of amber. And when he had laid out the carpet on the floor, he struck on the wire strings of his lute, and a girl whose face was veiled ran in and began to dance before us. Her face was veiled with a veil of gauze, but her feet were naked. Naked were her feet, and they moved over the carpet like little white pigeons. Never have I seen anything so marvellous, and the city in which she dances is but a day's journey from this place."

Now when the young Fisherman heard the words of his soul, he remembered that the little Mermaid had no feet and could not dance. And a great desire came over him, and he said to himself, "It is but a day's journey, and I can return to my love," and he laughed, and stood up in the shallow water, and strode towards the shore.

And when he had reached the dry shore he laughed again, and held out his arms to his Soul. And his Soul gave a great cry of joy and ran to meet him, and entered into him, and the young Fisherman saw stretched before him upon the sand that shadow of the body that is the body of the Soul.

And his Soul said to him, "Let us not tarry, but get hence at once, for the Sea-gods are jealous, and have monsters that do their bidding."

So they made haste, and all that night they journeyed beneath the moon, and all the next day they journeyed beneath the sun, and on the evening of the day they came to a city.

And the young Fisherman said to his Soul, "Is this the city in which she dances of whom thou did'st speak to me?"

And his Soul answered, "It is not this city, but another. Nevertheless let us enter in."

So they entered in and passed through the streets, and as they passed through the Street of the Jewellers the young fisherman saw a fair silver cup set forth in a booth. And his Soul said to him, "Take that silver cup and hide it."

So he took the cup and hid it in the fold of his tunic, and they went hurriedly out of the city.

And after they had gone a league from the city, the young Fisherman frowned, and flung the cup away, and said to his Soul, "Why did'st thou tell me to take this cup and hide it, for it was an evil thing to do?"

But his Soul answered him, "Be at peace, be at peace."

And on the evening of the second day they came to a city, and the young Fisherman said to his Soul, "Is this the city in which she dances of whom thou did'st speak to me?"

And his Soul answered him, "It is not this city, but another. Nevertheless let us enter in."

So they entered in and passed through the streets, and as they passed through the Street of the Sellers of Sandals, the young Fisherman saw a child standing by a jar of water. And his Soul said to him, "Smite that child." So he smote the child 'til it wept, and when he had done this they went hurriedly out of the city.

And after that they had gone a league from the city the young Fisherman grew wroth, and said to his Soul, "Why did'st thou tell me to smite the child, for it was an evil thing to do?"

But his Soul answered him, "Be at peace, be at peace."

And on the evening of the third day they came to a city, and the young Fisherman said to his Soul, "Is this the city in which she dances of whom thou did'st speak to me?"

And his Soul answered him, "It may be that it is this city, therefore let us enter in."

So they entered and passed through the streets, but nowhere could the young Fisherman find the river or the inn that stood by its side. And the people looked curiously at him, and he grew afraid and said to his Soul, "Let us go hence, for she who dances with white feet is not here."

But his Soul answered, "Nay, but let us tarry, for the night is dark and there will be robbers on the way."

So he sat him down in the market-place and rested, and after a time there went by a hooded merchant who had a cloak of cloth of Tartary, and bare a lantern of pierced horn at the end of a jointed reed. And the merchant said to him, "Why dost thou sit in the market-place, seeing that the booths are closed and the bales corded?"

And the young Fisherman answered him, "I can find no inn in this city, nor have I any kinsman who might give me shelter."

"Are we not all kinsmen?" said the merchant. "And did not one God make us? Therefore come with me, for I have a guest-chamber."

So the young Fisherman rose up and followed the merchant to his house. And when he had passed through a garden and entered into the house, the merchant brought him rose-water in a copper dish that he might wash his hands, and ripe melons that he might quench his thirst, and set a bowl of rice and a piece of roasted kid before him.

And after that he had finished, the merchant led him to the guest-chamber, bade him sleep and be at rest. And the young Fisherman gave him thanks, and kissed the ring that was on his hand, and flung himself down on the carpets of dyed goat's-hair. And when he had covered himself with a covering of black lambs-wool he fell asleep.

And three hours before dawn, and while it was still night, his Soul waked him, and said to him, "Rise up and go to the room of the merchant, even to the room in which he sleepeth, and slay him, and take from him his gold, for we have need of it."

And the young Fisherman crept towards the room of the merchant, and over the feet of the merchant there was lying a curved sword, and the tray by the side of the merchant held nine purses of gold. And he reached out his hand and touched the sword, and when he touched it the merchant started and awoke, and leaping up seized himself the sword and cried to the young Fisherman, "Dost thou return evil for good, and pay with the shedding of blood for the kindness that I have shown thee?"

And his Soul said to the young Fisherman, "Strike him," and he struck him and seized the nine purses of gold, and fled hastily through the garden, and set his face to the star that is the star of morning.

And when they had gone a league from the city, the young Fisherman beat his breast, and said to his Soul, "Why didst thou bid me slay the merchant and take his gold? Surely thou art evil."

But his Soul answered him, "Be at peace, be at peace."

"Nay," cried the young Fisherman, "I may not be at peace, for all that thou hast made me to do I hate. Thee also I hate, and I bid thee tell me why thou hast wrought with me in this manner."

And his Soul answered him, "When thou didst send me forth into the world with no heart, so I learned to do all these things and love them."

"What sayest thou?" murmured the young Fisherman.

"Thou knowest," answered his Soul, "thou knowest it well. Hast thou forgotten that thou gavest me no heart? I think not. And so trouble not thyself nor me, but be at peace, for there is no pain that thou shalt not give away, nor any pleasure that thou shalt not receive."

And when the young Fisherman heard these words he trembled and said to his Soul, "Nay, but thou art evil, and hast made me forget my love, and hast tempted me with temptations, and hast set my feet in the ways of sin."

And his Soul answered him, "Thou hast not forgotten that when thou didst send me forth into the world thou gavest me no heart. Come, let us go to another city, and make merry, for we have nine purses of gold."

But the young Fisherman took the nine purses of gold, and flung them down, and trampled on them.

"Nay," he cried, "but I will have nought to do with thee, nor will I journey with thee anywhere, but even as I sent thee away before, so will I send thee away now, for thou hast wrought me no good."

And he turned his back to the moon, and with the little knife that had the handle of green viper's skin he strove to cut from his feet that shadow of the body which is the body of the Soul.

Yet his Soul stirred not from him, nor paid heed to his command, but said to him, "The spell that the Witch told thee avails thee no more, for I may not leave thee, nor mayest thou drive me forth. Once in his life may a man send his Soul away, but he who receiveth back his Soul must keep it with him for ever, and this is his punishment and his reward."

And the young Fisherman grew pale and clenched his hands and cried, "She was a false Witch in that she told me not that."

"Nay," answered his Soul, "but she was true to Him she worships, and whose servant she will be ever."

And when the young Fisherman knew that he could no longer get rid of his Soul, and that it was an evil Soul and would abide with him always, he fell upon the ground weeping bitterly.

And when it was day, the young Fisherman rose up and said to his Soul, "I will bind my hands that I may not do thy bidding, and close my lips that I may not speak thy words, and I will return to the place where she whom I love has her dwelling. Even to the sea will I return, and to the little bay where she is wont to sing, and I will call to her and tell her the evil I have done and the evil thou hast wrought on me."

Then the young Fisherman closed his lips with the seal of silence and with a tight cord bound his hands, and journeyed back to the place from which he had come, even to the little bay where his love had been wont to sing. And ever did his Soul tempt him by the way, but he made it no answer, nor would he do any of the wickedness that it sought to make him to do, so great was the power of the love that was within him.

And when he had reached the shore of the sea, he loosed the cord from his hands, and took the seal of silence from his lips, and called to the little Mermaid. But she came not to his call, though he called to her all day long and besought her.

And his Soul mocked him and said, "Surely thou hast but little joy out of love. Thou art as one who in time of dearth pours water into a broken vessel. Thou givest away what thou hast, and nought is given to thee in return. It were better for thee to come with me, for I know where the Valley of Pleasure lies, and what things are wrought there."

But the young Fisherman answered not his Soul, but in a cleft of the rock he built himself a house, and abode there for the space of a year. And every morning he called to the Mermaid, and every noon he called to her again, and at night-time he spake her name. Yet never did she rise out of the sea to meet him, nor in any place of the sea could he find her, though he sought for her in the caves and in the green water, in the pools of the tide and in the wells that are at the bottom of the deep.

And ever did his Soul tempt him with evil, and whisper of terrible things. Yet did it not prevail against him, so great was the power of his love.

And after the year was over, the Soul thought within himself, "I have tempted my master with evil, and his love is stronger than I am. I will tempt him now with good, and it may be that he will come with me."

So he spake to the young Fisherman and said, "I have told thee of the joy of the world, and thou hast turned a deaf ear to me. Suffer me now to tell thee of the world's pain, and it may be that thou wilt hearken. For of a truth, pain is the Lord of this world, nor is there anyone who escapes from its net. There be some who lack raiment, and others who lack bread. There be widows who sit in purple, and widows who sit in rags. To and fro over the fens go the lepers, and they are cruel to each other. The beggars go up and down the highways, and their wallets are empty. Through the streets of the cities walks Famine, and the Plague sits at their gates. Come, let us go forth and mend these things, and make them not to be. Why should'st thou tarry here calling to thy love, seeing she comes not to thy call? And what is love, that thou should'st set this high store upon it?"

But the young Fisherman answered it nought, so great was the power of his love. And every morning he called to the Mermaid, and every noon he called to her again, and at night-time he spake her name. Yet never did she rise out of the sea to meet him, nor in any place of the sea could he find her, though he sought for her in the rivers of the sea, and in the valleys that are under the waves, in the sea that the night makes purple, and in the sea that the dawn leaves grey.

And after the second year was over, the Soul said to the young Fisherman at night-time as he sat alone, "Lo! now I have tempted thee with evil, and I have tempted thee with good, and thy love is stronger than I am. Why will I tempt thee no longer, but I pray thee to allow me to enter thy heart, that I may be one with thee even as before."

"Surely thou mayest enter," said the young Fisherman, "for in the days when with no heart thou didst go through the world thou must have much suffered."

"Alas!" cried his Soul, "I can find no place of entrance, so compassed about with love is this heart of thine."

"Yet I would that I could help thee," said the young Fisherman.

And as he spake there came a great cry of mourning from the sea, even the cry that men hear when one of the Sea-folk is dead. And the young Fisherman leapt up, and left his house, and ran down to the shore. And the black waves came hurrying to the shore, bearing with them a burden that was whiter than silver. White as the surf it was, and like a flower it tossed on the waves. And the surf took it from the waves, and the foam took it from the surf, and the shore received it, and lying at his feet the young Fisherman saw the body of the little Mermaid. Dead at his feet it was lying.

Weeping as one smitten with pain he flung himself down beside it, and he kissed the cold red of the mouth, and toyed with the wet amber of the hair. He flung himself down beside it on the sand, weeping as one trembling with joy, and in his brown arms he held it to his breast. Cold were the lips, yet he kissed them. Salt was the honey of the hair, yet he tasted it with a bitter joy. He kissed the closed eyelids, and the wild spray that lay upon their cups was less salt than his tears.

And to the dead thing he made confession. Into the shells of its ears he poured the harsh wine of his tale. He put the little hands round his neck, and with his fingers he touched the thin reed of the throat. Bitter, bitter was his joy, and full of strange gladness was his pain.

The black sea came nearer, and the white foam moaned like a leper. With white claws of foam the sea grabbled at the shore. From the palace of the Sea-King came the cry of mourning, and far out upon the sea the great Tritons blew hoarsely upon their horns.

"Flee away," said his Soul, "for ever doth the sea come nearer, and if thou tarriest it will slay thee. Flee away, for I am afraid, seeing that thy heart is closed against me by reason of the greatness of thy love. Flee away to a place of safety. Surely thou wilt not send me without a heart into another world?"

But the young Fisherman listened not to his Soul, but called on the little Mermaid and said, "Love is better than wisdom, and more precious than riches, and fairer than the feet of the daughters of men. The fires cannot destroy it, nor can the waters quench it. I called on thee at dawn, and thou didst not come to my call. The moon heard thy name, yet hadst thou no heed of me. For evilly had I left thee, and to my own hurt had I wandered away. Yet ever did thy love abide with me, and ever was it strong, nor did anything prevail against it, though I have looked upon evil and looked upon good. And now that thou art dead, surely I will die with thee also."

And his Soul besought him to depart, but he would not, so great was his love. And the sea came nearer, and sought to cover him with its waves, and when he knew that the end was at hand he kissed with mad lips the cold lips of the Mermaid and the heart that was within him brake. And as through the fullness of his love his heart did break, the Soul found an entrance and entered in, and was one with him even as before. And the sea covered the young Fisherman with its waves.

And in the morning the Priest went forth to bless the sea, for it had been troubled. And with him went the monks and the musicians, and the candle-bearers, and the swingers of censers, and a great company.

And when the Priest reached the shore he saw the young Fisherman lying drowned in the surf, and clasped in his arms was the body of the little Mermaid. And he drew back frowning, and having made the sign of the cross, he cried aloud and said, "I will not bless the sea, nor anything that is in it. Accursed be the Sea-folk, and accursed be all they who traffic with them. And as for him who for love's sake forsook God, and so lieth here with his lover slain by God's judgment, take up his body and the body of his lover, and bury them in the corner of the Field of the Fullers, and set no mark above them, nor sign of any kind, that none may know the place of their resting. For accursed were they in their lives, and accursed shall they be in their deaths also."

And the people did as he commanded, and in the corner of the Field of the Fullers, where no sweet herbs grew, they dug a deep pit, and laid the dead things within it.

And when the third year was over, and on a day that was a holy day, the Priest went up to the chapel that he might show to the people the wounds of the Lord and speak to them about the wrath of God.

And when he had robed himself with his robes, and entered in and bowed himself before the altar, he saw that the altar was covered with strange flowers that never had he seen before. Strange were they to look at, and of curious beauty, and their beauty troubled him, and their odour was sweet. And he felt glad, and understood not why he was glad.

And after that he had opened the tabernacle, and incensed the monstrance that was in it, and shown the fair wafer to the people, and hid it again behind the veil of veils, he began to speak to the people, desiring to speak to them of the wrath of God. But the beauty of the flowers troubled him, and their odour was sweet in his nostrils, and there came another word into his lips, and he spake not of the wrath of God, but of the God whose name is Love. And why he so spake, he knew not.

And when he had finished his word the people wept, and the Priest went back to the sacristy, and his eyes were full of tears. And the deacons came in and began to unrobe him, and took from him the alb and the girdle, the maniple and the stole. And he stood as one in a dream.

And after that they had unrobed him, he looked at them and said, "What are the flowers that stand on the altar, and whence do they come?"

And they answered him, "What flowers they are we cannot tell, but they come from the corner of the Fullers' Field." And the Priest trembled, and returned to his own house and prayed.

And in the morning, while it was still dawn, he went forth with the monks and the musicians, and the candle-bearers and the swingers of censers, and a great company, and came to the shore of the sea, and blessed the sea, and all the wild things that are in it. The Fauns also he blessed, and the little things that dance in the woodland, and the bright-eyed things that peer through the leaves. All the things in God's world he blessed, and the people were filled with joy and wonder. Yet never again in the corner of the Fullers' Field grew flowers of any kind, but the field remained barren even as before. Nor came the Sea-folk into the bay as they had been wont to do, for they went to another part of the sea.

A. Scott Berg

from
"Oysters and Pearls"
BEACH HOUSE ON THE MOON
1999

"Getting the Picture"
Sports Illustrated Magazine
2004

THERE CAN BE no doubt that Jimmy's read this biography that won the Pulitzer Prize in 1999. If you saw the opening shots of the video download for "Getting the Picture," you glimpsed a quick shot of *Lindbergh* before you saw Jimmy reading a copy of a *Sports Illustrated* swimsuit issue.

If you missed all that, however, here's more impressive evidence. Of the aviator's having landed in Paris, Scott Berg writes: "Everything changed for both the pilot and the planet." It's the same sentiment, as well as the same phrase, that Jimmy sings in "Oysters and Pearls."

"This moment when Lindbergh landed in Paris in 1927 was not only a great moment in the revolution in transportation," Berg once explained, "but also there was a great revolution going on in the world of communications. This was a moment when radio was everywhere in the civilized world, when newspaper syndicates could spread the word everywhere, when cable processes could send photographs around the world in a matter of minutes, and, indeed, for the first time, sound was being attached to motion pictures, so it's really the first time that the entire civilized world could share a single event instantaneously and simultaneously."

While Lindbergh himself is a fascinating subject, Berg's own work should not be overshadowed by that. Scott Berg was named after one of his mother's favorite writers (Fitzgerald), studied under Hemingway's noted biographer (Carlos Baker), and quickly became a master at his craft. When he was thirty-one, Berg received the National Book Award for his first published biography, *Max Perkins: Editor of Genius*.

His initial desire to write about Lindbergh stemmed from his belief that the aviation pioneer provided what Berg calls "a great window onto the twentieth century, the great American century." And though Lindbergh's story already had been told, time and time again, in bits and in pieces, those all had been based simply upon press clippings and folklore. Berg wanted to set the record straight.

In addition to his own writing talents, there existed thousands of sealed boxes of personal papers and materials which Charles Lindbergh had ordered not be opened until some fifty years after the death of his wife, Ann Morrow Lindbergh. His widow, however, granted Berg access to every one of those files, along with access to herself and to the five surviving Lindbergh children, as well as to a circle of close family friends. The result is this powerful, historical narrative that begins with the simple sentence: "For more than a day the world held its breath."

The remaining six hundred pages of Lindbergh's triumph and his tragedy read almost as fast and smooth as those first ten words. And as you follow the pages of that solo flight across the Atlantic, your mind will not be able to resist humming the melody that lifts the lyric, "Lindbergh left Long Island in 1927. / He thumbed his nose at gravity and climbed into the heaven."

The following selection is pretty much the ending of Berg's masterpiece, as well as of Lindbergh's life. As with a few others on Jimmy's short list of personal heroes, Lindbergh was buried on an island in the South Pacific. This is the way his life had ended; this is the way his story had ended; and this is the way this reader now ends, as well.

Additional suggested works by A. Scott Berg:

— *Max Perkins: Editor of Genius* (1978)

— *Lindbergh* (1998)

"Aloha"

a selection from
Lindbergh / Chapter XIX

ON AUGUST TWENTY-FIFTH, the grave and casket were completed; and Jon returned to Seattle. He expected to see his father again but realized there was a good chance he would be too late in returning.

Lindbergh's breathing became labored that afternoon, and he felt chest pains. Dr. Howell, who had been visiting twice a day, gave him aspirin with codeine, half-grain tablets which Lindbergh broke up, swallowing quarter-grain bits only when necessary. Because he steadily drank enough fluids, Howell never had to hook him up to an intravenous drip. He did keep an oxygen mask at Lindbergh's side, however, which he replaced that afternoon with a larger breathing apparatus. "Now, Doctor," Lindbergh asked that Sunday night, "is the calibre of the oxygen tube really large enough to supply me with the amount of oxygen I need?" In fact, it was not, as the lymphosarcoma was filling his lungs. Later that night, reaching over to adjust a valve so that he might get more air, his arm dropped and he drifted into a coma. Dr. Howell sedated him and planned to move him to the clinic the next day. Anne, Land, and a nurse remained by his side through the night, his wife holding his hand.

In the morning – Monday, August twenty-sixth – Lindbergh seemed at peace. After an early breakfast, Anne and Land went into the bedroom and found him barely breathing. The Howells arrived a few minutes after seven; and after examining him, the doctor said, "He's going now." Anne took his hand and could hardly believe how lifeless it had become since the night before. Land instinctively wanted to hold his father, but he knew how much he disliked being touched. And so, with his mother at one end of the bed, he sat at the other, putting his hand on his father's foot. For more than ten minutes they sat there as the room became increasingly still. "And then," recalled Land, "he just went."

Silently, everybody left the room, leaving Anne alone with Charles. She gave him a last kiss. She wanted to have a longer moment alone with him, but there was no time. He had prepared everybody to move him from his bed to his grave as swiftly as possible, not only to beat the invasion of the press but also for legal reasons.

Lindbergh had insisted that he not be embalmed. A "natural" burial was legal in Hawaii so long as it occurred within eight hours of death. But the law also prohibited interment until a death certificate had been signed by the coroner, and he was on "the other side" of the island. At Lindbergh's urging, Dr. Howell had already made preparations. He had filled out the certificate with everything except the date of death; he had apprised the coroner of the situation; and he had his son standing by to drive the document to him in Wailuku, two hours away. Howell followed all of Lindbergh's instructions to the letter. He dispatched his son; he summoned Tevi, on a construction job on the other side of the island; he notified the police, asking them to provide security around the cottage and the church; and he called the newspaper editor, telling him that Lindbergh had died and asking him to hold the news at least until noon.

Minutes later, the local radio station got word. Not three hours after Land had called Jon in Seattle to tell him their father had died, he heard it on the radio. A few women rushed to the church to sweep it clean and to strew ginger stalks and hibiscus onto the deep window ledges. John Hanchett and a dozen ranch hands pulled up to the Pechin guest cottage and unloaded the heavy eucalyptus casket. The Hudson Bay blanket arrived that morning.

Tevi, flown into Hana by private plane, arrived at the house to perform the most personal duties of the day. Lindbergh had asked the sixty-three-year-old laborer to dress him. Anne handed him the outfit Charles had selected – a pair of old, gray cotton pants and a khaki shirt; he would wear neither a belt, because of the metal buckle, nor shoes. Tevi, John Hanchett, and two ranch hands then carried the dressed corpse to the blanket-lined coffin and set him down, tucking in the sheets exactly as prescribed. Just as one of the men prepared to hammer down the lid, Anne called out, "No, wait." She approached for a final look and lost her composure. With tears in her eyes, she placed four white flowers inside the casket, which was finally nailed shut. Eight men carried the heavy box out to Hanchett's blue pickup. Tevi hopped in back so that he could ride alongside the coffin, which was covered with canvas.

It was early afternoon when the local police sergeant began his drive from the Pechin cottage down to the Kipahulu church, followed by Hanchett's truck, and a small convoy of other vehicles. As they passed the Ohe'o Stream, none of the sightseers at the Seven Sacred Pools had any idea that the funeral cortege of Charles Lindbergh was passing by. The service was scheduled for three o'clock, and Milton Howell had said he would talk to the press at four. But by two o'clock, the coffin had been carried inside to the front of the church, and all the intended guests were present – no more than fifteen people, most of the men in their work clothes. Candles flickered in the sconces and the smell of ginger filled the small church. Knowing that the serenity of the moment could not last much longer, Anne and Land asked for the service to begin.

In a moment of absolute tranquility just before the Reverend John Tincher spoke, a barefooted Hawaiian woman, who occasionally helped with the housekeeping at Argonauta, walked to the front of the church, her apron full of flowers. She knelt by the coffin; and, placing one blossom at a time, she covered it with a blanket of plumeria. Exactly as scripted, the service of silent prayer and Tincher's reading of five selections took less than twenty minutes.

Because the casket was so heavy, six or seven men carried it back to the truck, and John Hanchett drove it to the gravesite. It was difficult lowering the coffin into the deep stone-lined hole; and, as it was done, Tincher spoke the words of committal. People tossed flowers into the tomb, and Land actually climbed in to place one white plumeria blossom on the coffin for his mother. Henry Kahula led the singing of a Hawaiian hymn with three other voices; and the music, Land recalled, "just soared out and away with the wind and the crashing of the waves below us."

Only one local reporter was present for the service, respectfully in the background. By three o'clock, when the mourners were driving off, the first television crew was on its way to the church, not a half-mile away. The dozen members of the press who followed felt they had been tricked. But Milton Howell explained the situation and invited them to his house, where he answered all their questions.

For the last time, Charles Lindbergh captured the attention of the world media. News of his death commanded the entire upper-left corner of the front page of *The New York Times*. The paper paid further homage with a two-page obituary by Alden Whitman, a column of tributes, including one from the President of three weeks, Gerald Ford. The *Times* editorial, titled "Passing of a Hero," spoke of Lindbergh as "both the beneficiary and the victim of a celebrity experienced by no other American in this century." It was fitting, it noted, that he chose to die and be buried "in the utmost simplicity, far from the crowds that had hailed and repelled him in his lifetime." Beginning that afternoon, close to one thousand messages of condolence began to pour in, from around the world.

At two o'clock the following afternoon, two dozen people arrived at the Ho'omau Church for Lindbergh's memorial service. Another dozen reporters had arrived early to cover the event; and Anne Lindbergh invited them to take seats in the rear pews. Jon and Sam Pryor sat up front with Anne and Land. John Tincher, in his final hours on Maui, conducted the multifaith service, again with Henry Kahula. Anne was especially moved by the singing of the last hymn, a sublime rendition of "Hawaii Aloha." The entire program lasted less than thirty minutes, without any suggestion of Lindbergh's accomplishments. When it was over, Anne thanked each person who attended, even the reporters. She would return to the mainland later that week, and settle into a progressively reclusive widowhood in Connecticut, reducing her life to visits with her children and seventeen grandchildren. In time, she stopped going to Switzerland and Hawaii at all.

Lindbergh's *Autobiography of Values* would be published in 1978, exposing a more philosophical, even poetic, man than most readers expected. It concludes on a transcendental note. "After my death," he wrote, "the molecules of my being will return to the earth and the sky. They came from the stars. I am of the stars."

⁊

PERMISSIONS

PERMISSIONS

"Epilogue" excerpt from *Legends of the Fall* by Jim Harrison. Copyright ©1989 by Jim Harrison. Used by permission of Dell Publishing, a division of Random House, Inc.

Excerpt from *The Loss of El Dorado* by V. S. Naipaul. Copyright ©1969 by V. S. Naipaul. Used by permission of Alfred A. Knopf, a division of Random House, Inc.

Excerpt from *The Power of Myth* by Joseph Campbell & Bill Moyers. Copyright ©1988 by Apostrophe S Productions, Inc. and Bill Moyers and Alfred Van der Marck Editions, Inc. for itself and the estate of Joseph Campbell. Used by permission of Doubleday, a division of Random House, Inc.

Reprinted with the permission of St. Martin's Press:
Excerpt from *The Mango Opera* by Tom Corcoran. Copyright ©1998 by Tom Corcoran. Reprinted by permission of Thomas Dunne Books, an imprint of St. Martin's Press, LLC.

Reprinted with the permission of Simon & Schuster:
"The Gonzo Salvage Company" excerpt from *Generation of Swine: Tales of Shame and Degradation in the '80s* by Hunter S. Thompson. Copyright ©1988 by Hunter S. Thompson. All rights reserved. Reprinted with the permission of Simon and Schuster, Inc.

"Salvage is not Looting" excerpt from *Generation of Swine: Tales of Shame and Degradation in the '80s* by Hunter S. Thompson. Copyright ©1988 by Hunter S. Thompson. All rights reserved. Reprinted with the permission of Simon and Schuster, Inc.

Excerpt from *The Road Less Traveled* by M. Scott Peck, M.D.. Copyright ©1978 by M. Scott Peck, M.D. All rights reserved. Reprinted with the permission of Simon and Schuster, Inc.

APPRECIATIONS

THOUGH THEY TRULY DESERVE much more than this, we do wish to express our warmest thanks and deepest appreciation to those newfound friends in the copyrights and permissions departments of quite a few publishing houses and literary agencies. In addition to their reading all of those pages we submitted for inclusion in this volume, as well as then checking our reproduction – word for word – with the writer's original work, they extended the extra effort that enabled *The Occasional Margareader* to remain affordable for all of its readers.

Without a doubt, we could not have produced this book without the assistance of the following people (in alphabetical order):

Faith Freeman Barbato / *HarperCollins Publishers*

Trinity Boscardin / *St. Martin's Press*

Rosemarie Cerminaro / *Simon & Schuster*

Carol Christiansen / *Random House*

George E. Diskant / *Diskant & Associates*

Florence B. Eichin / *Penguin Group USA*

Agnes Fisher / *Simon & Schuster*

Deborah Foley / *Random House*

Victoria Fox / *Farrar, Straus and Giroux*

Bette Graber / *Random House*

Amy Hasselbeck / *William Morris Endeavor Entertainment*

Scarlett R. Huffman / *Harvard University Press*

Ron Hussey / *Houghton Mifflin Harcourt*

Dara Hyde / *Grove/Atlantic*

Quinn Marshall / *New Directions Publishing*

Anthony McDonald / *Houghton Mifflin Harcourt*

Sam Moore / *Penguin Group USA*

Jennifer Chang Rowley / *Random House*

Johnny Temple / *Akashic Books*

Alice Torello / *Random House*

Susan Walker / *Tried & True Foundation*

Hayley Yeeles / *Pollinger Limited*

Lydia Zelaya / *Simon & Schuster*

LAST AND MOST CERTAINLY NOT LEAST, the strongest of thanks are in order for all of our librarians throughout Cape Cod, Nantucket & Martha's Vineyard who have become interconnected through CLAMS, the Cape Libraries Automated Materials Sharing system.

Though it might well go without saying, let me say it just the same: Thanks. I could not have found a great many of these items without the time and effort of these librarians. Alas, however, some never made it into this volume.

I remains especially grateful to my hometown friends at the West Dennis Public Library, as well as those at the South Yarmouth Public Library, the Hyannis Public Library, the Osterville Village Library, the Sturgis Library in Barnstable, and the Brooks Library in Harwich. The fact that their entire collections are catalogued online has managed to save me hours of travel time amongst the various towns and villages, but their willingness (no, their eagerness!) in helping me find materials in other libraries just over the horizon and beyond has been an invaluable service to the readers of this book. On behalf of those readers, then, let me add yet another layer of gratitude.

THE LAST HUNDRED WORDS

DON DAVIDSON IS the editorial director and publisher of The Peninsula Press on Cape Cod, as well as the founding publisher of Jimmy Buffett's Margaritaville Books. He did attend school and earn some degrees, but he cannot recall any of his SAT scores, his GPA, or even his class rank. He has written some books, has edited a great many others, and has worked alongside a number of renowned writers. That's pretty much all there is to say about his career. On a more personal note, he still lives and works in his homeport of West Dennis on Cape Cod.

Made in the USA
Charleston, SC
13 March 2011